MG Concept
सबसे अलग

INSPECTOR चालीसा

Calculation का महाग्रंथ

Bilingual
for
All Govt. Competitive Exams
(SSC CGL/CHSL | CPO | MTS | GD | CAPF CDS | Railway NTPC – Group D | UP-SI DSSSB | CAT | MAT | Bank | CTET)

MOHIT GOYAL

M.Sc Physics PhD (I), Delhi University
Mathematics Talent Research Award Winner

5 Times Selected SSC CGL Inspector
[Ex-Group B Officer, Postal, Excise & CBI Inspector]

INSPECTOR चालीसा **Calculation का महाग्रंथ**

First Edition:-
Version 1.0: January 2026
Price: ₹250/-
Published by: Mohit Goyal
Reg off: Indirapuram, Ghaziabad-201014

I am always open to listen to your feedback and suggestion at my official email Id mentioned below. If you really love the Book Inspector चालीसा do share your thought with your friends on Social Media. Also you can use the hashtag #inspectorchalisa while sharing your thought on Social Media.

I wish you all the best for your bright career!

Mohit Goyal
Author

mgconcept.works@gmail.com
Contact us / WhatsApp:- 9711113573

Print Date : 01.01.2026

PREFACE

- Competitive दुनिया में ऐसा अधिकतर होता है कि आपको Examination Hall में सब कुछ आने के बावजूद यह एहसास होता है कि Speed की कमी की वजह से Paper उतना अच्छा नहीं कर पाए जितना हो सकता था, यहीं से मेरी किताब का purpose शुरु होता है।
- India में बच्चों की सबसे बड़ी समस्या है Calculation जिसके कारण कई बच्चे अपना Target achieve नहीं कर पाते इस Book के माध्यम से मेरा यह प्रयास है कि मैं एक बदलता हुआ भारत देख पाऊँ जहाँ बच्चे बिना लिखे Orally Calculation कर पाएं।
- मैने इस चालीसा में केवल वही Calculation रखने की कोशिश की है जो आपके Exam के हिसाब से Relevant हैं।
- मेरा दावा है अगर आप Daily अपनी जिंदगी में से 30 मिनट निकाल कर Practice करते हैं तो 6 महीनों में आपकी Calculation Speed कम से कम 5 गुना हो जाएगी।

आओ हम सब मिलकर एक नए भारत का निर्माण करते हैं।

जय हिन्द

INDEX

CALCULATE 10 × FASTER THAN BEFORE

ADDITION (जोड़)

Type-1

Hint :

7 + 67 =

☞ एक संख्या का दहाई (Tens) का अंक (digit) (6) के आगे zero मानकर दिमाग में (60) रखें फिर दोनों संख्याओं के इकाई (unit) के अंक (digit) जोड़कर (7 + 7) दिमाग वाली संख्या (60) में जोड़ दें, तो Answer आ जाएगा।

Solution:

Step – 1 ⇒ 6 0

↓

मान लिया

Step – 2 ⇒ 7 + 7 = 14

Step – 3 ⇒ 60 + 14 = $\boxed{74}$

एक बार में जल्दी से सब कुछ दिमाग में करना है।

Exercise

1. 7 + 67 =

(a) 75 (b) 74 (c) 81 (d) 71

2. 49 + 8 =

(a) 96 (b) 56 (c) 59 (d) 57

3. 88 + 8 =

(a) 96 (b) 94 (c) 103 (d) 98

4. **6 + 67 =**

(a) 51 (b) 57 (c) 73 (d) 59

5. **97 + 8 =**

(a) 103 (b) 105 (c) 108 (d) 111

6. **78 + 8 =**

(a) 90 (b) 99 (c) 88 (d) 86

7. **55 + 3 =**

(a) 72 (b) 66 (c) 58 (d) 69

8. **37 + 2 =**

(a) 39 (b) 48 (c) 41 (d) 51

9. **37 + 9 =**

(a) 44 (b) 46 (c) 41 (d) 51

10. **75 + 6 =**

(a) 88 (b) 94 (c) 87 (d) 81

11. **27 + 9 =**

(a) 35 (b) 41 (c) 36 (d) 33

12. **74 + 8 =**

(a) 90 (b) 78 (c) 70 (d) 82

13. **6 + 29 =**

(a) 45 (b) 65 (c) 33 (d) 35

14. **12 + 9 =**

(a) 31 (b) 34 (c) 21 (d) 26

15. **9 + 89 =**

(a) 91 (b) 98 (c) 108 (d) 118

16. **38 + 5 =**

(a) 49 (b) 54 (c) 63 (d) 43

17. 3 + 55 =

(a) 67 (b) 58 (c) 59 (d) 55

18. 69 + 5 =

(a) 74 (b) 84 (c) 77 (d) 78

19. 6 + 85 =

(a) 90 (b) 97 (c) 91 (d) 99

20. 69 + 8 =

(a) 80 (b) 67 (c) 87 (d) 77

21. 7 + 89 =

(a) 106 (b) 102 (c) 96 (d) 99

22. 66 + 8 =

(a) 74 (b) 88 (c) 78 (d) 72

23. 6 + 82 =

(a) 91 (b) 93 (c) 88 (d) 97

24. 4 + 29 =

(a) 34 (b) 45 (c) 43 (d) 33

25. 45 + 2 =

(a) 59 (b) 47 (c) 57 (d) 67

26. 6 + 29 =

(a) 34 (b) 35 (c) 43 (d) 33

27. 89 + 6 =

(a) 94 (b) 97 (c) 107 (d) 95

28. 4 + 53 =

(a) 59 (b) 68 (c) 67 (d) 57

29. 65 + 5 =

(a) 79 (b) 73 (c) 70 (d) 69

30. 7 + 49 =

(a) 66 (b) 59 (c) 64 (d) 56

31. 56 + 9 =

(a) 65 (b) 77 (c) 69 (d) 75

32. 6 + 99 =

(a) 103 (b) 106 (c) 105 (d) 104

33. 69 + 2 =

(a) 81 (b) 73 (c) 71 (d) 76

34. 9 + 42 =

(a) 54 (b) 51 (c) 61 (d) 53

35. 48 + 6 =

(a) 64 (b) 57 (c) 54 (d) 55

36. 8 + 76 =

(a) 96 (b) 84 (c) 91 (d) 86

37. 34 + 5 =

(a) 39 (b) 49 (c) 51 (d) 46

38. 3 + 85 =

(a) 87 (b) 102 (c) 88 (d) 93

39. 39 + 6 =

(a) 55 (b) 62 (c) 49 (d) 45

40. 3 + 78 =

(a) 91 (b) 89 (c) 81 (d) 87

41. 53 + 5 =

(a) 58 (b) 78 (c) 64 (d) 67

42. 4 + 59 =

(a) 63 (b) 68 (c) 64 (d) 67

43. 89 + 5 =

(a) 93 (b) 94 (c) 97 (d) 92

44. 6 + 79 =

(a) 87 (b) 85 (c) 82 (d) 86

45. 46 + 7 =

(a) 58 (b) 53 (c) 57 (d) 52

46. 8 + 69 =

(a) 78 (b) 75 (c) 79 (d) 77

47. 88 + 6 =

(a) 99 (b) 94 (c) 91 (d) 97

48. 3 + 24 =

(a) 29 (b) 32 (c) 38 (d) 27

49. 43 + 4 =

(a) 49 (b) 47 (c) 46 (d) 51

50. 7 + 42 =

(a) 52 (b) 57 (c) 47 (d) 49

51. 49 + 8 =

(a) 58 (b) 57 (c) 61 (d) 59

52. 8 + 57 =

(a) 62 (b) 61 (c) 68 (d) 65

53. 70 + 7 =

(a) 73 (b) 77 (c) 67 (d) 69

54. 6 + 59 =

(a) 62 (b) 61 (c) 71 (d) 65

55. 77 + 9 =

(a) 86 (b) 83 (c) 87 (d) 89

56. 8 + 85 =

(a) 91 (b) 99 (c) 96 (d) 93

57. 37 + 9 =

(a) 43 (b) 46 (c) 49 (d) 51

58. 84 + 8 =

(a) 93 (b) 95 (c) 92 (d) 94

59. 6 + 59 =

(a) 49 (b) 46 (c) 53 (d) 65

60. 57 + 7 =

(a) 64 (b) 46 (c) 53 (d) 65

61. 87 + 7 =

(a) 93 (b) 94 (c) 97 (d) 99

62. 6 + 55 =

(a) 66 (b) 63 (c) 56 (d) 61

63. 33 + 9 =

(a) 45 (b) 42 (c) 46 (d) 49

64. 87 + 9 =

(a) 93 (b) 98 (c) 91 (d) 96

65. 7 + 43 =

(a) 48 (b) 53 (c) 50 (d) 55

66. 98 + 7 =

(a) 102 (b) 105 (c) 104 (d) 107

67. 9 + 66 =

(a) 87 (b) 75 (c) 84 (d) 81

68. 88 + 8 =

(a) 94 (b) 91 (c) 98 (d) 96

69. 4 + 78 =
(a) 79 (b) 82 (c) 67 (d) 87

70. 77 + 5 =
(a) 89 (b) 93 (c) 81 (d) 82

71. 6 + 58 =
(a) 62 (b) 64 (c) 67 (d) 69

72. 9 + 68 =
(a) 77 (b) 74 (c) 72 (d) 75

73. 79 + 9 =
(a) 84 (b) 93 (c) 88 (d) 91

74. 8 + 63 =
(a) 79 (b) 84 (c) 73 (d) 71

75. 47 + 5 =
(a) 49 (b) 54 (c) 52 (d) 58

76. 9 + 58 =
(a) 59 (b) 54 (c) 62 (d) 67

77. 75 + 9 =
(a) 87 (b) 89 (c) 86 (d) 84

78. 8 + 36 =
(a) 44 (b) 47 (c) 51 (d) 42

79. 49 + 9 =
(a) 67 (b) 77 (c) 58 (d) 51

80. 6 + 88 =
(a) 93 (b) 94 (c) 97 (d) 99

81. 87 + 9 =
(a) 96 (b) 98 (c) 94 (d) 92

82. 6 + 98 =

(a) 103 (b) 104 (c) 108 (d) 105

83. 53 + 6 =

(a) 62 (b) 64 (c) 58 (d) 59

84. 5 + 58 =

(a) 61 (b) 63 (c) 65 (d) 67

85. 89 + 6 =

(a) 89 (b) 95 (c) 97 (d) 94

86. 49 + 6 =

(a) 54 (b) 58 (c) 55 (d) 53

87. 9 + 86 =

(a) 89 (b) 94 (c) 93 (d) 95

88. 66 + 6 =

(a) 77 (b) 74 (c) 72 (d) 78

89. 4 + 93 =

(a) 96 (b) 97 (c) 98 (d) 99

90. 49 + 7 =

(a) 66 (b) 55 (c) 54 (d) 56

91. 4 + 77 =

(a) 81 (b) 83 (c) 86 (d) 84

92. 44 + 6 =

(a) 53 (b) 52 (c) 50 (d) 49

93. 7 + 86 =

(a) 89 (b) 93 (c) 95 (d) 91

94. 88 + 5 =

(a) 95 (b) 98 (c) 96 (d) 93

95. 4 + 65 =

(a) 69 (b) 71 (c) 73 (d) 75

96. 38 + 5 =

(a) 44 (b) 48 (c) 43 (d) 47

97. 8 + 28 =

(a) 37 (b) 36 (c) 39 (d) 41

98. 57 + 8 =

(a) 64 (b) 67 (c) 62 (d) 65

99. 4 + 68 =

(a) 71 (b) 72 (c) 75 (d) 69

100. 82 + 6 =

(a) 89 (b) 85 (c) 88 (d) 95

101. 2 + 57 =

(a) 66 (b) 59 (c) 63 (d) 64

102. 67 + 5 =

(a) 74 (b) 72 (c) 77 (d) 63

103. 4 + 35 =

(a) 37 (b) 42 (c) 39 (d) 38

104. 62 + 5 =

(a) 64 (b) 67 (c) 59 (d) 69

105. 7 + 39 =

(a) 44 (b) 48 (c) 46 (d) 49

106. 65 + 9 =

(a) 77 (b) 74 (c) 69 (d) 78

107. 7 + 45 =

(a) 54 (b) 55 (c) 57 (d) 52

108. 81 + 5 =

(a) 96 (b) 89 (c) 84 (d) 86

109. 3 + 65 =

(a) 67 (b) 68 (c) 71 (d) 69

110. 38 + 8 =

(a) 45 (b) 47 (c) 46 (d) 49

111. 4 + 88 =

(a) 90 (b) 93 (c) 96 (d) 92

112. 27 + 6 =

(a) 35 (b) 33 (c) 37 (d) 39

113. 7 + 67 =

(a) 77 (b) 73 (c) 74 (d) 76

ADDITION (जोड़)

Type-1: Answer - Key

1.	(b)	**24.**	(d)	**47.**	(b)	**70.**	(d)	**93.**	(b)
2.	(d)	**25.**	(b)	**48.**	(d)	**71.**	(b)	**94.**	(d)
3.	(a)	**26.**	(b)	**49.**	(b)	**72.**	(a)	**95.**	(a)
4.	(c)	**27.**	(d)	**50.**	(d)	**73.**	(c)	**96.**	(c)
5.	(b)	**28.**	(d)	**51.**	(b)	**74.**	(d)	**97.**	(b)
6.	(d)	**29.**	(c)	**52.**	(d)	**75.**	(c)	**98.**	(d)
7.	(c)	**30.**	(d)	**53.**	(b)	**76.**	(d)	**99.**	(b)
8.	(a)	**31.**	(a)	**54.**	(d)	**77.**	(d)	**100.**	(c)
9.	(b)	**32.**	(c)	**55.**	(a)	**78.**	(a)	**101.**	(b)
10.	(d)	**33.**	(c)	**56.**	(d)	**79.**	(c)	**102.**	(b)
11.	(c)	**34.**	(b)	**57.**	(b)	**80.**	(b)	**103.**	(c)
12.	(d)	**35.**	(c)	**58.**	(c)	**81.**	(a)	**104.**	(b)
13.	(d)	**36.**	(b)	**59.**	(d)	**82.**	(b)	**105.**	(c)
14.	(c)	**37.**	(a)	**60.**	(a)	**83.**	(d)	**106.**	(b)
15.	(b)	**38.**	(c)	**61.**	(b)	**84.**	(b)	**107.**	(d)
16.	(d)	**39.**	(d)	**62.**	(d)	**85.**	(b)	**108.**	(d)
17.	(b)	**40.**	(c)	**63.**	(b)	**86.**	(c)	**109.**	(b)
18.	(a)	**41.**	(a)	**64.**	(d)	**87.**	(d)	**110.**	(c)
19.	(c)	**42.**	(a)	**65.**	(c)	**88.**	(c)	**111.**	(d)
20.	(d)	**43.**	(b)	**66.**	(b)	**89.**	(b)	**112.**	(b)
21.	(c)	**44.**	(b)	**67.**	(b)	**90.**	(d)	**113.**	(c)
22.	(a)	**45.**	(b)	**68.**	(d)	**91.**	(a)		
23.	(c)	**46.**	(d)	**69.**	(b)	**92.**	(c)		

Type-2

Hint :

23 + 47

☞ दोनों संख्याओं का दहाई (Tens) का अंक (digit) जोड़कर (2 + 4 = 6) के आगे zero मानकर (60) को दिमाग में रखें फिर दोनों संख्याओं के इकाई (unit) का अंक (digit) (3 + 7) दिमाग वाली संख्या (60) में जोड़ दें, तो Answer आ जाएगा।

Step – 1 = 2 + 4 = 6 → 0 ⇒ मान लिया

Step – 2 = 3 + 7 = 10

Step – 3 = 60 + 10 = 70

Exercise

1. **23 + 47 =**
   (a) 72 (b) 68 (c) 70 (d) 67
2. **48 + 55 =**
   (a) 101 (b) 103 (c) 105 (d) 107
3. **96 + 37 =**
   (a) 130 (b) 137 (c) 133 (d) 136
4. **43 + 86 =**
   (a) 126 (b) 129 (c) 134 (d) 123
5. **57 + 74 =**
   (a) 137 (b) 141 (c) 144 (d) 131

6. 43 + 39 =
(a) 82 (b) 87 (c) 83 (d) 79

7. 39 + 58 =
(a) 89 (b) 91 (c) 93 (d) 97

8. 78 + 87 =
(a) 168 (b) 165 (c) 164 (d) 167

9. 28 + 82 =
(a) 108 (b) 111 (c) 114 (d) 110

10. 97 + 79 =
(a) 178 (b) 179 (c) 176 (d) 175

11. 68 + 98 =
(a) 167 (b) 166 (c) 171 (d) 156

12. 48 + 54 =
(a) 102 (b) 107 (c) 111 (d) 106

13. 24 + 42 =
(a) 56 (b) 69 (c) 67 (d) 66

14. 76 + 67 =
(a) 163 (b) 155 (c) 144 (d) 143

15. 59 + 95 =
(a) 169 (b) 154 (c) 149 (d) 177

16. 63 + 36 =
(a) 90 (b) 103 (c) 105 (d) 99

17. 47 + 52 =
(a) 107 (b) 99 (c) 109 (d) 113

18. 77 + 87 =
(a) 159 (b) 168 (c) 175 (d) 164

19. 88 + 98 =

(a) 189 (b) 192 (c) 186 (d) 184

20. 78 + 52 =

(a) 145 (b) 155 (c) 137 (d) 130

21. 88 + 88 =

(a) 189 (b) 176 (c) 187 (d) 175

22. 89 + 37 =

(a) 145 (b) 148 (c) 138 (d) 126

23. 77 + 77 =

(a) 160 (b) 154 (c) 163 (d) 159

24. 99 + 99 =

(a) 196 (b) 199 (c) 203 (d) 198

25. 78 + 75 =

(a) 160 (b) 153 (c) 163 (d) 167

26. 73 + 67 =

(a) 155 (b) 140 (c) 135 (d) 130

27. 45 + 48 =

(a) 98 (b) 89 (c) 93 (d) 85

28. 51 + 42 =

(a) 86 (b) 93 (c) 97 (d) 77

29. 65 + 57 =

(a) 143 (b) 125 (c) 122 (d) 135

30. 82 + 57 =

(a) 155 (b) 148 (c) 136 (d) 139

31. 43 + 85 =

(a) 134 (b) 145 (c) 128 (d) 141

32. 28 + 98 =
(a) 143 (b) 155 (c) 138 (d) 126

33. 97 + 57 =
(a) 167 (b) 154 (c) 177 (d) 149

34. 49 + 37 =
(a) 89 (b) 79 (c) 90 (d) 86

35. 75 + 47 =
(a) 137 (b) 122 (c) 139 (d) 145

36. 88 + 98 =
(a) 197 (b) 189 (c) 179 (d) 186

37. 71 + 67 =
(a) 146 (b) 157 (c) 138 (d) 165

38. 57 + 75 =
(a) 133 (b) 164 (c) 154 (d) 132

39. 91 + 35 =
(a) 157 (b) 126 (c) 173 (d) 165

40. 47 + 37 =
(a) 96 (b) 78 (c) 97 (d) 84

41. 85 + 39 =
(a) 155 (b) 145 (c) 124 (d) 137

42. 95 + 82 =
(a) 177 (b) 197 (c) 179 (d) 190

43. 82 + 91 =
(a) 189 (b) 194 (c) 176 (d) 173

44. 98 + 67 =
(a) 199 (b) 180 (c) 170 (d) 165

45. 76 + 81 =

(a) 179 (b) 157 (c) 160 (d) 169

46. 34 + 56 =

(a) 55 (b) 47 (c) 90 (d) 49

47. 29 + 67 =

(a) 99 (b) 96 (c) 78 (d) 85

48. 97 + 71 =

(a) 168 (b) 180 (c) 193 (d) 199

49. 53 + 64 =

(a) 127 (b) 137 (c) 117 (d) 147

50. 82 + 46 =

(a) 134 (b) 128 (c) 143 (d) 138

51. 73 + 64 =

(a) 148 (b) 154 (c) 137 (d) 167

52. 19 + 76 =

(a) 109 (b) 95 (c) 89 (d) 99

53. 49 + 94 =

(a) 157 (b) 163 (c) 143 (d) 156

54. 65 + 77 =

(a) 125 (b) 156 (c) 167 (d) 142

55. 94 + 65 =

(a) 159 (b) 189 (c) 178 (d) 169

56. 64 + 73 =

(a) 157 (b) 148 (c) 166 (d) 137

57. 77 + 94 =

(a) 180 (b) 199 (c) 174 (d) 171

58. 34 + 43 =
(a) 66 (b) 79 (c) 77 (d) 55

59. 69 + 76 =
(a) 160 (b) 188 (c) 145 (d) 126

60. 35 + 53 =
(a) 77 (b) 97 (c) 55 (d) 88

61. 76 + 46 =
(a) 145 (b) 155 (c) 122 (d) 138

62. 19 + 91 =
(a) 115 (b) 123 (c) 128 (d) 110

63. 43 + 46 =
(a) 92 (b) 98 (c) 87 (d) 89

64. 91 + 97 =
(a) 179 (b) 168 (c) 158 (d) 188

65. 57 + 67 =
(a) 144 (b) 168 (c) 124 (d) 166

66. 58 + 88 =
(a) 146 (b) 176 (c) 157 (d) 188

67. 95 + 66 =
(a) 177 (b) 181 (c) 187 (d) 161

68. 35 + 76 =
(a) 145 (b) 166 (c) 111 (d) 177

69. 77 + 57 =
(a) 134 (b) 155 (c) 188 (d) 189

70. 53 + 59 =
(a) 127 (b) 147 (c) 167 (d) 112

71. 65 + 43 =
(a) 113 (b) 125 (c) 108 (d) 134

72. 46 + 64 =
(a) 119 (b) 128 (c) 145 (d) 110

73. 38 + 48 =
(a) 99 (b) 86 (c) 78 (d) 66

74. 57 + 23 =
(a) 69 (b) 89 (c) 80 (d) 92

75. 81 + 67 =
(a) 165 (b) 157 (c) 144 (d) 148

76. 66 + 66 =
(a) 154 (b) 137 (c) 132 (d) 147

77. 14 + 41 =
(a) 67 (b) 73 (c) 88 (d) 55

78. 65 + 32 =
(a) 88 (b) 93 (c) 97 (d) 104

79. 39 + 75 =
(a) 125 (b) 145 (c) 137 (d) 114

80. 58 + 30 =
(a) 88 (b) 98 (c) 69 (d) 76

81. 77 + 78 =
(a) 167 (b) 178 (c) 129 (d) 155

82. 28 + 82 =
(a) 122 (b) 135 (c) 110 (d) 144

83. 36 + 57 =
(a) 83 (b) 93 (c) 77 (d) 87

84. 77 + 79 =

(a) 165 (b) 155 (c) 156 (d) 176

85. 98 + 87 =

(a) 187 (b) 194 (c) 185 (d) 176

86. 54 + 58 =

(a) 122 (b) 113 (c) 135 (d) 112

87. 25 + 42 =

(a) 77 (b) 57 (c) 67 (d) 86

88. 67 + 86 =

(a) 167 (b) 189 (c) 177 (d) 153

89. 58 + 85 =

(a) 134 (b) 155 (c) 143 (d) 165

90. 73 + 36 =

(a) 121 (b) 134 (c) 109 (d) 117

91. 87 + 52 =

(a) 149 (b) 159 (c) 129 (d) 139

92. 35 + 77 =

(a) 132 (b) 112 (c) 122 (d) 162

93. 89 + 98 =

(a) 177 (b) 197 (c) 167 (d) 187

94. 52 + 79 =

(a) 144 (b) 151 (c) 121 (d) 131

95. 88 + 83 =

(a) 177 (b) 171 (c) 189 (d) 176

96. 75 + 77 =

(a) 142 (b) 157 (c) 152 (d) 174

97. 98 + 79 =
(a) 167 (b) 188 (c) 158 (d) 177

98. 46 + 78 =
(a) 123 (b) 124 (c) 157 (d) 138

99. 85 + 34 =
(a) 136 (b) 128 (c) 119 (d) 147

100. 76 + 45 =
(a) 155 (b) 121 (c) 147 (d) 161

101. 83 + 33 =
(a) 125 (b) 141 (c) 136 (d) 116

102. 59 + 62 =
(a) 133 (b) 141 (c) 121 (d) 135

103. 67 + 87 =
(a) 174 (b) 184 (c) 161 (d) 154

104. 55 + 89 =
(a) 124 (b) 155 (c) 144 (d) 165

105. 44 + 86 =
(a) 130 (b) 141 (c) 124 (d) 166

106. 58 + 87 =
(a) 157 (b) 178 (c) 136 (d) 145

107. 58 + 37 =
(a) 77 (b) 89 (c) 95 (d) 93

108. 87 + 35 =
(a) 143 (b) 156 (c) 155 (d) 122

109. 58 + 98 =
(a) 166 (b) 177 (c) 156 (d) 146

110. 67 + 91 =
(a) 158 (b) 168 (c) 178 (d) 148

111. 95 + 75 =
(a) 170 (b) 178 (c) 180 (d) 138

112. 85 + 93 =
(a) 149 (b) 168 (c) 183 (d) 178

113. 66 + 37 =
(a) 107 (b) 103 (c) 105 (d) 108

114. 85 + 43 =
(a) 128 (b) 148 (c) 136 (d) 156

115. 97 + 85 =
(a) 178 (b) 192 (c) 182 (d) 172

116. 91 + 83 =
(a) 184 (b) 174 (c) 164 (d) 155

117. 65 + 98 =
(a) 166 (b) 174 (c) 163 (d) 143

118. 76 + 71 =
(a) 147 (b) 138 (c) 159 (d) 129

Type-2: Answer - Key

1.	(c)	25.	(b)	49.	(c)	73.	(b)	97.	(d
2.	(b)	26.	(b)	50.	(b)	74.	(c)	98.	(b)
3.	(c)	27.	(c)	51.	(c)	75.	(d)	99.	(c)
4.	(b)	28.	(b)	52.	(b)	76.	(c)	100.	(b)
5.	(d)	29.	(c)	53.	(c)	77.	(d)	101.	(d)
6.	(a)	30.	(d)	54.	(d)	78.	(c)	102.	(c)
7.	(d)	31.	(c)	55.	(a)	79.	(d)	103.	(d)
8.	(b)	32.	(d)	56.	(d)	80.	(a)	104.	(c)
9.	(d)	33.	(b)	57.	(d)	81.	(d)	105.	(a)
10.	(c)	34.	(d)	58.	(c)	82.	(c)	106.	(d)
11.	(b)	35.	(b)	59.	(c)	83.	(b)	107.	(c)
12.	(a)	36.	(d)	60.	(d)	84.	(c)	108.	(d)
13.	(d)	37.	(c)	61.	(c)	85.	(c)	109.	(c)
14.	(d)	38.	(d)	62.	(d)	86.	(d)	110.	(a)
15.	(b)	39.	(b)	63.	(d)	87.	(c)	111.	(a)
16.	(d)	40.	(d)	64.	(d)	88.	(d)	112.	(d)
17.	(b)	41.	(c)	65.	(c)	89.	(c)	113.	(b)
18.	(d)	42.	(a)	66.	(a)	90.	(c)	114.	(a)
19.	(c)	43.	(d)	67.	(d)	91.	(d)	115.	(c)
20.	(d)	44.	(d)	68.	(c)	92.	(b)	116.	(b)
21.	(b)	45.	(b)	69.	(a)	93.	(d)	117.	(c)
22.	(d)	46.	(c)	70.	(d)	94.	(d)	118.	(a)
23.	(b)	47.	(b)	71.	(c)	95.	(b)		
24.	(d)	48.	(a)	72.	(d)	96.	(c)		

Type-3

Hint :

173 + 98 + 92 + 78 + 43 + 68 + 65 + 97

☞ पहली संख्या का सैंकड़ें (Hundred) वाले अंक (digit) (1) के आगे दो zero मानकर दिमाग में रखना है और बचे हुए सभी संख्याओं के दहाई (Tens) के अंकों (digit) को जोड़कर एक zero और दिमाग में रखना है और पहले सैंकड़ें (Hundred) की दिमाग में रखी संख्या में जोड़ना है, तो परिणाम 670 आता है। 670 को दिमाग में रखकर इकाई (unit) के अंक (digit) वाली सभी संख्याओं को दिमाग में रखी संख्या में जोड़ दें, तो Answer आ जाता है।

Step-1 ⇒ 1(00) → मान लिए

Step-2 ⇒ 7 + 9 + 9 + 7 + 4 + 6 + 6 + 9

⇒ 57<u>0</u> + 100 = 670
(0 मान)

Step-3 ⇒ 3 + 8 + 2 + 8 + 3 + 8 + 5 + 7

⇒ 670 + 44 = **714**

Exercise

1. 173 + 98 + 92 + 78 + 43 + 68 + 65 + 97

(a) 714 (b) 814 (c) 658 (d) 865

2. **84 + 93 + 94 + 73 + 57 + 37 + 41 + 82**
(a) 663 (b) 461 (c) 561 (d) 771

3. **69 + 96 + 93 + 43 + 47 + 55 + 59**
(a) 367 (b) 572 (c) 442 (d) 462

4. **19 + 69 + 39 + 49 + 89 + 79 + 34 + 81**
(a) 548 (b) 459 (c) 467 (d) 482

5. **73 + 47 + 58 + 68 + 78 + 97 + 80**
(a) 573 (b) 501 (c) 583 (d) 494

6. **45 + 37 + 46 + 27 + 46 + 2**
(a) 304 (b) 403 (c) 203 (d) 303

7. **47 + 34 + 46 + 89 + 72 + 71 + 64 + 22**
(a) 555 (b) 445 (c) 345 (d) 465

8. **35 + 64 + 78 + 45 + 76 + 79**
(a) 347 (b) 457 (c) 387 (d) 377

9. **64 + 76 + 81 + 89 + 72 + 43 + 64 + 74**
(a) 667 (b) 563 (c) 488 (d) 566

10. **34 + 64 + 75 + 95 + 82 + 46 + 64**
(a) 560 (b) 470 (c) 453 (d) 460

11. **75 + 57 + 81 + 34 + 64 + 95**
(a) 308 (b) 406 (c) 409 (d) 506

12. **54 + 86 + 95 + 86 + 75 + 77 + 67 + 25**
(a) 666 (b) 465 (c) 766 (d) 565

13. **34 + 64 + 54 + 84 + 75 + 95**
(a) 406 (b) 505 (c) 308 (d) 411

14. **74 + 64 + 82 + 47 + 71 + 67 + 94**
(a) 566 (b) 488 (c) 499 (d) 579

15. **97 + 11 + 11 + 35 + 73 + 99 + 99 + 38**
(a) 763 (b) 566 (c) 435 (d) 463

16. **66 + 88 + 51 + 13 + 56 + 80**
(a) 354 (b) 255 (c) 455 (d) 665

17. **60 + 95 + 60 + 76 + 55 + 75 + 88 + 26**
(a) 645 (b) 455 (c) 543 (d) 535

18. **07 + 99 + 57 + 81 + 35 + 64**
(a) 245 (b) 343 (c) 444 (d) 356

19. **44 + 64 + 57 + 81 + 67 + 94 + 28**
(a) 535 (b) 365 (c) 478 (d) 435

20. **67 + 82 + 88 + 64 + 57 + 94**
(a) 440 (b) 452 (c) 367 (d) 662

21. **64 + 49 + 57 + 10 + 83 + 06 + 77 + 77**
(a) 427 (b) 533 (c) 423 (d) 323

22. **88 + 26 + 07 + 99 + 89 + 50**
(a) 359 (b) 459 (c) 558 (d) 462

23. **58 + 10 + 34 + 54 + 68 + 97 + 41**
(a) 266 (b) 463 (c) 562 (d) 362

24. **88 + 43 + 64 + 75 + 71 + 21**
(a) 436 (b) 362 (c) 448 (d) 562

25. **79 + 27 + 64 + 72 + 35 + 44 + 17**
(a) 333 (b) 348 (c) 338 (d) 543

26. **46 + 54 + 17 + 64 + 75 + 84**
(a) 440 (b) 340 (c) 541 (d) 348

27. **17 + 73 + 84 + 95 + 35 + 67 + 88 + 10**
(a) 569 (b) 779 (c) 449 (d) 469

28. 80 + 80 + 81 + 34 + 74 + 95

(a) 453 (b) 444 (c) 555 (d) 654

29. 55 + 86 + 98 + 88 + 75 + 77 + 67 + 25

(a) 582 (b) 471 (c) 571 (d) 661

30. 35 + 49 + 57 + 97 + 75 + 95

(a) 518 (b) 611 (c) 508 (d) 408

31. 85 + 69 + 83 + 49 + 71 + 67 + 94

(a) 518 (b) 448 (c) 428 (d) 538

32. 97 + 19 + 17 + 35 + 73 + 99 + 98 + 38

(a) 668 (b) 676 (c) 476 (d) 575

33. 68 + 78 + 51 + 13 + 56 + 80

(a) 554 (b) 346 (c) 446 (d) 646

34. 67 + 95 + 56 + 76 + 85 + 75 + 88 + 26

(a) 664 (b) 378 (c) 468 (d) 568

35. 07 + 99 + 64 + 81 + 46 + 64

(a) 267 (b) 461 (c) 361 (d) 541

36. 87 + 44 + 99 + 81 + 67 + 94 + 28

(a) 500 (b) 502 (c) 601 (d) 408

37. 97 + 85 + 88 + 66 + 57 + 94

(a) 589 (b) 688 (c) 487 (d) 577

38. 71 + 85 + 76 + 77 + 77 + 64 + 49 + 57

(a) 556 (b) 776 (c) 666 (d) 456

39. 78 + 21 + 57 + 90 + 88 + 61 + 89

(a) 585 (b) 488 (c) 584 (d) 484

40. 85 + 58 + 45 + 66 + 79

(a) 444 (b) 333 (c) 438 (d) 533

41. **77 + 68 + 05 + 98 + 88 + 57**

(a) 393 (b) 473 (c) 483 (d) 433

42. **78 + 10 + 38 + 54 + 99 + 97 + 41**

(a) 447 (b) 557 (c) 417 (d) 317

43. **69 + 49 + 54 + 76 + 71 + 31**

(a) 450 (b) 350 (c) 555 (d) 452

44. **89 + 57 + 64 + 62 + 88 + 19 + 17**

(a) 445 (b) 399 (c) 497 (d) 396

45. **88 + 97 + 37 + 15 + 69 + 95**

(a) 401 (b) 407 (c) 503 (d) 350

46. **54 + 36 + 85 + 89 + 78 + 77 + 67 + 25**

(a) 511 (b) 411 (c) 533 (d) 423

47. **54 + 94 + 74 + 84 + 65 + 95**

(a) 466 (b) 546 (c) 448 (d) 365

48. **84 + 64 + 72 + 49 + 71 + 67 + 94**

(a) 602 (b) 401 (c) 507 (d) 501

49. **97 + 19 + 19 + 38 + 73 + 99**

(a) 436 (b) 543 (c) 345 (d) 447

50. **86 + 78 + 57 + 67 + 95 + 88**

(a) 663 (b) 471 (c) 473 (d) 575

51. **68 + 95 + 68 + 76 + 59 + 79 + 88 + 26**

(a) 764 (b) 481 (c) 679 (d) 559

52. **97 + 96 + 67 + 81 + 35 + 64**

(a) 542 (b) 544 (c) 440 (d) 641

53. **74 + 84 + 57 + 85 + 67 + 94 + 28**

(a) 689 (b) 489 (c) 588 (d) 479

54. 66 + 98 + 87 + 66 + 58 + 94

(a) 469 (b) 579 (c) 559 (d) 589

55. 19 + 36 + 45 + 76 + 77 + 64 + 49 + 57

(a) 323 (b) 453 (c) 556 (d) 423

56. 78 + 21 + 59 + 70 + 08 + 61 + 72

(a) 459 (b) 369 (c) 458 (d) 558

57. 94 + 47 + 43 + 68 + 77

(a) 269 (b) 439 (c) 329 (d) 427

58. 73 + 98 + 92 + 78 + 43 + 68 + 65 + 97 + 66 + 45

(a) 827 (b) 924 (c) 725 (d) 725

59. 84 + 93 + 94 + 73 + 65 + 23 + 57 + 37 + 41 + 82

(a) 779 (b) 984 (c) 724 (d) 649

60. 19 + 69 + 39 + 49 + 89 + 79 + 34 + 81 + 34 + 11

(a) 496 (b) 608 (c) 504 (d) 404

61. 73 + 47 + 58 + 68 + 56 + 33 + 78 + 97 + 80

(a) 590 (b) 680 (c) 790 (d) 874

62. 86 + 87 + 37 + 21 + 43 + 78 + 94 + 43 + 23 + 93 + 69

(a) 873 (b) 963 (c) 577 (d) 674

63. 45 + 37 + 46 + 27 + 46 + 25 + 46 + 74 + 48 + 92 + 79

(a) 765 (b) 565 (c) 668 (d) 475

64. **47 + 34 + 46 + 89 + 70 + 72 + 71 + 64 + 22 + 53**

(a) 669 (b) 755 (c) 568 (d) 478

65. **64 + 76 + 81 + 39 + 12 + 89+ 72 + 43 + 64 + 74**

(a) 614 (b) 524 (c) 674 (d) 513

66. **34 + 64 + 75 + 95 + 82 + 46 + 64 + 67 + 23 + 99**

(a) 789 (b) 649 (c) 569 (d) 779

67. **75 + 57 + 81 + 34 + 64 + 95 + 24 + 53**

(a) 448 (b) 493 (c) 353 (d) 483

68. **54 + 86 + 95 + 86 + 75 + 77 + 67 + 25 + 89 + 56**

(a) 730 (b) 711 (c) 710 (d) 620

69. **74 + 64 + 82 + 47 + 71 + 67 + 94 + 48 + 98**

(a) 735 (b) 845 (c) 569 (d) 645

70. **97 + 11 + 11 + 35 + 73 + 99 + 99 + 38 + 97 + 33**

(a) 694 (b) 883 (c) 593 (d) 795

71. **66 + 88 + 51 + 13 + 56 + 80 + 43 + 52**

(a) 648 (b) 449 (c) 488 (d) 359

72. **60 + 95 + 60 + 76 + 55 + 75 + 88 + 26**

(a) 535 (b) 645 (c) 743 (d) 434

73. **07 + 99 + 57 + 81 + 35 + 4 + 84 + 62**

(a) 579 (b) 669 (c) 389 (d) 429

74. **44 + 64 + 57 + 81 + 67 + 94 + 28 + 76 + 34**
(a) 579 (b) 545 (c) 389 (d) 489

75. **10 + 83 + 06 + 77 + 77 + 64 + 49 + 57 + 54 + 91**
(a) 778 (b) 888 (c) 458 (d) 568

76. **98 + 21 + 59 + 70 + 08 + 61 + 82 + 53 + 61**
(a) 447 (b) 513 (c) 524 (d) 443

77. **88 + 26 + 07 + 99 + 89 + 50 + 94 + 15 + 13**
(a) 533 (b) 491 (c) 587 (d) 481

78. **58 + 10 + 34 + 54 + 68 + 97 + 41 + 54 + 68**
(a) 574 (b) 544 (c) 484 (d) 584

79. **88 + 43 + 64 + 75 + 71 + 21 + 74 + 24**
(a) 533 (b) 460 (c) 587 (d) 481

80. **79 + 27 + 64 + 72 + 35 + 44 + 17 + 54 + 89**
(a) 783 (b) 583 (c) 491 (d) 481

81. **46 + 54 + 17 + 64 + 75 + 84 + 43 + 23 + 82**
(a) 488 (b) 583 (c) 584 (d) 398

82. **17 + 73 + 84 + 95 + 35 + 67 + 88 + 10 + 76 + 32**
(a) 677 (b) 666 (c) 577 (d) 487

83. **89 + 80 + 81 + 34 + 74 + 95 + 33 + 52**
(a) 477 (b) 538 (c) 438 (d) 432

84. **55 + 86 + 98 + 88 + 75 + 77 + 67 + 25 + 34 + 44**
(a) 650 (b) 760 (c) 649 (d) 450

85. **85 + 69 + 83 + 49 + 71 + 67 + 94 + 54 + 21**
(a) 573 (b) 593 (c) 669 (d) 793

86. **97 + 17 + 19 + 35 + 73 + 99 + 98 + 34**
(a) 790 (b) 472 (c) 572 (d) 484

87. **68 + 78 + 51 + 13 + 56 + 80 + 74 + 81 + 32**
(a) 653 (b) 463 (c) 533 (d) 433

88. **67 + 95 + 56 + 76 + 85 + 75 + 88 + 26 + 23 + 45**
(a) 636 (b) 566 (c) 578 (d) 486

89. **97 + 85 + 88 + 66 + 57 + 9 + 34**
(a) 356 (b) 546 (c) 448 (d) 436

90. **71 + 85 + 76 + 77 + 77 + 64 + 49 + 57 + 89 + 25**
(a) 670 (b) 472 (c) 570 (d) 480

91. **78 + 10 + 38 + 54 + 99 + 97 + 47 + 56**
(a) 380 (b) 484 (c) 479 (d) 578

92. **69 + 49 + 54 + 76 + 71 + 31 + 76 + 34 + 56**
(a) 518 (b) 516 (c) 661 (d) 417

93. **88 + 97 + 37 + 15 + 69 + 95 + 78 + 23 + 56 + 88**
(a) 666 (b) 746 (c) 656 (d) 646

94. **54 + 94 + 74 + 84 + 65 + 95 + 70 + 98 + 45**
(a) 679 (b) 589 (c) 788 (d) 658

95. **84 + 64 + 72 + 49 + 71 + 67 + 94 + 34 + 76**
(a) 514 (b) 623 (c) 611 (d) 725

96. **19 + 36 + 45 + 76 + 77 + 64 + 49 + 57 + 72**

(a) 584 (b) 495 (c) 594 (d) 398

97. **78 + 21 + 59 + 70 + 08 + 61 + 72 + 78 + 26 + 57**

(a) 621 (b) 524 (c) 420 (d) 530

98. **94 + 47 + 43 + 68 + 77 + 45 + 56 + 23**

(a) 453 (b) 554 (c) 445 (d) 489

99. **78 + 21 + 57 + 90 + 88 + 61 + 89 + 57 + 77**

(a) 788 (b) 517 (c) 618 (d) 422

100. **85 + 58 + 45 + 66 + 79 + 44 + 72 + 38 + 66**

(a) 654 (b) 553 (c) 755 (d) 352

101. **78 + 10 + 38 + 54 + 21 + 99 + 97 + 41 + 78**

(a) 614 (b) 517 (c) 616 (d) 516

102. **89 + 57 + 64 + 62 + 88 + 19 + 17 + 64 + 39 + 77**

(a) 576 (b) 578 (c) 479 (d) 678

Type-3: Answer - Key

1.	(a)	22.	(a)	43.	(b)	64.	(c)	85.	(b)
2.	(c)	23.	(d)	44.	(d)	65.	(a)	86.	(b)
3.	(d)	24.	(b)	45.	(a)	66.	(b)	87.	(c)
4.	(b)	25.	(c)	46.	(a)	67.	(d)	88.	(a)
5.	(b)	26.	(b)	47.	(a)	68.	(c)	89.	(d)
6.	(c)	27.	(d)	48.	(d)	69.	(d)	90.	(a)
7.	(b)	28.	(b)	49.	(c)	70.	(c)	91.	(c)
8.	(d)	29.	(c)	50.	(b)	71.	(b)	92.	(b)
9.	(b)	30.	(d)	51.	(d)	72.	(a)	93.	(d)
10.	(d)	31.	(a)	52.	(c)	73.	(d)	94.	(a)
11.	(b)	32.	(c)	53.	(b)	74.	(b)	95.	(c)
12.	(d)	33.	(b)	54.	(a)	75.	(d)	96.	(b)
13.	(a)	34.	(d)	55.	(d)	76.	(b)	97.	(d)
14.	(c)	35.	(c)	56.	(b)	77.	(d)	98.	(a)
15.	(d)	36.	(a)	57.	(c)	78.	(c)	99.	(c)
16.	(a)	37.	(c)	58.	(c)	79.	(b)	100.	(b)
17.	(d)	38.	(a)	59.	(d)	80.	(d)	101.	(d)
18.	(b)	39.	(d)	60.	(c)	81.	(a)	102.	(a)
19.	(d)	40.	(b)	61.	(a)	82.	(c)		
20.	(b)	41.	(a)	62.	(d)	83.	(b)		
21.	(c)	42.	(c)	63.	(b)	84.	(c)		

Type-4

Hint :

Type-4 / Type-5 / Type-6

☞ ये सभी Type [1, 2, 3] पर आधारित है। दिमाग में calculation कीजिए।

☞ पहले सैकड़े वाले अंक (Hundred digit) साथ में 0 0 फिर दहाई वाले अंक (Tens digit) साथ में 0 फिर इकाई अंक (Unit digit)।

Exercise

1. 153 + 278 + 654 + 321 + 243 + 126

(a) 1777 (b) 1678 (c) 1775 (d) 1778

2. 653 + 823 + 669 + 789 + 653

(a) 3345 (b) 3587 (c) 3488 (d) 4487

3. 887 + 778 + 894 + 326 + 125 + 257

(a) 3366 (b) 3165 (c) 3267 (d) 4268

4. 666 + 771 + 818 + 929 + 679 + 674

(a) 4537 (b) 5547 (c) 3627 (d) 6548

5. 774 + 474 + 694 + 884 + 994 + 63

(a) 3883 (b) 4287 (c) 4777 (d) 4885

6. 989 + 619 + 453 + 682 + 91

(a) 2444 (b) 3835 (c) 2834 (d) 3453

7. **212 + 323 + 914 + 420 + 680 + 741**
(a) 3680 (b) 2780 (c) 4290 (d) 3290

8. **425 + 645 + 945 + 854 + 814**
(a) 3585 (b) 3683 (c) 4183 (d) 3284

9. **851 + 648 + 751 + 645 + 958**
(a) 3553 (b) 3883 (c) 3853 (d) 4784

10. **215 + 546 + 851 + 356 + 9 + 574**
(a) 2453 (b) 2551 (c) 3541 (d) 2652

11. **141 + 451 + 656 + 252 + 895**
(a) 2395 (b) 2485 (c) 3795 (d) 2694

12. **484 + 656 + 758 + 154 + 785**
(a) 2738 (b) 3837 (c) 4377 (d) 2837

13. **417 + 548 + 656 + 958 + 187 + 517**
(a) 2689 (b) 4367 (c) 3283 (d) 3385

14. **435 + 645 + 487 + 487 + 254 + 785**
(a) 3592 (b) 3093 (c) 3993 (d) 2894

15. **252 + 356 + 645 + 784 + 589 + 258**
(a) 2785 (b) 3283 (c) 2985 (d) 2884

16. **147 + 548 + 784 + 689 + 369 + 258**
(a) 3784 (b) 4583 (c) 3494 (d) 2795

17. **354 + 645 + 958 + 784 + 678**
(a) 3419 (b) 2919 (c) 3449 (d) 2899

18. **159 + 858 + 645 + 948 + 287**
(a) 2789 (b) 2887 (c) 2897 (d) 3697

19. **125 + 456 + 987 + 132 + 485 + 558**
(a) 2743 (b) 2844 (c) 2955 (d) 3243

20. 193 + 378 + 854 + 351

(a) 1777 (b) 1776 (c) 1686 (d) 1896

21. 763 + 923 + 769 + 599 + 653

(a) 3808 (b) 3507 (c) 2907 (d) 3707

22. 897 + 758 + 864 + 576

(a) 3696 (b) 3095 (c) 2967 (d) 3345

23. 676 + 991 + 588 + 959 + 579 + 774

(a) 4538 (b) 4434 (c) 4567 (d) 4237

24. 876 + 548 + 773 + 234 + 121

(a) 2552 (b) 4453 (c) 3252 (d) 3355

25. 794 + 884 + 574 + 764 + 554 + 854

(a) 4525 (b) 4626 (c) 4724 (d) 4424

26. 449 + 669 + 763 + 752 + 81 + 123 + 214

(a) 3055 (b) 4451 (c) 3051 (d) 2452

27. 972 + 533 + 674 + 452 + 650 + 841

(a) 4431 (b) 5451 (c) 4122 (d) 4424

28. 925 + 965 + 445 + 884 + 784

(a) 5008 (b) 4578 (c) 4004 (d) 4003

29. 981 + 468 + 541 + 465 + 598

(a) 2553 (b) 3053 (c) 4053 (d) 5553

30. 125 + 456 + 851 + 536 + 9 + 599 + 67 + 245

(a) 2888 (b) 4883 (c) 3888 (d) 4898

31. 814 + 641 + 656 + 522 + 885 + 851 + 536

(a) 6905 (b) 5908 (c) 4905 (d) 5598

ADDITION (जोड़)

32. 984 + 756 + 658 + 554 + 885 + 45 + 234

(a) 4116 (b) 3716 (c) 4446 (d) 5161

33. 617 + 864 + 856 + 768 + 557 + 617

(a) 4557 (b) 4279 (c) 3790 (d) 4789

34. 835 + 745 + 887 + 467 + 784 + 786

(a) 5545 (b) 6447 (c) 4504 (d) 4605

35. 373 + 458 + 654 + 321 + 345 + 123

(a) 2575 (b) 2274 (c) 2477 (d) 3325

36. 753 + 553 + 689 + 469 + 653

(a) 3377 (b) 3218 (c) 4818 (d) 3117

37. 986 + 758 + 464 + 826 + 123 + 321

(a) 3478 (b) 3378 (c) 3688 (d) 3278

38. 798 + 454 + 660 + 856 + 954 + 756

(a) 5577 (b) 3380 (c) 2377 (d) 4478

39. 956 + 675 + 484 + 676 + 87

(a) 4187 (b) 3678 (c) 2878 (d) 2688

40. 872 + 643 + 464 + 580 + 870 + 741

(a) 4360 (b) 4280 (c) 4375 (d) 4170

41. 225 + 645 + 845 + 954 + 914

(a) 3384 (b) 2583 (c) 3583 (d) 4578

42. 641 + 648 + 301 + 645 + 958 + 342 + 121

(a) 3656 (b) 4566 (c) 3256 (d) 3568

43. 755 + 546 + 851 + 466 + 9 + 574

(a) 2722 (b) 3201 (c) 4421 (d) 4203

44. 354 + 551 + 659 + 252 + 895

(a) 3122 (b) 3212 (c) 2814 (d) 2711

45. 450 + 466 + 598 + 764 + 795 + 22+ 121

(a) 3116 (b) 3246 (c) 3216 (d) 3566

46. 459 + 550 + 675 + 950 + 187 + 517

(a) 3488 (b) 3268 (c) 3337 (d) 3338

47. 405 + 955 + 588 + 487 + 254 + 785 + 135

(a) 4609 (b) 3789 (c) 3609 (d) 3580

48. 653 + 823 + 669 + 789 + 653 + 245 + 121

(a) 3953 (b) 4255 (c) 4273 (d) 5774

49. 887 + 778 + 894 + 326 + 356 + 122

(a) 4468 (b) 4661 (c) 4363 (d) 3363

50. 666 + 771 + 818 + 443 + 929 + 679 + 674

(a) 4780 (b) 4980 (c) 4790 (d) 5780

51. 774 + 474 + 694 + 884 + 994 + 634 + 342 + 442

(a) 5339 (b) 5388 (c) 5238 (d) 5536

52. 489 + 619 + 453 + 682 + 91 + 34 + 71

(a) 2540 (b) 2439 (c) 2242 (d) 3240

53. 212 + 323 + 914 + 420 + 680 + 741

(a) 3491 (b) 3290 (c) 2493 (d) 3494

54. 234 + 134 + 425 + 645 + 945 + 854 + 814

(a) 3106 (b) 3366 (c) 4051 (d) 3486

55. 851 + 648 + 751 + 645 + 958

(a) 3553 (b) 3455 (c) 4154 (d) 3853

56. 215 + 546 + 851 + 356 + 9 + 574 + 111 + 325

(a) 2788 (b) 3277 (c) 2987 (d) 2928

57. 154 + 451 + 656 + 252 + 895 + 132

(a) 2346 (b) 2542 (c) 2540 (d) 2441

58. 484 + 656 + 758 + 154 + 785 + 121 + 174

(a) 3132 (b) 3433 (c) 3237 (d) 3720

59. 417 + 548 + 656 + 958 + 187 + 517

(a) 3385 (b) 4573 (c) 4184 (d) 3283

60. 435 + 645 + 487 + 487 + 254 + 785

(a) 2783 (b) 3093 (c) 2886 (d) 2884

61. 252 + 356 + 645 + 784 + 589 + 258 + 144 + 154

(a) 3883 (b) 3182 (c) 4434 (d) 3272

62. 147 + 548 + 784 + 689 + 369 + 258 + 245 + 121

(a) 3161 (b) 3262 (c) 4271 (d) 4571

63. 354 + 645 + 958 + 784 + 678 + 245 + 167

(a) 3932 (b) 3631 (c) 4833 (d) 3831

64. 159 + 858 + 645 + 948 + 287 + 243 + 143

(a) 3144 (b) 2541 (c) 3040 (d) 3283

65. 125 + 456 + 987 + 132 + 485 + 558

(a) 2242 (b) 2654 (c) 2743 (d) 2844

66. 193 + 378 + 854 + 351 + 321 + 92

(a) 1979 (b) 2189 (c) 3190 (d) 2788

67. 435 + 763 + 923 + 769 + 599 + 653

(a) 4142 (b) 4241 (c) 3342 (d) 3543

68. 897 + 758 + 864 + 576 + 312 + 214

(a) 3724 (b) 3323 (c) 3522 (d) 3621

69. 676 + 991 + 558 + 959 + 579 + 774

(a) 4437 (b) 4537 (c) 4347 (d) 4148

70. 794 + 884 + 574 + 764 + 554 + 854 + 234

(a) 4759 (b) 4257 (c) 4658 (d) 4966

71. 449 + 669 + 763 + 852 + 81 + 132

(a) 2948 (b) 2846 (c) 3156 (d) 2946

72. 449669 + 763 + 7852 + 81 + 134

(a) 458499 (b) 428897 (c) 469899 (d) 568899

73. 972 + 533 + 674 + 452 + 650 + 841

(a) 3824 (b) 4242 (c) 3923 (d) 4122

74. 925 + 965 + 445 + 884 + 784

(a) 4104 (b) 3803 (c) 4003 (d) 4005

75. 981 + 468 + 541 + 465 + 598 + 341

(a) 3495 (b) 3394 (c) 3485 (d) 3395

76. 125 + 456 + 851 + 536 + 9 + 599 + 234

(a) 2711 (b) 2810 (c) 3111 (d) 3520

77. 814 + 641 + 656 + 522 + 885 + 134

(a) 3553 (b) 4152 (c) 3652 (d) 5152

78. 984 + 756 + 658 + 554 + 885

(a) 3837 (b) 3738 (c) 4128 (d) 3838

79. 617 + 864 + 856 + 768 + 557 + 617

(a) 4217 (b) 4416 (c) 4279 (d) 4118

ADDITION (जोड़)

80. **835 + 745 + 887 + 467 + 784 + 786 + 124 + 342**

(a) 4871 (b) 4880 (c) 4471 (d) 4970

81. **245 + 373 + 458 + 654 + 321**

(a) 2352 (b) 2051 (c) 2352 (d) 4970

82. **753 + 553 + 689 + 469 + 653 + 341**

(a) 3668 (b) 3758 (c) 3458 (d) 3548

83. **986 + 758 + 464 + 826 + 423**

(a) 3457 (b) 4164 (c) 3686 (d) 2767

84. **664 + 981 + 554 + 941 + 642 + 650 + 456**

(a) 5438 (b) 5638 (c) 4888 (d) 5538

85. **846 + 548 + 783 + 234 + 342**

(a) 2854 (b) 2743 (c) 3753 (d) 2753

86. **798 + 454 + 660 + 856 + 954 + 756**

(a) 4688 (b) 4478 (c) 3778 (d) 4589

87. **956 + 675 + 484 + 676 + 87 + 367**

(a) 3245 (b) 3344 (c) 4445 (d) 4655

88. **872 + 643 + 464 + 580 + 870 + 741**

(a) 4260 (b) 4370 (c) 4170 (d) 4371

89. **225 + 645 + 845 + 954 + 914 + 452**

(a) 3934 (b) 4135 (c) 4136 (d) 4035

90. **641 + 648 + 301 + 645 + 95 + 456**

(a) 2678 (b) 2786 (c) 2866 (d) 2787

91. **755 + 546 + 851 + 466 + 9 + 574**

(a) 3201 (b) 3133 (c) 3002 (d) 2901

92. **354 + 551 + 659 + 252 + 895**

(a) 2812 (b) 2614 (c) 2711 (d) 3013

93. 450 + 466 + 598 + 764 + 795 + 423 + 167
(a) 3037 (b) 3764 (c) 3573 (d) 3663

94. 459 + 550 + 675 + 950 + 187 + 517 + 341 + 245
(a) 4925 (b) 3924 (c) 5924 (d) 4124

95. 405 + 955 + 588 + 487 + 254 + 785
(a) 3575 (b) 3673 (c) 3474 (d) 4176

96. 156 + 153 + 278 + 654 + 321 + 345
(a) 1907 (b) 2006 (c) 2167 (d) 2377

97. 653 + 823 + 669 + 789 + 653 + 564 + 233
(a) 4485 (b) 4274 (c) 4184 (d) 4384

98. 666 + 771 + 818 + 812 + 929 + 679 + 674
(a) 5349 (b) 4442 (c) 5648 (d) 4347

99. 774 + 474 + 694 + 884 + 994 + 634
(a) 4653 (b) 3455 (c) 2754 (d) 4454

100. 989 + 619 + 453 + 682 + 91 + 456
(a) 3380 (b) 3290 (c) 3491 (d) 4194

101. 212 + 323 + 914 + 420 + 680 + 741 + 234
(a) 2923 (b) 4124 (c) 3525 (d) 3524

102. 425 + 645 + 945 + 854 + 814 + 467
(a) 4555 (b) 4249 (c) 4350 (d) 4150

103. 851 + 648 + 751 + 645 + 958 + 421
(a) 4274 (b) 4772 (c) 5274 (d) 3675

104. 215 + 546 + 851 + 356 + 9 + 574
(a) 4274 (b) 2652 (c) 4941 (d) 2551

105. 325 + 484 + 656 + 758 + 154 + 785
(a) 3361 (b) 3162 (c) 3463 (d) 3663

Type-4: Answer - Key

1.	(c)	22.	(b)	43.	(b)	64.	(d)	85.	(d)
2.	(b)	23.	(c)	44.	(d)	65.	(c)	86.	(b)
3.	(c)	24.	(a)	45.	(c)	66.	(b)	87.	(a)
4.	(a)	25.	(d)	46.	(d)	67.	(a)	88.	(c)
5.	(a)	26.	(c)	47.	(c)	68.	(d)	89.	(d)
6.	(c)	27.	(c)	48.	(a)	69.	(b)	90.	(b)
7.	(d)	28.	(d)	49.	(d)	70.	(c)	91.	(a)
8.	(b)	29.	(b)	50.	(b)	71.	(d)	92.	(c)
9.	(c)	30.	(a)	51.	(c)	72.	(a)	93.	(d)
10.	(b)	31.	(c)	52.	(b)	73.	(d)	94.	(b)
11.	(a)	32.	(a)	53.	(b)	74.	(c)	95.	(c)
12.	(d)	33.	(b)	54.	(c)	75.	(b)	96.	(a)
13.	(c)	34.	(c)	55.	(d)	76.	(b)	97.	(d)
14.	(b)	35.	(b)	56.	(c)	77.	(c)	98.	(a)
15.	(d)	36.	(d)	57.	(c)	78.	(a)	99.	(d)
16.	(d)	37.	(a)	58.	(a)	79.	(c)	100.	(b)
17.	(a)	38.	(d)	59.	(d)	80.	(d)	101.	(d)
18.	(c)	39.	(c)	60.	(b)	81.	(b)	102.	(d)
19.	(a)	40.	(d)	61.	(b)	82.	(c)	103.	(a)
20.	(b)	41.	(c)	62.	(a)	83.	(a)	104.	(d)
21.	(d)	42.	(a)	63.	(d)	84.	(c)	105.	(b)

Type-5

1. **886 + 664 + 43 + 8**
(a) 1602 (b) 1601 (c) 1702 (d) 1803

2. **994 + 44 + 12 + 9**
(a) 1158 (b) 1257 (c) 1049 (d) 1059

3. **994 + 980 + 613 + 64 + 4**
(a) 2464 (b) 2576 (c) 2655 (d) 2726

4. **414 + 14 + 04 + 84 + 7**
(a) 525 (b) 523 (c) 648 (d) 438

5. **919 + 82 + 32 + 42 + 89 + 9 + 3 + 2 + 1**
(a) 1179 (b) 1278 (c) 1478 (d) 1269

6. **442 + 642 + 600 + 225 + 40 + 48 + 94 + 64 + 31 + 9 + 8 + 7**
(a) 2313 (b) 2214 (c) 3111 (d) 2210

7. **989 + 587 + 37 + 76 + 72 + 89 + 67**
(a) 1816 (b) 1917 (c) 1918 (d) 2177

8. **777 + 267 + 99 + 79 + 36 + 51**
(a) 1411 (b) 1208 (c) 1309 (d) 1419

9. **553 + 465 + 63 + 75 + 64**
(a) 1321 (b) 1420 (c) 1220 (d) 1322

10. **83 + 767 + 998 + 466 + 756 + 628 + 997 + 4512**
(a) 9207 (b) 9205 (c) 8909 (d) 7607

11. **99 + 43 + 681 + 532 + 447 + 74**
(a) 1977 (b) 1886 (c) 1676 (d) 1876

12. 24 + 464 + 756 + 124 + 98

(a) 1567 (b) 1466 (c) 1367 (d) 1577

13. 751 + 35 + 54 + 63 + 77 + 88 + 51 + 13 + 56 + 80 + 99

(a) 1257 (b) 1471 (c) 1678 (d) 1367

14. 223 + 369 + 78 + 13 + 31 + 521 + 99 + 108 + 30 + 677467 + 99

(a) 679038 (b) 718237 (c) 657888 (d) 869048

15. 885 + 665 + 73 + 64 + 91 + 435 + 958 + 232 + 856 + 568 + 992

(a) 6818 (b) 5816 (c) 4819 (d) 5819

16. 971 + 716 + 05 + 677 + 751 + 446 + 825 + 65

(a) 4565 (b) 5756 (c) 4456 (d) 4366

17. 982 + 15 + 933 + 69 + 999 + 823 + 43

(a) 5455 (b) 4456 (c) 4536 (d) 3864

18. 819 + 23 + 407 + 798 + 723 + 85 + 181

(a) 3036 (b) 3346 (c) 2426 (d) 2833

19. 998 + 76 + 823

(a) 2898 (b) 2687 (c) 3177 (d) 1897

20. 879 + 884 + 43 + 897

(a) 2525 (b) 2801 (c) 2703 (d) 2704

21. 874 + 64 + 75 + 95

(a) 1118 (b) 1108 (c) 1288 (d) 1178

22. 597 + 154 + 356 + 56 + 582

(a) 1745 (b) 1846 (c) 1945 (d) 1946

23. **564 + 16 + 57 + 80 + 689**
(a) 1446 (b) 1305 (c) 1406 (d) 1706

24. **879 + 87 + 52 + 54 + 71 + 7 + 5 + 3 + 1**
(a) 1258 (b) 1179 (c) 1169 (d) 1159

25. **556 + 992 + 840 + 675 + 57 + 87 + 50 + 46 + 31 + 8 + 7 + 6**
(a) 3334 (b) 3576 (c) 2745 (d) 3355

26. **812 + 642 + 544 + 792 + 874 + 560 + 65 + 49 + 89 + 7**
(a) 4333 (b) 4434 (c) 4235 (d) 4236

27. **649 + 757 + 37 + 78 + 73 + 54 + 67**
(a) 1715 (b) 1618 (c) 1814 (d) 1616

28. **999 + 289 + 94 + 76 + 36 + 51**
(a) 1646 (b) 1443 (c) 1545 (d) 1444

29. **873 + 499 + 54 + 81 + 54**
(a) 1361 (b) 1662 (c) 1463 (d) 1561

30. **50 + 877 + 898 + 496 + 556 + 698 + 797 + 5814**
(a) 11285 (b) 10186 (c) 11288 (d) 14176

31. **98 + 53 + 971 + 462 + 857 + 55**
(a) 2394 (b) 2496 (c) 2586 (d) 2836

32. **54 + 644 + 576 + 214 + 98**
(a) 1586 (b) 1687 (c) 1886 (d) 1987

33. **571 + 35 + 54 + 93 + 87 + 89 + 51 + 14 + 56 + 89 + 88**
(a) 1317 (b) 1477 (c) 1517 (d) 1227

34. **465 + 370 + 87 + 55 + 31 + 521 + 79 + 788 + 99 + 677 + 467 + 99**

(a) 3648 (b) 3737 (c) 3738 (d) 4838

35. **895 + 505 + 74 + 64 + 98 + 435 + 968 + 452 + 956 + 568 + 992**

(a) 6007 (b) 6608 (c) 7809 (d) 7007

36. **988 + 716 + 05 + 679 + 756 + 756 + 895 + 64**

(a) 4103 (b) 4303 (c) 5033 (d) 4859

37. **953 + 15 + 949 + 69 + 999 + 843 + 456 + 919 + 56 + 577 + 789 + 786 + 79 + 951**

(a) 7551 (b) 9055 (c) 8842 (d) 8441

38. **15 + 949 + 69 + 999 + 919 + 56 + 577 + 789 + 786 + 79 + 951**

(a) 5890 (b) 6189 (c) 8889 (d) 7889

39. **860 + 988 + 716 + 05 + 679 + 756 + 756 + 895 + 64**

(a) 5821 (b) 5818 (c) 5719 (d) 6219

40. **530 + 895 + 505 + 74 + 64 + 98 + 435 + 968 + 452 + 956 + 568 + 992**

(a) 6537 (b) 6634 (c) 7838 (d) 5338

Type-5: Answer - Key

1.	(b)	9.	(c)	17.	(d)	25.	(d)	33.	(d)
2.	(d)	10.	(a)	18.	(a)	26.	(b)	34.	(c)
3.	(c)	11.	(d)	19.	(d)	27.	(a)	35.	(a)
4.	(b)	12.	(b)	20.	(c)	28.	(c)	36.	(d)
5.	(a)	13.	(d)	21.	(b)	29.	(d)	37.	(d)
6.	(d)	14.	(a)	22.	(a)	30.	(b)	38.	(b)
7.	(b)	15.	(d)	23.	(c)	31.	(b)	39.	(c)
8.	(c)	16.	(c)	24.	(d)	32.	(a)	40.	(a)

Type-6

1.

994
439
726
890
49
23
41
958

(a) 4522 (b) 4120
(c) 3120 (d) 5523

2.

887
941
428
182
64
94
312
582

(a) 3680 (b) 3770
(c) 3490 (d) 2589

3. 132
43
167
32
432
56
421
77

(a) 1360
(b) 1459
(c) 1560
(d) 1470

4. 111
39
324
67
457
14
569
18

(a) 1489
(b) 1599
(c) 1799
(d) 1379

5. 56
121
67
345
15
342
36
321

(a) 1412
(b) 1313
(c) 1404
(d) 1303

6. 990
490
678
45
235
23
451
47

(a) 2959
(b) 3839
(c) 2858
(d) 2859

7.
25
234
12
323
56
341
78
521

(a) 1590 (b) 1480 (c) 1689 (d) 1788

8.
145
17
678
90
267
56
780
59

(a) 2041
(b) 1993
(c) 2092
(d) 1892

9.
223
54
678
28
456
46
378
76

(a) 1839 (b) 1939
(c) 1749 (d) 1579

10.
654
21
345
49
451
34
459
34

(a) 2148
(b) 2457
(c) 2747
(d) 2047

11. 342

77

289

79

356

23

69

59

(a) 1764 (b) 1344

(c) 1294 (d) 1474

12. 59

456

48

378

289

78

358

46

(a) 1714 (b) 1712 (c) 1913 (d) 1814

13. 445
89
234
654
46
678
89
49

(a) 2321 (b) 1944
(c) 2083 (d) 2284

14. 342
37
567
54
78
235
48
790

(a) 2151 (b) 2551 (c) 2441 (d) 2351

15. 267
37
789
26
674
93
367
59

(a) 2213 (b) 2312 (c) 1933 (d) 2614

16. 723
65
189
37
548
378
32
49

(a) 1923 (b) 2121 (c) 2223 (d) 2021

17. 368
67
785
34
712
45
53
570

(a) 2634 (b) 2744
(c) 3444 (d) 2444

18. 116
65
452
31
678
58
789
24

(a) 3113 (b) 2833 (c) 2213 (d) 2323

19.

478
69
237
59
677
568
69
367

(a) 2723 (b) 2524
(c) 3125 (d) 2234

20.

978
45
876
34
75
632
59
478

(a) 3387 (b) 3177
(c) 2777 (d) 3377

21. 447
63
321
57
233
334
50
543

(a) 1292 (b) 2048 (c) 1881 (d) 1873

22. 453
78
340
71
589
55
34
673

(a) 3133 (b) 2692
(c) 2583 (d) 2293

23. 904
85
783
489
342
59
689
475

(a) 3736 (b) 3435
(c) 3826 (d) 2626

24. 44
678
34
678
589
66
879
34

(a) 3002 (b) 3004
(c) 3203 (d) 3304

25.

$$\begin{array}{r} 479 \\ 57 \\ 897 \\ 40 \\ 345 \\ 78 \\ 650 \\ 65 \\ \hline \end{array}$$

(a) 2812 (b) 2311

(c) 2611 (d) 1912

26.

$$\begin{array}{r} 782 \\ 43 \\ 785 \\ 66 \\ 543 \\ 87 \\ 289 \\ 67 \\ \hline \end{array}$$

(a) 2872 (b) 2763

(c) 2762 (d) 2662

27. 765
39
290
48
793
37
567
79

(a) 2488 (b) 2618
(c) 2318 (d) 2718

28. 359
76
258
75
159
45
357
24

(a) 1454 (b) 1353 (c) 1233 (d) 1343

29. 229
44
334
55
779
111
49
556

(a) 2467 (b) 2157
(c) 2777 (d) 2557

30. 189
45
719
28
267
78
489
26

(a) 1841 (b) 1187
(c) 1942 (d) 1747

31. 557
49
54
789
12
782
59
456

(a) 2678 (b) 3168
(c) 2758 (d) 1848

32. 452
58
426
36
258
75
124
42

(a) 2678 (b) 3168
(c) 1471 (d) 1848

33. 24
789
35
345
30
563
23
754

(a) 2563 (b) 2354
(c) 2663 (d) 2573

34. 345
47
789
23
578
23
451
24

(a) 2470 (b) 2280
(c) 3180 (d) 2191

35. 255
68
980
28
543
68
356
76

(a) 3374 (b) 2470
(c) 2573 (d) 2374

36. 765
23
456
678
18
567
34
426

(a) 2877 (b) 3167
(c) 2466 (d) 2967

37. 432
54
423
79
234
67
456
66

(a) 1912 (b) 1714
(c) 2313 (d) 1811

38. 34
679
76
543
68
543
79
55

(a) 2177 (b) 2378
(c) 2077 (d) 2567

39.
```
345
 77
546
 89
111
 47
333
 98
```
(a) 1646 (b) 1686
(c) 1866 (d) 2356

40.
```
333
 57
234
 65
168
 92
345
 57
```
(a) 1455 (b) 1351
(c) 1552 (d) 1251

Type-6: Answer - Key

1.	(b)	**9.**	(b)	**17.**	(a)	**25.**	(c)	**33.**	(a)
2.	(c)	**10.**	(d)	**18.**	(c)	**26.**	(d)	**34.**	(b)
3.	(a)	**11.**	(c)	**19.**	(b)	**27.**	(b)	**35.**	(d)
4.	(b)	**12.**	(b)	**20.**	(b)	**28.**	(b)	**36.**	(d)
5.	(d)	**13.**	(d)	**21.**	(b)	**29.**	(b)	**37.**	(d)
6.	(a)	**14.**	(a)	**22.**	(d)	**30.**	(a)	**38.**	(c)
7.	(a)	**15.**	(b)	**23.**	(c)	**31.**	(c)	**39.**	(a)
8.	(c)	**16.**	(d)	**24.**	(a)	**32.**	(c)	**40.**	(b)

Type-7

Hint :

☞ सभी अंक को एक flow में जोड़ना है बिना रूके।

Exercise

1. **226789**
(a) 34 (b) 44 (c) 54 (d) 24

2. **334567**
(a) 48 (b) 38 (c) 28 (d) 27

3. **897886**
(a) 56 (b) 36 (c) 66 (d) 46

4. **8874567966**
(a) 76 (b) 66 (c) 86 (d) 77

5. **864182763**
(a) 44 (b) 45 (c) 55 (d) 65

6. **9711039673**
(a) 55 (b) 25 (c) 38 (d) 46

7. **8894329768321**
(a) 80 (b) 67 (c) 70 (d) 50

8. **5893796456839028**
(a) 92 (b) 72 (c) 82 (d) 62

9. **6874565792109**
(a) 69 (b) 89 (c) 79 (d) 59

10. **787674379772787**
(a) 76 (b) 86 (c) 96 (d) 78

11. 78275429709810440806

(a) 89 (b) 79 (c) 69 (d) 91

12. 81780448458026325 8645

(a) 98 (b) 178 (c) 148 (d) 188

13. 99183677885773568 1556

(a) 134 (b) 114 (c) 125 (d) 124

14. 75841236894253214678

(a) 95 (b) 85 (c) 55 (d) 115

15. 153549875605468 7634

(a) 86 (b) 66 (c) 96 (d) 116

16. 37253648975658623549

(a) 111 (b) 107 (c) 108 (d) 105

17. 65698125469782564

(a) 93 (b) 95 (c) 83 (d) 78

18. 415287956238956235

(a) 102 (b) 89 (c) 90 (d) 80

19. 9258795689533658

(a) 106 (b) 107 (c) 86 (d) 98

20. 72356489575896544375

(a) 114 (b) 112 (c) 122 (d) 98

21. 35468975246587455 76

(a) 118 (b) 108 (c) 138 (d) 106

22. 71254632589546243 21

(a) 68 (b) 92 (c) 79 (d) 82

23. 946587623588945 63

(a) 98 (b) 88 (c) 78 (d) 68

24. 79658762358894563

(a) 101 (b) 86 (c) 76 (d) 96

25. 975082836546826347

(a) 83 (b) 73 (c) 93 (d) 63

26. 46358692387959862

(a) 100 (b) 110 (c) 102 (d) 107

27. 2275824315469

(a) 48 (b) 68 (c) 58 (d) 78

28. 4533456795813264

(a) 65 (b) 75 (c) 85 (d) 95

29. 89788615489513

(a) 82 (b) 53 (c) 59 (d) 62

30. 887456796655423 5498

(a) 114 (b) 111 (c) 117 (d) 122

31. 8641827631265897

(a) 77 (b) 68 (c) 83 (d) 87

32. 9711039673586924 51256

(a) 89 (b) 99 (c) 79 (d) 59

33. 35622468894329768321

(a) 88 (b) 67 (c) 97 (d) 98

34. 58937964568390282563

(a) 108 (b) 118 (c) 109 (d) 106

35. 687456525463579 2109

(a) 114 (b) 118 (c) 84 (d) 94

36. 48251665489756 2546

(a) 77 (b) 93 (c) 109 (d) 83

37. 7254782754297098104408

(a) 104 (b) 102 (c) 103 (d) 107

38. 912461234580263258645

(a) 84 (b) 86 (c) 96 (d) 88

39. 3562455735681556

(a) 71 (b) 76 (c) 81 (d) 82

40. 77546836894253214678

(a) 107 (b) 105 (c) 109 (d) 104

41. 556789164789545

(a) 89 (b) 99 (c) 79 (d) 69

42. 4523618888864533456

(a) 77 (b) 117 (c) 97 (d) 118

43. 995621354666253286

(a) 88 (b) 78 (c) 68 (d) 98

44. 5962356784573355966

(a) 105 (b) 104 (c) 107 (d) 103

45. 546812166516489763

(a) 99 (b) 77 (c) 88 (d) 78

46. 3541658745233039673

(a) 84 (b) 74 (c) 44 (d) 94

47. 79854621356849854115

(a) 111 (b) 102 (c) 101 (d) 104

48. 59421536513564987

(a) 83 (b) 85 (c) 86 (d) 82

49. 92726549810440789

(a) 88 (b) 87 (c) 85 (d) 75

50. 798614236458851281266

(a) 103 (b) 102 (c) 106 (d) 75

51. 70648952355485356

(a) 76 (b) 85 (c) 96 (d) 86

52. 254168597485125614678

(a) 104 (b) 105 (c) 107 (d) 114

53. 5526487452365689153

(a) 107 (b) 104 (c) 94 (d) 84

54. 958623564597485614678

(a) 118 (b) 117 (c) 127 (d) 121

55. 862356459748561 46

(a) 99 (b) 89 (c) 79 (d) 88

56. 26487452365 6891

(a) 72 (b) 76 (c) 62 (d) 68

Type-7: Answer - Key

1.	(a)	12.	(a)	24.	(a)	36.	(b)	48.	(a)
2.	(c)	13.	(d)	25.	(c)	37.	(c)	49.	(c)
3.	(d)	14.	(a)	26.	(a)	38.	(b)	50.	(b)
4.	(b)	15.	(c)	27.	(c)	39.	(b)	51.	(b)
5.	(b)	16.	(b)	28.	(b)	40.	(b)	52.	(a)
6.	(d)	17.	(a)	29.	(a)	41.	(a)	53.	(c)
7.	(c)	18.	(c)	30.	(b)	42.	(c)	54.	(a)
8.	(a)	19.	(d)	31.	(c)	43.	(a)	55.	(b)
9.	(a)	20.	(b)	32.	(b)	44.	(b)	56.	(b)
10.	(c)	21.	(d)	33.	(d)	45.	(c)		
11.	(d)	22.	(c)	34.	(a)	46.	(a)		
		23.	(a)	35.	(d)	47.	(c)		

ADDITION (जोड़)

Type-8

Hint :

☞ कही से भी शुरू करके आखिर तक जोड़ना है बिना लिखे।

Exercise

1.

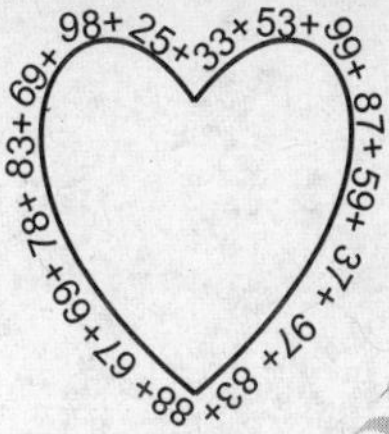

(a) 1035 (b) 1125 (c) 1145 (d) 1255

2.

(a) 1035 (b) 1145 (c) 1075 (d) 1026

3.

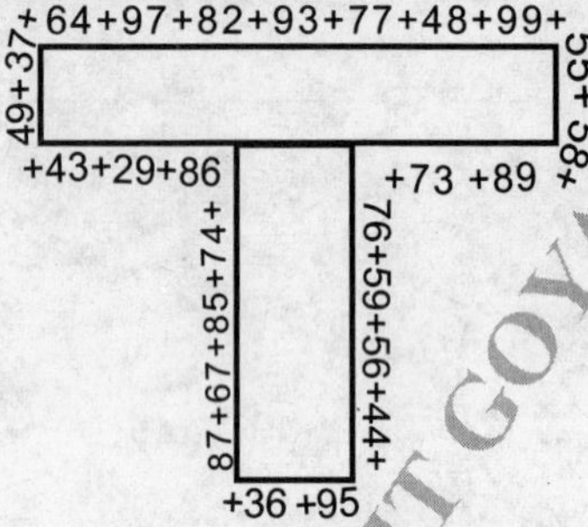

(a) 1685 (b) 1791 (c) 1758 (d) 1885

4.

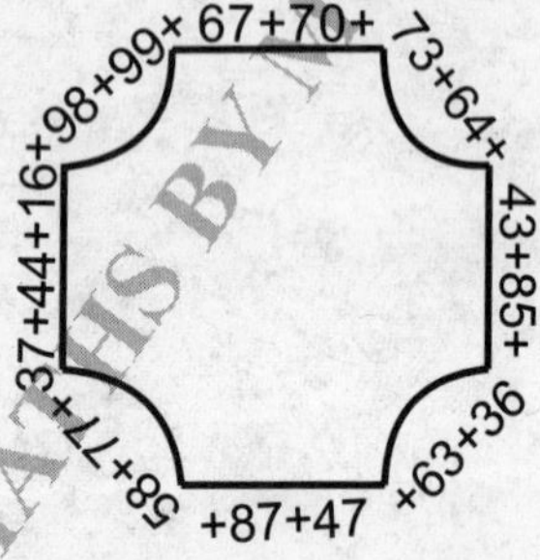

(a) 1064 (b) 1086 (c) 1164 (d) 1196

5.

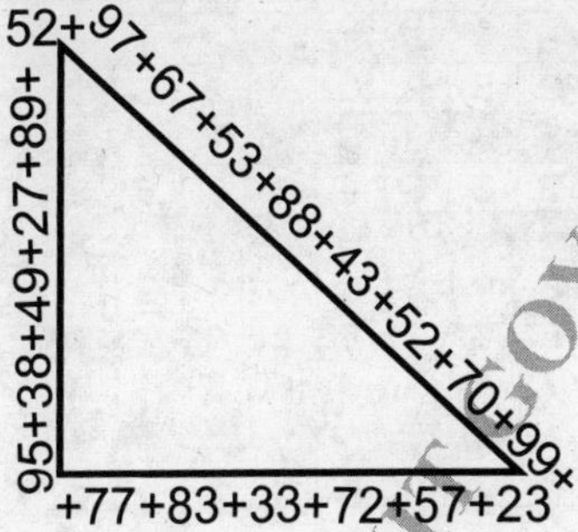

(a) 1165 (b) 1264 (c) 1284 (d) 1168

6.

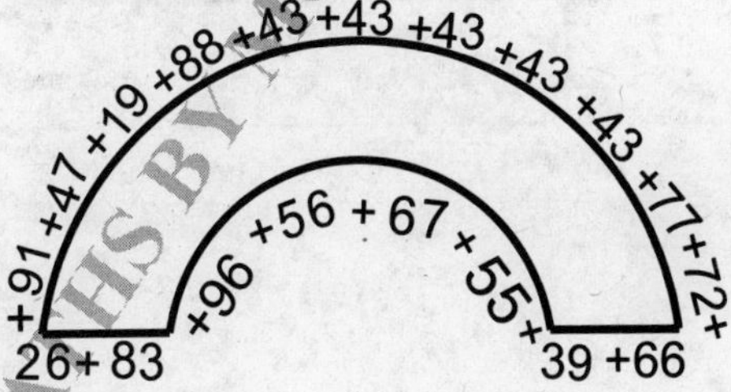

(a) 1097 (b) 1198 (c) 1087 (d) 1077

INSPECTOR चालीसा

8	7	8	9	6	5	6	6	6	8	6	6	9	8
8	5	2	4	6	9	7	8	2	1	4	6	8	7
7	2	6	8	2	5	9	3	9	8	5	2	8	6
5	5	4	7	8	5	2	3	6	9	4	8	8	7
7	8	9	4	2	3	5	4	4	5	6	6	7	5
8	4	5	6	4	5	7	8	8	9	1	2	3	4
8	2	4	6	8	9	6	6	6	3	2	1	1	3
9	9	9	6	5	4	7	8	9	6	2	2	1	2
3	6	5	8	7	4	5	9	6	5	4	8	9	1
9	8	7	6	5	4	8	6	9	8	5	4	7	8
4	2	1	5	3	2	8	6	8	9	5	5	4	5

Type-8: Answer - Key

1. (b)	**3.** (c)	**5.** (b)
2. (a)	**4.** (a)	**6.** (a)

SUBTRACTION (घटाव)

Type-1

Hint :

☞ Single digit का subtraction सभी कर लेते है कोशिश करिए कि कुछ लिखा ना जाए।

Hint :

76 – 71

(जब दोनों संख्या का पहला अंक (digit) समान है)

☞ जब दहाई का अंक (Tens digit) समान होता है तो सीधा घटा देते है, और Answer (5) निकल जाता है।

98 – 65

(जब पहले वाली संख्या के दोनों अंक बड़े हों)

☞ सबसे पहले दहाई के अंक (Tens digit) घटाने है (9 – 6) = 3 के आगे एक zero मानकर (30) संख्या को दिमाग में रखे और इकाई की संख्या (Unit digit) (8 – 5) घटा देंगे जो (3) प्राप्त होता हो तो दिमाग में रखी संख्या (30) में (3) add कर देंगे तो Answer 33 आ जाएगा।

73 – 47

(जब पहले वाली संख्या का पहला अंक बड़ा हो पर दूसरा छोटा)

☞ सबसे पहले दहाई के अंक (Tens digit) घटाओ [7 – 4 = 3] के आगे zero मान लो (30) दिमाग में रखो और इकाई (unit) के

अंक घटाने पर (3 – 7 = – 4) आ रहा है तो 30 में से 4 घटा दो 26 आ जाएगा पर सब mind में करना है।

522 – 217

☞ 522 – 217 starting के दो अंक पकड़ कर घटाओ (52 – 21 = 31) आगे एक zero मान लो 310। अब (2 – 7 = – 5) 310 में से 5 घटा दो 305 आ जाएगा।

1782 – 1184

☞ 1782 – 1184 starting के दो अंक पकड़ कर घटाओ (17 – 11 = 6) आगे दो zero मान लो 600 अब (82 – 84 = – 2) 600 में से 2 घटा दो 598 आ जाएगा।

☞ 100, 1000, 10000, 100000 में से जब भी किसी संख्या को Unit digit को 10 में से घटाएँ बाकि को 9 में से

e.g. 100000 – 1 3 4 5 7 जब zero और घटाने वाली
↓ ↓ ↓ ↓ ↓ संख्या के अंक (digit) दोनों
8 6 5 4 3 समान हैं

e.g. 10000 – 0 1 7 3 अगर अंक (digit) और zero
↓ ↓ ↓ ↓ समान नहीं है तो बाद वाली संख्या
9 8 2 7 में पहले zero लगाकर समान करें
फिर वैसे ही करें जैसे ऊपर किया है।

Exercise

1. 65 – 3

(a) 58 (b) 62 (c) 52 (d) 64

2. 48 – 9

(a) 42 (b) 38 (c) 39 (d) 29

3. 56 – 7

(a) 49 (b) 48 (c) 50 (d) 47

4. 96 – 7

(a) 88 (b) 92 (c) 79 (d) 89

5. 93 – 8

(a) 85 (b) 86 (c) 84 (d) 87

6. 47 – 5

(a) 42 (b) 43 (c) 39 (d) 44

7. 56 – 8

(a) 49 (b) 48 (c) 38 (d) 46

8. 23 – 8

(a) 14 (b) 15 (c) 18 (d) 13

9. 34 – 7

(a) 27 (b) 19 (c) 16 (d) 18

10. 46 – 9

(a) 28 (b) 38 (c) 37 (d) 27

11. 58 – 9

(a) 47 (b) 52 (c) 39 (d) 49

12. 63 – 7

(a) 57 (b) 56 (c) 58 (d) 46

13. 64 – 8

(a) 46 (b) 36 (c) 56 (d) 48

14. 98 – 9

(a) 89 (b) 79 (c) 88 (d) 91

15. 88 – 9

(a) 87 (b) 79 (c) 69 (d) 78

16. 79 – 9

(a) 73 (b) 60 (c) 71 (d) 70

17. 46 – 7

(a) 29 (b) 39 (c) 41 (d) 37

18. 74 – 8

(a) 57 (b) 46 (c) 66 (d) 56

19. 63 – 5

(a) 48 (b) 58 (c) 59 (d) 49

20. 97 – 9

(a) 77 (b) 68 (c) 88 (d) 78

21. 43 – 6

(a) 34 (b) 37 (c) 26 (d) 38

22. 88 – 7

(a) 81 (b) 79 (c) 75 (d) 83

23. 86 – 4

(a) 83 (b) 86 (c) 82 (d) 78

24. 85 – 7

(a) 78 (b) 77 (c) 68 (d) 74

25. 89 – 6

(a) 85 (b) 74 (c) 65 (d) 83

26. 72 – 9

(a) 66 (b) 63 (c) 62 (d) 53

27. 92 – 4

(a) 78 (b) 88 (c) 82 (d) 79

28. 72 – 8

(a) 64 (b) 67 (c) 69 (d) 66

29. 88 – 9

(a) 69 (b) 72 (c) 79 (d) 78

30. 43 – 7

(a) 36 (b) 37 (c) 26 (d) 35

31. 48 – 6

(a) 39 (b) 42 (c) 44 (d) 49

32. 68 – 9

(a) 57 (b) 61 (c) 59 (d) 49

33. 96 – 7

(a) 89 (b) 79 (c) 91 (d) 86

34. 102 – 5

(a) 87 (b) 97 (c) 93 (d) 88

35. 112 – 9

(a) 107 (b) 103 (c) 105 (d) 108

36. 114 – 8

(a) 103 (b) 109 (c) 106 (d) 102

37. 116 – 7

(a) 108 (b) 109 (c) 111 (d) 107

38. 126 – 9

(a) 108 (b) 117 (c) 111 (d) 107

39. 123 – 8

(a) 115 (b) 119 (c) 112 (d) 116

40. 134 – 6

(a) 118 (b) 126 (c) 128 (d) 119

41. 136 – 8

(a) 127 (b) 129 (c) 126 (d) 128

42. 133 – 7

(a) 124 (b) 122 (c) 128 (d) 126

43. 149 – 6

(a) 146 (b) 143 (c) 145 (d) 133

44. 152 – 9

(a) 145 (b) 148 (c) 143 (d) 134

45. 165 – 8

(a) 55 (b) 157 (c) 138 (d) 149

46. 183 – 5

(a) 168 (b) 158 (c) 148 (d) 178

47. 174 – 9

(a) 163 (b) 165 (c) 155 (d) 168

48. 177 – 8

(a) 169 (b) 135 (c) 158 (d) 149

49. 165 – 9

(a) 146 (b) 156 (c) 119 (d) 157

50. 194 – 6

(a) 186 (b) 178 (c) 188 (d) 168

51. 204 – 8

(a) 196 (b) 186 (c) 177 (d) 156

SUBTRACTION (घटाव)

52. 214 – 9

(a) 204 (b) 203 (c) 205 (d) 197

53. 243 – 7

(a) 233 (b) 237 (c) 238 (d) 236

54. 286 – 9

(a) 277 (b) 267 (c) 248 (d) 273

55. 374 – 8

(a) 368 (b) 366 (c) 356 (d) 364

56. 491 – 6

(a) 487 (b) 483 (c) 485 (d) 385

57. 516 – 7

(a) 508 (b) 509 (c) 409 (d) 506

58. 608 – 9

(a) 593 (b) 589 (c) 599 (d) 597

59. 816 – 7

(a) 809 (b) 797 (c) 805 (d) 789

60. 819 – 9

(a) 811 (b) 810 (c) 814 (d) 799

61. 923 – 4

(a) 919 (b) 989 (c) 1009 (d) 1003

62. 1012 – 9

(a) 1003 (b) 989 (c) 1009 (d) 1004

63. 1023 – 4

(a) 1017 (b) 998 (c) 1019 (d) 1003

64. 1119 – 8

(a) 1109 (b) 1111 (c) 1099 (d) 1117

65. 1120 – 3
(a) 1117 (b) 1114 (c) 1097 (d) 1115

66. 1481 – 7
(a) 1475 (b) 1474 (c) 1165 (d) 1434

67. 1591 – 8
(a) 1587 (b) 1482 (c) 1583 (d) 1578

68. 1608 – 8
(a) 1601 (b) 1600 (c) 1599 (d) 1593

69. 2048 – 7
(a) 2044 (b) 2031 (c) 2042 (d) 2041

70. 2056 – 8
(a) 2046 (b) 2048 (c) 2038 (d) 2028

71. 2093 – 9
(a) 2077 (b) 2084 (c) 2087 (d) 2083

72. 3100 – 7
(a) 3211 (b) 3207 (c) 3093 (d) 3199

73. 3217 – 8
(a) 3211 (b) 3207 (c) 3209 (d) 3199

74. 5000 – 9
(a) 4981 (b) 4991 (c) 4987 (d) 4792

75. 4000 – 8
(a) 3892 (b) 3897 (c) 3992 (d) 3982

76. 3000 – 7
(a) 2897 (b) 2899 (c) 2995 (d) 2993

77. 1000 – 9
(a) 9991 (b) 987 (c) 989 (d) 991

78. 2250 – 7

(a) 2233 (b) 2243 (c) 2153 (d) 2239

79. 2310 – 3

(a) 2293 (b) 2297 (c) 2307 (d) 2303

80. 2450 – 9

(a) 2444 (b) 2441 (c) 2391 (d) 2399

81. 2225 – 8

(a) 2217 (b) 2219 (c) 2214 (d) 2197

82. 1600 – 9

(a) 1594 (b) 1483 (c) 1591 (d) 1499

83. 1700 – 8

(a) 1692 (b) 1582 (c) 1571 (d) 1694

84. 1800 – 4

(a) 1797 (b) 1786 (c) 1796 (d) 1698

85. 2500 – 7

(a) 2493 (b) 2443 (c) 2393 (d) 2373

86. 76 – 71

(a) 7 (b) 9 (c) 5 (d) 11

87. 98 – 65

(a) 37 (b) 33 (c) 44 (d) 23

88. 91 – 83

(a) 8 (b) 13 (c) 7 (d) 9

89. 97 – 85

(a) 14 (b) 13 (c) 12 (d) 17

90. 85 – 43

(a) 44 (b) 33 (c) 42 (d) 52

91. 66 – 37

(a) 28 (b) 39 (c) 19 (d) 29

92. 93 – 81

(a) 16 (b) 12 (c) 18 (d) 14

93. 97 – 75

(a) 25 (b) 23 (c) 27 (d) 22

94. 91 – 67

(a) 24 (b) 26 (c) 21 (d) 28

95. 91 – 58

(a) 35 (b) 32 (c) 33 (d) 37

96. 87 – 35

(a) 54 (b) 53 (c) 52 (d) 42

97. 57 – 37

(a) 20 (b) 33 (c) 27 (d) 35

98. 98 – 57

(a) 32 (b) 41 (c) 21 (d) 35

99. 88 – 53

(a) 44 (b) 47 (c) 35 (d) 27

100. 86 – 44

(a) 42 (b) 47 (c) 37 (d) 48

101. 89 – 55

(a) 36 (b) 34 (c) 41 (d) 27

102. 88 – 33

(a) 58 (b) 55 (c) 57 (d) 48

103. 62 – 59

(a) 3 (b) 7 (c) 9 (d) 5

104. 87 – 33

(a) 54 (b) 44 (c) 64 (d) 48

105. 76 – 45

(a) 33 (b) 44 (c) 31 (d) 32

106. 85 – 34

(a) 49 (b) 63 (c) 51 (d) 55

107. 98 – 79

(a) 23 (b) 21 (c) 19 (d) 24

108. 88 – 83

(a) 7 (b) 5 (c) 11 (d) 9

109. 79 – 52

(a) 27 (b) 29 (c) 37 (d) 24

110. 98 – 89

(a) 8 (b) 9 (c) 11 (d) 7

111. 77 – 35

(a) 52 (b) 39 (c) 42 (d) 47

112. 87 – 52

(a) 45 (b) 65 (c) 39 (d) 35

113. 73 – 36

(a) 35 (b) 37 (c) 42 (d) 48

114. 95 – 58

(a) 41 (b) 37 (c) 42 (d) 48

115. 86 – 67

(a) 19 (b) 44 (c) 38 (d) 51

116. 42 – 25

(a) 19 (b) 17 (c) 21 (d) 14

117. 58 – 54

(a) 4 (b) 3 (c) 2 (d) 7

118. 98 – 87

(a) 13 (b) 11 (c) 23 (d) 31

119. 79 – 27

(a) 57 (b) 63 (c) 42 (d) 52

120. 56 – 36

(a) 20 (b) 23 (c) 24 (d) 28

121. 82 – 28

(a) 57 (b) 48 (c) 54 (d) 49

122. 78 – 47

(a) 33 (b) 29 (c) 31 (d) 42

123. 58 – 30

(a) 28 (b) 23 (c) 31 (d) 18

124. 75 – 39

(a) 38 (b) 46 (c) 36 (d) 26

125. 65 – 32

(a) 44 (b) 33 (c) 39 (d) 28

126. 41 – 14

(a) 27 (b) 18 (c) 23 (d) 29

127. 67 – 43

(a) 44 (b) 27 (c) 34 (d) 24

128. 81 – 67

(a) 14 (b) 15 (c) 17 (d) 21

129. 57 – 23

(a) 37 (b) 33 (c) 34 (d) 38

SUBTRACTION (घटाव)

130. 48 – 31

(a) 19 (b) 17 (c) 23 (d) 15

131. 64 – 46

(a) 19 (b) 28 (c) 18 (d) 27

132. 65 – 43

(a) 27 (b) 22 (c) 24 (d) 34

133. 59 – 53

(a) 9 (b) 6 (c) 11 (d) 14

134. 76 – 57

(a) 19 (b) 14 (c) 17 (d) 29

135. 75 – 37

(a) 39 (b) 38 (c) 28 (d) 48

136. 95 – 66

(a) 24 (b) 29 (c) 37 (d) 49

137. 88 – 28

(a) 69 (b) 71 (c) 60 (d) 58

138. 67 – 50

(a) 27 (b) 17 (c) 19 (d) 23

139. 99 – 61

(a) 38 (b) 41 (c) 28 (d) 49

140. 46 – 33

(a) 15 (b) 13 (c) 17 (d) 16

141. 91 – 19

(a) 67 (b) 72 (c) 77 (d) 82

142. 76 – 46

(a) 30 (b) 37 (c) 39 (d) 28

143. 53 – 35

(a) 28 (b) 18 (c) 14 (d) 19

144. 76 – 69

(a) 9 (b) 7 (c) 11 (d) 06

145. 43 – 31

(a) 11 (b) 14 (c) 12 (d) 16

146. 94 – 77

(a) 18 (b) 17 (c) 23 (d) 27

147. 79 – 33

(a) 55 (b) 48 (c) 44 (d) 46

148. 91 – 82

(a) 14 (b) 9 (c) 11 (d) 13

149. 95 – 84

(a) 14 (b) 9 (c) 11 (d) 15

150. 97 – 71

(a) 26 (b) 36 (c) 17 (d) 27

151. 79 – 33

(a) 55 (b) 48 (c) 44 (d) 46

152. 90 – 81

(a) 14 (b) 9 (c) 11 (d) 7

153. 46 – 26

(a) 24 (b) 27 (c) 22 (d) 20

154. 56 – 36

(a) 32 (b) 26 (c) 23 (d) 20

155. 99 – 30

(a) 69 (b) 38 (c) 42 (d) 27

SUBTRACTION (घटाव)

156. 89 – 80

(a) 8 (b) 9 (c) 14 (d) 17

157. 66 – 31

(a) 37 (b) 39 (c) 35 (d) 43

158. 48 – 33

(a) 15 (b) 18 (c) 22 (d) 17

159. 98 – 47

(a) 57 (b) 53 (c) 51 (d) 49

160. 100 – 12

(a) 78 (b) 67 (c) 83 (d) 88

161. 100 – 13

(a) 58 (b) 63 (c) 87 (d) 86

162. 100 – 16

(a) 84 (b) 94 (c) 87 (d) 74

163. 100 – 17

(a) 76 (b) 84 (c) 83 (d) 88

164. 100 – 19

(a) 88 (b) 89 (c) 81 (d) 23

165. 100 – 31

(a) 69 (b) 86 (c) 77 (d) 93

166. 100 – 61

(a) 48 (b) 39 (c) 44 (d) 41

167. 100 – 58

(a) 42 (b) 47 (c) 39 (d) 52

168. 100 – 52

(a) 48 (b) 37 (c) 49 (d) 55

169. 100 – 96

(a) 07 (b) 04 (c) 14 (d) 18

170. 100 – 24

(a) 68 (b) 76 (c) 92 (d) 84

171. 100 – 33

(a) 67 (b) 77 (c) 57 (d) 87

172. 100 – 66

(a) 44 (b) 39 (c) 35 (d) 34

173. 100 – 42

(a) 68 (b) 59 (c) 58 (d) 71

174. 100 – 32

(a) 68 (b) 63 (c) 48 (d) 79

175. 100 – 68

(a) 38 (b) 32 (c) 47 (d) 36

176. 100 – 39

(a) 64 (b) 69 (c) 61 (d) 51

177. 100 – 34

(a) 66 (b) 56 (c) 46 (d) 29

178. 100 – 36

(a) 64 (b) 44 (c) 53 (d) 58

179. 100 – 43

(a) 67 (b) 57 (c) 47 (d) 59

180. 100 – 63

(a) 37 (b) 39 (c) 35 (d) 43

181. 100 – 90

(a) 13 (b) 10 (c) 19 (d) 15

182. 1000 – 912
(a) 99 (b) 78 (c) 88 (d) 86

183. 1000 – 143
(a) 767 (b) 857 (c) 787 (d) 954

184. 1000 – 102
(a) 789 (b) 888 (c) 898 (d) 890

185. 1000 – 343
(a) 766 (b) 657 (c) 659 (d) 767

186. 1000 – 613
(a) 567 (b) 478 (c) 387 (d) 277

187. 1000 – 471
(a) 689 (b) 529 (c) 479 (d) 229

188. 1000 – 712
(a) 278 (b) 268 (c) 288 (d) 168

189. 1000 – 729
(a) 273 (b) 376 (c) 272 (d) 271

190. 1000 – 216
(a) 784 (b) 786 (c) 777 (d) 778

191. 1000 – 225
(a) 765 (b) 885 (c) 775 (d) 478

192. 1000 – 543
(a) 477 (b) 457 (c) 469 (d) 387

193. 1000 – 625
(a) 385 (b) 265 (c) 375 (d) 465

194. 1000 – 512
(a) 488 (b) 578 (c) 168 (d) 638

195. 1000 – 721

(a) 389 (b) 279 (c) 489 (d) 569

196. 1000 – 861

(a) 139 (b) 149 (c) 159 (d) 148

197. 1000 – 815

(a) 145 (b) 195 (c) 175 (d) 185

198. 1000 – 824

(a) 166 (b) 176 (c) 188 (d) 146

199. 1000 – 724

(a) 196 (b) 266 (c) 276 (d) 356

200. 1000 – 676

(a) 324 (b) 434 (c) 344 (d) 424

201. 1000 – 576

(a) 564 (b) 424 (c) 514 (d) 258

202. 1000 – 529

(a) 577 (b) 421 (c) 471 (d) 381

203. 1000 – 484

(a) 516 (b) 426 (c) 518 (d) 636

204. 1000 – 441

(a) 469 (b) 579 (c) 559 (d) 465

205. 1000 – 361

(a) 637 (b) 648 (c) 539 (d) 639

206. 1000 – 324

(a) 676 (b) 677 (c) 786 (d) 456

207. 1000 – 289

(a) 721 (b) 812 (c) 711 (d) 613

SUBTRACTION (घटाव)

208. 1000 – 256

(a) 756 (b) 734 (c) 744 (d) 624

209. 1000 – 64

(a) 936 (b) 956 (c) 846 (d) 348

210. 1000 – 125

(a) 775 (b) 875 (c) 645 (d) 726

211. 1000 – 917

(a) 89 (b) 73 (c) 83 (d) 123

212. 10000 – 1431

(a) 8669 (b) 8759 (c) 8849 (d) 8569

213. 10000 – 1728

(a) 8272 (b) 8377 (c) 8478 (d) 8772

214. 10000 – 1331

(a) 8789 (b) 8669 (c) 8468 (d) 8923

215. 10000 – 6431

(a) 4568 (b) 3569 (c) 4576 (d) 3456

216. 10000 – 7829

(a) 2572 (b) 3674 (c) 2172 (d) 2171

217. 10000 – 5432

(a) 4569 (b) 3678 (c) 4468 (d) 4568

218. 10000 – 6089

(a) 3781 (b) 3911 (c) 4713 (d) 3917

219. 10000 – 1024

(a) 6789 (b) 5676 (c) 7986 (d) 8976

220. 10000 – 2096

(a) 7605 (b) 7904 (c) 6740 (d) 844

221. 10000 – 196

(a) 9807 (b) 9694 (c) 9803 (d) 9804

222. 10000 – 616

(a) 9344 (b) 7683 (c) 9285 (d) 9384

223. 10000 – 1225

(a) 8775 (b) 6775 (c) 7885 (d) 7845

224. 100000 – 98732

(a) 1278 (b) 1348 (c) 1268 (d) 1458

225. 100000 – 41607

(a) 56788 (b) 57873 (c) 58343 (d) 58393

226. 100000 – 90134

(a) 9866 (b) 88967 (c) 9666 (d) 7865

227. 100000 – 16012

(a) 84588 (b) 83988 (c) 73578 (d) 67889

228. 100000 – 20178

(a) 78223 (b) 79434 (c) 69822 (d) 79822

229. 100000 – 11407

(a) 89563 (b) 88593 (c) 78493 (d) 87463

230. 50 – 12

(a) 37 (b) 28 (c) 38 (d) 42

231. 50 – 26

(a) 27 (b) 24 (c) 16 (d) 18

232. 50 – 34

(a) 14 (b) 19 (c) 16 (d) 13

233. 50 – 41

(a) 11 (b) 7 (c) 9 (d) 8

234. 50 – 37

(a) 16 (b) 13 (c) 23 (d) 19

235. 50 – 27

(a) 23 (b) 17 (c) 27 (d) 14

236. 50 – 23

(a) 28 (b) 27 (c) 17 (d) 31

237. 50 – 18

(a) 41 (b) 33 (c) 32 (d) 37

238. 50 – 21

(a) 36 (b) 28 (c) 29 (d) 27

239. 50 – 31

(a) 17 (b) 19 (c) 29 (d) 21

240. 50 – 24

(a) 26 (b) 22 (c) 29 (d) 27

241. 50 – 36

(a) 14 (b) 17 (c) 31 (d) 27

242. 50 – 16

(a) 34 (b) 41 (c) 44 (d) 14

243. 50 – 28

(a) 22 (b) 27 (c) 23 (d) 12

244. 50 – 38

(a) 13 (b) 12 (c) 15 (d) 23

245. 50 – 32

(a) 13 (b) 17 (c) 18 (d) 19

246. 50 – 21

(a) 24 (b) 31 (c) 32 (d) 29

247. 50 – 8

(a) 13 (b) 42 (c) 37 (d) 44

248. 50 – 33

(a) 13 (b) 16 (c) 17 (d) 21

249. 50 – 41

(a) 7 (b) 9 (c) 11 (d) 13

250. 50 – 25

(a) 21 (b) 23 (c) 27 (d) 25

251. 50 – 43

(a) 6 (b) 14 (c) 7 (d) 9

252. 75 – 51

(a) 23 (b) 24 (c) 34 (d) 31

253. 75 – 43

(a) 32 (b) 42 (c) 37 (d) 44

254. 75 – 42

(a) 37 (b) 29 (c) 35 (d) 33

255. 75 – 37

(a) 48 (b) 38 (c) 29 (d) 35

256. 75 – 28

(a) 47 (b) 24 (c) 42 (d) 48

257. 75 – 63

(a) 21 (b) 14 (c) 12 (d) 17

258. 75 – 54

(a) 21 (b) 24 (c) 34 (d) 22

259. 75 – 38

(a) 38 (b) 49 (c) 41 (d) 37

SUBTRACTION (घटाव)

260. 75 – 34

(a) 33 (b) 36 (c) 41 (d) 23

261. 75 – 57

(a) 28 (b) 18 (c) 15 (d) 19

262. 75 – 47

(a) 28 (b) 18 (c) 15 (d) 19

263. 75 – 14

(a) 67 (b) 61 (c) 63 (d) 58

264. 75 – 21

(a) 44 (b) 56 (c) 54 (d) 47

265. 75 – 31

(a) 44 (b) 56 (c) 54 (d) 47

266. 75 – 12

(a) 73 (b) 63 (c) 54 (d) 64

267. 75 – 16

(a) 55 (b) 49 (c) 59 (d) 29

268. 75 – 23

(a) 52 (b) 42 (c) 37 (d) 58

269. 75 – 41

(a) 44 (b) 59 (c) 34 (d) 35

270. 75 – 58

(a) 19 (b) 22 (c) 17 (d) 16

271. 75 — 62

(a) 27 (b) 24 (c) 18 (d) 13

272. 75 — 39

(a) 38 (b) 36 (c) 39 (d) 46

273. 75 — 29

(a) 44 (b) 56 (c) 46 (d) 26

274. 75 — 19

(a) 66 (b) 56 (c) 49 (d) 28

275. 75 — 11

(a) 64 (b) 58 (c) 34 (d) 44

276. 75 — 26

(a) 47 (b) 59 (c) 49 (d) 38

277. 75 — 49

(a) 26 (b) 46 (c) 28 (d) 24

278. 75 — 69

(a) 16 (b) 13 (c) 6 (d) 9

279. 116 — 107

(a) 8 (b) 12 (c) 9 (d) 6

280. 126 — 104

(a) 24 (b) 28 (c) 22 (d) 32

281. 196 — 137

(a) 59 (b) 69 (c) 39 (d) 55

282. 184 — 173

(a) 14 (b) 12 (c) 21 (d) 11

283. 169 — 108

(a) 63 (b) 59 (c) 71 (d) 61

284. 294 — 143

(a) 144 (b) 153 (c) 151 (d) 162

285. 375 — 294

(a) 81 (b) 57 (c) 75 (d) 162

286. 473 — 365

(a) 133 (b) 129 (c) 108 (d) 109

287. 514 — 216

(a) 378 (b) 298 (c) 167 (d) 248

288. 520 — 314

(a) 216 (b) 326 (c) 208 (d) 206

289. 686 — 423

(a) 367 (b) 263 (c) 262 (d) 442

290. 943 — 472

(a) 478 (b) 472 (c) 471 (d) 473

291. 333 — 176

(a) 212 (b) 155 (c) 157 (d) 127

292. 512 — 216

(a) 366 (b) 293 (c) 176 (d) 296

293. 520 — 314

(a) 226 (b) 206 (c) 209 (d) 211

294. 286 — 104

(a) 173 (b) 184 (c) 182 (d) 193

295. 126 — 109

(a) 19 (b) 17 (c) 147 (d) 124

296. 375 — 177

(a) 201 (b) 283 (c) 193 (d) 198

297. 333 — 186

(a) 147 (b) 157 (c) 167 (d) 177

298. 522 — 217

(a) 371 (b) 309 (c) 305 (d) 408

299. 685 — 413

(a) 272 (b) 377 (c) 275 (d) 255

300. 470 — 193

(a) 288 (b) 277 (c) 367 (d) 283

301. 212 — 147

(a) 73 (b) 55 (c) 86 (d) 65

302. 912 — 614

(a) 298 (b) 388 (c) 397 (d) 287

303. 908 — 170

(a) 689 (b) 539 (c) 738 (d) 588

304. 943 — 179

(a) 666 (b) 789 (c) 767 (d) 764

305. 982 — 375

(a) 708 (b) 609 (c) 607 (d) 470

306. 861 — 473

(a) 388 (b) 578 (c) 356 (d) 478

307. 625 — 196

(a) 467 (b) 429 (c) 349 (d) 479

308. 625 — 144

(a) 452 (b) 347 (c) 488 (d) 481

309. 625 — 169

(a) 466 (b) 456 (c) 379 (d) 446

310. 625 — 279

(a) 388 (b) 476 (c) 396 (d) 346

311. 625 — 324

(a) 311 (b) 316 (c) 301 (d) 241

SUBTRACTION (घटाव)

312. 625 — 121
(a) 501 (b) 504 (c) 408 (d) 344

313. 625 — 576
(a) 58 (b) 49 (c) 69 (d) 39

314. 625 — 441
(a) 288 (b) 245 (c) 184 (d) 388

315. 625 — 484
(a) 224 (b) 147 (c) 141 (d) 432

316. 729 — 526
(a) 305 (b) 203 (c) 327 (d) 207

317. 729 — 441
(a) 288 (b) 378 (c) 489 (d) 248

318. 729 — 676
(a) 46 (b) 73 (c) 53 (d) 64

319. 729 — 484
(a) 245 (b) 443 (c) 244 (d) 348

320. 729 — 289
(a) 479 (b) 440 (c) 260 (d) 340

321. 729 — 144
(a) 588 (b) 379 (c) 585 (d) 289

322. 729 — 196
(a) 438 (b) 333 (c) 533 (d) 443

323. 729 — 216
(a) 513 (b) 334 (c) 544 (d) 223

324. 843 — 760
(a) 78 (b) 83 (c) 94 (d) 88

325. 891 — 712

(a) 423 (b) 178 (c) 179 (d) 289

326. 812 — 643

(a) 169 (b) 177 (c) 158 (d) 166

327. 808 — 579

(a) 328 (b) 229 (c) 246 (d) 178

328. 743 — 502

(a) 244 (b) 241 (c) 249 (d) 141

329. 759 — 489

(a) 327 (b) 270 (c) 348 (d) 237

330. 696 — 489

(a) 306 (b) 207 (c) 211 (d) 171

331. 688 — 477

(a) 211 (b) 312 (c) 217 (d) 167

332. 573 — 409

(a) 256 (b) 165 (c) 164 (d) 157

333. 1234 — 1104

(a) 230 (b) 342 (c) 130 (d) 137

334. 1806 — 1092

(a) 744 (b) 714 (c) 621 (d) 524

335. 2702 — 2160

(a) 542 (b) 652 (c) 457 (d) 522

336. 1784 — 1182

(a) 722 (b) 508 (c) 802 (d) 602

337. 1268 — 1140

(a) 231 (b) 138 (c) 128 (d) 348

338. 3410 — 2600

(a) 720 (b) 810 (c) 430 (d) 780

339. 1703 — 1500

(a) 203 (b) 304 (c) 230 (d) 320

340. 1608 — 1248

(a) 345 (b) 346 (c) 360 (d) 405

341. 2116 — 1107

(a) 1009 (b) 1059 (c) 1097 (d) 1021

342. 3126 — 2107

(a) 1099 (b) 1019 (c) 1239 (d) 1469

343. 2196 — 1137

(a) 1233 (b) 1159 (c) 1059 (d) 1345

344. 4184 — 2173

(a) 2313 (b) 2140 (c) 2211 (d) 2011

345. 4286 — 1104

(a) 3182 (b) 3218 (c) 2488 (d) 2655

346. 3272 — 1372

(a) 2190 (b) 1245 (c) 1899 (d) 1900

347. 4294 — 2143

(a) 2151 (b) 2321 (c) 2177 (d) 2155

348. 3375 — 1194

(a) 2181 (b) 2287 (c) 2161 (d) 2344

349. 5473 — 1365

(a) 4418 (b) 3488 (c) 4108 (d) 4488

350. 6514 — 4216

(a) 2368 (b) 4388 (c) 2178 (d) 2298

351. 5250 — 2314

(a) 2936 (b) 2743 (c) 2866 (d) 3129

352. 2686 — 1423

(a) 1233 (b) 1263 (c) 1364 (d) 1466

353. 8943 — 6472

(a) 2477 (b) 2471 (c) 2373 (d) 3171

354. 6333 — 4176

(a) 2477 (b) 3477 (c) 2157 (d) 2341

355. 9572 — 6216

(a) 3344 (b) 3376 (c) 3216 (d) 3356

356. 2024 — 1326

(a) 698 (b) 788 (c) 339 (d) 478

357. 4100 — 1326

(a) 2877 (b) 2177 (c) 2774 (d) 4232

358. 4234 — 3623

(a) 813 (b) 611 (c) 733 (d) 781

359. 4048 — 2916

(a) 1141 (b) 1131 (c) 1132 (d) 1142

360. 2314 — 1814

(a) 503 (b) 607 (c) 608 (d) 500

361. 6500 — 2136

(a) 4364 (b) 3344 (c) 3565 (d) 4466

362. 7600 — 1756

(a) 5890 (b) 5743 (c) 5844 (d) 6444

363. 9400 — 4354

(a) 5575 (b) 5248 (c) 5046 (d) 5246

364. 6600 — 3450

(a) 3350 (b) 3150 (c) 3320 (d) 2740

365. 4200 — 3680

(a) 543 (b) 670 (c) 520 (d) 423

366. 9800 — 4616

(a) 5288 (b) 5287 (c) 5181 (d) 5184

367. 2314 — 1807

(a) 571 (b) 408 (c) 509 (d) 507

368. 116 — 37

(a) 79 (b) 67 (c) 49 (d) 68

369. 109 — 73

(a) 49 (b) 39 (c) 48 (d) 36

370. 174 — 86

(a) 88 (b) 86 (c) 87 (d) 89

371. 128 — 44

(a) 28 (b) 48 (c) 84 (d) 76

372. 168 — 79

(a) 64 (b) 87 (c) 69 (d) 89

373. 254 — 74

(a) 155 (b) 168 (c) 180 (d) 122

374. 286 — 68

(a) 215 (b) 216 (c) 221 (d) 218

375. 394 — 47

(a) 357 (b) 248 (c) 347 (d) 278

376. 319 — 73

(a) 246 (b) 270 (c) 218 (d) 229

377. 543 — 68

(a) 455 (b) 377 (c) 475 (d) 380

378. 704 — 29

(a) 570 (b) 675 (c) 486 (d) 457

379. 216 — 86

(a) 164 (b) 178 (c) 130 (d) 128

380. 432 — 74

(a) 348 (b) 358 (c) 288 (d) 268

381. 904 — 76

(a) 818 (b) 828 (c) 678 (d) 738

382. 898 — 76

(a) 822 (b) 732 (c) 739 (d) 638

383. 184 — 73

(a) 114 (b) 141 (c) 112 (d) 111

384. 116 — 87

(a) 37 (b) 48 (c) 39 (d) 29

385. 126 — 74

(a) 55 (b) 52 (c) 42 (d) 48

386. 196 — 37

(a) 149 (b) 128 (c) 133 (d) 159

387. 184 — 73

(a) 131 (b) 111 (c) 121 (d) 114

388. 286 — 69

(a) 231 (b) 218 (c) 217 (d) 219

389. 272 — 77

(a) 189 (b) 179 (c) 195 (d) 199

SUBTRACTION (घटाव)

390. 294 — 43

(a) 234 (b) 248 (c) 251 (d) 239

391. 375 — 98

(a) 255 (b) 268 (c) 277 (d) 237

392. 473 — 65

(a) 411 (b) 408 (c) 378 (d) 468

393. 514 — 28

(a) 486 (b) 386 (c) 466 (d) 487

394. 520 — 63

(a) 477 (b) 466 (c) 430 (d) 457

395. 686 — 97

(a) 540 (b) 480 (c) 583 (d) 589

396. 943 — 72

(a) 878 (b) 782 (c) 827 (d) 871

397. 333 — 76

(a) 279 (b) 268 (c) 257 (d) 178

398. 512 — 66

(a) 536 (b) 446 (c) 477 (d) 426

399. 729 — 64

(a) 579 (b) 665 (c) 375 (d) 455

400. 512 — 81

(a) 443 (b) 431 (c) 445 (d) 478

401. 216 — 64

(a) 154 (b) 152 (c) 138 (d) 124

402. 625 — 81

(a) 543 (b) 534 (c) 448 (d) 544

403. 676 — 81
(a) 589 (b) 595 (c) 539 (d) 549

404. 729 — 64
(a) 667 (b) 669 (c) 665 (d) 765

405. 824 — 81
(a) 785 (b) 743 (c) 697 (d) 674

406. 576 — 81
(a) 495 (b) 447 (c) 387 (d) 358

407. 196 — 81
(a) 117 (b) 115 (c) 169 (d) 127

408. 225 — 64
(a) 176 (b) 171 (c) 161 (d) 186

409. 1024 — 326
(a) 678 (b) 588 (c) 698 (d) 479

410. 1100 — 616
(a) 395 (b) 640 (c) 574 (d) 484

411. 1234 — 623
(a) 611 (b) 721 (c) 824 (d) 638

412. 2048 — 916
(a) 1372 (b) 1132 (c) 1232 (d) 1141

413. 2314 — 814
(a) 1502 (b) 1401 (c) 1500 (d) 1480

414. 2500 — 136
(a) 2364 (b) 2296 (c) 2129 (d) 2366

415. 1800 — 616
(a) 1376 (b) 1184 (c) 1285 (d) 1188

416. 1400 — 354

(a) 1046 (b) 1179 (c) 1059 (d) 1178

417. 1400 — 396

(a) 1104 (b) 1374 (c) 1134 (d) 1004

418. 3600 — 756

(a) 2748 (b) 2784 (c) 2844 (d) 2355

419. 4200 — 680

(a) 3632 (b) 3520 (c) 3160 (d) 3320

420. 5500 — 450

(a) 5130 (b) 5275 (c) 5050 (d) 4870

421. 2116 — 137

(a) 1870 (b) 1979 (c) 1876 (d) 1489

422. 3109 — 273

(a) 2838 (b) 2855 (c) 2836 (d) 2780

423. 4174 — 786

(a) 3477 (b) 3388 (c) 3189 (d) 3890

424. 9128 — 644

(a) 8484 (b) 8375 (c) 7575 (d) 6877

425. 8168 — 479

(a) 6688 (b) 7489 (c) 7689 (d) 7859

426. 3254 — 174

(a) 2370 (b) 3080 (c) 2784 (d) 2480

427. 6286 — 968

(a) 5577 (b) 5319 (c) 4898 (d) 5318

428. 4394 — 947

(a) 3367 (b) 3510 (c) 3447 (d) 2896

429. **8319 — 773**
(a) 7856 (b) 7850 (c) 7546 (d) 6446

430. **8543 — 968**
(a) 7955 (b) 7488 (c) 7575 (d) 6565

431. **1704 — 829**
(a) 782 (b) 875 (c) 372 (d) 495

432. **6216 — 986**
(a) 5230 (b) 5180 (c) 5140 (d) 4877

433. **8432 — 674**
(a) 6647 (b) 6897 (c) 5780 (d) 7758

434. **2904 — 876**
(a) 2028 (b) 2785 (c) 2382 (d) 2277

435. **1898 — 476**
(a) 1477 (b) 1498 (c) 1422 (d) 1482

436. **4116 — 907**
(a) 3349 (b) 3209 (c) 3088 (d) 3175

437. **5126 — 904**
(a) 4349 (b) 4222 (c) 4422 (d) 4375

438. **7196 — 637**
(a) 6559 (b) 6679 (c) 4689 (d) 5559

439. **8184 — 973**
(a) 7749 (b) 7123 (c) 7129 (d) 7211

440. **6286 — 709**
(a) 5577 (b) 5278 (c) 5166 (d) 5379

441. **9272 — 637**
(a) 8635 (b) 8455 (c) 8258 (d) 8535

442. 4294 — 943
(a) 3754 (b) 3573 (c) 3266 (d) 3351

443. 6375 — 998
(a) 5278 (b) 5128 (c) 5377 (d) 4877

444. 8473 — 365
(a) 8070 (b) 8137 (c) 8108 (d) 8288

445. 9514 — 216
(a) 9218 (b) 9298 (c) 8977 (d) 9237

446. 7520 — 394
(a) 7227 (b) 7336 (c) 7126 (d) 7339

447. 8686 — 423
(a) 7588 (b) 8264 (c) 8263 (d) 8788

448. 6943 — 472
(a) 6477 (b) 6671 (c) 6471 (d) 5567

449. 9333 — 676
(a) 8657 (b) 7790 (c) 8355 (d) 8183

450. 8512 — 216
(a) 8270 (b) 7760 (c) 7681 (d) 8296

451. 8111 — 933
(a) 6978 (b) 7245 (c) 7178 (d) 7777

452. 7999 — 811
(a) 6822 (b) 7188 (c) 7358 (d) 6898

453. 6666 — 544
(a) 6122 (b) 6374 (c) 5979 (d) 6342

454. 7384 — 916
(a) 5869 (b) 4877 (c) 6554 (d) 6468

455. 8666 — 669
(a) 7784 (b) 7997 (c) 7368 (d) 6849

Type-1: Answer - Key

1.	(b)	26.	(b)	51.	(a)	76.	(d)	101.	(b)
2.	(c)	27.	(b)	52.	(c)	77.	(d)	102.	(b)
3.	(a)	28.	(a)	53.	(d)	78.	(b)	103.	(a)
4.	(d)	29.	(c)	54.	(a)	79.	(c)	104.	(a)
5.	(a)	30.	(a)	55.	(b)	80.	(b)	105.	(c)
6.	(a)	31.	(b)	56.	(c)	81.	(a)	106.	(c)
7.	(b)	32.	(c)	57.	(b)	82.	(c)	107.	(c)
8.	(b)	33.	(a)	58.	(c)	83.	(a)	108.	(b)
9.	(a)	34.	(b)	59.	(a)	84.	(c)	109.	(a)
10.	(c)	35.	(b)	60.	(b)	85.	(a)	110.	(b)
11.	(d)	36.	(c)	61.	(a)	86.	(c)	111.	(c)
12.	(b)	37.	(b)	62.	(a)	87.	(b)	112.	(d)
13.	(c)	38.	(b)	63.	(c)	88.	(a)	113.	(b)
14.	(a)	39.	(a)	64.	(b)	89.	(c)	114.	(b)
15.	(b)	40.	(c)	65.	(a)	90.	(c)	115.	(a)
16.	(d)	41.	(d)	66.	(b)	91.	(d)	116.	(b)
17.	(b)	42.	(d)	67.	(c)	92.	(b)	117.	(a)
18.	(c)	43.	(b)	68.	(b)	93.	(d)	118.	(b)
19.	(b)	44.	(c)	69.	(d)	94.	(a)	119.	(d)
20.	(c)	45.	(b)	70.	(b)	95.	(c)	120.	(a)
21.	(b)	46.	(d)	71.	(b)	96.	(c)	121.	(c)
22.	(a)	47.	(b)	72.	(c)	97.	(a)	122.	(c)
23.	(c)	48.	(a)	73.	(c)	98.	(b)	123.	(a)
24.	(a)	49.	(b)	74.	(b)	99.	(c)	124.	(c)
25.	(d)	50.	(c)	75.	(c)	100.	(a)	125.	(b)

Type-1: Answer - Key

126. (a)	151. (d)	176. (c)	201. (b)	226. (a)
127. (d)	152. (b)	177. (a)	202. (c)	227. (b)
128. (a)	153. (d)	178. (a)	203. (a)	228. (d)
129. (c)	154. (d)	179. (b)	204. (c)	229. (b)
130. (b)	155. (a)	180. (a)	205. (d)	230. (c)
131. (c)	156. (b)	181. (b)	206. (a)	231. (b)
132. (b)	157. (c)	182. (c)	207. (c)	232. (c)
133. (b)	158. (a)	183. (b)	208. (c)	233. (c)
134. (a)	159. (c)	184. (c)	209. (a)	234. (b)
135. (b)	160. (d)	185. (b)	210. (b)	235. (a)
136. (b)	161. (c)	186. (c)	211. (c)	236. (b)
137. (c)	162. (a)	187. (b)	212. (d)	237. (c)
138. (b)	163. (c)	188. (c)	213. (a)	238. (c)
139. (a)	164. (c)	189. (d)	214. (b)	239. (b)
140. (b)	165. (a)	190. (a)	215. (b)	240. (a)
141. (b)	166. (b)	191. (c)	216. (d)	241. (a)
142. (a)	167. (a)	192. (b)	217. (d)	242. (a)
143. (b)	168. (a)	193. (c)	218. (b)	243. (a)
144. (b)	169. (b)	194. (a)	219. (d)	244. (b)
145. (c)	170. (b)	195. (b)	220. (b)	245. (c)
146. (b)	171. (a)	196. (a)	221. (d)	246. (d)
147. (d)	172. (d)	197. (d)	222. (d)	247. (b)
148. (b)	173. (c)	198. (b)	223. (a)	248. (c)
149. (c)	174. (a)	199. (c)	224. (c)	249. (b)
150. (a)	175. (b)	200. (a)	225. (d)	250. (d)

Type-1: Answer - Key

251. (c)	276. (c)	301. (d)	326. (a)	351. (a)
252. (b)	277. (a)	302. (a)	327. (b)	352. (b)
253. (a)	278. (c)	303. (c)	328. (b)	353. (b)
254. (d)	279. (c)	304. (d)	329. (b)	354. (c)
255. (b)	280. (c)	305. (c)	330. (b)	355. (d)
256. (a)	281. (a)	306. (a)	331. (a)	356. (a)
257. (c)	282. (d)	307. (b)	332. (c)	357. (c)
258. (a)	283. (d)	308. (d)	333. (c)	358. (b)
259. (d)	284. (c)	309. (b)	334. (b)	359. (c)
260. (c)	285. (a)	310. (d)	335. (a)	360. (d)
261. (b)	286. (c)	311. (c)	336. (d)	361. (a)
262. (a)	287. (b)	312. (b)	337. (c)	362. (c)
263. (b)	288. (d)	313. (b)	338. (b)	363. (c)
264. (c)	289. (b)	314. (c)	339. (a)	364. (b)
265. (a)	290. (c)	315. (c)	340. (c)	365. (c)
266. (b)	291. (c)	316. (b)	341. (a)	366. (d)
267. (c)	292. (d)	317. (a)	342. (b)	367. (d)
268. (a)	293. (b)	318. (c)	343. (c)	368. (a)
269. (c)	294. (c)	319. (a)	344. (d)	369. (d)
270. (c)	295. (b)	320. (b)	345. (a)	370. (a)
271. (d)	296. (d)	321. (c)	346. (d)	371. (c)
272. (b)	297. (a)	322. (c)	347. (a)	372. (d)
273. (c)	298. (c)	323. (a)	348. (a)	373. (c)
274. (b)	299. (a)	324. (b)	349. (c)	374. (d)
275. (a)	300. (b)	325. (c)	350. (d)	375. (c)

Type-1: Answer - Key

376. (a)	**392.** (b)	**408.** (c)	**424.** (a)	**440.** (a)
377. (c)	**393.** (a)	**409.** (c)	**425.** (c)	**441.** (a)
378. (b)	**394.** (d)	**410.** (d)	**426.** (b)	**442.** (d)
379. (c)	**395.** (d)	**411.** (a)	**427.** (d)	**443.** (c)
380. (b)	**396.** (d)	**412.** (b)	**428.** (c)	**444.** (c)
381. (b)	**397.** (c)	**413.** (c)	**429.** (c)	**445.** (b)
382. (a)	**398.** (b)	**414.** (a)	**430.** (c)	**446.** (c)
383. (d)	**399.** (b)	**415.** (b)	**431.** (b)	**447.** (c)
384. (d)	**400.** (b)	**416.** (a)	**432.** (a)	**448.** (c)
385. (b)	**401.** (b)	**417.** (d)	**433.** (d)	**449.** (a)
386. (d)	**402.** (d)	**418.** (c)	**434.** (a)	**450.** (d)
387. (b)	**403.** (b)	**419.** (b)	**435.** (c)	**451.** (c)
388. (c)	**404.** (c)	**420.** (c)	**436.** (b)	**452.** (b)
389. (c)	**405.** (b)	**421.** (b)	**437.** (b)	**453.** (a)
390. (c)	**406.** (a)	**422.** (c)	**438.** (a)	**454.** (d)
391. (c)	**407.** (b)	**423.** (b)	**439.** (d)	**455.** (b)

MULTIPLICATION (गुणा)

Type-1

Hint :

19 × 8

☞ पहले की संख्या का दहाई का अंक (Tens digit) (1) को दूसरे संख्या के इकाई के अंक (Unit digit) (8) में गुणा करके (8 × 1) आगे एक zero लगाकर (80) दिमाग में रखना है तथा बाद में इकाई की संख्या को गुणा करके दिमाग में रखी संख्या से जोड़ देना है तो Answer निकल जाएगा।

19 × 8

Step - 1 = 8 × 1 = 80 → मान लेना है और संख्या को दिमाग में रखना है।

Step - 2 = 9 × 8 = 72

Step - 3 = 80 + 72 = [152]

सारी calculation दिमाग में करनी है बिना पेन और पेपर का प्रयोग करें।

Exercise

1. 19 × 8

(a) 165 (b) 150 (c) 142 (d) 152

2. 48 × 9

(a) 443 (b) 342 (c) 355 (d) 432

3. 42 × 5

(a) 233 (b) 235 (c) 210 (d) 198

4. 86 × 8

(a) 688 (b) 598 (c) 483 (d) 572

5. 94 × 8

(a) 688 (b) 577 (c) 752 (d) 875

6. 78 × 8

(a) 685 (b) 624 (c) 589 (d) 587

7. 88 × 4

(a) 355 (b) 423 (c) 352 (d) 488

8. 78 × 7

(a) 577 (b) 588 (c) 546 (d) 466

9. 15 × 6

(a) 88 (b) 79 (c) 95 (d) 90

10. 67 × 6

(a) 423 (b) 402 (c) 507 (d) 388

11. 34 × 6

(a) 208 (b) 204 (c) 209 (d) 206

12. 71 × 8

(a) 566 (b) 577 (c) 568 (d) 468

13. 85 × 8

(a) 593 (b) 687 (c) 674 (d) 680

14. 43 × 7

(a) 301 (b) 308 (c) 311 (d) 299

15. 65 × 5

(a) 344 (b) 322 (c) 325 (d) 334

16. 17 × 8

(a) 124 (b) 136 (c) 129 (d) 122

17. 85 × 7

(a) 455 (b) 582 (c) 354 (d) 595

18. 99 × 9

(a) 881 (b) 891 (c) 789 (d) 888

19. 22 × 9

(a) 173 (b) 201 (c) 187 (d) 198

20. 49 × 6

(a) 255 (b) 247 (c) 294 (d) 199

21. 66 × 8

(a) 388 (b) 397 (c) 528 (d) 409

22. 57 × 5

(a) 285 (b) 255 (c) 277 (d) 293

23. 22 × 9

(a) 197 (b) 188 (c) 198 (d) 166

24. 15 × 7

(a) 105 (b) 111 (c) 118 (d) 256

25. 97 × 5

(a) 466 (b) 755 (c) 389 (d) 485

26. 18 × 6

(a) 109 (b) 210 (c) 177 (d) 108

27. 56 × 6

(a) 236 (b) 388 (c) 336 (d) 244

28. 33 × 4

(a) 133 (b) 132 (c) 146 (d) 128

29. 98 × 7

(a) 668 (b) 587 (c) 688 (d) 686

30. 64 × 9

(a) 439 (b) 572 (c) 576 (d) 466

31. 87 × 4

(a) 288 (b) 397 (c) 377 (d) 348

32. 75 × 9

(a) 557 (b) 659 (c) 675 (d) 688

33. 57 × 6

(a) 342 (b) 345 (c) 286 (d) 436

34. 98 × 7

(a) 476 (b) 688 (c) 582 (d) 686

35. 74 × 9

(a) 666 (b) 486 (c) 544 (d) 651

36. 51 × 7

(a) 287 (b) 356 (c) 387 (d) 357

37. 64 × 4

(a) 213 (b) 279 (c) 264 (d) 256

38. 73 × 7

(a) 521 (b) 531 (c) 541 (d) 511

39. 54 × 9

(a) 486 (b) 466 (c) 388 (d) 489

40. 88 × 4

(a) 269 (b) 342 (c) 352 (d) 334

41. 24 × 7

(a) 177 (b) 168 (c) 218 (d) 213

42. 48 × 8

(a) 344 (b) 384 (c) 287 (d) 299

43. 65 × 6

(a) 297 (b) 394 (c) 390 (d) 401

44. 83 × 6

(a) 498 (b) 388 (c) 397 (d) 488

45. 64 × 3

(a) 179 (b) 184 (c) 192 (d) 217

46. 44 × 7

(a) 305 (b) 341 (c) 308 (d) 317

47. 31 × 8

(a) 288 (b) 258 (c) 284 (d) 248

48. 45 × 7

(a) 287 (b) 345 (c) 315 (d) 214

49. 99 × 3

(a) 277 (b) 244 (c) 287 (d) 297

50. 27 × 7

(a) 189 (b) 201 (c) 188 (d) 148

51. 84 × 9

(a) 654 (b) 756 (c) 746 (d) 755

52. 69 × 9

(a) 522 (b) 631 (c) 537 (d) 621

53. 73 × 9

(a) 747 (b) 654 (c) 657 (d) 648

54. 55 × 7

(a) 388 (b) 385 (c) 401 (d) 389

55. 39 × 5

(a) 198 (b) 195 (c) 185 (d) 192

56. 44 × 7

(a) 299 (b) 307 (c) 298 (d) 308

57. 46 × 8

(a) 368 (b) 354 (c) 367 (d) 388

58. 25 × 9

(a) 225 (b) 237 (c) 342 (d) 321

59. 63 × 6

(a) 298 (b) 348 (c) 378 (d) 358

60. 46 × 7

(a) 334 (b) 325 (c) 421 (d) 322

61. 15 × 4

(a) 60 (b) 72 (c) 59 (d) 67

62. 85 × 9

(a) 744 (b) 647 (c) 585 (d) 765

63. 51 × 7

(a) 283 (b) 357 (c) 277 (d) 347

64. 74 × 4

(a) 256 (b) 312 (c) 246 (d) 296

65. 44 × 8

(a) 456 (b) 326 (c) 352 (d) 248

66. 74 × 5

(a) 370 (b) 377 (c) 287 (d) 297

67. 31 × 4

(a) 189 (b) 144 (c) 242 (d) 124

68. 29 × 9

(a) 266 (b) 316 (c) 268 (d) 261

69. 15 × 7

(a) 109 (b) 208 (c) 106 (d) 105

70. 33 × 8

(a) 266 (b) 264 (c) 278 (d) 371

71. 64 × 5

(a) 325 (b) 319 (c) 320 (d) 298

72. 47 × 8

(a) 379 (b) 297 (c) 386 (d) 376

73. 78 × 9

(a) 709 (b) 658 (c) 702 (d) 708

74. 94 × 8

(a) 752 (b) 691 (c) 699 (d) 748

75. 51 × 4

(a) 208 (b) 340 (c) 304 (d) 204

76. 29 × 8

(a) 344 (b) 334 (c) 232 (d) 343

77. 48 × 8

(a) 384 (b) 488 (c) 348 (d) 287

78. 37 × 5

(a) 188 (b) 286 (c) 175 (d) 185

79. 44 × 8

(a) 333 (b) 352 (c) 455 (d) 387

80. 32 × 8

(a) 278 (b) 357 (c) 256 (d) 316

81. 19 × 8

(a) 144 (b) 217 (c) 126 (d) 152

82. 56 × 4

(a) 224 (b) 348 (c) 324 (d) 144

83. 71 × 7

(a) 466 (b) 497 (c) 377 (d) 487

84. 56 × 6

(a) 368 (b) 336 (c) 435 (d) 438

85. 96 × 6

(a) 577 (b) 485 (c) 487 (d) 576

86. 37 × 6

(a) 222 (b) 333 (c) 342 (d) 224

87. 64 × 8

(a) 552 (b) 412 (c) 512 (d) 421

88. 95 × 8

(a) 860 (b) 743 (c) 560 (d) 760

89. 76 × 7

(a) 534 (b) 532 (c) 482 (d) 434

90. 95 × 5

(a) 347 (b) 477 (c) 475 (d) 425

91. 34 × 8

(a) 271 (b) 272 (c) 371 (d) 477

92. 61 × 7

(a) 528 (b) 378 (c) 427 (d) 424

93. 73 × 9

(a) 578 (b) 658 (c) 657 (d) 577

94. 62 × 9

(a) 588 (b) 685 (c) 558 (d) 498

95. 73 × 6

(a) 459 (b) 488 (c) 438 (d) 389

96. 16 × 8

(a) 128 (b) 228 (c) 218 (d) 197

97. 76 × 5

(a) 370 (b) 389 (c) 480 (d) 380

98. 36 × 9

(a) 427 (b) 226 (c) 324 (d) 328

99. 46 × 7

(a) 482 (b) 237 (c) 521 (d) 322

100. 85 × 5

(a) 573 (b) 425 (c) 524 (d) 348

101. 55 × 7

(a) 385 (b) 267 (c) 497 (d) 681

102. 77 × 6

(a) 566 (b) 376 (c) 462 (d) 391

103. 99 × 8

(a) 792 (b) 618 (c) 629 (d) 682

104. 37 × 7

(a) 368 (b) 259 (c) 348 (d) 485

105. 43 × 7

(a) 301 (b) 402 (c) 209 (d) 389

106. 52 × 9

(a) 488 (b) 358 (c) 468 (d) 308

107. 31 × 4

(a) 254 (b) 124 (c) 233 (d) 125

108. 71 × 9

(a) 639 (b) 589 (c) 429 (d) 279

109. 17 × 6

(a) 111 (b) 114 (c) 211 (d) 102

110. 69 × 7

(a) 485 (b) 483 (c) 328 (d) 284

111. 34 × 9

(a) 308 (b) 206 (c) 306 (d) 316

112. 61 × 7

(a) 421 (b) 427 (c) 328 (d) 423

113. 91 × 4

(a) 345 (b) 364 (c) 268 (d) 464

114. 85 × 9

(a) 826 (b) 365 (c) 564 (d) 765

115. 34 × 9

(a) 408 (b) 306 (c) 508 (d) 409

116. 96 × 4

(a) 388 (b) 374 (c) 384 (d) 495

117. 38 × 7

(a) 486 (b) 278 (c) 266 (d) 186

118. 49 × 8

(a) 382 (b) 392 (c) 422 (d) 398

119. 51 × 6

(a) 299 (b) 438 (c) 306 (d) 206

120. 53 × 4
(a) 212 (b) 343 (c) 214 (d) 413

121. 57 × 9
(a) 417 (b) 513 (c) 313 (d) 414

122. 59 × 3
(a) 188 (b) 277 (c) 177 (d) 127

123. 61 × 7
(a) 428 (b) 589 (c) 347 (d) 427

124. 63 × 8
(a) 504 (b) 511 (c) 408 (d) 509

125. 75 × 8
(a) 597 (b) 600 (c) 792 (d) 409

126. 77 × 3
(a) 233 (b) 241 (c) 231 (d) 344

127. 46 × 6
(a) 178 (b) 266 (c) 286 (d) 276

128. 48 × 7
(a) 336 (b) 446 (c) 284 (d) 345

129. 84 × 9
(a) 468 (b) 756 (c) 655 (d) 845

130. 67 × 9
(a) 589 (b) 609 (c) 603 (d) 409

131. 69 × 9
(a) 568 (b) 524 (c) 621 (d) 423

132. 77 × 7
(a) 429 (b) 589 (c) 539 (d) 588

133. 73 × 5

(a) 475 (b) 236 (c) 365 (d) 385

134. 75 × 7

(a) 524 (b) 525 (c) 631 (d) 527

135. 64 × 8

(a) 623 (b) 428 (c) 512 (d) 431

136. 28 × 9

(a) 233 (b) 422 (c) 325 (d) 252

137. 29 × 6

(a) 174 (b) 242 (c) 254 (d) 179

138. 33 × 7

(a) 345 (b) 245 (c) 231 (d) 317

139. 35 × 4

(a) 140 (b) 247 (c) 147 (d) 257

140. 45 × 9

(a) 324 (b) 405 (c) 325 (d) 204

141. 43 × 7

(a) 298 (b) 301 (c) 281 (d) 391

142. 48 × 9

(a) 432 (b) 429 (c) 452 (d) 442

143. 83 × 8

(a) 664 (b) 565 (c) 486 (d) 583

144. 77 × 5

(a) 358 (b) 385 (c) 482 (d) 345

145. 55 × 4

(a) 227 (b) 321 (c) 220 (d) 311

146. 96 × 9

(a) 844 (b) 864 (c) 758 (d) 984

147. 99 × 7

(a) 589 (b) 259 (c) 639 (d) 693

148. 34 × 8

(a) 277 (b) 272 (c) 473 (d) 127

149. 61 × 5

(a) 259 (b) 439 (c) 305 (d) 407

150. 16 × 8

(a) 128 (b) 329 (c) 348 (d) 126

151. 76 × 9

(a) 568 (b) 684 (c) 852 (d) 482

152. 88 × 8

(a) 704 (b) 809 (c) 697 (d) 702

153. 27 × 6

(a) 284 (b) 166 (c) 162 (d) 211

154. 55 × 4

(a) 220 (b) 246 (c) 321 (d) 421

155. 25 × 6

(a) 148 (b) 247 (c) 251 (d) 150

156. 18 × 5

(a) 101 (b) 90 (c) 109 (d) 103

157. 45 × 7

(a) 421 (b) 324 (c) 239 (d) 315

158. 77 × 9

(a) 583 (b) 693 (c) 581 (d) 482

159. 89 × 4

(a) 346 (b) 283 (c) 429 (d) 356

160. 56 × 4

(a) 245 (b) 224 (c) 321 (d) 423

161. 23 × 8

(a) 149 (b) 243 (c) 177 (d) 184

162. 45 × 8

(a) 423 (b) 256 (c) 360 (d) 243

163. 79 × 5

(a) 348 (b) 395 (c) 428 (d) 521

164. 66 × 8

(a) 429 (b) 432 (c) 528 (d) 618

165. 42 × 7

(a) 239 (b) 294 (c) 428 (d) 285

166. 82 × 4

(a) 438 (b) 238 (c) 328 (d) 418

167. 38 × 9

(a) 354 (b) 352 (c) 342 (d) 482

168. 75 × 6

(a) 496 (b) 382 (c) 450 (d) 385

169. 98 × 7

(a) 573 (b) 784 (c) 686 (d) 926

170. 76 × 8

(a) 708 (b) 520 (c) 788 (d) 608

171. 88 × 4

(a) 355 (b) 452 (c) 352 (d) 482

MULTIPLICATION (गुणा)

172. 57 × 9

(a) 513 (b) 488 (c) 312 (d) 471

173. 49 × 7

(a) 423 (b) 473 (c) 343 (d) 237

174. 75 × 8

(a) 599 (b) 600 (c) 702 (d) 489

175. 66 × 4

(a) 277 (b) 268 (c) 467 (d) 264

176. 48 × 8

(a) 348 (b) 384 (c) 288 (d) 386

177. 58 × 4

(a) 256 (b) 232 (c) 332 (d) 143

178. 68 × 8

(a) 456 (b) 444 (c) 544 (d) 354

179. 77 × 5

(a) 542 (b) 488 (c) 385 (d) 295

180. 99 × 7

(a) 563 (b) 494 (c) 792 (d) 693

181. 33 × 9

(a) 288 (b) 297 (c) 377 (d) 189

182. 77 × 5

(a) 385 (b) 455 (c) 387 (d) 428

183. 86 × 4

(a) 248 (b) 349 (c) 346 (d) 344

184. 72 × 8

(a) 571 (b) 576 (c) 481 (d) 376

185. 59 × 7

(a) 333 (b) 413 (c) 514 (d) 418

186. 47 × 9

(a) 373 (b) 425 (c) 423 (d) 521

187. 67 × 7

(a) 488 (b) 572 (c) 489 (d) 469

188. 71 × 4

(a) 148 (b) 284 (c) 198 (d) 488

189. 44 × 7

(a) 297 (b) 314 (c) 308 (d) 428

190. 81 × 4

(a) 348 (b) 324 (c) 328 (d) 445

191. 47 × 8

(a) 376 (b) 286 (c) 426 (d) 327

192. 72 × 4

(a) 346 (b) 288 (c) 428 (d) 388

193. 81 × 7

(a) 488 (b) 587 (c) 567 (d) 427

194. 52 × 8

(a) 416 (b) 318 (c) 278 (d) 417

195. 69 × 9

(a) 523 (b) 421 (c) 524 (d) 621

196. 74 × 6

(a) 442 (b) 824 (c) 511 (d) 444

197. 52 × 6

(a) 312 (b) 322 (c) 421 (d) 248

198. 47 × 6

(a) 216 (b) 282 (c) 248 (d) 328

199. 93 × 4

(a) 372 (b) 377 (c) 482 (d) 522

200. 47 × 7

(a) 417 (b) 561 (c) 329 (d) 427

201. 81 × 9

(a) 849 (b) 729 (c) 824 (d) 769

Type-1: Answer - Key

1.	(d)	26.	(d)	51.	(b)	76.	(c)	101.	(a)
2.	(d)	27.	(c)	52.	(d)	77.	(a)	102.	(c)
3.	(c)	28.	(b)	53.	(c)	78.	(d)	103.	(a)
4.	(a)	29.	(d)	54.	(b)	79.	(b)	104.	(b)
5.	(c)	30.	(c)	55.	(b)	80.	(c)	105.	(a)
6.	(b)	31.	(d)	56.	(d)	81.	(d)	106.	(c)
7.	(c)	32.	(c)	57.	(a)	82.	(a)	107.	(b)
8.	(c)	33.	(a)	58.	(a)	83.	(b)	108.	(a)
9.	(d)	34.	(d)	59.	(c)	84.	(b)	109.	(d)
10.	(b)	35.	(a)	60.	(d)	85.	(d)	110.	(b)
11.	(b)	36.	(d)	61.	(a)	86.	(a)	111.	(c)
12.	(c)	37.	(d)	62.	(d)	87.	(c)	112.	(b)
13.	(d)	38.	(d)	63.	(b)	88.	(d)	113.	(b)
14.	(a)	39.	(a)	64.	(d)	89.	(b)	114.	(d)
15.	(c)	40.	(c)	65.	(c)	90.	(c)	115.	(b)
16.	(b)	41.	(b)	66.	(a)	91.	(b)	116.	(c)
17.	(d)	42.	(b)	67.	(d)	92.	(c)	117.	(c)
18.	(b)	43.	(c)	68.	(d)	93.	(c)	118.	(b)
19.	(d)	44.	(a)	69.	(d)	94.	(c)	119.	(c)
20.	(c)	45.	(c)	70.	(b)	95.	(c)	120.	(a)
21.	(c)	46.	(c)	71.	(c)	96.	(a)	121.	(b)
22.	(a)	47.	(d)	72.	(d)	97.	(d)	122.	(c)
23.	(c)	48.	(c)	73.	(c)	98.	(c)	123.	(d)
24.	(a)	49.	(d)	74.	(a)	99.	(d)	124.	(a)
25.	(d)	50.	(a)	75.	(d)	100.	(b)	125.	(b)

Type-1: Answer - Key

126. (c)	141. (b)	156. (b)	171. (c)	186. (c)
127. (d)	142. (a)	157. (d)	172. (a)	187. (d)
128. (a)	143. (a)	158. (b)	173. (c)	188. (b)
129. (b)	144. (b)	159. (d)	174. (b)	189. (c)
130. (c)	145. (c)	160. (b)	175. (d)	190. (b)
131. (c)	146. (b)	161. (d)	176. (b)	191. (a)
132. (c)	147. (d)	162. (c)	177. (b)	192. (b)
133. (c)	148. (b)	163. (b)	178. (c)	193. (c)
134. (b)	149. (c)	164. (c)	179. (c)	194. (a)
135. (c)	150. (a)	165. (b)	180. (d)	195. (d)
136. (d)	151. (b)	166. (c)	181. (b)	196. (d)
137. (a)	152. (a)	167. (c)	182. (a)	197. (a)
138. (c)	153. (c)	168. (c)	183. (d)	198. (b)
139. (a)	154. (a)	169. (c)	184. (b)	199. (a)
140. (b)	155. (d)	170. (d)	185. (b)	200. (c)
				201. (b)

Type-2

Hint :

47
×2 3

☞ दोनों संख्याओं के इकाई के अंकों (Unit digits) को आपस में गुणा (7 × 3) = (21) करके एक को लिख देना है और शेष हासिल को दिमाग में रखना है, उसके बाद एक दूसरे के इकाई अंकों के साथ दहाई के अंकों का कैंची का गुणा करके जोड़ना है और जो हासिल बच गया था उसे भी जोड़ देना है और नए हासिल को दिमाग में रखना है उसके बाद एक दूसरे के दहाई अंक को गुणा करना है और हासिल को जोड़ देना है, तो Answer निकल आएगा।

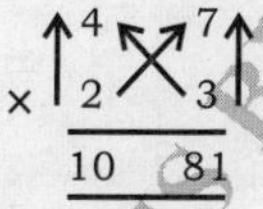

Step - 1 :- 7 × 3 = 2(1) → लिख देना
2 → दिमाग में रखना

Step - 2 :-

$\underline{(3\times4)} + \underline{(2\times7)} +$ हासिल

$\downarrow \quad \downarrow$

12 + 14 + 2 = 2⑧ → लिख देना

2 → दिमाग में रखना

Step - 3 :- 4 × 2 = 8 + हासिल = 8 + 2 = 10

Answer = $\boxed{1081}$

कोशिश करनी है कि पूरा answer बिना लिखे दिमाग में calculate करके आए।

Exercise

1. 47 × 23

(a) 1182 (b) 973 (c) 1271 (d) 1081

2. 48 × 55

(a) 2465 (b) 2340 (c) 2640 (d) 2751

3. 28 × 82

(a) 2296 (b) 2473 (c) 3166 (d) 3156

4. 52 × 47

(a) 2348 (b) 2444 (c) 2548 (d) 3441

5. 63 × 31

(a) 1953 (b) 1843 (c) 1984 (d) 1875

6. 32 × 23

(a) 882 (b) 634 (c) 736 (d) 846

7. 32 × 75

(a) 2358 (b) 2510 (c) 2400 (d) 2695

8. 22 × 88

(a) 1876 (b) 1936 (c) 2116 (d) 2286

9. 87 × 53

(a) 4611 (b) 4826 (c) 5111 (d) 5246

10. 98 × 65

(a) 6570 (b) 6280 (c) 6370 (d) 7770

11. 38 × 88

(a) 4234 (b) 4325 (c) 3344 (d) 4233

12. 38 × 41

(a) 1558 (b) 1778 (c) 1754 (d) 1423

13. 93 × 41

(a) 4823 (b) 3714 (c) 3813 (d) 3588

14. 53 × 13

(a) 678 (b) 849 (c) 687 (d) 689

15. 49 × 78

(a) 4722 (b) 5210 (c) 3822 (d) 4579

16. 82 × 91

(a) 7566 (b) 8416 (c) 7462 (d) 6895

17. 49 × 26

(a) 1247 (b) 1274 (c) 1877 (d) 1884

18. 71 × 31

(a) 2422 (b) 2105 (c) 2201 (d) 2341

19. 58 × 97

(a) 5626 (b) 6628 (c) 7162 (d) 5429

20. 53 × 41

(a) 2747 (b) 2173 (c) 2477 (d) 2275

21. 38 × 83

(a) 3457 (b) 4214 (c) 3154 (d) 3555

22. 92 × 39

(a) 3588 (b) 4158 (c) 4289 (d) 3654

23. 58 × 24

(a) 1582 (b) 1782 (c) 1392 (d) 1222

24. 73 × 49

(a) 3577 (b) 4578 (c) 5172 (d) 6277

25. 69 × 28

(a) 1824 (b) 1932 (c) 2012 (d) 3431

26. 44 × 76

(a) 3242 (b) 2347 (c) 3344 (d) 2578

27. 57 × 95

(a) 5417 (b) 5864 (c) 4515 (d) 5415

28. 62 × 75

(a) 4650 (b) 4886 (c) 5578 (d) 4784

29. 42 × 88

(a) 4166 (b) 3871 (c) 3856 (d) 3696

30. 55 × 98

(a) 5388 (b) 5790 (c) 5390 (d) 5570

31. 75 × 59

(a) 4824 (b) 4425 (c) 5524 (d) 5570

32. 82 × 85

(a) 6180 (b) 6870 (c) 7271 (d) 6970

33. 71 × 45

(a) 4175 (b) 2837 (c) 3195 (d) 4710

34. 25 × 75

(a) 1875 (b) 1978 (c) 1615 (d) 1855

35. 35 × 19

(a) 746 (b) 665 (c) 855 (d) 745

36. 74 × 88

(a) 8592 (b) 8521 (c) 6512 (d) 7515

37. 93 × 24

(a) 3452 (b) 5412 (c) 2232 (d) 4522

38. 77 × 29

(a) 2577 (b) 3322 (c) 2233 (d) 4721

39. 38 × 66

(a) 3509 (b) 2508 (c) 2718 (d) 2919

40. 95 × 97

(a) 1014 (b) 1125 (c) 9215 (d) 9518

41. 22 × 45

(a) 1220 (b) 1011 (c) 1419 (d) 990

42. 58 × 28

(a) 1725 (b) 1624 (c) 1875 (d) 4523

43. 92 × 38

(a) 3856 (b) 4498 (c) 3496 (d) 4166

44. 87 × 53

(a) 4611 (b) 7744 (c) 5522 (d) 6213

45. 98 × 65

(a) 7740 (b) 8482 (c) 6370 (d) 9170

46. 38 × 88
(a) 4588 (b) 3344 (c) 5233 (d) 2714

47. 53 × 46
(a) 5218 (b) 4458 (c) 2829 (d) 2438

48. 98 × 85
(a) 9230 (b) 3712 (c) 8330 (d) 1040

49. 73 × 52
(a) 3250 (b) 3796 (c) 3276 (d) 3866

50. 77 × 43
(a) 3311 (b) 5412 (c) 4214 (d) 5545

51. 33 × 26
(a) 1155 (b) 1075 (c) 1088 (d) 858

52. 61 × 45
(a) 3412 (b) 2870 (c) 2745 (d) 3841

53. 81 × 49
(a) 4277 (b) 4130 (c) 3969 (d) 5269

54. 81 × 31
(a) 4111 (b) 2821 (c) 2511 (d) 3122

55. 58 × 84
(a) 5877 (b) 4872 (c) 6174 (d) 7122

56. 73 × 41
(a) 4895 (b) 4985 (c) 2993 (d) 5143

57. 38 × 33
(a) 1247 (b) 1258 (c) 1254 (d) 1823

58. 99 × 49
(a) 6278 (b) 4855 (c) 4199 (d) 4851

59. 57 × 24

(a) 1588 (b) 1368 (c) 1868 (d) 1744

60. 39 × 28

(a) 1472 (b) 1092 (c) 1728 (d) 1453

61. 74 × 76

(a) 5624 (b) 5829 (c) 8426 (d) 5944

62. 62 × 78

(a) 4836 (b) 5826 (c) 7826 (d) 4986

63. 87 × 45

(a) 4815 (b) 4755 (c) 5716 (d) 3915

64. 65 × 79

(a) 5545 (b) 5135 (c) 5715 (d) 6815

65. 78 × 38

(a) 4826 (b) 2926 (c) 2964 (d) 2546

66. 45 × 87

(a) 4145 (b) 3915 (c) 5217 (d) 4716

67. 77 × 82

(a) 6583 (b) 6314 (c) 7515 (d) 6218

68. 82 × 75

(a) 6150 (b) 6582 (c) 6472 (d) 7510

69. 95 × 45

(a) 4720 (b) 5217 (c) 4275 (d) 5610

70. 49 × 81

(a) 4769 (b) 7123 (c) 5969 (d) 3969

71. 65 × 42

(a) 3172 (b) 2730 (c) 2890 (d) 3720

Type-2: Answer - Key

1.	(d)	**15.**	(c)	**29.**	(d)	**43.**	(c)	**57.**	(c)
2.	(c)	**16.**	(c)	**30.**	(c)	**44.**	(a)	**58.**	(d)
3.	(a)	**17.**	(b)	**31.**	(b)	**45.**	(c)	**59.**	(b)
4.	(b)	**18.**	(c)	**32.**	(d)	**46.**	(b)	**60.**	(b)
5.	(a)	**19.**	(a)	**33.**	(c)	**47.**	(d)	**61.**	(a)
6.	(c)	**20.**	(b)	**34.**	(a)	**48.**	(c)	**62.**	(a)
7.	(c)	**21.**	(c)	**35.**	(b)	**49.**	(b)	**63.**	(d)
8.	(b)	**22.**	(a)	**36.**	(c)	**50.**	(a)	**64.**	(b)
9.	(a)	**23.**	(c)	**37.**	(c)	**51.**	(d)	**65.**	(c)
10.	(c)	**24.**	(a)	**38.**	(c)	**52.**	(c)	**66.**	(b)
11.	(c)	**25.**	(b)	**39.**	(b)	**53.**	(c)	**67.**	(b)
12.	(a)	**26.**	(c)	**40.**	(c)	**54.**	(c)	**68.**	(a)
13.	(c)	**27.**	(d)	**41.**	(d)	**55.**	(b)	**69.**	(c)
14.	(d)	**28.**	(a)	**42.**	(b)	**56.**	(c)	**70.**	(d)
								71.	(b)

Type-3

Square (वर्ग)

Hint :

$(42)^2$

☞ वर्ग (Square) करते वक्त सबसे पहले इकाई के अंक (Unit digit) (2) का वर्ग करना है तो (4) उसके बाद इकाई अंक (Unit digit) (2), दहाई का अंक (Tens digit) (4) का गुणा करके (4 × 2) = 8 का दुबारा से (2) गुणा करके (8 × 2) = (16) यानि 6 लिख देना है। एक (हासिल) आगे चला जाएगा, फिर दहाई के अंक (Tens digit) के रूप में (16 + 1) = (17) जोड़ दिया जाए और Answer निकल जाएगा।

Step - 1 ⇒ $(42)^2$ → ④

Step - 2 ⇒ (4 × 2) × 2 = 1⑥ → लिख देना है
1 → एक हासिल है जो आगे चला जाएगा।

Step - 3 ⇒ $(4)^2$ = 16 + हासिल (1) = 17

Answer 1764 दिमाग में करना हैं बिना पेन के।

Exercise

1. 21^2

(a) 521 (b) 562 (c) 441 (d) 742

2. 22^2

(a) 526 (b) 854 (c) 254 (d) 484

3. 27^2

(a) 893 (b) 826 (c) 729 (d) 927

4. 31^2

(a) 1123 (b) 961 (c) 2139 (d) 1523

5. 32^2

(a) 1522 (b) 1823 (c) 1023 (d) 1024

6. 33^2

(a) 1328 (b) 1089 (c) 1272 (d) 1184

7. 42^2

(a) 1764 (b) 1965 (c) 1824 (d) 2064

8. 43^2

(a) 1859 (b) 1957 (c) 1849 (d) 1758

9. 48^2

(a) 2583 (b) 2304 (c) 3173 (d) 3104

10. 52^2

(a) 3217 (b) 2704 (c) 3582 (d) 3712

11. 55^2

(a) 3812 (b) 4123 (c) 3025 (d) 3472

12. 63^2

(a) 4239 (b) 3969 (c) 4729 (d) 3859

13. 67^2

(a) 5829 (b) 4489 (c) 5219 (d) 5379

14. 72^2

(a) 5879 (b) 4623 (c) 7184 (d) 5184

15. 74^2

(a) 5876 (b) 5774 (c) 7154 (d) 5476

16. 78^2

(a) 6084 (b) 6124 (c) 6384 (d) 7445

17. 82^2

(a) 7134 (b) 6724 (c) 8124 (d) 9412

18. 85^2

(a) 7225 (b) 8427 (c) 8265 (d) 7524

19. 91^2

(a) 8581 (b) 8281 (c) 8178 (d) 8321

20. 92^2

(a) 9464 (b) 9128 (c) 8565 (d) 8464

21. 89^2

(a) 8942 (b) 7859 (c) 7921 (d) 9128

22. 66^2

(a) 5472 (b) 4356 (c) 4238 (d) 5236

23. 43^2

(a) 2129 (b) 1849 (c) 1982 (d) 2099

24. 31^2

(a) 1023 (b) 1129 (c) 1161 (d) 961

25. 56^2

(a) 3729 (b) 4236 (c) 3136 (d) 5216

26. 96^2

(a) 8729 (b) 9236 (c) 9216 (d) 8246

27. 57^2

(a) 3578 (b) 4129 (c) 3379 (d) 3249

28. 34^2

(a) 1246 (b) 1156 (c) 1736 (d) 1826

29. 47^2

(a) 2726 (b) 2237 (c) 3126 (d) 2209

30. 94^2

(a) 9126 (b) 8336 (c) 8836 (d) 7126

31. 55^2

(a) 3025 (b) 3519 (c) 4225 (d) 4682

32. 79^2

(a) 8524 (b) 4562 (c) 7526 (d) 6241

33. 18^2

(a) 0421 (b) 0324 (c) 0823 (d) 0752

34. 93^2

(a) 9569 (b) 8641 (c) 8649 (d) 9997

35. 59^2

(a) 5217 (b) 4281 (c) 3582 (d) 3481

36. 99^2

(a) 9823 (b) 9801 (c) 7148 (d) 8719

37. 35^2

(a) 1427 (b) 1225 (c) 1823 (d) 1985

38. 95^2

(a) 9712 (b) 9345 (c) 7424 (d) 9025

39. 41^2

(a) 1831 (b) 1681 (c) 1754 (d) 1982

40. 77^2

(a) 6230 (b) 5929 (c) 7524 (d) 8543

41. 49^2

(a) 2811 (b) 3210 (c) 4102 (d) 2401

42. 97^2

(a) 9409 (b) 9994 (c) 8526 (d) 2401

43. 46^2

(a) 2511 (b) 3128 (c) 2116 (d) 4128

44. 88^2

(a) 7744 (b) 8542 (c) 4582 (d) 9562

45. 33^2

(a) 1289 (b) 1428 (c) 1199 (d) 1089

46. 73^2

(a) 5899 (b) 5246 (c) 5843 (d) 5329

47. 57^2

(a) 3289 (b) 3249 (c) 3199 (d) 3089

48. 64^2

(a) 4094 (b) 4046 (c) 4096 (d) 4044

49. 48^2

(a) 2485 (b) 2304 (c) 3141 (d) 4144

50. 55^2

(a) 3175 (b) 3025 (c) 4128 (d) 3946

51. 44^2

(a) 2328 (b) 2346 (c) 1936 (d) 2476

52. 58^2
(a) 3416 (b) 3374 (c) 4517 (d) 3364

53. 23^2
(a) 0523 (b) 0659 (c) 0749 (d) 0529

54. 41^2
(a) 1872 (b) 1749 (c) 1681 (d) 1284

55. 75^2
(a) 5526 (b) 5625 (c) 6517 (d) 7419

56. 44^2
(a) 2116 (b) 2814 (c) 1936 (d) 2456

57. 35^2
(a) 1426 (b) 1225 (c) 1784 (d) 4513

58. 90^2
(a) 8271 (b) 9410 (c) 8123 (d) 8100

59. 11^2
(a) 231 (b) 134 (c) 121 (d) 413

60. 60^2
(a) 3781 (b) 4126 (c) 5124 (d) 3600

61. 73^2
(a) 5529 (b) 5329 (c) 4589 (d) 7126

62. 24^2
(a) 472 (b) 752 (c) 826 (d) 576

63. 42^2
(a) 1873 (b) 1764 (c) 1894 (d) 1955

64. 84^2
(a) 7186 (b) 7284 (c) 8410 (d) 7056

65. 85^2

(a) 7354 (b) 7225 (c) 8145 (d) 9125

66. 69^2

(a) 4966 (b) 5211 (c) 4761 (d) 4951

67. 98^2

(a) 9604 (b) 9947 (c) 8543 (d) 8624

68. 65^2

(a) 4225 (b) 4785 (c) 6712 (d) 7525

Type-3: Answer - Key

1.	(c)	15.	(d)	29.	(d)	43.	(c)	57.	(b)
2.	(d)	16.	(a)	30.	(c)	44.	(a)	58.	(d)
3.	(c)	17.	(b)	31.	(a)	45.	(d)	59.	(c)
4.	(b)	18.	(a)	32.	(d)	46.	(d)	60.	(d)
5.	(d)	19.	(b)	33.	(b)	47.	(b)	61.	(b)
6.	(b)	20.	(d)	34.	(c)	48.	(c)	62.	(d)
7.	(a)	21.	(c)	35.	(d)	49.	(b)	63.	(b)
8.	(c)	22.	(b)	36.	(b)	50.	(b)	64.	(d)
9.	(b)	23.	(b)	37.	(b)	51.	(c)	65.	(b)
10.	(b)	24.	(d)	38.	(d)	52.	(d)	66.	(c)
11.	(c)	25.	(c)	39.	(b)	53.	(d)	67.	(a)
12.	(b)	26.	(c)	40.	(b)	54.	(c)	68.	(a)
13.	(b)	27.	(d)	41.	(d)	55.	(b)		
14.	(d)	28.	(b)	42.	(a)	56.	(c)		

Type-4

Hint :

$(123)^2$

☞ बड़ी संख्या का वर्ग (Square) निकालने के लिए हम संख्या को दो भागों में लाईन खींच देते है उसके बाद लाईन के R.H.S. वाले भाग (3) का वर्ग (Square) लिखना है (09) इसके बाद L.H.S. वाली संख्या का वर्ग (Square) करना है उसके बाद एक दूसरे से गुणा करना है (12 × 3) और प्राप्त संख्या का 2 से गुणा करके नीचे से L.H.S. से एक अंक छोड़कर लिखकर जोड़ देना है और Answer निकल जाएगा।

$(123)^2$

Step - 1 ⇒ 12 | 3

Step - 2 ⇒

12	3
144	09

Step - 3 ⇒ (12 × 3) × 2 = 72

Step - 4 ⇒

12	3
144	09
7	2

Step - 5 ⇒

12	3 ⊗
144	09 ⊕
7	2
151	29

Exercise

1. 102^2
(a) 10806 (b) 12461 (c) 10404 (d) 11740

2. 108^2
(a) 11664 (b) 17256 (c) 14256 (d) 12367

3. 114^2
(a) 13580 (b) 12996 (c) 12289 (d) 12703

4. 121^2
(a) 14726 (b) 18942 (c) 14641 (d) 17842

5. 125^2
(a) 18952 (b) 17526 (c) 16253 (d) 15625

6. 144^2
(a) 21453 (b) 21534 (c) 20736 (d) 18729

7. 135^2
(a) 18743 (b) 18225 (c) 19743 (d) 19742

8. 204^2
(a) 41616 (b) 45163 (c) 52164 (d) 51616

9. 212^2
(a) 48746 (b) 51239 (c) 44944 (d) 51426

10. 303^2
(a) 89512 (b) 95123 (c) 94126 (d) 91809

11. 1008^2
(a) 1016064 (b) 1067513 (c) 2145382 (d) 1054361

12. 1107^2
(a) 1225364 (b) 1425312 (c) 1342561 (d) 1225449

13. 2102^2

(a) 4512631 (b) 4845263
(c) 4418404 (d) 5142361

14. 182^2

(a) 33412 (b) 41253 (c) 45126 (d) 33124

15. 198^2

(a) 51265 (b) 39204 (c) 41320 (d) 41203

16. 145^2

(a) 21025 (b) 21234 (c) 21252 (d) 21204

17. 150^2

(a) 21342 (b) 22500 (c) 21340 (d) 13256

18. 122^2

(a) 14884 (b) 17854 (c) 16253 (d) 14523

19. 143^2

(a) 21403 (b) 25341 (c) 25130 (d) 20449

20. 176^2

(a) 30976 (b) 31446 (c) 32458 (d) 32104

21. 156^2

(a) 25741 (b) 24156 (c) 24336 (d) 27130

22. 223^2

(a) 51270 (b) 49729 (c) 51245 (d) 64129

23. 353^2

(a) 2145509 (b) 124609
(c) 125480 (d) 141253

24. 1198^2

(a) 1435204 (b) 1523412
(c) 2145123 (d) 1423512

25. 1108^2

(a) 1235464 (b) 1227664
(c) 1754267 (d) 2142534

26. 2502^2

(a) 6260004 (b) 6254234
(c) 6225341 (d) 6251236

27. 903^2

(a) 8154123 (b) 815409
(c) 812148 (d) 8157476

28. 404^2

(a) 165246 (b) 156246
(c) 163216 (d) 187456

29. 4008^2

(a) 16064064 (b) 16364064
(c) 16164064 (d) 16264064

30. 5008^2

(a) 27153461 (b) 25080064
(c) 28415310 (d) 54274156

31. 2001^2

(a) 4004009 (b) 40451230
(c) 4004001 (d) 51400230

32. 3102^2

(a) 9712503 (b) 93652134
(c) 9622404 (d) 8854213

33. 4120^2

(a) 1678400 (b) 1754234
(c) 16974400 (d) 1823402

34. 2420^2
(a) 5678500 (b) 5856400
(c) 6576220 (d) 7546200

35. 2184^2
(a) 4769856 (b) 41522686
(c) 4712527 (d) 4715296

36. 4102^2
(a) 17845264 (b) 18542634
(c) 16826404 (d) 16741404

37. 2586^2
(a) 6687346 (b) 6687496
(c) 6687396 (d) 4512538

38. 1142^2
(a) 1243164 (b) 1304164
(c) 1452616 (d) 1542685

39. 2103^2
(a) 4452179 (b) 4422609
(c) 5412569 (d) 8452358

40. 1244^2
(a) 1547536 (b) 6541256
(c) 1124468 (d) 1245236

41. 1750^2
(a) 4120600 (b) 3062500
(c) 3140524 (d) 1545124

42. 1852^2
(a) 3429904 (b) 4108404
(c) 3521054 (d) 4150230

Type-4: Answer - Key

1.	(c)	10.	(d)	19.	(d)	28.	(c)	37.	(c)
2.	(a)	11.	(a)	20.	(a)	29.	(a)	38.	(b)
3.	(b)	12.	(d)	21.	(c)	30.	(b)	39.	(b)
4.	(c)	13.	(c)	22.	(b)	31.	(c)	40.	(a)
5.	(d)	14.	(d)	23.	(b)	32.	(c)	41.	(b)
6.	(c)	15.	(b)	24.	(a)	33.	(c)	42.	(a)
7.	(b)	16.	(a)	25.	(b)	34.	(b)		
8.	(a)	17.	(b)	26.	(a)	35.	(a)		
9.	(c)	18.	(a)	27.	(b)	36.	(c)		

Type-5

Cube (घन)

Hint :

$(a + b)^3 = a^3 . 3a^2b . 3ab^2 . b^3$

$(12)^3$

Cube solve करने के लिए हम इस formula को सीधा दिमाग में solve करेगें।

सबसे पहले इकाई के अंक (Unit digit) (2) का cube करके लिख देना (8) है उसके बाद इकाई के अंक (Unit digit) का वर्ग (Square) (4) और दहाई के अंक (Tens digit) (1) और उसे गुणा करना है (12) लिख देना है और (1) हासिल आगे चला जाएगा उसके बाद दहाई के अंक (Tens digit) (1) का वर्ग (Square) और इकाई के अंक (Unit digit) (2) को 3 से गुणा कर देना जो (6) आएगा और पिछले हासिल (1) को जोड़ देना (7) अब दहाई के अंक (Tens digit) का cube करना है।

Step - 1 $\Rightarrow 8 \Rightarrow (2)^3 = 8$

Step - 2 $\Rightarrow 2 \Rightarrow 3 \times 1 \times (2)^2 = 3 \times 4 = \text{(1)}2$ हासिल

Step - 3 $\Rightarrow 7 \Rightarrow 3 \times (1)^2 \times 2 +$ हासिल $(1) = 7$

Step - 4 $\Rightarrow 1 \Rightarrow (1)^3 = 1$

Step - 5 $\Rightarrow \boxed{1728}$

Exercise

1. 5^3

(a) 225 (b) 125 (c) 145 (d) 147

2. 6^3

(a) 317 (b) 246 (c) 326 (d) 216

3. 7^3

(a) 343 (b) 333 (c) 413 (d) 354

4. 8^3

(a) 614 (b) 512 (c) 412 (d) 611

5. 9^3

(a) 729 (b) 849 (c) 949 (d) 844

6. 10^3

(a) 1203 (b) 1000 (c) 1100 (d) 1402

7. 11^3

(a) 1421 (b) 1331 (c) 1524 (d) 1221

8. 12^3

(a) 1828 (b) 1728 (c) 1978 (d) 1823

9. 13^3

(a) 2241 (b) 2177 (c) 2197 (d) 2457

10. 14^3

(a) 2874 (b) 2844 (c) 2973 (d) 2744

11. 15^3

(a) 3375 (b) 4125 (c) 4377 (d) 5237

12. 21^3

(a) 9741 (b) 9261 (c) 8261 (d) 97451

13. 16^3

(a) 4096 (b) 4426 (c) 4086 (d) 4356

14. 34^3

(a) 41235 (b) 38458 (c) 39304 (d) 41204

15. 44^3

(a) 85184 (b) 75244 (c) 74125 (d) 86174

16. 47^3

(a) 112022 (b) 103823 (c) 104710 (d) 102524

17. 92^3

(a) 888678 (b) 778654 (c) 778688 (d) 687418

18. 36^3

(a) 46656 (b) 54166 (c) 51744 (d) 61423

19. 63^3

(a) 325047 (b) 250047 (c) 412505 (d) 245133

20. 52^3

(a) 141604 (b) 140608 (c) 110608 (d) 141618

21. 58^3

(a) 195112 (b) 214313 (c) 245135 (d) 241253

22. 23^3

(a) 12456 (b) 14523 (c) 12167 (d) 21547.

Type-5: Answer - Key

1.	(b)	6.	(b)	11.	(a)	16.	(b)	21.	(a)
2.	(d)	7.	(b)	12.	(b)	17.	(c)	22.	(c)
3.	(a)	8.	(b)	13.	(a)	18.	(a)		
4.	(b)	9.	(c)	14.	(c)	19.	(b)		
5.	(a)	10.	(d)	15.	(a)	20.	(b)		

Type-6

Hint :

$6^2 \times 3$

☞ ऊपर तरीका बताया है वैसे सबसे पहले पहली संख्या (First Number) $(6)^2$ का वर्ग (Square) करना है और फिर जो तरीका ऊपर बताया गया है गुणा करने का वैसे करके उत्तर निकल जाएगा।

बिना लिखे दिमाग में हल हो जाएगा

Step - 1 $\Rightarrow 6^2 \times 3 = 36 \times 3$

Step - 2 $\Rightarrow 36 \times 3 = \boxed{108}$

Exercise

1. **$6^2 \times 3$**

(a) 117 (b) 121 (c) 108 (d) 107

2. **$4^2 \times 8$**

(a) 118 (b) 128 (c) 138 (d) 157

3. **$7^2 \times 3$**

(a) 177 (b) 125 (c) 147 (d) 157

4. **$9^2 \times 4$**

(a) 325 (b) 324 (c) 425 (d) 342

5. **$8^2 \times 8$**

(a) 512 (b) 751 (c) 714 (d) 622

6. $9^2 \times 3$
(a) 255 (b) 342 (c) 243 (d) 413

7. $7^2 \times 5$
(a) 425 (b) 245 (c) 535 (d) 247

8. $5^2 \times 8$
(a) 320 (b) 401 (c) 300 (d) 200

9. $12^2 \times 2$
(a) 328 (b) 338 (c) 288 (d) 208

10. $13^2 \times 2$
(a) 588 (b) 541 (c) 328 (d) 338

11. $25^2 \times 4$
(a) 2500 (b) 3400 (c) 2811 (d) 2520

12. $21^2 \times 4$
(a) 1965 (b) 1764 (c) 1751 (d) 1944

13. $9^2 \times 6$
(a) 486 (b) 456 (c) 476 (d) 436

14. $7^2 \times 8$
(a) 412 (b) 392 (c) 592 (d) 492

15. $8^2 \times 3$
(a) 198 (b) 192 (c) 412 (d) 199

16. $7^2 \times 4$
(a) 186 (b) 241 (c) 196 (d) 355

17. $9^2 \times 8$
(a) 685 (b) 648 (c) 782 (d) 948

18. $6^2 \times 4$
(a) 134 (b) 154 (c) 144 (d) 164

19. $5^2 \times 5$

(a) 214 (b) 324 (c) 125 (d) 245

20. $4^2 \times 7$

(a) 112 (b) 114 (c) 136 (d) 144

21. $6^2 \times 8$

(a) 741 (b) 288 (c) 481 (d) 348

22. $13^2 \times 2$

(a) 338 (b) 429 (c) 518 (d) 658

23. $19^2 \times 2$

(a) 848 (b) 942 (c) 822 (d) 722

24. $26^2 \times 4$

(a) 2808 (b) 3104 (c) 2704 (d) 2814

25. $23^2 \times 4$

(a) 2116 (b) 3126 (c) 4117 (d) 2416

26. $10^2 \times 8$

(a) 810 (b) 780 (c) 821 (d) 800

27. $30^2 \times 3$

(a) 2700 (b) 3100 (c) 2870 (d) 2840

28. $29^2 \times 5$

(a) 4305 (b) 4205 (c) 4808 (d) 4207

29. $23^2 \times 9$

(a) 4701 (b) 4601 (c) 4761 (d) 4401

30. $27^2 \times 8$

(a) 6819 (b) 7182 (c) 5832 (d) 6812

31. $28^2 \times 2$

(a) 1758 (b) 1978 (c) 1568 (d) 1914

32. $20^2 \times 2$

(a) 901 (b) 809 (c) 799 (d) 800

33. $22^2 \times 3$

(a) 1452 (b) 1755 (c) 1458 (d) 1342

34. $4^2 \times 27$

(a) 522 (b) 432 (c) 342 (d) 436

35. $3^2 \times 22$

(a) 240 (b) 188 (c) 198 (d) 274

36. $9^2 \times 21$

(a) 1701 (b) 1808 (c) 1670 (d) 1960

37. $8^2 \times 11$

(a) 708 (b) 704 (c) 806 (d) 944

38. $9^2 \times 30$

(a) 2440 (b) 2430 (c) 3410 (d) 4130

39. $7^2 \times 28$

(a) 1372 (b) 1432 (c) 1312 (d) 1321

40. $5^2 \times 18$

(a) 561 (b) 450 (c) 750 (d) 520

41. $2^2 \times 25$

(a) 201 (b) 100 (c) 203 (d) 301

42. $8^2 \times 13$

(a) 942 (b) 832 (c) 736 (d) 854

43. $7^2 \times 29$

(a) 1562 (b) 1421 (c) 1524 (d) 1723

44. $7^2 \times 16$

(a) 784 (b) 842 (c) 824 (d) 948

45. $9^2 \times 19$

(a) 1549 (b) 1539 (c) 1748 (d) 1854

46. $7^2 \times 17$

(a) 853 (b) 833 (c) 924 (d) 1023

47. $8^2 \times 14$

(a) 955 (b) 1146 (c) 896 (d) 2143

48. $7^2 \times 12$

(a) 748 (b) 781 (c) 588 (d) 794

49. $9^2 \times 9$

(a) 729 (b) 849 (c) 1122 (d) 1472

50. $6^2 \times 9$

(a) 344 (b) 334 (c) 324 (d) 314

51. $5^2 \times 6$

(a) 120 (b) 160 (c) 170 (d) 150

52. $6^2 \times 7$

(a) 242 (b) 252 (c) 342 (d) 312

53. $13^2 \times 6$

(a) 1104 (b) 1014 (c) 1204 (d) 1064

54. $19^2 \times 2$

(a) 824 (b) 832 (c) 722 (d) 942

55. $26^2 \times 4$

(a) 2704 (b) 2174 (c) 3104 (d) 3244

56. $9^2 \times 22$

(a) 1782 (b) 1942 (c) 2184 (d) 1977

57. $7^2 \times 15$

(a) 853 (b) 735 (c) 844 (d) 966

58. $9^2 \times 26$

(a) 2347 (b) 2106 (c) 2713 (d) 1176

59. $8^2 \times 21$

(a) 1454 (b) 1344 (c) 1858 (d) 1726

60. $9^2 \times 23$

(a) 1853 (b) 1843 (c) 1863 (d) 1873

61. $12^2 \times 19$

(a) 2788 (b) 2736 (c) 3417 (d) 3174

62. $8^2 \times 16$

(a) 1125 (b) 1024 (c) 1726 (d) 1446

63. $9^2 \times 18$

(a) 1746 (b) 1978 (c) 1458 (d) 1941

64. $13^2 \times 8$

(a) 1488 (b) 1347 (c) 1352 (d) 2113

65. $21^2 \times 5$

(a) 2205 (b) 3105 (c) 2145 (d) 2748

66. $21^2 \times 7$

(a) 3087 (b) 3141 (c) 2179 (d) 3177

67. $17^2 \times 18$

(a) 5202 (b) 5302 (c) 5452 (d) 5122

Type-6: Answer - Key

1.	(c)	15.	(b)	29.	(c)	43.	(b)	57.	(b)
2.	(b)	16.	(c)	30.	(c)	44.	(a)	58.	(b)
3.	(c)	17.	(b)	31.	(c)	45.	(b)	59.	(b)
4.	(b)	18.	(c)	32.	(d)	46.	(b)	60.	(c)
5.	(a)	19.	(c)	33.	(a)	47.	(c)	61.	(b)
6.	(c)	20.	(a)	34.	(b)	48.	(c)	62.	(b)
7.	(b)	21.	(b)	35.	(c)	49.	(a)	63.	(c)
8.	(d)	22.	(a)	36.	(a)	50.	(c)	64.	(c)
9.	(c)	23.	(d)	37.	(b)	51.	(d)	65.	(a)
10.	(d)	24.	(c)	38.	(b)	52.	(b)	66.	(a)
11.	(a)	25.	(a)	39.	(a)	53.	(b)	67.	(a)
12.	(b)	26.	(d)	40.	(b)	54.	(c)		
13.	(a)	27.	(a)	41.	(b)	55.	(a)		
14.	(b)	28.	(b)	42.	(b)	56.	(a)		

Type-7

Hint :

$2^2 \times 3^2$

☞ पहली संख्या का वर्ग (Square) करना है फिर दूसरी संख्या का वर्ग (Square) करके आपस में गुणा करके Answer निकल जाएगा।

Step - 1 $\Rightarrow 4 \times 9$

Step - 1 $\Rightarrow \boxed{36}$

Exercise

1. **$2^2 \times 3^2$**
(a) 38 (b) 47 (c) 48 (d) 36

2. **$4^2 \times 3^2$**
(a) 144 (b) 154 (c) 164 (d) 174

3. **$6^2 \times 3^2$**
(a) 354 (b) 324 (c) 344 (d) 334

4. **$5^2 \times 4^2$**
(a) 400 (b) 501 (c) 621 (d) 485

5. **$3^3 \times 2^2$**
(a) 118 (b) 108 (c) 121 (d) 119

6. **$4^3 \times 2^2$**
(a) 342 (b) 256 (c) 326 (d) 412

7. **$5^3 \times 2^2$**
(a) 498 (b) 500 (c) 648 (d) 524

8. $6^3 \times 2^2$

(a) 944 (b) 942 (c) 864 (d) 866

9. $7^3 \times 3^2$

(a) 3087 (b) 3247 (c) 4127 (d) 3471

10. $8^3 \times 10^2$

(a) 52100 (b) 51200 (c) 52200 (d) 53100

11. $9^3 \times 2^2$

(a) 3118 (b) 2913 (c) 2916 (d) 3148

12. $4^3 \times 9^2$

(a) 5124 (b) 6174 (c) 5184 (d) 7142

13. $8^3 \times 9^2$

(a) 41472 (b) 51423 (c) 47123 (d) 52714

14. $8^3 \times 4^2$

(a) 9412 (b) 1122 (c) 8192 (d) 7412

15. $3^3 \times 4^2$

(a) 432 (b) 521 (c) 743 (d) 652

16. $6^3 \times 5^2$

(a) 5741 (b) 5400 (c) 6140 (d) 7410

17. $9^3 \times 7^2$

(a) 35721 (b) 37172 (c) 41277 (d) 42175

18. $5^3 \times 8^2$

(a) 9100 (b) 10200 (c) 12030 (d) 8000

19. $6^3 \times 3^2$

(a) 1944 (b) 1964 (c) 1934 (d) 1914

20. $7^3 \times 10^2$

(a) 34300 (b) 41300 (c) 51204 (d) 52134

MULTIPLICATION (गुणा)

21. $6^3 \times 4^2$

(a) 3436 (b) 4436 (c) 3456 (d) 1904

22. $9^3 \times 3^2$

(a) 7161 (b) 7423 (c) 6561 (d) 6264

23. $5^3 \times 3^2$

(a) 1125 (b) 1234 (c) 2417 (d) 3141

24. $9^3 \times 4^2$

(a) 12566 (b) 13674 (c) 14266 (d) 11664

25. $3^3 \times 5^2$

(a) 755 (b) 846 (c) 675 (d) 945

26. $8^3 \times 2^2$

(a) 2048 (b) 3174 (c) 3148 (d) 3521

27. $2^3 \times 4^2$

(a) 248 (b) 128 (c) 230 (d) 314

28. $6^3 \times 7^2$

(a) 10584 (b) 14823 (c) 17523 (d) 13245

29. $7^3 \times 3^2$

(a) 3094 (b) 4123 (c) 3087 (d) 2379

30. $3^3 \times 6^2$

(a) 984 (b) 972 (c) 1234 (d) 1423

31. $6^3 \times 2^2$

(a) 945 (b) 865 (c) 1024 (d) 864

32. $9^3 \times 5^2$

(a) 18225 (b) 19334 (c) 17423 (d) 19452

33. $7^3 \times 8^2$

(a) 25123 (b) 31452 (c) 21952 (d) 18962

Type-7: Answer - Key

1.	(d)	**8.**	(c)	**15.**	(a)	**22.**	(c)	**29.**	(c)
2.	(a)	**9.**	(a)	**16.**	(b)	**23.**	(a)	**30.**	(b)
3.	(b)	**10.**	(b)	**17.**	(a)	**24.**	(d)	**31.**	(d)
4.	(a)	**11.**	(c)	**18.**	(d)	**25.**	(c)	**32.**	(a)
5.	(b)	**12.**	(c)	**19.**	(a)	**26.**	(a)	**33.**	(c)
6.	(b)	**13.**	(a)	**20.**	(a)	**27.**	(b)		
7.	(b)	**14.**	(c)	**21.**	(c)	**28.**	(a)		

Type-8

Hint :

$$\begin{array}{r} 637 \\ \times 5 \\ \hline \\ \hline \end{array}$$

☞ तीन अंकों की संख्या के साथ गुणा करते वक्त सबसे पहले (5) का गुणा तीसरे अंक जो सैंकड़े का अंक (Hundred digit) है (6) से करना है जो (3000) और आगे दो zero मानकर दिमाग में रखना है उसके बाद 5 का गुणा दूसरी संख्या जो दहाई का अंक (Tens digit) है (3) से गुणा करके (15) में आगे zero मानकर (150) दिमाग वाली संख्या से जोड़ देना है। उसके बाद पहली संख्या (7) को जो इकाई का अंक (Unit digit) है 5 से गुणा करके दूसरी दिमाग वाली संख्या से जोड़ देना है तो Answer आ जाएगा।

$$\begin{array}{r} 637 \\ \times 5 \\ \hline \\ \hline \end{array}$$

Step – 1 = 6 × 5 = 30[00] → मान लेना

Step – 2 = 3 × 5 = 15[0] → मान लेना

Step – 3 = 7 × 5 = 35

Step – 4 = 3000 + 150 + 35 = 3185

दिमाग में करके आ जाएगा बिना लिखे।

Exercise

1. 637 × 5

(a) 3325 (b) 3185 (c) 4621 (d) 4125

2. 862 × 4

(a) 3448 (b) 3784 (c) 4288 (d) 3472

3. 957 × 6

(a) 5841 (b) 6744 (c) 5742 (d) 8412

4. 188 × 6

(a) 1184 (b) 1128 (c) 1429 (d) 1388

5. 667 × 9

(a) 7021 (b) 6003 (c) 7482 (d) 8423

6. 670 × 4

(a) 3740 (b) 2870 (c) 3890 (d) 2680

7. 490 × 3

(a) 1560 (b) 1740 (c) 1470 (d) 1571

8. 862 × 5

(a) 4510 (b) 4310 (c) 6214 (d) 1784

9. 691 × 3

(a) 2163 (b) 2201 (c) 2073 (d) 3174

10. 554 × 7

(a) 3748 (b) 3878 (c) 2317 (d) 3824

11. 578 × 9

(a) 5302 (b) 5374 (c) 5202 (d) 5207

12. 184 × 7

(a) 1384 (b) 1478 (c) 1288 (d) 1497

13. 214 × 7

(a) 1498 (b) 2471 (c) 2318 (d) 1718

14. 807 × 9

(a) 7423 (b) 7263 (c) 7164 (d) 7842

15. 814 × 8

(a) 6512 (b) 6814 (c) 6614 (d) 7414

16. 957 × 5

(a) 4885 (b) 4785 (c) 5158 (d) 4962

17. 882 × 9

(a) 5813 (b) 6754 (c) 8412 (d) 7938

18. 607 × 8

(a) 4962 (b) 6126 (c) 4856 (d) 7818

19. 199 × 7

(a) 1455 (b) 1393 (c) 1742 (d) 1423

20. 837 × 9

(a) 9542 (b) 8562 (c) 7533 (d) 9413

21. 879 × 4

(a) 4523 (b) 3516 (c) 4171 (d) 3416

22. 456 × 3

(a) 1395 (b) 1368 (c) 1563 (d) 1497

23. 862 × 5

(a) 4724 (b) 4310 (c) 5120 (d) 6210

24. 553 × 6
(a) 3318 (b) 3328 (c) 3428 (d) 3408

25. 998 × 9
(a) 10210 (b) 9419 (c) 8982 (d) 7541

26. 990 × 5
(a) 4950 (b) 6412 (c) 6250 (d) 5270

27. 852 × 4
(a) 4528 (b) 3408 (c) 3740 (d) 4120

28. 477 × 6
(a) 3262 (b) 3178 (c) 4128 (d) 2862

29. 168 × 6
(a) 1106 (b) 1008 (c) 1427 (d) 1348

30. 967 × 9
(a) 8703 (b) 9408 (c) 7034 (d) 8073

31. 689 × 4
(a) 2874 (b) 3178 (c) 2756 (d) 3179

32. 569 × 3
(a) 1887 (b) 1788 (c) 1707 (d) 1978

33. 859 × 5
(a) 4523 (b) 4895 (c) 4295 (d) 4719

34. 681 × 3
(a) 2144 (b) 2343 (c) 3143 (d) 2043

35. 354 × 7
(a) 3174 (b) 3418 (c) 2478 (d) 3178

36. 678 × 9
(a) 6102 (b) 6212 (c) 7128 (d) 8142

37. 194 × 7

(a) 1427 (b) 1358 (c) 1484 (d) 1472

38. 324 × 8

(a) 2678 (b) 3178 (c) 3219 (d) 2592

39. 977 × 9

(a) 8793 (b) 9413 (c) 8425 (d) 9493

40. 544 × 8

(a) 4352 (b) 5231 (c) 6231 (d) 8412

41. 257 × 5

(a) 1457 (b) 1285 (c) 3142 (d) 1474

42. 472 × 9

(a) 4236 (b) 4382 (c) 4138 (d) 4248

43. 517 × 8

(a) 4136 (b) 4214 (c) 4126 (d) 4314

44. 329 × 7

(a) 2345 (b) 3142 (c) 4123 (d) 2303

45. 447 × 9

(a) 4123 (b) 4023 (c) 5142 (d) 3122

46. 479 × 4

(a) 1472 (b) 1623 (c) 1916 (d) 2179

47. 496 × 3

(a) 1528 (b) 1874 (c) 1858 (d) 1488

48. 332 × 5

(a) 1861 (b) 1660 (c) 2178 (d) 1891

49. 551 × 8

(a) 4408 (b) 5268 (c) 5128 (d) 6213

50. 928 × 8

(a) 8413 (b) 7424 (c) 10235 (d) 9425

51. 477 × 5

(a) 2453 (b) 2385 (c) 3412 (d) 4225

52. 192 × 4

(a) 768 (b) 878 (c) 942 (d) 714

53. 827 × 6

(a) 5142 (b) 4962 (c) 4912 (d) 5412

54. 131 × 6

(a) 786 (b) 854 (c) 866 (d) 948

55. 668 × 9

(a) 6123 (b) 6012 (c) 8182 (d) 6192

56. 655 × 4

(a) 2820 (b) 2620 (c) 4123 (d) 3140

57. 499 × 3

(a) 1497 (b) 1741 (c) 1487 (d) 1456

58. 872 × 5

(a) 4850 (b) 5160 (c) 4360 (d) 5421

59. 886 × 3

(a) 3146 (b) 2817 (c) 2658 (d) 2918

60. 434 × 7

(a) 3240 (b) 3038 (c) 4128 (d) 3718

61. 679 × 9

(a) 7112 (b) 8123 (c) 6111 (d) 6414

62. 188 × 7

(a) 1875 (b) 1436 (c) 1876 (d) 1316

63. 234 × 8
(a) 1872 (b) 1942 (c) 2171 (d) 2437

64. 855 × 9
(a) 8415 (b) 7695 (c) 9425 (d) 9541

65. 881 × 8
(a) 7048 (b) 8412 (c) 7028 (d) 8124

66. 955 × 5
(a) 4855 (b) 4775 (c) 5124 (d) 5145

67. 889 × 9
(a) 8001 (b) 8101 (c) 7910 (d) 9102

68. 608 × 8
(a) 4864 (b) 5164 (c) 5128 (d) 5714

69. 562 × 7
(a) 4134 (b) 3934 (c) 4125 (d) 5172

70. 821 × 9
(a) 7349 (b) 7389 (c) 7229 (d) 7489

71. 879 × 4
(a) 3516 (b) 3718 (c) 4116 (d) 4217

72. 456 × 3
(a) 1918 (b) 1368 (c) 2148 (d) 2311

73. 862 × 5
(a) 4310 (b) 4872 (c) 5110 (d) 4723

74. 553 × 8
(a) 4520 (b) 5172 (c) 6225 (d) 4424

75. 998 × 3
(a) 2994 (b) 3144 (c) 4194 (d) 3415

76. 748 × 4

(a) 2992 (b) 3100 (c) 4128 (d) 2919

77. 521 × 9

(a) 5144 (b) 4389 (c) 4689 (d) 5219

78. 423 × 6

(a) 2538 (b) 3148 (c) 4124 (d) 3155

79. 561 × 3

(a) 1683 (b) 1643 (c) 1663 (d) 1653

80. 621 × 4

(a) 3144 (b) 2463 (c) 2484 (d) 2313

81. 741 × 3

(a) 2234 (b) 2534 (c) 3144 (d) 2223

82. 561 × 5

(a) 2805 (b) 3145 (c) 7841 (d) 3155

83. 712 × 6

(a) 4326 (b) 5122 (c) 4272 (d) 5123

84. 521 × 3

(a) 1623 (b) 1563 (c) 2174 (d) 1542

85. 4.6 × 4 =

(a) 19.4 (b) 18.4 (c) 17.3 (d) 21.4

86. 2.5 × 7 =

(a) 19.4 (b) 17.5 (c) 18.9 (d) 19.8

87. 7.5 × 4 =

(a) 30 (b) 31.4 (c) 24.1 (d) 29

Type-8: Answer - Key

1.	(b)	19.	(b)	37.	(b)	55.	(b)	73.	(a)
2.	(a)	20.	(c)	38.	(d)	56.	(b)	74.	(d)
3.	(c)	21.	(b)	39.	(a)	57.	(a)	75.	(a)
4.	(b)	22.	(b)	40.	(a)	58.	(c)	76.	(a)
5.	(b)	23.	(b)	41.	(b)	59.	(c)	77.	(c)
6.	(d)	24.	(a)	42.	(d)	60.	(b)	78.	(a)
7.	(c)	25.	(c)	43.	(a)	61.	(c)	79.	(a)
8.	(b)	26.	(a)	44.	(d)	62.	(d)	80.	(c)
9.	(c)	27.	(b)	45.	(b)	63.	(a)	81.	(d)
10.	(b)	28.	(d)	46.	(c)	64.	(b)	82.	(a)
11.	(c)	29.	(b)	47.	(d)	65.	(a)	83.	(c)
12.	(c)	30.	(a)	48.	(b)	66.	(b)	84.	(b)
13.	(a)	31.	(c)	49.	(a)	67.	(a)	85.	(b)
14.	(b)	32.	(c)	50.	(b)	68.	(a)	86.	(b)
15.	(a)	33.	(c)	51.	(b)	69.	(b)	87.	(a)
16.	(b)	34.	(d)	52.	(a)	70.	(b)		
17.	(d)	35.	(c)	53.	(b)	71.	(a)		
18.	(c)	36.	(a)	54.	(a)	72.	(b)		

DIVISION (विभाजन)

Type-1

Hint :

$$\frac{171}{9}$$

☞ भाग करने की विधि (Division Method) 9 को इकाई का अंक (Unit digit) (1) से गुणा किया जाएगा तो अंतिम संख्या 9 आ जाएगी। अब दो अंक 17 को 9 से भाग दिया जाता है लगभग एक बार में जाता है तो हमारा Answer option का use करके आ जाएगा।

Example 1:

$\frac{171}{9}$ → 19

Example 2:

$\frac{252}{63}$ लगभग 4 बार option में देखकर 2 को

3 × (4) = 2

→ Unit digit

Exercise

1. 120 / 15 =

(a) 6 (b) 9 (c) 8 (d) 7.5

2. 171 / 9 =

(a) 17 (b) 19 (c) 18 (d) 16

3. **112 / 16 =**
(a) 8 (b) 6 (c) 7 (d) 9

4. **168 / 7 =**
(a) 26 (b) 23 (c) 22 (d) 24

5. **117 / 9 =**
(a) 12 (b) 13 (c) 14 (d) 16

6. **140 / 28 =**
(a) 5 (b) 6 (c) 7 (d) 4.5

7. **165 / 33 =**
(a) 5 (b) 4.5 (c) 5.5 (d) 6

8. **120 / 24 =**
(a) 4 (b) 5 (c) 6 (d) 7

9. **144 / 36 =**
(a) 6 (b) 7 (c) 4 (d) 8

10. **132 / 22 =**
(a) 8 (b) 7 (c) 5 (d) 6

11. **189 / 21 =**
(a) 7 (b) 9 (c) 8 (d) 6

12. **96 / 24 =**
(a) 3 (b) 6 (c) 4 (d) 5

13. **216 / 27 =**
(a) 7 (b) 8 (c) 9 (d) 6

14. **192 / 48 =**
(a) 3 (b) 6 (c) 5 (d) 4

15. **252 / 63 =**
(a) 6 (b) 3 (c) 7 (d) 4

16. 774 / 43 =

(a) 18 (b) 19 (c) 16 (d) 17

17. 270 / 18 =

(a) 14 (b) 13 (c) 15 (d) 16

18. 621 / 27 =

(a) 23 (b) 21 (c) 26 (d) 24

19. 1098 / 61 =

(a) 28 (b) 19 (c) 21 (d) 18

20. 462 / 33 =

(a) 13 (b) 14 (c) 11 (d) 12

21. 338 / 26 =

(a) 12 (b) 16 (c) 13 (d) 14

22. 2491 / 47 =

(a) 53 (b) 47 (c) 49 (d) 43

23. 1494 / 83 =

(a) 19 (b) 18 (c) 16 (d) 17

24. 4512 / 96 =

(a) 47 (b) 49 (c) 42 (d) 52

25. 1178 / 31 =

(a) 28 (b) 34 (c) 38 (d) 39

26. 1178 / 38 =

(a) 29 (b) 41 (c) 32 (d) 31

27. 210 / 42 =

(a) 6 (b) 4 (c) 5 (d) 3

28. 688 / 86 =

(a) 8 (b) 7 (c) 6 (d) 9

29. 546 / 7 =

(a) 79 (b) 78 (c) 77 (d) 76

30. 672 / 8 =
(a) 78 (b) 74 (c) 88 (d) 84

31. 285 / 57 =
(a) 4 (b) 7 (c) 5 (d) 6

32. 297 / 99 =
(a) 4 (b) 2 (c) 2.3 (d) 3

33. 344 / 8 =
(a) 33 (b) 34 (c) 47 (d) 43

34. 752 / 8 =
(a) 84 (b) 83 (c) 94 (d) 93

35. 320 / 5 =
(a) 65 (b) 64 (c) 58 (d) 62

36. 124 / 4 =
(a) 31 (b) 28 (c) 32 (d) 27

37. 308 / 7 =
(a) 42 (b) 44 (c) 54 (d) 48

38. 621 / 9 =
(a) 69 (b) 68 (c) 67 (d) 71

39. 756 / 9 =
(a) 86 (b) 78 (c) 84 (d) 74

40. 248 / 8 =
(a) 28 (b) 32 (c) 29 (d) 31

41. 332 / 4 =
(a) 86 (b) 83 (c) 76 (d) 73

42. 891 / 9 =
(a) 91 (b) 98 (c) 93 (d) 99

43. 336 / 6 =
(a) 56 (b) 54 (c) 59 (d) 51

44. 756 / 84 =
(a) 9 (b) 8 (c) 7 (d) 6

45. 639 / 9 =
(a) 69 (b) 68 (c) 71 (d) 72

46. 525 / 7 =
(a) 55 (b) 75 (c) 67.5 (d) 65

47. 603 / 9 =
(a) 68 (b) 67 (c) 66 (d) 63

48. 512 / 8 =
(a) 69 (b) 59 (c) 64 (d) 54

49. 664 / 8 =
(a) 73 (b) 78 (c) 88 (d) 83

50. 427 / 7 =
(a) 61 (b) 63 (c) 57 (d) 59

51. 322 / 7 =
(a) 44 (b) 46 (c) 47 (d) 48

52. 504 / 8 =
(a) 68 (b) 58 (c) 63 (d) 53

53. 177 / 3 =
(a) 61 (b) 57 (c) 59 (d) 58

54. 760 / 8 =
(a) 95 (b) 94 (c) 96 (d) 93

55. 497 / 7 =
(a) 69 (b) 72 (c) 68 (d) 71

56. 175 / 5 =
(a) 35 (b) 33 (c) 37 (d) 39

57. 204 / 4 =
(a) 49 (b) 52 (c) 53 (d) 51

58. 138 / 3 =
(a) 43 (b) 42 (c) 46 (d) 48

59. 189 / 3 =
(a) 67 (b) 63 (c) 59 (d) 61

60. 301 / 7 =
(a) 48 (b) 43 (c) 46 (d) 47

61. 335 / 5 =
(a) 65 (b) 67 (c) 63 (d) 69

62. 693 / 7 =
(a) 99 (b) 89 (c) 98 (d) 78

63. 704 / 8 =
(a) 93 (b) 83 (c) 88 (d) 78

64. 147 / 3 =
(a) 47 (b) 51 (c) 49 (d) 53

65. 225 / 5 =
(a) 41 (b) 43 (c) 47 (d) 45

66. 222 / 37 =
(a) 6 (b) 7 (c) 8 (d) 5

Type-1: Answer - Key

1.	(c)	**14.**	(d)	**28.**	(a)	**42.**	(d)	**56.**	(a)
2.	(b)	**15.**	(d)	**29.**	(b)	**43.**	(a)	**57.**	(d)
3.	(c)	**16.**	(a)	**30.**	(d)	**44.**	(a)	**58.**	(c)
4.	(d)	**17.**	(c)	**31.**	(c)	**45.**	(c)	**59.**	(b)
5.	(b)	**18.**	(a)	**32.**	(d)	**46.**	(b)	**60.**	(b)
6.	(a)	**19.**	(d)	**33.**	(d)	**47.**	(b)	**61.**	(b)
7.	(a)	**20.**	(b)	**34.**	(c)	**48.**	(c)	**62.**	(a)
8.	(b)	**21.**	(c)	**35.**	(b)	**49.**	(d)	**63.**	(c)
9.	(c)	**22.**	(a)	**36.**	(a)	**50.**	(a)	**64.**	(c)
10.	(d)	**23.**	(b)	**37.**	(b)	**51.**	(b)	**65.**	(d)
11.	(b)	**24.**	(a)	**38.**	(a)	**52.**	(c)	**66.**	(a)
12.	(c)	**25.**	(c)	**39.**	(c)	**53.**	(c)		
13.	(b)	**26.**	(d)	**40.**	(d)	**54.**	(a)		
		27.	(c)	**41.**	(b)	**55.**	(d)		

DIVISION (विभाजन)

Type-2

Hint :

$$\frac{6}{5}$$

☞ भाग करते समय हम देखते है जब 6 को 5 से भाग दिया जाता है तो एक बार में चला जाता है और $\left(\frac{1}{5}\right)$ बच जाता है। जिसका मतलब (1 + 0.20) है जो हमारा Answer है।

$$\frac{6}{5} = \boxed{1.20}$$

Exercise

1. 6 / 5 =
(a) 6 (b) 1.2 (c) 8 (d) 7.5

2. 42 / 5 =
(a) 8.3 (b) 8.2 (c) 8.4 (d) 8.6

3. 35 / 4 =
(a) 8.75 (b) 8.25 (c) 8.45 (d) 8.65

4. 72 / 5 =
(a) 14.4 (b) 14.6 (c) 14.8 (d) 14.2

5. 21 / 4 =
(a) 5.5 (b) 5.25 (c) 5.75 (d) 5.45

6. 35 / 8 =
(a) 4.25 (b) 4.75 (c) 4.375 (d) 4.275

7. 91 / 5 =
(a) 18.4 (b) 18.3 (c) 18.1 (d) 18.2

8. 48 / 5 =

(a) 9.6 (b) 9.4 (c) 9.8 (d) 9.2

9. 117 / 4 =

(a) 29.45 (b) 29.25 (c) 29.75 (d) 29.35

10. 96 / 5 =

(a) 19.4 (b) 19.1 (c) 19.2 (d) 19.3

11. 84 / 5 =

(a) 16.8 (b) 16.6 (c) 16.4 (d) 16.75

12. 77 / 20 =

(a) 3.65 (b) 3.75 (c) 3.45 (d) 3.85

13. 48 / 25 =

(a) 1.94 (b) 1.92 (c) 1.86 (d) 1.88

14. 72 / 25 =

(a) 2.68 (b) 2.66 (c) 2.86 (d) 2.88

15. 112 / 25 =

(a) 4.48 (b) 4.84 (c) 4.36 (d) 4.24

16. 63 / 20 =

(a) 3.05 (b) 3.25 (c) 3.15 (d) 3.35

17. 114 / 5 =

(a) 21.8 (b) 23.8 (c) 22.8 (d) 23.2

18. 188 / 5 =

(a) 35.6 (b) 36.6 (c) 38.4 (d) 37.6

19. 44 / 5 =

(a) 8.8 (b) 7.8 (c) 8.2 (d) 7.2

20. 102 / 5 =

(a) 20.2 (b) 20.5 (c) 21.4 (d) 20.4

21. 84 / 5 =

(a) 16.8 (b) 16.6 (c) 17.8 (d) 15.8

22. 88 / 5 =
(a) 16.7 (b) 17.4 (c) 17.6 (d) 16.8

23. 143 / 4 =
(a) 35.50 (b) 35.75 (c) 35.45 (d) 35.25

24. 33 / 4 =
(a) 8.50 (b) 8.25 (c) 8.75 (d) 8.45

25. 19 / 8 =
(a) 2.375 (b) 2.675 (c) 2.350 (d) 2.325

26. 23 / 8 =
(a) 2.625 (b) 2.675 (c) 2.875 (d) 2.825

27. 99 / 4 =
(a) 24.75 (b) 24.25 (c) 24.50 (d) 24.65

28. 103 / 8 =
(a) 12.625 (b) 12.675 (c) 12.825 (d) 12.875

29. 19 / 16 =
(a) 1.25 (b) 1.18 (c) 1.17 (d) 1.16

30. 33 / 4 =
(a) 8.25 (b) 8.75 (c) 8.50 (d) 8.45

31. 98 / 16 =
(a) 6.150 (b) 6.125 (c) 6.175 (d) 6.234

32. 290 / 40 =
(a) 7.50 (b) 7.75 (c) 7.25 (d) 7.65

33. 656 / 64 =
(a) 9.75 (b) 9.65 (c) 10.25 (d) 10.75

34. 498 / 32 =
(a) 15.67 (b) 15.56 (c) 15.75 (d) 15.46

35. 68 / 16 =
(a) 4.125 (b) 4.75 (c) 4.15 (d) 4.25

36. 132 / 8 =
(a) 16.25 (b) 17.5 (c) 17.25 (d) 16.5

37. 78 / 4 =
(a) 19.5 (b) 19.25 (c) 19.8 (d) 19.75

38. 124 / 8 =
(a) 15.6 (b) 15.5 (c) 15.3 (d) 15.4

39. 735 / 70 =
(a) 10.4 (b) 10.6 (c) 10.5 (d) 10.7

40. 88 / 25 =
(a) 3.52 (b) 3.54 (c) 3.25 (d) 3.45

41. 115 / 25 =
(a) 4.7 (b) 4.5 (c) 4.4 (d) 4.6

42. 47 / 25 =
(a) 1.78 (b) 1.77 (c) 1.88 (d) 1.89

43. 93 / 8 =
(a) 11.675 (b) 11.625 (c) 11.750 (d) 11.725

44. 55 / 8 =
(a) 6.825 (b) 6.875 (c) 6.625 (d) 6.675

45. 576 / 25 =
(a) 23.16 (b) 23.02 (c) 23.04 (d) 23.12

46. 216 / 25 =
(a) 8.64 (b) 8.46 (c) 8.65 (d) 8.75

47. 346 / 25 =
(a) 13.45 (b) 13.48 (c) 13.54 (d) 13.84

48. 96 / 25 =
(a) 3.64 (b) 3.84 (c) 3.92 (d) 3.74

Type-2: Answer - Key

1.	(b)	**11.**	(a)	**21.**	(a)	**31.**	(b)	**41.**	(d)
2.	(c)	**12.**	(d)	**22.**	(c)	**32.**	(c)	**42.**	(c)
3.	(a)	**13.**	(b)	**23.**	(b)	**33.**	(c)	**43.**	(b)
4.	(a)	**14.**	(d)	**24.**	(b)	**34.**	(b)	**44.**	(b)
5.	(b)	**15.**	(a)	**25.**	(a)	**35.**	(d)	**45.**	(c)
6.	(c)	**16.**	(c)	**26.**	(c)	**36.**	(d)	**46.**	(a)
7.	(d)	**17.**	(c)	**27.**	(a)	**37.**	(a)	**47.**	(d)
8.	(a)	**18.**	(d)	**28.**	(d)	**38.**	(b)	**48.**	(b)
9.	(b)	**19.**	(a)	**29.**	(b)	**39.**	(c)		
10.	(c)	**20.**	(d)	**30.**	(a)	**40.**	(a)		

Type-3

Hint :

$$\frac{16}{3}$$

☞ जब (16) को (3) से भाग करने पर लगभग (5) बार जाता है और $\left(\frac{1}{3}\right)$ बचता है जिससे हमारा Answer (5 + 0.33) 5.33 निकल जाएगा।

Exercise

1. 16 / 3 =
(a) 5.25 (b) 5.75 (c) 5.33 (d) 5.66

2. 17 / 3 =
(a) 5.75 (b) 5.33 (c) 5.65 (d) 5.66

3. 101 / 3 =
(a) 33.33 (b) 33.66 (c) 34.66 (d) 34.33

4. 50 / 6 =
(a) 8.33 (b) 8.66 (c) 8.25 (d) 8.75

5. 13 / 6 =
(a) 2.33 (b) 2.133 (c) 2.166 (d) 2.66

6. 16 / 6 =
(a) 2.33 (b) 2.75 (c) 2.66 (d) 2.96

7. 27 / 7 =
(a) 3.75 (b) 3.96 (c) 3.85 (d) 3.69

8. 20 / 9 =
(a) 2.33 (b) 2.22 (c) 2.44 (d) 2.11

9. 24 / 11 =
(a) 2.24 (b) 2.14 (c) 2.16 (d) 2.18

10. 95 / 7 =
(a) 13.57 (b) 13.28 (c) 13.42 (d) 13.85

11. 42 / 9 =
(a) 4.66 (b) 4.33 (c) 4.75 (d) 4.45

12. 95 / 3 =
(a) 31.25 (b) 31.33 (c) 31.75 (d) 31.66

13. 23 / 6 =
(a) 3.85 (b) 3.833 (c) 3.66 (d) 3.866

14. 17 / 6 =
(a) 2.825 (b) 2.866 (c) 2.875 (d) 2.833

15. 29 / 6 =
(a) 4.85 (b) 4.833 (c) 4.66 (d) 4.866

16. 49 / 9 =
(a) 5.55 (b) 5.33 (c) 5.44 (d) 5.66

17. 28 / 11 =
(a) 2.54 (b) 2.45 (c) 2.27 (d) 2.72

18. 36 / 7 =
(a) 5.28 (b) 5.15 (c) 5.14 (d) 5.25

19. 25 / 9 =
(a) 2.88 (b) 2.66 (c) 2.63 (d) 2.77

20. 37 / 9 =
(a) 4.11 (b) 4.22 (c) 4.21 (d) 4.33

21. 13 / 12 =
(a) 1.83 (b) 1.083 (c) 1.86 (d) 1.086

22. 31 / 11 =
(a) 2.18 (b) 2.27 (c) 2.81 (d) 2.72

23. 31 / 3 =
(a) 10.25 (b) 10.66 (c) 10.22 (d) 10.33

24. 28 / 9 =
(a) 3.11 (b) 3.33 (c) 3.09 (d) 3.22

25. 89 / 9 =
(a) 9.77 (b) 9.88 (c) 9.99 (d) 9.66

26. 80 / 7 =
(a) 11.34 (b) 11.28 (c) 11.43 (d) 11.57

27. 16 / 15 =
(a) 1.066 (b) 1.033 (c) 1.106 (d) 1.013

28. 32 / 15 =
(a) 2.033 (b) 2.33 (c) 2.133 (d) 2.22

29. 114 / 7 =
(a) 16.43 (b) 16.57 (c) 16.14 (d) 16.28

30. 94 / 9 =
(a) 10.44 (b) 10.33 (c) 10.66 (d) 10.55

31. 143 / 3 =
(a) 46.66 (b) 47.66 (c) 47.77 (d) 47.33

32. 112 / 9 =
(a) 12.33 (b) 12.55 (c) 12.44 (d) 12.66

33. 51 / 7 =
(a) 7.14 (b) 7.43 (c) 7.28 (d) 7.54

34. 106 / 7 =
(a) 15.43 (b) 15.28 (c) 15.57 (d) 15.14

35. 38 / 7 =
(a) 5.71 (b) 5.57 (c) 5.28 (d) 5.43

36. 90 / 11 =
(a) 8.27 (b) 9.09 (c) 8.18 (d) 8.88

37. 17 / 15 =
(a) 1.11 (b) 1.133 (c) 1.122 (d) 1.166

38. 106 / 11 =
(a) 9.63 (b) 9.36 (c) 9.72 (d) 9.27

39. 124 / 9 =
(a) 13.77 (b) 13.66 (c) 13.33 (d) 13.88

40. 111 / 11 =
(a) 10.18 (b) 10.09 (c) 11.11 (d) 10.11

41. 97 / 9 =
(a) 10.66 (b) 10.88 (c) 10.77 (d) 10.99

42. 58 / 11 =
(a) 5.54 (b) 5.36 (c) 5.45 (d) 5.27

Type-3: Answer - Key

1.	(c)	**10.**	(a)	**19.**	(d)	**28.**	(c)	**37.**	(b)
2.	(d)	**11.**	(a)	**20.**	(a)	**29.**	(d)	**38.**	(a)
3.	(b)	**12.**	(d)	**21.**	(b)	**30.**	(a)	**39.**	(a)
4.	(a)	**13.**	(b)	**22.**	(c)	**31.**	(b)	**40.**	(b)
5.	(c)	**14.**	(d)	**23.**	(d)	**32.**	(c)	**41.**	(c)
6.	(c)	**15.**	(b)	**24.**	(a)	**33.**	(c)	**42.**	(d)
7.	(c)	**16.**	(c)	**25.**	(b)	**34.**	(d)		
8.	(b)	**17.**	(a)	**26.**	(c)	**35.**	(d)		
9.	(d)	**18.**	(c)	**27.**	(a)	**36.**	(c)		

Type-4

Hint :

$$\frac{3.6}{2}$$

☞ Divide करते वक्त Decimal को भूलकर संख्या पर ध्यान देना है कि Number क्या आएगा? 36 को जब 2 से भाग दिया जाता है तो 18 आता है एक अंक (digit) बाद Decimal लगा है तो एक अंक (digit) बाद Decimal लगा दो।

$\frac{3.6}{2}$ 1.8

Exercise

1. 3.6 / 2 =

(a) 1.6 (b) 1.4 (c) 1.8 (d) 1.9

2. 4.9 / 7 =

(a) 0.8 (b) 0.9 (c) 0.6 (d) 0.7

3. 13.2 / 4 =

(a) 3.5 (b) 3.3 (c) 3.8 (d) 3.2

4. 8.1 / 9 =

(a) 0.7 (b) 0.8 (c) 1.9 (d) 0.9

5. 23.5 / 5 =

(a) 4.5 (b) 4.7 (c) 4.3 (d) 4.9

6. 21.6 / 6 =

(a) 3.6 (b) 4.1 (c) 3.4 (d) 3.8

7. 7.8 / 3 =
(a) 2.4 (b) 2.5 (c) 2.6 (d) 2.3

8. 33.6 / 4 =
(a) 8.9 (b) 8.2 (c) 7.9 (d) 8.4

9. 12 / 8 =
(a) 1.5 (b) 1.2 (c) 1.4 (d) 1.6

10. 5.5 / 5 =
(a) 1.2 (b) 1.25 (c) 1.1 (d) 1.5

11. 8.2 / 2 =
(a) 4.2 (b) 4.3 (c) 4.1 (d) 4.4

12. 52.8 / 6 =
(a) 9.3 (b) 8.3 (c) 8.8 (d) 8.6

13. 22.4 / 7 =
(a) 3.3 (b) 3.2 (c) 3.4 (d) 3.6

14. 4.8 / 3 =
(a) 1.7 (b) 1.3 (c) 1.8 (d) 1.6

15. 9.2 / 4 =
(a) 2.3 (b) 2.8 (c) 2.1 (d) 2.5

16. 3.74 / 2 =
(a) 1.82 (b) 1.78 (c) 1.92 (d) 1.87

17. 1.96 / 7 =
(a) 0.28 (b) 0.26 (c) 0.24 (d) 0.29

18. 8.33 / 7 =
(a) 1.21 (b) 1.19 (c) 1.23 (d) 1.18

19. 5 / 4 =
(a) 1.50 (b) 1.20 (c) 1.25 (d) 1.125

20. 3.8 / 4 =
(a) 0.89 (b) 0.95 (c) 0.92 (d) 0.88

21. 4.38 / 3 =
(a) 1.46 (b) 1.64 (c) 1.45 (d) 1.54

22. 4.05 / 9 =
(a) 0.55 (b) 0.44 (c) 0.45 (d) 0.54

23. 9.55 / 5 =
(a) 1.93 (b) 1.87 (c) 1.91 (d) 1.89

24. 2.52 / 6 =
(a) 0.37 (b) 0.42 (c) 0.47 (d) 0.43

25. 1.92 / 8 =
(a) 0.24 (b) 0.26 (c) 0.29 (d) 0.19

26. 65.8 / 7 =
(a) 9.3 (b) 9.2 (c) 9.5 (d) 9.4

27. 76.5 / 9 =
(a) 8.6 (b) 8.5 (c) 8.4 (d) 8.3

28. 44.4 / 6 =
(a) 6.9 (b) 7.9 (c) 8.4 (d) 7.4

29. 0.96 / 4 =
(a) 0.24 (b) 0.36 (c) 0.26 (d) 0.23

30. 8.46 / 9 =
(a) 0.98 (b) 0.95 (c) 0.94 (d) 0.96

31. 35.14 / 7 =
(a) 5.2 (b) 5.3 (c) 5.02 (d) 5.03

32. 33.2 / 4 =
(a) 8.5 (b) 8.3 (c) 7.8 (d) 8.2

33. 28.5 / 5 =
(a) 5.5 (b) 5.9 (c) 5.3 (d) 5.7

34. 14.2 / 2 =
(a) 7.2 (b) 7.1 (c) 6.9 (d) 6.8

35. 28.5 / 3 =
(a) 9.5 (b) 9.6 (c) 9.4 (d) 9.3

36. 31.6 / 4 =
(a) 7.7 (b) 7.6 (c) 7.8 (d) 7.9

37. 29.1 / 3 =
(a) 9.6 (b) 9.8 (c) 9.7 (d) 9.5

38. 10.8 / 3 =
(a) 3.8 (b) 3.6 (c) 3.5 (d) 3.7

39. 23.6 / 4 =
(a) 5.9 (b) 5.4 (c) 6.1 (d) 6.4

40. 12.6 / 3 =
(a) 4.8 (b) 4.3 (c) 4.2 (d) 4.1

41. 22.8 / 4 =
(a) 6.2 (b) 5.7 (c) 5.6 (d) 5.2

42. 0.8 / 2 =
(a) 0.4 (b) 0.6 (c) 0.2 (d) 0.16

43. 3.15 / 5 =
(a) 0.67 (b) 0.65 (c) 0.61 (d) 0.63

44. 6.8 / 4 =
(a) 1.6 (b) 1.8 (c) 1.7 (d) 1.9

45. 9.8 / 2 =
(a) 4.8 (b) 4.9 (c) 4.7 (d) 4.4

46. 36.4 / 7 =
(a) 5.5 (b) 5.4 (c) 5.2 (d) 5.1

47. 137.6 / 2 =
(a) 68.6 (b) 66.6 (c) 66.8 (d) 68.8

48. 538.4 / 4 =
(a) 132.6 (b) 134.6 (c) 132.1 (d) 134.1

49. 13.2 / 11 =
(a) 1.2 (b) 1.3 (c) 1.1 (d) 1.4

50. 36.27 / 9 =
(a) 4.03 (b) 4.3 (c) 4.33 (d) 4.6

51. 9.2 / 4 =
(a) 2.6 (b) 2.3 (c) 2.5 (d) 2.4

52. 0.42 / 6 =
(a) 0.68 (b) 0.7 (c) 0.86 (d) 0.07

53. 1.68 / 8 =
(a) 0.23 (b) 0.31 (c) 0.21 (d) 0.25

54. 51 / 6 =
(a) 8.6 (b) 8.2 (c) 8.5 (d) 8.3

55. 2.52 / 6 =
(a) 0.47 (b) 0.44 (c) 0.45 (d) 0.42

56. 35.2 / 8 =
(a) 4.4 (b) 4.9 (c) 4.5 (d) 4.6

57. 0.456 / 3 =
(a) 0.152 (b) 0.125 (c) 0.162 (d) 0.142

58. 578.4 / 3 =
(a) 190.8 (b) 192.8 (c) 193.8 (d) 191.8

59. 843.6 / 3 =
(a) 280.2 (b) 282.2 (c) 281.2 (d) 283.2

60. 22.1 / 17 =
(a) 1.4 (b) 1.2 (c) 1.5 (d) 1.3

61. 7.47 / 3 =
(a) 2.47 (b) 2.49 (c) 2.51 (d) 2.39

62. 41.6 / 8 =
(a) 5.2 (b) 5.4 (c) 5.7 (d) 5.5

63. 1.26 / 6 =
(a) 0.27 (b) 0.23 (c) 0.21 (d) 0.24

64. 18.85 / 5 =
(a) 3.57 (b) 3.77 (c) 3.75 (d) 3.66

65. 7.8 / 2 =
(a) 3.7 (b) 3.8 (c) 3.6 (d) 3.9

66. 11.1 / 3 =
(a) 3.5 (b) 3.6 (c) 3.9 (d) 3.7

67. 55.3 / 7 =
(a) 7.7 (b) 7.5 (c) 7.9 (d) 7.8

68. 1.68 / 6 =
(a) 0.28 (b) 0.26 (c) 0.23 (d) 0.29

69. 724.2 / 6 =
(a) 120.2 (b) 121.6 (c) 120.7 (d) 121.7

70. 562.5 / 9 =
(a) 61.5 (b) 62.5 (c) 61.75 (d) 63.5

71. 12.5 / 25 =
(a) 0.5 (b) 0.4 (c) 0.3 (d) 0.6

72. 8.46 / 9 =
(a) 0.93 (b) 0.94 (c) 0.95 (d) 0.96

73. 52.8 / 6 =
(a) 8.7 (b) 8.6 (c) 8.8 (d) 8.9

74. 9.96 / 4 =
(a) 2.45 (b) 2.47 (c) 2.48 (d) 2.49

75. 17.56 / 4 =

(a) 4.39 (b) 4.36 (c) 4.41 (d) 4.42

76. 72.8 / 8 =

(a) 9.2 (b) 9.1 (c) 8.9 (d) 9.3

77. 16.8 / 7 =

(a) 2.6 (b) 2.5 (c) 2.4 (d) 2.2

78. 44.4 / 6 =

(a) 7.5 (b) 7.2 (c) 7.7 (d) 7.4

79. 56.8 / 8 =

(a) 6.8 (b) 7.1 (c) 7.3 (d) 7.2

80. 218.5 / 5 =

(a) 43.7 (b) 42.7 (c) 43.5 (d) 42.5

81. 362.4 / 8 =

(a) 42.5 (b) 45.2 (c) 45.3 (d) 43.5

82. 28.4 / 40 =

(a) 0.69 (b) 0.72 (c) 0.75 (d) 0.71

83. 22.4 / 7 =

(a) 3.3 (b) 3.5 (c) 3.6 (d) 3.2

84. 13.2 / 4 =

(a) 3.3 (b) 3.6 (c) 3.2 (d) 3.5

Type-4: Answer - Key

1.	(c)	18.	(b)	35.	(a)	52.	(d)	69.	(c)
2.	(d)	19.	(c)	36.	(d)	53.	(c)	70.	(b)
3.	(b)	20.	(b)	37.	(c)	54.	(c)	71.	(a)
4.	(d)	21.	(a)	38.	(b)	55.	(d)	72.	(b)
5.	(b)	22.	(c)	39.	(a)	56.	(a)	73.	(c)
6.	(a)	23.	(c)	40.	(c)	57.	(a)	74.	(d)
7.	(c)	24.	(b)	41.	(b)	58.	(b)	75.	(a)
8.	(d)	25.	(a)	42.	(a)	59.	(c)	76.	(b)
9.	(a)	26.	(d)	43.	(d)	60.	(d)	77.	(c)
10.	(c)	27.	(b)	44.	(c)	61.	(b)	78.	(d)
11.	(c)	28.	(d)	45.	(b)	62.	(a)	79.	(b)
12.	(c)	29.	(a)	46.	(c)	63.	(c)	80.	(a)
13.	(b)	30.	(c)	47.	(d)	64.	(b)	81.	(c)
14.	(d)	31.	(c)	48.	(b)	65.	(d)	82.	(d)
15.	(a)	32.	(b)	49.	(a)	66.	(d)	83.	(d)
16.	(d)	33.	(d)	50.	(a)	67.	(c)	84.	(a)
17.	(a)	34.	(b)	51.	(b)	68.	(a)		

Type-5

Hint :

$$\frac{0.81}{0.9}$$

☞ Decimal हटाकर पहले सीधा Divide करिए और देखिए कि अंश (Numerator) में Decimal दो अंक (Digit) पहले है और हर (Denominator) में एक अंक (Digit) पहले तो हमने देखा कि अंश (Numerator) में ज्यादा है और हर (Denominator) में कम है तो Net (2 – 1) = (1) होगा यानि एक place ऊपर वाले (Numerator) में एक Zero बचेगा तो (81) को (9) से भाग (Divide) करने पर (9) भागफल (Quotient) आता है और Net 1 place पहले जो आया वहाँ Decimal लगा देना है।

$$\frac{0.81}{0.9} = \boxed{0.9}$$

Exercise

1. 0.81 / 0.9 =

(a) 9 (b) 90 (c) 0.09 (d) 0.9

2. 0.45 / 0.5 =

(a) 90 (b) 0.09 (c) 9 (d) 0.9

3. 0.07 / 0.7 =

(a) 0.1 (b) 0.01 (c) 1 (d) 10

4. 2.8 / 0.4 =

(a) 0.7 (b) 7 (c) 70 (d) 0.07

DIVISION (विभाजन)

5. 0.352 / 1.6 =
(a) 0.22 (b) 0.27 (c) 2.2 (d) 2.7

6. 0.72 / 0.008 =
(a) 9 (b) 0.9 (c) 90 (d) 900

7. 0.30 / 0.6 =
(a) 5 (b) 0.5 (c) 50 (d) 0.05

8. 0.72 / 0.9 =
(a) 80 (b) 0.8 (c) 8 (d) 0.08

9. 4.2 / 0.6 =
(a) 0.7 (b) 70 (c) 7 (d) 0.07

10. 0.234 / 0.03 =
(a) 0.88 (b) 8.8 (c) 78 (d) 7.8

11. 0.22 / 0.044 =
(a) 5 (b) 50 (c) 0.5 (d) 500

12. 0.09 / 0.1 =
(a) 9 (b) 90 (c) 0.9 (d) 0.09

13. 0.36 / 0.4 =
(a) 9 (b) 90 (c) 0.9 (d) 0.09

14. 0.04 / 0.1 =
(a) 40 (b) 0.4 (c) 4 (d) 0.04

15. 5.18 / 0.7 =
(a) 72 (b) 74 (c) 7.2 (d) 7.4

16. 0.55 / 0.05 =
(a) 11 (b) 1.1 (c) 110 (d) 0.11

17. 0.06 / 0.1 =
(a) 0.6 (b) 6 (c) 60 (d) 0.06

18. 0.63 / 0.7 =
(a) 90 (b) 0.9 (c) 0.09 (d) 9

19. 4.26 / 0.6 =
(a) 71 (b) 7.1 (c) 0.71 (d) 6.6

20. 83.7 / 0.9 =
(a) 930 (b) 93 (c) 9.6 (d) 9.3

21. 0.66 / 0.03 =
(a) 22 (b) 220 (c) 2.2 (d) 0.22

22. 0.24 / 0.8 =
(a) 3 (b) 0.03 (c) 0.3 (d) 30

23. 0.18 / 0.6 =
(a) 0.03 (b) 3 (c) 0.3 (d) 30

24. 11.9 / 1.7 =
(a) 0.9 (b) 9 (c) 70 (d) 7

25. 4.52 / 0.2 =
(a) 22.1 (b) 22.6 (c) 2.21 (d) 2.26

26. 0.56 / 0.02 =
(a) 28 (b) 2.8 (c) 280 (d) 0.28

27. 0.06 / 0.6 =
(a) 0.01 (b) 0.11 (c) 0.1 (d) 1.1

28. 8.4 / 0.6 =
(a) 12 (b) 14 (c) 15 (d) 16

29. 4.36 / 0.4 =
(a) 10.4 (b) 11.4 (c) 10.8 (d) 10.9

30. 0.415 / 0.83 =
(a) 0.6 (b) 0.7 (c) 0.5 (d) 0.35

Type-5: Answer - Key

1.	(d)	**7.**	(b)	**13.**	(c)	**19.**	(b)	**25.**	(b)
2.	(d)	**8.**	(b)	**14.**	(b)	**20.**	(b)	**26.**	(a)
3.	(a)	**9.**	(c)	**15.**	(d)	**21.**	(a)	**27.**	(c)
4.	(b)	**10.**	(d)	**16.**	(a)	**22.**	(c)	**28.**	(b)
5.	(a)	**11.**	(a)	**17.**	(a)	**23.**	(c)	**29.**	(d)
6.	(c)	**12.**	(c)	**18.**	(b)	**24.**	(d)	**30.**	(c)

Type-6

Unitary Method:

Hint :

$3 \rightarrow 12$

$16 \rightarrow ??$

☞ Unitary Method को multiplier देखकर हल करना है यहाँ (3) का मान (12) के बराबर है जो (4) का multiplier है इसी प्रकार 16 का multiplier (4) 64 होगा। सब कुछ दिमाग में करना है सिर्फ observe करके।

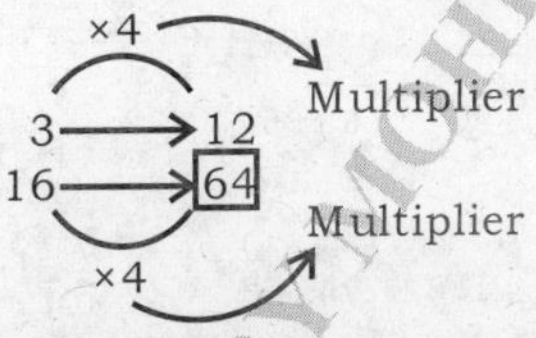

Exercise

1. **$3 \rightarrow 12$**

$16 \rightarrow ? =$

(a) 48 (b) 64 (c) 80 (d) 96

2. **$5 \rightarrow 44$**

$15 \rightarrow ? =$

(a) 154 (b) 176 (c) 132 (d) 135

3. $2 \rightarrow 12$
$27 \rightarrow ? =$
(a) 189 (b) 135 (c) 216 (d) 162

4. $12 \rightarrow 48$
$14 \rightarrow ? =$
(a) 56 (b) 70 (c) 80 (d) 63

5. $4 \rightarrow 68$
$12 \rightarrow ? =$
(a) 192 (b) 180 (c) 204 (d) 216

6. $13 \rightarrow 117$
$9 \rightarrow ? =$
(a) 72 (b) 81 (c) 108 (d) 90

7. $6 \rightarrow 102$
$5 \rightarrow ? =$
(a) 75 (b) 90 (c) 80 (d) 85

8. $15 \rightarrow 180$
$12 \rightarrow ? =$
(a) 144 (b) 156 (c) 132 (d) 168

9. $31 \rightarrow 6200$
$15 \rightarrow ? =$
(a) 3300 (b) 3600 (c) 3000 (d) 3150

10. $5 \rightarrow 115$
$3 \rightarrow ? =$
(a) 69 (b) 81 (c) 45 (d) 54

11. $17 \rightarrow 119$
$19 \rightarrow ? =$
(a) 114 (b) 133 (c) 152 (d) 171

12. **$12 \rightarrow 132$**

$15 \rightarrow ? =$

(a) 180 (b) 165 (c) 195 (d) 175

13. **$13 \rightarrow 41600$**

$5 \rightarrow ? =$

(a) 15,000 (b) 16,500 (c) 14,500 (d) 16,000

14. **$20 \rightarrow 2400$**

$8 \rightarrow ? =$

(a) 960 (b) 720 (c) 920 (d) 1040

15. **$4 \rightarrow 63$**

$12 \rightarrow ? =$

(a) 189 (b) 168 (c) 252 (d) 192

16. **$17 \rightarrow 544$**

$5 \rightarrow ? =$

(a) 140 (b) 160 (c) 130 (d) 150

17. **$1140 \rightarrow 5700$**

$17 \rightarrow ? =$

(a) 68 (b) 102 (c) 85 (d) 119

18. **$30 \rightarrow 650$**

$24 \rightarrow ? =$

(a) 480 (b) 528 (c) 456 (d) 520

19. **$4 \rightarrow 220$**

$10 \rightarrow ? =$

(a) 440 (b) 880 (c) 550 (d) 660

20. **$15 \rightarrow 120$**

$12.5 \rightarrow ? =$

(a) 100 (b) 108 (c) 96 (d) 105

21. $9 \rightarrow 171$

$12 \rightarrow ? =$

(a) 240 (b) 312 (c) 228 (d) 216

22. $16 \rightarrow 112$

$3.5 \rightarrow ? =$

(a) 21 (b) 24.5 (c) 28 (d) 27.5

23. $7 \rightarrow 168$

$11 \rightarrow ? =$

(a) 253 (b) 286 (c) 251 (d) 264

24. $28 \rightarrow 140$

$3.4 \rightarrow ? =$

(a) 17 (b) 18 (c) 16 (d) 15

25. $33 \rightarrow 165$

$7.8 \rightarrow ? =$

(a) 37 (b) 40 (c) 39 (d) 41

26. $36 \rightarrow 144$

$9.5 \rightarrow ? =$

(a) 36 (b) 38 (c) 35 (d) 40

27. $22 \rightarrow 132$

$12.5 \rightarrow ? =$

(a) 80 (b) 72 (c) 60 (d) 75

28. $21 \rightarrow 189$

$23 \rightarrow ? =$

(a) 207 (b) 161 (c) 217 (d) 184

29. $24 \rightarrow 9600$

$25 \rightarrow ? =$

(a) 12,500 (b) 10,000

(c) 7,500 (d) 15,000

30. $27 \rightarrow 21600$

$12 \rightarrow ? =$

(a) 10,800 (b) 9,600 (c) 8,400 (d) 7,200

31. $48 \rightarrow 1920$

$32 \rightarrow ? =$

(a) 1440 (b) 1080 (c) 1280 (d) 1664

32. $6.3 \rightarrow 25.2$

$1.5 \rightarrow ? =$

(a) 6 (b) 9 (c) 7.5 (d) 12

33. $43 \rightarrow 77.4$

$5 \rightarrow ? =$

(a) 7.5 (b) 8 (c) 7 (d) 9

34. $18 \rightarrow 270$

$1.5 \rightarrow ? =$

(a) 25 (b) 25.5 (c) 22.5 (d) 24

35. $0.01 \rightarrow 25$

$100 \rightarrow ? =$

(a) 2,50,000 (b) 25,000

(c) 2,500 (d) 25,00,000

36. $0.04 \rightarrow 360$

$100 \rightarrow ? =$

(a) 9,000 (b) 9,00,000

(c) 90,000 (d) 90,00,000

37. $25\% \rightarrow 45$

$100\% \rightarrow ? =$

(a) 270 (b) 90 (c) 540 (d) 180

38. $12.5\% \rightarrow 30$
$100\% \rightarrow ? =$
(a) 210 (b) 250 (c) 270 (d) 240

39. $68\% \rightarrow 476$
$100\% \rightarrow ? =$
(a) 700 (b) 600 (c) 900 (d) 800

40. $20\% \rightarrow 450$
$100\% \rightarrow ? =$
(a) 2500 (b) 2750 (c) 2250 (d) 2150

41. $60\% \rightarrow 8$
$45\% \rightarrow ? =$
(a) 5 (b) 4 (c) 6 (d) 7

42. $36\% \rightarrow 198$
$100\% \rightarrow ? =$
(a) 520 (b) 550 (c) 510 (d) 540

43. $80\% \rightarrow 14.4$
$100\% \rightarrow ? =$
(a) 15 (b) 16 (c) 17 (d) 18

44. $28\% \rightarrow 1120$
$100\% \rightarrow ? =$
(a) 4000 (b) 5000 (c) 3000 (d) 6000

45. $128\% \rightarrow 2560$
$32\% \rightarrow ? =$
(a) 480 (b) 600 (c) 640 (d) 540

46. $12\% \rightarrow 450$
$100\% \rightarrow ? =$
(a) 3750 (b) 3250 (c) 3500 (d) 3600

47. **6% → 200**

4% → ? =

(a) 125 (b) 133.33 (c) 150 (d) 166.66

48. **49% → 1470**

36% → ? =

(a) 1152 (b) 1250 (c) 1296 (d) 1080

49. **8% → 26**

100% → ? =

(a) 312 (b) 650 (c) 416 (d) 325

50. **43% → 7740**

100% → ? =

(a) 15,000 (b) 18,000 (c) 16,000 (d) 17,500

51. **114% → 2850**

108% → ? =

(a) 2900 (b) 2500 (c) 2700 (d) 2750

52. **36% → 162**

100% → ? =

(a) 480 (b) 360 (c) 450 (d) 375

53. **62.5% → 125**

58.33% → ? =

(a) 166.66 (b) 113.33 (c) 116.66 (d) 133.33

54. **110% → 8800**

112.5% → ? =

(a) 9000 (b) 9900 (c) 9500 (d) 9600

55. **14.28% → 2856**

15.5% → ? =

(a) 3200 (b) 3250 (c) 3150 (d) 3100

56. 7% → 5460

100% → ? =

(a) 84,000 (b) 78,000 (c) 91,000 (d) 75,000

57. 9% → 639

10% → ? =

(a) 710 (b) 720 (c) 750 (d) 690

58. 0.09% → 45

100% → ? =

(a) 51,000 (b) 48,000 (c) 47,500 (d) 50,000

59. 0.16% → 240

8% → ? =

(a) 13,500 (b) 12,000 (c) 10,000 (d) 10,800

60. 0.25% → 48

100% → ? =

(a) 18,500 (b) 16,800 (c) 19,200 (d) 17,500

61. 0.25% → 720

100% → ? =

(a) 2,50,000 (b) 2,75,000
(c) 2,88,000 (d) 3,00,000

62. 0.25% → 112

100% → ? =

(a) 47,500 (b) 45,000 (c) 42,600 (d) 44,800

63. 0.36% → 108

100% → ? =

(a) 30,000 (b) 27,000 (c) 24,000 (d) 25,000

64. 0.36% → 144

100% → ? =

(a) 30,000 (b) 40,000 (c) 36,000 (d) 50,000

65. **0.49% → 1470**
100% → ? =
(a) 4,00,000 (b) 3,50,000
(c) 5,00,000 (d) 3,00,000

66. **0.49% → 15**
98% → ? =
(a) 3000 (b) 5000 (c) 7000 (d) 3500

67. **0.64% → 32**
100% → ? =
(a) 8000 (b) 5000 (c) 4000 (d) 6000

68. **0.64% → 256**
10% → ? =
(a) 5000 (b) 6000 (c) 4000 (d) 3000

69. **0.64% → 13**
2.56% → ? =
(a) 50 (b) 60 (c) 52 (d) 54

70. **0.81% → 162**
100% → ? =
(a) 25,000 (b) 20,000 (c) 27,000 (d) 30,000

71. **0.81% → 8.1**
18% → ? =
(a) 180 (b) 150 (c) 120 (d) 210

72. **0.81% → 243**
100% → ? =
(a) 25,000 (b) 27,000 (c) 36,000 (d) 30,000

73. **0.64% → 192**
0.49% → ? =
(a) 126 (b) 142 (c) 147 (d) 154

74. 1.2% → 13.2

1.1% → ? =

(a) 11.1 (b) 12.1 (c) 10.10 (d) 9.9

75. 1.21% → 242

11% → ? =

(a) 2310 (b) 2200 (c) 2420 (d) 1980

76. 1.44% → 72

24% → ? =

(a) 1200 (b) 1600 (c) 1350 (d) 1440

77. 1.44% → 57.6

12% → ? =

(a) 480 (b) 360 (c) 600 (d) 720

78. 1.69% → 338

100% → ? =

(a) 21,000 (b) 20,000 (c) 24,000 (d) 25,000

79. 1.96% → 98

100% → ? =

(a) 4000 (b) 6000 (c) 5000 (d) 4500

80. 2.25% → 90

30% → ? =

(a) 1500 (b) 1000 (c) 1350 (d) 1200

81. 2.25% → 18

100% → ? =

(a) 720 (b) 800 (c) 600 (d) 900

82. 5 → 6

4 → ? =

(a) 4.8 (b) 5.4 (c) 4.5 (d) 8.4

83. $5 \to 42$

$8 \to ? =$

(a) 62.4 (b) 64 (c) 67.2 (d) 64.8

84. $4 \to 35$

$100 \to ? =$

(a) 750 (b) 850 (c) 700 (d) 875

85. $4 \to 21$

$3 \to ? =$

(a) 15.15 (b) 15.75 (c) 15.45 (d) 15.25

86. $16 \to 98$

$24 \to ? =$

(a) 145 (b) 142 (c) 147 (d) 144

87. $5 \to 44$

$7 \to ? =$

(a) 53.9 (b) 61.6 (c) 57.4 (d) 69.3

88. $25 \to 72$

$4 \to ? =$

(a) 11.52 (b) 12.54 (c) 10.12 (d) 14.40

89. $20 \to 63$

$7 \to ? =$

(a) 21.05 (b) 22.50 (c) 21.50 (d) 22.05

90. $2 \to 3.6$

$5 \to ? =$

(a) 8.5 (b) 8 (c) 9.5 (d) 9

91. $4 \to 9.2$

$5 \to ? =$

(a) 10.75 (b) 11.25 (c) 11.5 (d) 10.5

92. $5 \rightarrow 28.5$
$4 \rightarrow ? =$
(a) 20.8 (b) 22.8 (c) 23.2 (d) 24.4

93. $6 \rightarrow 51$
$5 \rightarrow ? =$
(a) 42.5 (b) 45 (c) 40 (d) 43.5

94. $9 \rightarrow 8.1$
$14 \rightarrow ? =$
(a) 13.3 (b) 11.2 (c) 12.6 (d) 10.5

95. $3 \rightarrow 7.8$
$4 \rightarrow ? =$
(a) 10.4 (b) 9.8 (c) 9.2 (d) 10.8

96. $5 \rightarrow 3.15$
$4 \rightarrow ? =$
(a) 2.48 (b) 2.52 (c) 2.60 (d) 2.16

97. $7 \rightarrow 35.14$
$5 \rightarrow ? =$
(a) 27.25 (b) 24.5 (c) 23 (d) 25.1

98. $6 \rightarrow 1.26$
$5 \rightarrow ? =$
(a) 1.025 (b) 1.02 (c) 1.05 (d) 0.975

99. $3 \rightarrow 11.1$
$5 \rightarrow ? =$
(a) 16.5 (b) 17.5 (c) 18.5 (d) 19.5

100. $4 \rightarrow 22.8$
$16 \rightarrow ? =$
(a) 92.1 (b) 88.9 (c) 91.2 (d) 89.8

DIVISION (विभाजन)

101. $6 \rightarrow 52.8$

$5 \rightarrow ? =$

(a) 46 (b) 44 (c) 48 (d) 45

102. $9 \rightarrow 8.46$

$10 \rightarrow ? =$

(a) 9.4 (b) 9.6 (c) 9.5 (d) 9.2

103. $7 \rightarrow 16.8$

$8 \rightarrow ? =$

(a) 19.2 (b) 18.4 (c) 20.8 (d) 22.4

104. $8 \rightarrow 56.8$

$9 \rightarrow ? =$

(a) 58.5 (b) 67.5 (c) 64.8 (d) 63.9

105. $8 \rightarrow 41.6$

$5 \rightarrow ? =$

(a) 25 (b) 24 (c) 26 (d) 27

106. $4 \rightarrow 23.6$

$7 \rightarrow ? =$

(a) 42 (b) 41.3 (c) 43.4 (d) 37.1

107. $6 \rightarrow 44.4$

$5 \rightarrow ? =$

(a) 37 (b) 35 (c) 36 (d) 38

108. $17 \rightarrow 22.1$

$9 \rightarrow ? =$

(a) 10.8 (b) 12.6 (c) 11.7 (d) 13.5

109. $11 \rightarrow 13.2$

$6 \rightarrow ? =$

(a) 7.2 (b) 7.8 (c) 6.6 (d) 8.4

110. 14 → 72.8

5 → ? =

(a) 27.5 (b) 26 (c) 24 (d) 25

111. 7 → 65.8

8 → ? =

(a) 78.4 (b) 72.8 (c) 71.4 (d) 75.2

112. 2 → 1/6

3 → ? =

(a) 1/5 (b) 1/3 (c) 2/3 (d) 1/4

113. 5 → 1/20

4 → ? =

(a) 1/16 (b) 1/20 (c) 1/30 (d) 1/25

114. 3 → 1/7

7 → ? =

(a) 1/3 (b) 1/4 (c) 2/7 (d) 1/5

115. 5 → 1/12

30 → ? =

(a) 1/3 (b) 1/2 (c) 1/4 (d) 1/5

116. 7 → 1/14

2 → ? =

(a) 1/49 (b) 2/49 (c) 1/98 (d) 1/4

117. 3 → 1/8

24 → ? =

(a) 1 (b) 1/2 (c) 2 (d) 2/3

118. 12 → 1/7

5 → ? =

(a) 5/84 (b) 4/49 (c) 5/42 (d) 5/49

119. 16 → 1/8

32 → ? =

(a) 1/8 (b) 1/16 (c) 1/2 (d) 1/4

120. 15 → 1/4

5 → ? =

(a) 1/3 (b) 1/12 (c) 1/6 (d) 1/4

121. 9 → 1/20

7 → ? =

(a) 7/90 (b) 9/140 (c) 7/180 (d) 9/70

122. 14 → 1/5

35 → ? =

(a) 1/3 (b) 1/4 (c) 1/2 (d) 2/3

123. 6 → 1/4

30 → ? =

(a) 5/4 (b) 1/4 (c) 1/16 (d) 1/8

124. 6 → 5/12

4 → ? =

(a) 2/5 (b) 5/18 (c) 4/15 (d) 5/12

125. 5 → 2/3

3 → ? =

(a) 2/5 (b) 4/9 (c) 3/5 (d) 3/10

126. 15 → 4/7

5 → ? =

(a) 4/21 (b) 5/21 (c) 5/14 (d) 4/35

127. 3 → 12/7

16 → ? =

(a) 48/21 (b) 64/7 (c) 96/21 (d) 32/7

128. $5 \rightarrow 4/11$

$15 \rightarrow ? =$

(a) 20/11 (b) 15/11 (c) 12/11 (d) 30/11

129. $4 \rightarrow 3/5$

$3 \rightarrow ? =$

(a) 3/10 (b) 9/20 (c) 4/3 (d) 6/20

130. $15 \rightarrow 2/9$

$45 \rightarrow ? =$

(a) 2/3 (b) 3/2 (c) 1/3 (d) 3/4

Type-6: Answer - Key

1. (b)	27. (d)	53. (c)	79. (c)	105. (c)
2. (c)	28. (a)	54. (a)	80. (d)	106. (b)
3. (d)	29. (b)	55. (d)	81. (b)	107. (a)
4. (a)	30. (b)	56. (b)	82. (a)	108. (c)
5. (c)	31. (c)	57. (a)	83. (c)	109. (a)
6. (b)	32. (a)	58. (d)	84. (d)	110. (b)
7. (d)	33. (d)	59. (b)	85. (b)	111. (d)
8. (a)	34. (c)	60. (c)	86. (c)	112. (d)
9. (c)	35. (a)	61. (c)	87. (b)	113. (d)
10. (a)	36. (b)	62. (d)	88. (a)	114. (a)
11. (b)	37. (d)	63. (a)	89. (d)	115. (b)
12. (b)	38. (d)	64. (b)	90. (d)	116. (a)
13. (d)	39. (a)	65. (d)	91. (c)	117. (a)
14. (a)	40. (c)	66. (a)	92. (b)	118. (a)
15. (a)	41. (c)	67. (b)	93. (a)	119. (d)
16. (b)	42. (b)	68. (c)	94. (c)	120. (b)
17. (c)	43. (d)	69. (c)	95. (a)	121. (c)
18. (d)	44. (a)	70. (b)	96. (b)	122. (c)
19. (c)	45. (c)	71. (a)	97. (d)	123. (a)
20. (a)	46. (a)	72. (d)	98. (c)	124. (b)
21. (c)	47. (b)	73. (c)	99. (c)	125. (a)
22. (b)	48. (d)	74. (b)	100. (c)	126. (a)
23. (d)	49. (d)	75. (b)	101. (b)	127. (b)
24. (a)	50. (b)	76. (a)	102. (a)	128. (c)
25. (c)	51. (c)	77. (a)	103. (a)	129. (b)
26. (b)	52. (c)	78. (b)	104. (d)	130. (a)

DECIMAL (दशमलव)

Type-1

Hint :

⇒ **5.6 × 8**

(5 + 0.6) × 8

Step-1 ⇒ 5 को 8 से गुणा करिए और संख्या को दिमाग में रखिए।

Step-2 ⇒ 6 को 8 से गुणा करिए (48) एक अंक (digit) पहले Decimal लगा देना है। (4.8) को दिमाग में रखिए।

Step-3 ⇒ 40 + 4.8 = $\boxed{44.8}$

Answer दिमाग मे निकल जाएगा।

Exercise

- **MULTIPLICATION IN DECIMAL:-**

1. 4.6 × 4 = ?
(a) 16.4 (b) 17.4 (c) 18.4 (d) 1.84

2. 2.3 × 9 = ?
(a) 21.7 (b) 20.7 (c) 18.7 (d) 19.7

3. 6.4 × 5 = ?
(a) 32.5 (b) 31 (c) 32 (d) 32.4

4. 7.2 × 9 = ?
(a) 62.8 (b) 60.8 (c) 63.8 (d) 64.8

5. 8.1 × 8 = ?
(a) 65.8 (b) 64.8 (c) 63.8 (d) 80.8

6. 9.4 × 3 = ?
(a) 27.6 (b) 27.2 (c) 28.2 (d) 28.4

7. 6.2 × 9 = ?
(a) 55.8 (b) 50.8 (c) 58.8 (d) 57.9

8. 3.3 × 4 = ?
(a) 12.3 (b) 13.5 (c) 13.2 (d) 14.2

9. 5.2 × 7 = ?
(a) 35.6 (b) 36.4 (c) 37.4 (d) 38.4

10. 9.3 × 2 = ?
(a) 17.6 (b) 18.8 (c) 18.6 (d) 19.2

11. 8.4 × 2 = ?
(a) 14.2 (b) 16.8 (c) 17.6 (d) 16.6

12. 7.1 × 6 = ?
(a) 45.6 (b) 43.2 (c) 42.6 (d) 43.6

13. 9.8 × 2 = ?
(a) 8.4 (b) 12.6 (c) 10.6 (d) 19.6

14. 1.8 × 7 = ?
(a) 8.4 (b) 12.6 (c) 10.6 (d) 96

15. 1.9 × 6 = ?
(a) 10.4 (b) 12.4 (c) 11.4 (d) 11.6

16. 2.1 × 6 = ?
(a) 12.8 (b) 12.6 (c) 12.4 (d) 10.6

17. 2.5 × 7 = ?
(a) 12.5 (b) 15 (c) 17.5 (d) 15.5

18. 2.8 × 4 = ?
(a) 10.2 (b) 13.2 (c) 12.2 (d) 11.2

19. 3.1 × 7 = ?
(a) 22.3 (b) 21.7 (c) 22.7 (d) 23.1

20. 3.2 × 6 = ?
(a) 21.2 (b) 18.2 (c) 19.2 (d) 1.92

21. 3.4 × 5 = ?
(a) 17 (b) 17.5 (c) 16 (d) 18

22. 4.4 × 5 = ?
(a) 21.5 (b) 21 (c) 22 (d) 22.5

23. 4.7 × 7 = ?
(a) 29.9 (b) 32.9 (c) 31.9 (d) 32.3

24. 5.4 × 8 = ?
(a) 45.2 (b) 44.4 (c) 43.2 (d) 41.2

25. 5.5 × 8 = ?
(a) 45 (b) 44 (c) 43 (d) 44.5

26. 5.6 × 9 = ?
(a) 51.4 (b) 50 (c) 50.4 (d) 51.6

27. 5.9 × 4 = ?
(a) 24.6 (b) 23.6 (c) 22.6 (d) 23.4

28. 6.2 × 7 = ?
(a) 43.2 (b) 49.4 (c) 43.4 (d) 44.4

29. 6.4 × 3 = ?
(a) 20.6 (b) 19.2 (c) 18.2 (d) 16.6

30. 7.1 × 5 = ?
(a) 33.5 (b) 36.5 (c) 37.5 (d) 35.5

31. 7.2 × 5 = ?
(a) 36 (b) 37 (c) 35 (d) 35.5

32. 7.3 × 7 = ?
(a) 49.1 (b) 52.7 (c) 51.1 (d) 53.9

33. 7.5 × 4 = ?
(a) 31.4 (b) 30 (c) 32 (d) 35

34. 8.2 × 6 = ?
(a) 49.4 (b) 51.4 (c) 48.2 (d) 49.2

35. 8.4 × 5 = ?
(a) 42 (b) 41 (c) 42.5 (d) 43

36. 9.4 × 7 = ?
(a) 68.4 (b) 65.8 (c) 66 (d) 66.8

37. 7.9 × 6 = ?
(a) 48.4 (b) 48.2 (c) 47.4 (d) 46.7

38. 4.4 × 4 = ?
(a) 17.4 (b) 18.6 (c) 18.4 (d) 17.6

39. 5.5 × 5 = ?
(a) 28.25 (b) 27.5 (c) 25.5 (d) 28.5

40. 6.6 × 6 = ?
(a) 36.6 (b) 38.6 (c) 39.6 (d) 39.3

41. 7.7 × 7 = ?
(a) 51.9 (b) 52.9 (c) 49.7 (d) 53.9

42. 8.8 × 8 = ?
(a) 72.4 (b) 71 (c) 70.4 (d) 77.4

43. 9.9 × 9 = ?
(a) 88.1 (b) 89.1 (c) 88.9 (d) 98.1

44. 3.3 × 3 = ?
(a) 8.1 (b) 6.6 (c) 9.9 (d) 9.3

45. 2.2 × 2 = ?
(a) 0.44 (b) 4.4 (c) 6.4 (d) 5.4

46. 1.4 × 7 = ?
(a) 9.8 (b) 0.98 (c) 9.08 (d) 98

47. 1.8 × 5 = ?
(a) 8 (b) 9 (c) 9.2 (d) 6

48. 0.9 × 9 = ?
(a) 8.1 (b) 9 (c) 9.2 (d) 6

49. 9.3 × 3 = ?
(a) 2.89 (b) 28.9 (c) 27.9 (d) 2.79

50. 6.4 × 4 = ?
(a) 25.6 (b) 24.6 (c) 26.6 (d) 32.6

51. 8.7 × 7 = ?
(a) 59.4 (b) 60.9 (c) 61.9 (d) 34.6

52. 5.4 × 4 = ?
(a) 2.06 (b) 22.4 (c) 21.6 (d) 20.6

53. 8.3 × 3 = ?
(a) 25.9 (b) 24.9 (c) 2.49 (d) 23.9

54. 6.7 × 5 = ?
(a) 63.5 (b) 3.35 (c) 32.5 (d) 33.5

55. 3.3 × 7 = ?
(a) 22.1 (b) 21.1 (c) 24.1 (d) 23.1

56. 9.6 × 4 = ?
(a) 26.4 (b) 38.4 (c) 3.84 (d) 33.4

57. 4.2 × 9 = ?
(a) 35.8 (b) 37.8 (c) 36.8 (d) 38

58. 3.6 × 9 = ?
(a) 3.34 (b) 31.2 (c) 32.4 (d) 33.4

59. 8.8 × 9 = ?
(a) 79.2 (b) 7.29 (c) 88.2 (d) 78.2

60. 7.6 × 9 = ?
(a) 69.4 (b) 68.6 (c) 68.4 (d) 68.2

61. 8.3 × 8 = ?
(a) 66.8 (b) 6.74 (c) 65.4 (d) 66.4

62. 9.2 × 8 = ?
(a) 73.6 (b) 78.6 (c) 72.6 (d) 77.6

63. 4.5 × 3 = ?
(a) 15.5 (b) 13.5 (c) 10.5 (d) 14

64. 3.5 × 7 = ?
(a) 22.5 (b) 21.5 (c) 24.5 (d) 54.5

65. 5.5 × 9 = ?
(a) 4.95 (b) 48.5 (c) 51.4 (d) 49.5

66. 2.5 × 7 = ?
(a) 17.5 (b) 1.75 (c) 15.5 (d) 16.5

67. 6.5 × 7 = ?
(a) 46.5 (b) 45.5 (c) 45 (d) 44

68. 8.5 × 5 = ?
(a) 45 (b) 44 (c) 42.5 (d) 43.5

69. 7.5 × 5 = ?
(a) 39.5 (b) 33.5 (c) 36.5 (d) 37.5

70. 9.5 × 9 = ?
(a) 82.5 (b) 84.5 (c) 85.5 (d) 88.5

71. 8.7 × 5 = ?
(a) 41.5 (b) 43.5 (c) 42.5 (d) 44.5

72. 4.8 × 5 = ?
(a) 24 (b) 25 (c) 23 (d) 22

73. 9.8 × 5 = ?
(a) 47 (b) 49 (c) 48 (d) 40

74. 8.6 × 3 = ?
(a) 28 (b) 26.8 (c) 25.8 (d) 25.4

75. 8.4 × 7 = ?
(a) 59.8 (b) 58.8 (c) 59 (d) 59.2

76. 9.2 × 3 = ?
(a) 26.7 (b) 72.6 (c) 2.76 (d) 27.6

77. 6.6 × 8 = ?
(a) 0.528 (b) 5.28 (c) 52.8 (d) 528

78. 9.1 × 9 = ?
(a) 8.91 (b) 81.9 (c) 83.9 (d) 98.1

79. 8.1 × 9 = ?
(a) 72.9 (b) 73.9 (c) 74.9 (d) 77.3

80. 7.1 × 9 = ?
(a) 63.3 (b) 63.9 (c) 64.9 (d) 65

81. 4.1 × 9 = ?
(a) 36 (b) 39 (c) 36.9 (d) 46

82. 3.2 × 6 = ?
(a) 1.92 (b) 19.4 (c) 20.2 (d) 19.2

83. 6.1 × 9 = ?
(a) 54.3 (b) 54.9 (c) 55.6 (d) 58.9

84. 7.1 × 3 = ?
(a) 22.3 (b) 31.2 (c) 21.3 (d) 23.1

85. 8.4 × 7 = ?
(a) 30.8 (b) 58.8 (c) 56.2 (d) 54.4

86. 9.3 × 6 = ?
(a) 54.8 (b) 55.8 (c) 54.4 (d) 55.9

87. 5.3 × 7 = ?
(a) 38.5 (b) 39 (c) 37.1 (d) 36.1

88. 7 × 3.3 = ?
(a) 23.3 (b) 23.1 (c) 22.1 (d) 24.3

89. 8 × 8.1 = ?
(a) 64.8 (b) 66.8 (c) 63.8 (d) 58.2

90. 8 × 7.9 = ?
(a) 62.3 (b) 6.32 (c) 63.2 (d) 70.2

91. 5 × 5.5 = ?
(a) 5.55 (b) 55.5 (c) 25.5 (d) 27.5

92. 7 × 1.4 = ?
(a) 9.8 (b) 8.8 (c) 9.6 (d) 8.9

93. 2 × 9.3 = ?
(a) 19.6 (b) 18.6 (c) 17.6 (d) 15.4

94. 7 × 4.8 = ?
(a) 34.6 (b) 32.6 (c) 33.6 (d) 36.6

95. 8 × 5.5 = ?
(a) 44.5 (b) 42 (c) 43 (d) 44

96. 4 × 9.6 = ?
(a) 39 (b) 38.4 (c) 36.2 (d) 37.4

97. 9 × 9.1 = ?
(a) 81.9 (b) 82.9 (c) 80.3 (d) 88.1

98. 3 × 9.3 = ?
(a) 28.3 (b) 27.9 (c) 26.9 (d) 30.9

99. 5 × 6.7 = ?
(a) 34.7 (b) 33 (c) 33.5 (d) 32.5

100. 7 × 8.7 = ?
(a) 61.9 (b) 60.9 (c) 66.9 (d) 63.3

101. 7 × 5.3 = ?
(a) 76.1 (b) 35.5 (c) 37.1 (d) 36.1

102. 6 × 7.9 = ?
(a) 49 (b) 48.4 (c) 4.74 (d) 47.4

103. 3 × 9.4 = ?
(a) 28.2 (b) 28.5 (c) 2.84 (d) 28.4

104. $7 \times 6.5 = ?$

(a) 48.5 (b) 45.5 (c) 43.5 (d) 46.5

105. $7 \times 8.4 = ?$

(a) 5.88 (b) 57.5 (c) 58.8 (d) 59.8

106. $9 \times 7.7 = ?$

(a) 70.6 (b) 67.3 (c) 70.7 (d) 69.3

107. $8 \times 8.8 = ?$

(a) 86 (b) 70.4 (c) 70.2 (d) 71

108. $6 \times 7.9 = ?$

(a) 45.4 (b) 46.4 (c) 47.4 (d) 48.7

109. $5 \times 9.8 = ?$

(a) 50 (b) 47 (c) 48 (d) 49

110. $5 \times 3.3 = ?$

(a) 16.5 (b) 17.5 (c) 15.6 (d) 15.5

111. $7 \times 1.8 = ?$

(a) 1.26 (b) 12.6 (c) 12.4 (d) 13.6

112. $9 \times 9.8 = ?$

(a) 89.9 (b) 88.2 (c) 89.1 (d) 88

113. $8 \times 6.6 = ?$

(a) 54.4 (b) 52.8 (c) 53.2 (d) 55.8

114. $8 \times 6.7 = ?$

(a) 55.6 (b) 54.6 (c) 54 (d) 53.6

115. $9 \times 7.7 = ?$

(a) 67.3 (b) 69.3 (c) 66.3 (d) 70.3

Type-1: Answer - Key

1.	(c)	24.	(c)	47.	(b)	70.	(c)	93.	(b)
2.	(b)	25.	(b)	48.	(a)	71.	(b)	94.	(c)
3.	(c)	26.	(c)	49.	(c)	72.	(a)	95.	(d)
4.	(d)	27.	(b)	50.	(a)	73.	(b)	96.	(b)
5.	(b)	28.	(c)	51.	(b)	74.	(c)	97.	(a)
6.	(c)	29.	(b)	52.	(c)	75.	(b)	98.	(b)
7.	(a)	30.	(d)	53.	(b)	76.	(d)	99.	(c)
8.	(c)	31.	(a)	54.	(d)	77.	(c)	100.	(b)
9.	(b)	32.	(c)	55.	(d)	78.	(b)	101.	(c)
10.	(c)	33.	(b)	56.	(b)	79.	(a)	102.	(d)
11.	(b)	34.	(d)	57.	(b)	80.	(b)	103.	(a)
12.	(c)	35.	(a)	58.	(c)	81.	(c)	104.	(b)
13.	(d)	36.	(b)	59.	(a)	82.	(d)	105.	(c)
14.	(b)	37.	(c)	60.	(c)	83.	(b)	106.	(d)
15.	(c)	38.	(d)	61.	(d)	84.	(c)	107.	(b)
16.	(b)	39.	(b)	62.	(a)	85.	(b)	108.	(c)
17.	(c)	40.	(c)	63.	(b)	86.	(b)	109.	(d)
18.	(d)	41.	(d)	64.	(c)	87.	(c)	110.	(a)
19.	(b)	42.	(c)	65.	(d)	88.	(b)	111.	(b)
20.	(c)	43.	(b)	66.	(a)	89.	(a)	112.	(b)
21.	(a)	44.	(c)	67.	(b)	90.	(c)	113.	(b)
22.	(c)	45.	(b)	68.	(c)	91.	(d)	114.	(d)
23.	(b)	46.	(a)	69.	(d)	92.	(a)	115.	(b)

Type-2

Hint :

$\Rightarrow$ **90.7 × 8**

Step-1 $\Rightarrow 90 \times 8 = 720$

Step-2 $\Rightarrow 8 \times 7 = 5.6$

Step-3 $\Rightarrow 720 + 5.6 = \boxed{725.6}$

Exercise

1. **14.3 × 3 = ?**
(a) 44.9 (b) 41.9 (c) 42.9 (d) 43.9

2. **11.4 × 4 = ?**
(a) 42.6 (b) 45.6 (c) 44.6 (d) 43.6

3. **11.8 × 9 = ?**
(a) 160.2 (b) 105.2 (c) 10.62 (d) 106.2

4. **12.6 × 8 = ?**
(a) 99.8 (b) 102.8 (c) 100.8 (d) 96.8

5. **12.9 × 5 = ?**
(a) 65.5 (b) 64.5 (c) 6.45 (d) 65.4

6. **13.3 × 6 = ?**
(a) 78.8 (b) 78.9 (c) 79.8 (d) 79.9

7. **13.8 × 5 = ?**
(a) 67 (b) 66 (c) 68 (d) 69

8. **13.8 × 8 = ?**
(a) 110.4 (b) 111 (c) 111.4 (d) 1.104

9. **12.3 × 7 = ?**
(a) 85.1 (b) 88.1 (c) 86.1 (d) 87.1

10. 14.2 × 3 = ?
(a) 43.6 (b) 45.6 (c) 44.6 (d) 42.6

11. 14.1 × 9 = ?
(a) 130.2 (b) 126.9 (c) 125.9 (d) 128.9

12. 14.9 × 5 = ?
(a) 74.5 (b) 75.4 (c) 75.5 (d) 76.5

13. 15.3 × 7 = ?
(a) 112 (b) 106.1 (c) 107.1 (d) 109.1

14. 15.7 × 5 = ?
(a) 78.2 (b) 78.5 (c) 78 (d) 79.5

15. 16.4 × 4 = ?
(a) 64.6 (b) 66.7 (c) 65.6 (d) 66.6

16. 16.6 × 8 = ?
(a) 218.8 (b) 133.3 (c) 131.8 (d) 132.8

17. 16.3 × 7 = ?
(a) 115.1 (b) 114.1 (c) 141.1 (d) 111.4

18. 19.2 × 5 = ?
(a) 96 (b) 97 (c) 98 (d) 99

19. 19.4 × 6 = ?
(a) 112.4 (b) 115.4 (c) 116.4 (d) 118.4

20. 24.5 × 4 = ?
(a) 97 (b) 98 (c) 99 (d) 96

21. 35.6 × 5 = ?
(a) 178.5 (b) 175 (c) 177 (d) 178

22. 41.2 × 5 = ?
(a) 206 (b) 208 (c) 204 (d) 203

23. 62.1 × 8 = ?
(a) 499.8 (b) 495.8 (c) 496.8 (d) 498.8

24. 84.4 × 5 = ?
(a) 441 (b) 422 (c) 421 (d) 420

25. 90.7 × 8 = ?
(a) 730 (b) 762 (c) 725.6 (d) 745.6

26. 46.3 × 4 = ?
(a) 190.2 (b) 185.2 (c) 188.2 (d) 186.2

27. 18.1 × 8 = ?
(a) 142.8 (b) 145.8 (c) 144.8 (d) 164.8

28. 11.3 × 7 = ?
(a) 80.1 (b) 79.1 (c) 78.1 (d) 77.1

29. 12.3 × 3 = ?
(a) 37.9 (b) 35.9 (c) 38.9 (d) 36.9

30. 12.7 × 7 = ?
(a) 88.9 (b) 87.9 (c) 89.9 (d) 90.9

31. 13.1 × 6 = ?
(a) 79.6 (b) 75.6 (c) 78.6 (d) 77.6

32. 13.4 × 8 = ?
(a) 110.2 (b) 107.2 (c) 108.2 (d) 109.2

33. 13.6 × 5 = ?
(a) 70 (b) 66 (c) 69 (d) 68

34. 13.9 × 9 = ?
(a) 123 (b) 126.3 (c) 124.1 (d) 125.1

35. 12.8 × 6 = ?
(a) 75 (b) 77.8 (c) 76.8 (d) 79.8

36. 14.6 × 4 = ?
(a) 56.7 (b) 58.4 (c) 57 (d) 57.4

37. 14.3 × 7 = ?
(a) 102.1 (b) 102 (c) 99.1 (d) 100.1

38. 15.2 × 5 = ?
(a) 77.5 (b) 77 (c) 76 (d) 76.5

39. 15.8 × 6 = ?
(a) 99.8 (b) 94.8 (c) 95.8 (d) 96.8

40. 16.5 × 5 = ?
(a) 82 (b) 83.5 (c) 80.5 (d) 82.5

41. 16.8 × 7 = ?
(a) 118.6 (b) 117.6 (c) 116.7 (d) 118.7

42. 16.1 × 9 = ?
(a) 147 (b) 145.9 (c) 144.9 (d) 145.1

43. 17.4 × 6 = ?
(a) 103.4 (b) 105.4 (c) 104.6 (d) 104.4

44. 20.2 × 5 = ?
(a) 101.5 (b) 101 (c) 102 (d) 102.5

45. 29.2 × 5 = ?
(a) 146.6 (b) 146.5 (c) 145 (d) 146

46. 38.4 × 7 = ?
(a) 286.9 (b) 268.8 (c) 269.8 (d) 296.8

47. 52.4 × 6 = ?
(a) 316.4 (b) 315.2 (c) 314.4 (d) 341.4

48. 71.4 × 5 = ?
(a) 358 (b) 357 (c) 356 (d) 360

49. 92.2 × 5 = ?
(a) 461 (b) 462 (c) 463 (d) 461.5

50. 44.4 × 5 = ?
(a) 222.5 (b) 221.5 (c) 222 (d) 223

51. 53.4 × 3 = ?
(a) 161.2 (b) 160.2 (c) 162.2 (d) 168.2

52. 10.2 × 5 = ?
(a) 50.5 (b) 52 (c) 53 (d) 51

53. 11.7 × 7 = ?
(a) 82.9 (b) 89.1 (c) 81.9 (d) 81.1

54. 12.4 × 7 = ?
(a) 86.8 (b) 88.8 (c) 87.5 (d) 85.8

55. 12.8 × 5 = ?
(a) 63.5 (b) 64 (c) 63 (d) 64.5

56. 13.2 × 7 = ?
(a) 93.6 (b) 93.4 (c) 92.4 (d) 94.4

57. 13.5 × 4 = ?
(a) 56 (b) 55 (c) 53 (d) 54

58. 13.7 × 3 = ?
(a) 41.1 (b) 45.1 (c) 42.1 (d) 43.3

59. 12.8 × 9 = ?
(a) 110 (b) 115.2 (c) 116.2 (d) 117

60. 14.4 × 5 = ?
(a) 110 (b) 75 (c) 72 (d) 94

61. 14.7 × 7 = ?
(a) 111 (b) 110 (c) 105.9 (d) 102.9

62. 14.8 × 5 = ?
(a) 75 (b) 74 (c) 73 (d) 79

63. 15.4 × 6 = ?
(a) 92.4 (b) 95.4 (c) 93.4 (d) 92.6

64. 15.9 × 3 = ?
(a) 46.7 (b) 48.7 (c) 47.7 (d) 49.7

65. 16.2 × 7 = ?
(a) 114 (b) 113.4 (c) 118.4 (d) 115.2

66. 16.6 × 8 = ?
(a) 137.8 (b) 138 (c) 132.8 (d) 139.2

67. 16.9 × 8 = ?
(a) 135 (b) 132 (c) 134.2 (d) 135.2

68. 18.2 × 4 = ?
(a) 72.6 (b) 72.8 (c) 78 (d) 75.8

69. 17.8 × 5 = ?
(a) 98 (b) 88 (c) 89 (d) 82

70. 21.6 × 4 = ?
(a) 86.2 (b) 84 (c) 87.4 (d) 86.4

71. 33.3 × 3 = ?
(a) 109 (b) 99.9 (c) 100.9 (d) 99

72. 42.4 × 5 = ?
(a) 214 (b) 222 (c) 212 (d) 220

73. 53.5 × 6 = ?
(a) 321 (b) 320 (c) 341 (d) 371

74. 82.1 × 5 = ?
(a) 460 (b) 410.5 (c) 420.5 (d) 411

75. 91.6 × 6 = ?
(a) 556 (b) 559.6 (c) 549.6 (d) 556.9

76. 48.8 × 5 = ?
(a) 248 (b) 240.4 (c) 254 (d) 244

77. 70.4 × 5 = ?
(a) 366 (b) 352 (c) 356 (d) 378

78. 79.2 × 3 = ?
(a) 239.7 (b) 236 (c) 237.6 (d) 236.7

79. 88.1 × 8 = ?
(a) 708.8 (b) 708 (c) 709 (d) 704.8

80. 21.4 × 6 = ?
(a) 124.8 (b) 128.4 (c) 124 (d) 126

81. 30.4 × 5 = ?
(a) 162 (b) 158 (c) 152 (d) 158.2

82. 10.7 × 6 = ?
(a) 62 (b) 68.2 (c) 72 (d) 64.2

83. 60.8 × 7 = ?
(a) 425.6 (b) 426.6 (c) 436.6 (d) 432.6

84. 90.1 × 9 = ?
(a) 824 (b) 810.9 (c) 813.9 (d) 812.9

85. 81.6 × 6 = ?
(a) 489.6 (b) 496 (c) 469 (d) 498.6

86. 91.3 × 3 = ?
(a) 243 (b) 283 (c) 273.9 (d) 276.3

87. 31.2 × 8 = ?
(a) 296 (b) 256.8 (c) 238.8 (d) 249.6

88. 20.8 × 6 = ?
(a) 124.8 (b) 120 (c) 142 (d) 126.8

89. 40.7 × 7 = ?
(a) 28.49 (b) 2.849 (c) 286.9 (d) 284.9

90. 70.7 × 9 = ?
(a) 666 (b) 636.3 (c) 63.63 (d) 663.3

91. 84.5 × 2 = ?
(a) 170 (b) 179 (c) 169 (d) 168

92. 27.7 × 5 = ?
(a) 169 (b) 138.5 (c) 140.5 (d) 139.5

93. 33.4 × 3 = ?
(a) 111 (b) 112 (c) 100.2 (d) 102.2

94. 25.4 × 5 = ?
(a) 127 (b) 128 (c) 130 (d) 132

95. 50.8 × 8 = ?
(a) 404.4 (b) 406.4 (c) 408 (d) 460

96. 80.8 × 6 = ?
(a) 494.8 (b) 488.8 (c) 474.8 (d) 484.8

Type-2: Answer - Key

1.	(c)	20.	(b)	39.	(b)	58.	(a)	77.	(b)
2.	(b)	21.	(d)	40.	(d)	59.	(b)	78.	(c)
3.	(d)	22.	(a)	41.	(b)	60.	(c)	79.	(d)
4.	(c)	23.	(c)	42.	(c)	61.	(d)	80.	(b)
5.	(b)	24.	(b)	43.	(d)	62.	(b)	81.	(c)
6.	(c)	25.	(c)	44.	(b)	63.	(a)	82.	(d)
7.	(d)	26.	(b)	45.	(d)	64.	(c)	83.	(a)
8.	(a)	27.	(c)	46.	(b)	65.	(b)	84.	(b)
9.	(c)	28.	(b)	47.	(c)	66.	(c)	85.	(a)
10.	(d)	29.	(d)	48.	(b)	67.	(d)	86.	(c)
11.	(b)	30.	(a)	49.	(a)	68.	(b)	87.	(d)
12.	(a)	31.	(c)	50.	(c)	69.	(c)	88.	(a)
13.	(c)	32.	(b)	51.	(b)	70.	(d)	89.	(d)
14.	(b)	33.	(d)	52.	(d)	71.	(b)	90.	(b)
15.	(c)	34.	(d)	53.	(c)	72.	(c)	91.	(c)
16.	(d)	35.	(c)	54.	(a)	73.	(a)	92.	(b)
17.	(b)	36.	(b)	55.	(b)	74.	(b)	93.	(c)
18.	(a)	37.	(d)	56.	(c)	75.	(c)	94.	(a)
19.	(c)	38.	(c)	57.	(d)	76.	(d)	95.	(b)
								96.	(d)

Type-3

Hint :

⇒ **23 × 0.09**

Step-1 ⇒ 23 × 9 = 207

Step-2 ⇒ 2 अंक (digit) पहले Decimal लगा दीजिए 2.07 Answer आ जाएगा।

Exercise

1. 62 × 0.3 = ?
(a) 18.6 (b) 1.86 (c) 16.8 (d) 186

2. 31 × 0.4 = ?
(a) 13.4 (b) 12.4 (c) 1.24 (d) 12.04

3. 77 × 0.2 = ?
(a) 1.54 (b) 14.5 (c) 16.4 (d) 15.4

4. 71 × 0.4 = ?
(a) 27.4 (b) 26.4 (c) 28.4 (d) 28.6

5. 49 × 0.4 = ?
(a) 20.4 (b) 19.6 (c) 1.96 (d) 18.6

6. 69 × 0.3 = ?
(a) 21.7 (b) 20.4 (c) 20.7 (d) 2.07

7. 13 × 0.006 = ?
(a) 0.078 (b) 0.78 (c) 7.8 (d) 78

8. 23 × 0.09 = ?
(a) 27.0 (b) 2.70 (c) 20.7 (d) 2.07

9. 77 × 0.03 = ?
(a) 23.1 (b) 2.31 (c) 2.76 (d) 2.51

10. 46 × 0.04 = ?
(a) 1.64 (b) 18.4 (c) 1.84 (d) 1.48

11. 56 × 0.02 = ?
(a) 11.2 (b) 112 (c) 12.1 (d) 1.12

12. 95 × 0.6 = ?
(a) 57 (b) 56 (c) 54 (d) 55

13. 42 × 0.7 = ?
(a) 2.96 (b) 29.4 (c) 27.4 (d) 2.94

14. 97 × 0.08 = ?
(a) 67.6 (b) 7.67 (c) 7.76 (d) 77.6

15. 74 × 0.5 = ?
(a) 0.37 (b) 38 (c) 37 (d) 370

16. 46 × 0.07 = ?
(a) 32.2 (b) 3.02 (c) 3.78 (d) 3.22

17. 57 × 0.5 = ?
(a) 30.5 (b) 28.5 (c) 29.5 (d) 27.5

18. 92 × 0.5 = ?
(a) 49 (b) 45 (c) 46 (d) 48

19. 99 × 0.4 = ?
(a) 36.6 (b) 33.6 (c) 38.6 (d) 39.6

20. 78 × 0.04 = ?
(a) 4.12 (b) 76.2 (c) 6.12 (d) 3.12

21. 39 × 0.05 = ?
(a) 1.95 (b) 2.95 (c) 19.5 (d) 195

22. 72 × 0.4 = ?
(a) 28.08 (b) 288 (c) 28.8 (d) 2.88

23. 94 × 0.07 = ?
(a) 5.58 (b) 6.58 (c) 9.58 (d) 10.58

24. 85 × 0.07 = ?
(a) 3.95 (b) 6.05 (c) 5.95 (d) 59.5

25. 26 × 0.05 = ?
(a) 130 (b) 13 (c) 0.13 (d) 1.3

26. 47 × 0.9 = ?
(a) 4.32 (b) 32.4 (c) 4.23 (d) 42.3

27. 93 × 0.08 = ?
(a) 7.44 (b) 74.4 (c) 7.04 (d) 74

28. 18 × 0.03 = ?
(a) 5.4 (b) 0.54 (c) 540 (d) 5.04

29. 19 × 0.003 = ?
(a) 57 (b) 0.057 (c) 5.7 (d) 0.57

30. 48 × 0.5 = ?
(a) 2.04 (b) 2.4 (c) 24 (d) 240

31. 49 × 0.6 = ?
(a) 294 (b) 28.4 (c) 29.4 (d) 2.94

32. 61 × 0.7 = ?
(a) 77.7 (b) 42.7 (c) 4.27 (d) 72.4

33. 33 × 0.2 = ?
(a) 6.6 (b) 66 (c) 0.66 (d) 6.06

34. 81 × 0.05 = ?
(a) 41.5 (b) 40.5 (c) 405 (d) 4.05

35. 22 × 0.8 = ?
(a) 1.86 (b) 18.6 (c) 1.76 (d) 17.6

36. 23 × 0.09 = ?
(a) 4.07 (b) 3.07 (c) 2.07 (d) 20.7

37. 14 × 0.04 = ?
(a) 0.56 (b) 56 (c) 0.056 (d) 5.6

38. 15 × 0.009 = ?
(a) 0.0135 (b) 0.135 (c) 1.35 (d) 13.5

39. 17 × 0.6 = ?
(a) 11.2 (b) 102 (c) 1.02 (d) 10.2

40. 66 × 0.4 = ?
(a) 2.46 (b) 264 (c) 2.64 (d) 26.4

41. 73 × 0.3 = ?
(a) 22 (b) 22.9 (c) 21.9 (d) 20.9

42. 33 × 0.6 = ?
(a) 1.98 (b) 19.8 (c) 20 (d) 22.8

43. 84 × 0.3 = ?
(a) 25.5 (b) 2.52 (c) 25.2 (d) 2.02

44. 36 × 0.4 = ?
(a) 12.04 (b) 14.4 (c) 1.44 (d) 14.04

45. 24 × 0.3 = ?
(a) 0.72 (b) 72 (c) 7.02 (d) 7.2

46. 76 × 0.8 = ?
(a) 60.8 (b) 6.08 (c) 7.08 (d) 70.8

47. 86 × 0.005 = ?
(a) 0.043 (b) 4.3 (c) 0.43 (d) 43

48. 59 × 0.08 = ?
(a) 4.02 (b) 4.72 (c) 47.2 (d) 472

49. 67 × 0.002 = ?
(a) 0.134 (b) 13.4 (c) 1.34 (d) 134

50. 54 × 0.9 = ?
(a) 4.86 (b) 48.6 (c) 4.06 (d) 40.6

51. 96 × 0.03 = ?
(a) 2.80 (b) 28.8 (c) 2.88 (d) 0.288

52. 52 × 0.5 = ?
(a) 13 (b) 13.5 (c) 2.6 (d) 26

53. 25 × 0.5 = ?

(a) 1.66 (b) 16.6 (c) 12.5 (d) 1.26

54. 12 × 0.6 = ?

(a) 72 (b) 7.2 (c) 2.7 (d) 27

55. 75 × 0.2 = ?

(a) 15 (b) 0.15 (c) 1.5 (d) 30

56. 17 × 0.07 = ?

(a) 11.09 (b) 11.90 (c) 1.19 (d) 119

57. 58 × 0.005 = ?

(a) 0.029 (b) 29 (c) 2.9 (d) 0.29

58. 65 × 0.006 = ?

(a) 3.9 (b) 0.39 (c) 39 (d) 0.039

59. 31 × 0.4 = ?

(a) 12.4 (b) 1.24 (c) 124 (d) 14.2

60. 82 × 0.6 = ?

(a) 50 (b) 4.92 (c) 49.2 (d) 48.2

61. 57 × 0.6 = ?

(a) 3.82 (b) 34.2 (c) 38.2 (d) 3.42

62. 74 × 0.6 = ?

(a) 404 (b) 40.4 (c) 4.44 (d) 44.4

63. 91 × 0.7 = ?

(a) 62.7 (b) 6.37 (c) 63.7 (d) 66.7

64. 34 × 0.2 = ?

(a) 6.8 (b) 68 (c) 0.68 (d) 680

65. 13 × 0.006 = ?

(a) 0.87 (b) 0.078 (c) 7.8 (d) 0.78

66. 35 × 0.02 = ?

(a) 7 (b) 0.07 (c) 0.7 (d) 70

67. 16 × 0.5 = ?
(a) 0.08 (b) 8 (c) 80 (d) 0.8

68. 83 × 0.9 = ?
(a) 77.4 (b) 7.47 (c) 747 (d) 74.7

69. 82 × 0.02 = ?
(a) 14.6 (b) 1.64 (c) 16.4 (d) 164

70. 89 × 0.05 = ?
(a) 5.45 (b) 44.5 (c) 54.4 (d) 4.45

71. 62 × 0.4 = ?
(a) 28.4 (b) 24.8 (c) 2.48 (d) 2.84

72. 53 × 0.7 = ?
(a) 3.17 (b) 3.71 (c) 37.1 (d) 31.7

73. 98 × 0.8 = ?
(a) 77.4 (b) 74.8 (c) 7.84 (d) 78.4

74. 64 × 0.06 = ?
(a) 3.84 (b) 38.4 (c) 34.6 (d) 3.48

75. 97 × 0.04 = ?
(a) 4.78 (b) 3.80 (c) 3.88 (d) 38.8

76. 45 × 0.06 = ?
(a) 2.07 (b) 270 (c) 27 (d) 2.7

77. 38 × 0.06 = ?
(a) 21.8 (b) 2.28 (c) 22.8 (d) 228

78. 87 × 0.8 = ?
(a) 69.9 (b) 6.96 (c) 69.6 (d) 66.9

79. 34 × 0.05 = ?
(a) 1.7 (b) 17 (c) 0.17 (d) 170

80. 43 × 0.06 = ?
(a) 24.8 (b) 2.58 (c) 2.48 (d) 4.58

81. $35 \times 0.4 = ?$
(a) 7 (b) 12 (c) 14 (d) 1.4

82. $44 \times 0.7 = ?$
(a) 32.8 (b) 3.08 (c) 3.3 (d) 30.8

83. $63 \times 0.008 = ?$
(a) 0.504 (b) 5.4 (c) 5.04 (d) 50.4

84. $27 \times 0.6 = ?$
(a) 12.2 (b) 18.2 (c) 16.2 (d) 1.62

85. $43 \times 0.07 = ?$
(a) 5.01 (b) 30.1 (c) 3.01 (d) 6.1

86. $44 \times 0.05 = ?$
(a) 2.2 (b) 22 (c) 2.4 (d) 3.4

87. $28 \times 0.3 = ?$
(a) 9.6 (b) 8.4 (c) 2.1 (d) 0.84

88. $29 \times 0.07 = ?$
(a) 2.30 (b) 20.3 (c) 2.03 (d) 203

89. $88 \times 0.04 = ?$
(a) 4.72 (b) 2.53 (c) 3.65 (d) 3.52

90. $13 \times 0.09 = ?$
(a) 1.17 (b) 117 (c) 11.7 (d) 1.07

91. $68 \times 0.008 = ?$
(a) 0.445 (b) 0.544 (c) 5.44 (d) 54.4

92. $79 \times 0.06 = ?$
(a) 47.4 (b) 7.74 (c) 4.74 (d) 6.74

93. $99 \times 0.05 = ?$
(a) 459 (b) 495 (c) 49.5 (d) 4.95

Type-3: Answer - Key

1.	(a)	**20.**	(d)	**39.**	(d)	**58.**	(b)	**77.**	(b)
2.	(b)	**21.**	(a)	**40.**	(d)	**59.**	(a)	**78.**	(c)
3.	(d)	**22.**	(c)	**41.**	(c)	**60.**	(c)	**79.**	(a)
4.	(c)	**23.**	(b)	**42.**	(b)	**61.**	(b)	**80.**	(b)
5.	(b)	**24.**	(c)	**43.**	(c)	**62.**	(d)	**81.**	(c)
6.	(c)	**25.**	(d)	**44.**	(b)	**63.**	(c)	**82.**	(d)
7.	(a)	**26.**	(d)	**45.**	(d)	**64.**	(a)	**83.**	(a)
8.	(d)	**27.**	(a)	**46.**	(a)	**65.**	(b)	**84.**	(c)
9.	(b)	**28.**	(b)	**47.**	(c)	**66.**	(c)	**85.**	(c)
10.	(c)	**29.**	(b)	**48.**	(b)	**67.**	(b)	**86.**	(a)
11.	(d)	**30.**	(c)	**49.**	(a)	**68.**	(d)	**87.**	(b)
12.	(a)	**31.**	(c)	**50.**	(b)	**69.**	(b)	**88.**	(c)
13.	(b)	**32.**	(b)	**51.**	(c)	**70.**	(d)	**89.**	(d)
14.	(c)	**33.**	(a)	**52.**	(d)	**71.**	(b)	**90.**	(a)
15.	(c)	**34.**	(d)	**53.**	(c)	**72.**	(c)	**91.**	(b)
16.	(d)	**35.**	(d)	**54.**	(b)	**73.**	(d)	**92.**	(c)
17.	(b)	**36.**	(c)	**55.**	(a)	**74.**	(a)	**93.**	(d)
18.	(c)	**37.**	(a)	**56.**	(c)	**75.**	(c)		
19.	(d)	**38.**	(b)	**57.**	(d)	**76.**	(d)		

Type-4

Hint :

⇒ **0.8 × 0.97**

Step-1 ⇒ अगर दोनों में Decimal है तो 8 × 90 = 720

Step-2 ⇒ 8 × 7 = 56

Step-3 ⇒ 720 + 56 = 776 तीन अंक (digit) पहले Decimal लगा देना है 0.776 Answer आ जाएगा।

Exercise

1. 8.2 × 0.6 = ?
(a) 0.392 (b) 4.92 (c) 3.92 (d) 0.492

2. 8.4 × 0.2 = ?
(a) 168 (b) 16.8 (c) 1.68 (d) 0.168

3. 8.3 × 0.04 = ?
(a) 3.32 (b) 0.332 (c) 3.23 (d) 0.323

4. 9.8 × 0.8 = ?
(a) 784 (b) 78.4 (c) 0.784 (d) 7.84

5. 2.4 × 0.3 = ?
(a) 0.72 (b) 7.2 (c) 3.6 (d) 0.36

6. 3.4 × 0.7 = ?
(a) 34 (b) 3.38 (c) 2.38 (d) 3.28

7. 8.8 × 0.6 = ?
(a) 5.08 (b) 5.28 (c) 4.28 (d) 7.08

8. 0.23 × 0.4 = ?
(a) 0.029 (b) 0.92 (c) 9.2 (d) 0.092

9. 6.8 × 0.8 = ?
(a) 44.4 (b) 5.44 (c) 54.4 (d) 4.44

10. 0.4 × 8.3 = ?
(a) 33.2 (b) 0.332 (c) 3.32 (d) 3.2

11. 0.5 × 3.3 = ?
(a) 1.65 (b) 2.05 (c) 3.50 (d) 16.5

12. 4.7 × 0.7 = ?
(a) 3.92 (b) 4.28 (c) 4.65 (d) 3.29

13. 0.7 × 0.62 = ?
(a) 4.34 (b) 0.434 (c) 34.3 (d) 0.344

14. 0.4 × 9.6 = ?
(a) 4.84 (b) 3.04 (c) 3.84 (d) 4.08

15. 0.9 × 0.36 = ?
(a) 0.424 (b) 4.24 (c) 3.24 (d) 0.324

16. 0.9 × 7.7 = ?
(a) 63.9 (b) 6.93 (c) 69.3 (d) 0.693

17. 3.4 × 0.2 = ?
(a) 34 (b) 6.8 (c) 0.68 (d) 68

18. 0.49 × 0.9 = ?
(a) 0.441 (b) 4.41 (c) 44.1 (d) 1.44

19. 0.4 × 0.49 = ?
(a) 2.96 (b) 2.46 (c) 1.96 (d) 0.196

20. 4.6 × 0.4 = ?
(a) 12.8 (b) 1.84 (c) 2.84 (d) 18.4

21. 6.3 × 0.8 = ?
(a) 6.04 (b) 4.05 (c) 5.04 (d) 3.98

22. 4.4 × 0.3 = ?
(a) 13.2 (b) 2.23 (c) 3.32 (d) 1.32

23. 8.2 × 0.2 = ?
(a) 1.64 (b) 16.4 (c) 23.4 (d) 21

24. 0.8 × 0.97 = ?
(a) 3.77 (b) 0.776 (c) 7.76 (d) 77.6

25. 10.2 × 0.5 = ?
(a) 4.1 (b) 51 (c) 5.1 (d) 0.51

26. 16.5 × 0.5 = ?
(a) 10.25 (b) 5.25 (c) 9.25 (d) 8.25

27. 13.1 × 0.6 = ?
(a) 8.86 (b) 7.86 (c) 8.46 (d) 9.36

28. 19.4 × 0.6 = ?
(a) 1117.4 (b) 1.164 (c) 11.64 (d) 116.4

29. 0.8 × 16.6 = ?
(a) 13.28 (b) 12.86 (c) 14.28 (d) 15.48

30. 0.9 × 0.91 = ?
(a) 81.9 (b) 0.819 (c) 9.08 (d) 4.08

31. 0.7 × 16.8 = ?
(a) 2.46 (b) 3.76 (c) 1.176 (d) 11.76

32. 0.5 × 4.88 = ?
(a) 62.8 (b) 3.24 (c) 2.44 (d) 5.44

33. 4.4 × 0.4 = ?
(a) 1.76 (b) 2.86 (c) 3.64 (d) 1.64

34. 2.8 × 0.4 = ?
(a) 2.12 (b) 1.12 (c) 4.62 (d) 9.62

35. 7.1 × 0.9 = ?
(a) 8.24 (b) 6.19 (c) 8.32 (d) 6.39

36. 2.7 × 0.6 = ?
(a) 2.02 (b) 2.31 (c) 1.62 (d) 4.64

37. 2.2 × 0.8 = ?
(a) 1.76 (b) 3.06 (c) 3.76 (d) 3.84

38. 1.4 × 0.05 = ?
(a) 70 (b) 0.07 (c) 7 (d) 0.7

39. 8.4 × 0.3 = ?
(a) 2.02 (b) 3.02 (c) 2.52 (d) 5.64

40. 0.72 × 0.5 = ?
(a) 32 (b) 3.6 (c) 36 (d) 0.36

41. 7.9 × 0.6 = ?
(a) 3.72 (b) 4.74 (c) 5.44 (d) 6.72

42. 0.7 × 9.2 = ?
(a) 21 (b) 4.64 (c) 6.44 (d) 8.44

43. 4.7 × 0.7 = ?
(a) 2.09 (b) 34 (c) 6.39 (d) 3.29

44. 0.8 × 5.4 = ?
(a) 32.4 (b) 4.32 (c) 5.02 (d) 5

45. 0.3 × 0.83 = ?
(a) 0.249 (b) 2.49 (c) 9.05 (d) 6.8

46. 0.6 × 0.93 = ?
(a) 5.58 (b) 4.58 (c) 0.558 (d) 5.59

47. 4.7 × 0.3 = ?
(a) 2.31 (b) 1.41 (c) 2.45 (d) 7.31

48. 0.35 × 0.2 = ?
(a) 0.7 (b) 7 (c) 70 (d) 0.07

49. 0.64 × 0.4 = ?
(a) 3.06 (b) 0.256 (c) 2.56 (d) 25.6

50. 7.7 × 0.3 = ?
(a) 2.51 (b) 3.51 (c) 2.31 (d) 5.81

51. 7.4 × 0.5 = ?
(a) 43 (b) 37 (c) 0.37 (d) 3.7

52. 11.2 × 0.8 = ?
(a) 9.69 (b) 8.96 (c) 5.96 (d) 4.86

53. 44.4 × 0.5 = ?
(a) 22.2 (b) 0.222 (c) 2.22 (d) 222

54. 13.5 × 0.4 = ?
(a) 2.54 (b) 54 (c) 5.4 (d) 0.54

55. 20.2 × 0.5 = ?
(a) 12.1 (b) 45 (c) 42 (d) 10.1

56. 0.5 × 15.6 = ?
(a) 31 (b) 7.8 (c) 4.8 (d) 21

57. 0.5 × 0.254 = ?
(a) 127 (b) 12.7 (c) 0.127 (d) 1.27

58. 0.6 × 52.4 = ?
(a) 31.44 (b) 34.44 (c) 32.78 (d) 44

59. 0.8 × 9.07 = ?
(a) 6.756 (b) 2.756 (c) 5.76 (d) 7.256

60. 3.3 × 0.03 = ?
(a) 9.9 (b) 0.099 (c) 0.99 (d) 99

61. 3.2 × 0.6 = ?
(a) 3.87 (b) 12.2 (c) 1.92 (d) 2.42

62. 6.1 × 0.9 = ?
(a) 5.49 (b) 4.87 (c) 2.89 (d) 6.39

63. 4.3 × 0.7 = ?
(a) 4.1 (b) 33.1 (c) 30.1 (d) 3.01

64. 1.3 × 0.6 = ?
(a) 7.8 (b) 0.78 (c) 3.87 (d) 4.82

65. 9.9 × 0.04 = ?
(a) 32.6 (b) 36.9 (c) 0.396 (d) 3.96

66. 0.12 × 0.5 = ?
(a) 3 (b) 6 (c) 0.6 (d) 0.06

67. 2.9 × 0.7 = ?
(a) 6 (b) 2.03 (c) 3.09 (d) 4.03

68. 5.5 × 0.4 = ?
(a) 0.22 (b) 4 (c) 2.2 (d) 22

69. 0.6 × 4.6 = ?
(a) 4 (b) 2.76 (c) 4.76 (d) 5.98

70. $3.1 \times 0.7 = ?$
(a) 5.73 (b) 2.17 (c) 4.32 (d) 6.52

71. $0.8 \times 5.4 = ?$
(a) 5.73 (b) 3.82 (c) 4.32 (d) 6.52

72. $0.3 \times 6.4 = ?$
(a) 5.92 (b) 4.32 (c) 19.2 (d) 1.92

73. $0.5 \times 3.3 = ?$
(a) 1.65 (b) 2.85 (c) 4 (d) 4.3

74. $8.6 \times 0.5 = ?$
(a) 4 (b) 4.3 (c) 5.76 (d) 5.3

75. $0.25 \times 0.4 = ?$
(a) 100 (b) 1 (c) 0.1 (d) 10

76. $0.81 \times 0.3 = ?$
(a) 0.423 (b) 3.65 (c) 34 (d) 0.243

77. $0.19 \times 0.3 = ?$
(a) 5.7 (b) 0.057 (c) 57 (d) 0.57

78. $2.6 \times 0.3 = ?$
(a) 0.39 (b) 78 (c) 0.78 (d) 7.8

79. $3.3 \times 0.4 = ?$
(a) 1.32 (b) 3.62 (c) 4.75 (d) 4.72

80. $9.1 \times 0.7 = ?$
(a) 5.86 (b) 4.87 (c) 6.37 (d) 4.88

81. $0.3 \times 0.73 = ?$
(a) 4.19 (b) 0.219 (c) 0.459 (d) 2.19

82. $9.8 \times 0.8 = ?$
(a) 4.82 (b) 7.88 (c) 6.94 (d) 7.84

83. $12.8 \times 0.5 = ?$
(a) 6.4 (b) 36 (c) 4.4 (d) 3.4

84. $48.8 \times 0.5 = ?$
(a) 44.4 (b) 48 (c) 24.4 (d) 58

85. 13.6 × 0.3 = ?

(a) 6.28 (b) 4.08 (c) 8 (d) 9.05

86. 0.5 × 30.4 = ?

(a) 42 (b) 9.2 (c) 4.2 (d) 15.2

87. 0.6 × 10.7 = ?

(a) 6.62 (b) 8.02 (c) 6.42 (d) 9.2

88. 0.4 × 16.4 = ?

(a) 6.56 (b) 8.76 (c) 9 (d) 7.56

89. 0.3 × 53.4 = ?

(a) 124.2 (b) 162.2 (c) 15.02 (d) 16.02

Type-4: Answer - Key

1.	(b)	**19.**	(d)	**37.**	(a)	**55.**	(d)	**73.**	(a)
2.	(c)	**20.**	(b)	**38.**	(b)	**56.**	(b)	**74.**	(b)
3.	(b)	**21.**	(c)	**39.**	(c)	**57.**	(c)	**75.**	(c)
4.	(d)	**22.**	(d)	**40.**	(d)	**58.**	(a)	**76.**	(d)
5.	(a)	**23.**	(a)	**41.**	(b)	**59.**	(d)	**77.**	(b)
6.	(c)	**24.**	(b)	**42.**	(c)	**60.**	(b)	**78.**	(c)
7.	(b)	**25.**	(c)	**43.**	(d)	**61.**	(c)	**79.**	(a)
8.	(d)	**26.**	(d)	**44.**	(b)	**62.**	(a)	**80.**	(c)
9.	(b)	**27.**	(b)	**45.**	(a)	**63.**	(d)	**81.**	(b)
10.	(c)	**28.**	(c)	**46.**	(c)	**64.**	(b)	**82.**	(d)
11.	(a)	**29.**	(a)	**47.**	(b)	**65.**	(c)	**83.**	(a)
12.	(d)	**30.**	(b)	**48.**	(d)	**66.**	(d)	**84.**	(c)
13.	(b)	**31.**	(d)	**49.**	(b)	**67.**	(b)	**85.**	(b)
14.	(c)	**32.**	(c)	**50.**	(c)	**68.**	(c)	**86.**	(d)
15.	(d)	**33.**	(a)	**51.**	(d)	**69.**	(b)	**87.**	(c)
16.	(b)	**34.**	(b)	**52.**	(b)	**70.**	(b)	**88.**	(a)
17.	(c)	**35.**	(d)	**53.**	(a)	**71.**	(c)	**89.**	(d)
18.	(a)	**36.**	(c)	**54.**	(c)	**72.**	(d)		

Type-5

Hint :

$\Rightarrow$ **28 × 1.50**

[1 + 0.5] × 28

Step-1 $\Rightarrow$ 28 × 1 = 28

Step-2 $\Rightarrow$ 50 देखकर पता लगना चाहिए कि 28 का आधा 14

Step-3 $\Rightarrow$ 28 + 14 = $\boxed{42}$

Note:

$0.20 \rightarrow 20\% \rightarrow \frac{1}{5}$ होता है

$0.25 \rightarrow 25\% \rightarrow \frac{1}{4}$ होता है

$0.50 \rightarrow 50\% \rightarrow \frac{1}{2}$ होता है

$0.75 \rightarrow 75\% \rightarrow \frac{3}{4}$ होता है

$0.125 \rightarrow 12.5 \rightarrow \frac{1}{8}$ होता है

Exercise

1. 28 × 1.50 = ?

(a) 40 (b) 42 (c) 41 (d) 42.5

2. 20 × 9.50 = ?

(a) 190 (b) 180 (c) 192 (d) 170

3. **7 × 3.50 = ?**
(a) 24.5 (b) 24 (c) 23.5 (d) 25

4. **14 × 15.50 = ?**
(a) 219 (b) 207 (c) 407 (d) 217

5. **30 × 13.50 = ?**
(a) 306 (b) 405 (c) 400 (d) 505

6. **13 × 20.50 = ?**
(a) 266.5 (b) 268 (c) 438 (d) 248.5

7. **8 × 14.50 = ?**
(a) 126 (b) 116 (c) 115 (d) 120

8. **60 × 11.50 = ?**
(a) 660 (b) 770 (c) 690 (d) 459

9. **33 × 20.50 = ?**
(a) 760 (b) 656.5 (c) 672 (d) 676.5

10. **90 × 12.50 = ?**
(a) 1025 (b) 1125 (c) 1235 (d) 1245

11. **92 × 8.50 = ?**
(a) 782 (b) 672 (c) 682 (d) 762

12. **30 × 11.50 = ?**
(a) 344 (b) 355 (c) 345 (d) 455

13. **5 × 36.50 = ?**
(a) 180 (b) 182.5 (c) 180.5 (d) 190

14. **12 × 24.50 = ?**
(a) 290 (b) 293 (c) 294 (d) 294.5

15. **88 × 1.50 = ?**
(a) 328 (b) 131.2 (c) 130 (d) 132

16. **20 × 6.50 = ?**
(a) 130 (b) 110 (c) 121 (d) 133

17. **18 × 15.50 = ?**
(a) 260 (b) 276 (c) 279 (d) 479

18. 40 × 21.50 = ?
(a) 678 (b) 860 (c) 780 (d) 870

19. 23 × 9.50 = ?
(a) 219.5 (b) 453 (c) 218 (d) 218.5

20. 44 × 7.50 = ?
(a) 330 (b) 333 (c) 332 (d) 331

21. 64 × 6.50 = ?
(a) 415 (b) 456 (c) 416 (d) 566

22. 30 × 12.50 = ?
(a) 385 (b) 375 (c) 376 (d) 379

23. 16 × 12.50 = ?
(a) 20 (b) 400 (c) 40 (d) 200

24. 96 × 2.50 = ?
(a) 240 (b) 24 (c) 48 (d) 200

25. 5 × 24.50 = ?
(a) 121 (b) 122.5 (c) 245 (d) 220

26. 40 × 8.50 = ?
(a) 330 (b) 450 (c) 340 (d) 320

27. 70 × 8.50 = ?
(a) 655 (b) 585 (c) 598 (d) 595

28. 10 × 20.50 = ?
(a) 205 (b) 304 (c) 405 (d) 320

29. 14 × 7.50 = ?
(a) 112 (b) 100 (c) 105 (d) 115

30. 18 × 8.50 = ?
(a) 153 (b) 150 (c) 163 (d) 343

31. 17 × 11.50 = ?
(a) 233 (b) 238 (c) 195.5 (d) 200.5

32. 40 × 18.50 = ?
(a) 470 (b) 478 (c) 740 (d) 744

33. 42 × 2.50 = ?
(a) 105 (b) 285 (c) 75 (d) 108

34. 7 × 42.50 = ?
(a) 300.5 (b) 453 (c) 297.5 (d) 548

35. 7 × 60.50 = ?
(a) 423.5 (b) 432 (c) 445.5 (d) 764

36. 48 × 3.50 = ?
(a) 328 (b) 164 (c) 168 (d) 248

37. 13 × 7.50 = ?
(a) 97.5 (b) 98 (c) 9.75 (d) 37.5

38. 46 × 11.50 = ?
(a) 540 (b) 549 (c) 529 (d) 521

39. 72 × 2.50 = ?
(a) 240 (b) 360 (c) 180 (d) 18

40. 18 × 9.50 = ?
(a) 342 (b) 431 (c) 181 (d) 171

41. 9 × 11.50 = ?
(a) 103.5 (b) 105.5 (c) 104 (d) 205

42. 8 × 20.50 = ?
(a) 244 (b) 164 (c) 186 (d) 174

43. 18 × 15.50 = ?
(a) 209 (b) 289 (c) 279 (d) 249

44. 4 × 22.50 = ?
(a) 92 (b) 80 (c) 100 (d) 90

45. 98 × 1.50 = ?
(a) 147 (b) 140 (c) 427 (d) 149

46. 24 × 4.50 = ?
(a) 102 (b) 108 (c) 106 (d) 105

47. 40 × 14.50 = ?
(a) 568 (b) 588 (c) 580 (d) 542

48. 14 × 12.50 = ?
(a) 150 (b) 175 (c) 185 (d) 195

49. 70 × 4.50 = ?
(a) 361 (b) 325 (c) 565 (d) 315

50. 70 × 11.50 = ?
(a) 805 (b) 809 (c) 803 (d) 808

51. 88 × 4.50 = ?
(a) 336 (b) 376 (c) 396 (d) 386

52. 60 × 9.50 = ?
(a) 570 (b) 549 (c) 560 (d) 590

53. 82 × 1.50 = ?
(a) 136 (b) 133 (c) 123 (d) 231

54. 20 × 12.50 = ?
(a) 250 (b) 230 (c) 435 (d) 255

55. 16 × 2.50 = ?
(a) 32 (b) 40 (c) 38 (d) 52

56. 5 × 24.50 = ?
(a) 122 (b) 132 (c) 122.5 (d) 210

57. 13 × 12.50 = ?
(a) 345 (b) 156 (c) 160.5 (d) 162.5

58. 26 × 4.50 = ?
(a) 117 (b) 118 (c) 327 (d) 119

59. 12 × 8.50 = ?
(a) 112 (b) 102 (c) 100 (d) 122

60. 50 × 21.50 = ?
(a) 1050 (b) 1145 (c) 1100 (d) 1075

61. 54 × 6.50 = ?
(a) 351 (b) 431 (c) 359 (d) 341

62. 42 × 8.50 = ?
(a) 356 (b) 357 (c) 355 (d) 364

63. 46 × 15.50 = ?
(a) 715 (b) 731 (c) 713 (d) 733

64. 42 × 9.50 = ?
(a) 399 (b) 398 (c) 400 (d) 500

65. 62 × 1.50 = ?
(a) 92 (b) 93 (c) 97 (d) 95

66. 7 × 24.50 = ?
(a) 94 (b) 162.5 (c) 171.5 (d) 175

67. 13 × 12.50 = ?
(a) 175 (b) 162.5 (c) 182.5 (d) 165

68. 6 × 15.50 = ?
(a) 92 (b) 94 (c) 93 (d) 95

69. 17 × 40.50 = ?
(a) 688.5 (b) 688 (c) 988 (d) 690

70. 20 × 6.50 = ?
(a) 132 (b) 120 (c) 130 (d) 110

71. 16 × 11.50 = ?
(a) 154 (b) 186 (c) 184 (d) 194

72. 16 × 9.50 = ?
(a) 152 (b) 167 (c) 165 (d) 158

73. 92 × 3.50 = ?
(a) 324 (b) 342 (c) 322 (d) 333

74. 43 × 3.50 = ?
(a) 150 (b) 150.5 (c) 151.5 (d) 159

75. 20 × 15.50 = ?
(a) 312 (b) 330 (c) 320 (d) 310

76. 80 × 12.50 = ?
(a) 1000 (b) 100 (c) 100.5 (d) 2000

77. 40 × 20.50 = ?

(a) 845 (b) 810 (c) 820 (d) 815

78. 40 × 8.50 = ?

(a) 320 (b) 385 (c) 346 (d) 340

79. 4 × 15.50 = ?

(a) 62 (b) 65 (c) 66 (d) 59

80. 43 × 7.50 = ?

(a) 342 (b) 333 (c) 322 (d) 322.5

81. 42 × 3.50 = ?

(a) 174 (b) 147 (c) 117 (d) 417

82. 62 × 11.50 = ?

(a) 713 (b) 653 (c) 715 (d) 783

83. 23 × 2.50 = ?

(a) 58.5 (b) 56.6 (c) 57.5 (d) 57

84. 4 × 19.50 = ?

(a) 80 (b) 76 (c) 88 (d) 78

85. 82 × 3.50 = ?

(a) 287 (b) 278 (c) 872 (d) 227

86. 92 × 8.50 = ?

(a) 781 (b) 782 (c) 784 (d) 785

87. 60 × 15.50 = ?

(a) 933 (b) 960 (c) 930 (d) 940

88. 43 × 3.50 = ?

(a) 150.5 (b) 160 (c) 155.5 (d) 164

89. 42 × 20.50 = ?

(a) 810 (b) 478 (c) 830 (d) 861

90. $8 \times 15.50 = ?$

(a) 125 (b) 124 (c) 122 (d) 123

91. $40 \times 12.50 = ?$

(a) 450 (b) 400 (c) 500 (d) 502

92. $70 \times 10.50 = ?$

(a) 735 (b) 765 (c) 775 (d) 675

93. $77 \times 10.50 = ?$

(a) 881 (b) 805 (c) 808.5 (d) 809

94. $8 \times 16.50 = ?$

(a) 132 (b) 133 (c) 321 (d) 122

95. $82 \times 1.50 = ?$

(a) 241 (b) 123 (c) 143 (d) 156

96. $32 \times 4.50 = ?$

(a) 215 (b) 145 (c) 144 (d) 164

97. $83 \times 7.50 = ?$

(a) 622.5 (b) 633 (c) 165 (d) 265

98. $42 \times 8.50 = ?$

(a) 367 (b) 345 (c) 357 (d) 544

Type-5: Answer - Key

1.	(b)	21.	(c)	41.	(a)	61.	(a)	81.	(b)
2.	(a)	22.	(b)	42.	(b)	62.	(b)	82.	(a)
3.	(a)	23.	(d)	43.	(c)	63.	(c)	83.	(c)
4.	(d)	24.	(a)	44.	(d)	64.	(a)	84.	(d)
5.	(b)	25.	(b)	45.	(a)	65.	(b)	85.	(a)
6.	(a)	26.	(c)	46.	(b)	66.	(c)	86.	(b)
7.	(b)	27.	(d)	47.	(c)	67.	(b)	87.	(c)
8.	(c)	28.	(a)	48.	(b)	68.	(c)	88.	(a)
9.	(d)	29.	(c)	49.	(d)	69.	(a)	89.	(d)
10.	(b)	30.	(a)	50.	(a)	70.	(c)	90.	(b)
11.	(a)	31.	(c)	51.	(c)	71.	(c)	91.	(c)
12.	(c)	32.	(c)	52.	(a)	72.	(a)	92.	(a)
13.	(b)	33.	(a)	53.	(c)	73.	(c)	93.	(c)
14.	(c)	34.	(c)	54.	(a)	74.	(b)	94.	(a)
15.	(d)	35.	(a)	55.	(b)	75.	(d)	95.	(b)
16.	(a)	36.	(c)	56.	(c)	76.	(a)	96.	(c)
17.	(c)	37.	(a)	57.	(d)	77.	(c)	97.	(a)
18.	(b)	38.	(c)	58.	(a)	78.	(d)	98.	(c)
19.	(d)	39.	(c)	59.	(b)	79.	(a)		
20.	(a)	40.	(d)	60.	(d)	80.	(d)		

Type-6

Hint :

12 × 2.25

[2 + 0.25] × 12

Step-1 ⇒ 12 × 2 = 24

Step-2 ⇒ $\cancel{12} \times \frac{1}{\cancel{4}} = 3$

Step-3 ⇒ 24 + 3 = $\boxed{27}$ Answer

दिमाग में करना है।

Exercise

1. 12 × 2.25 = ?
(a) 26 (b) 27 (c) 25 (d) 24

2. 12 × 6.125 = ?
(a) 75.5 (b) 77.5 (c) 76 (d) 73.5

3. 96 × 4.125 = ?
(a) 394 (b) 399 (c) 396 (d) 398

4. 14 × 4.25 = ?
(a) 59.5 (b) 55.5 (c) 54.5 (d) 58.5

5. 12 × 8.125 = ?
(a) 98 (b) 97.5 (c) 56.5 (d) 59

6. 28 × 7.25 = ?
(a) 207 (b) 305 (c) 205 (d) 203

7. 80 × 6.25 = ?
(a) 5000 (b) 400 (c) 500 (d) 50

8. $4 \times 12.25 = ?$
(a) 40 (b) 49 (c) 42 (d) 48

9. $15 \times 6.50 = ?$
(a) 97.5 (b) 94 (c) 95.5 (d) 92.25

10. $18 \times 4.25 = ?$
(a) 72 (b) 57 (c) 77.5 (d) 76.5

11. $24 \times 7.25 = ?$
(a) 176 (b) 175 (c) 174 (d) 177

12. $70 \times 6.25 = ?$
(a) 425 (b) 437.5 (c) 438.5 (d) 445

13. $13 \times 6.25 = ?$
(a) 82.25 (b) 81 (c) 78 (d) 81.25

14. $96 \times 4.25 = ?$
(a) 409 (b) 407 (c) 408 (d) 410

15. $8 \times 14.25 = ?$
(a) 114 (b) 118 (c) 115 (d) 116

16. $32 \times 7.125 = ?$
(a) 282 (b) 224 (c) 228 (d) 227

17. $54 \times 10.25 = ?$
(a) 553.5 (b) 555.5 (c) 545 (d) 542

18. $88 \times 4.125 = ?$
(a) 375 (b) 366 (c) 393 (d) 363

19. $36 \times 9.25 = ?$
(a) 363 (b) 320 (c) 333 (d) 323

20. $13 \times 3.25 = ?$
(a) 42.25 (b) 43.25 (c) 44.5 (d) 45

21. $72 \times 8.125 = ?$
(a) 536 (b) 595 (c) 585 (d) 587

22. $80 \times 7.125 = ?$
(a) 570 (b) 560 (c) 535 (d) 575

23. 12 × 8.125 = ?
(a) 98.5 (b) 97.5 (c) 99 (d) 100

24. 24 × 6.25 = ?
(a) 155 (b) 145 (c) 150 (d) 165

25. 48 × 8.25 = ?
(a) 396 (b) 346 (c) 386 (d) 336

26. 70 × 6.25 = ?
(a) 440 (b) 438.5 (c) 437.5 (d) 439

27. 30 × 4.25 = ?
(a) 127.5 (b) 126 (c) 128.5 (d) 135

28. 17 × 4.25 = ?
(a) 76 (b) 75.25 (c) 74 (d) 72.25

29. 18 × 6.25 = ?
(a) 65.5 (b) 112.5 (c) 110 (d) 62.5

30. 16 × 4.25 = ?
(a) 68 (b) 69 (c) 58 (d) 321

31. 15 × 2.25 = ?
(a) 32.25 (b) 34.25 (c) 33.75 (d) 35

32. 84 × 9.25 = ?
(a) 779 (b) 771 (c) 770 (d) 777

33. 40 × 13.25 = ?
(a) 565 (b) 535 (c) 530 (d) 545

34. 32 × 15.25 = ?
(a) 483 (b) 488 (c) 480 (d) 654

35. 16 × 6.125 = ?
(a) 98 (b) 99 (c) 100 (d) 96

36. 64 × 9.125 = ?
(a) 587 (b) 658 (c) 583 (d) 584

37. 88 × 4.25 = ?
(a) 326 (b) 374 (c) 393 (d) 366

38. 72 × 10.125 = ?
(a) 729 (b) 762 (c) 769 (d) 723

39. 64 × 10.25 = ?
(a) 655 (b) 665 (c) 656 (d) 565

40. 8 × 6.125 = ?
(a) 49 (b) 48 (c) 4.9 (d) 40

41. 40 × 5.125 = ?
(a) 202 (b) 207 (c) 205 (d) 404

42. 30 × 4.25 = ?
(a) 127.5 (b) 126 (c) 125.5 (d) 145

43. 8 × 9.25 = ?
(a) 73 (b) 84 (c) 75 (d) 74

44. 64 × 4.125 = ?
(a) 245 (b) 266 (c) 264 (d) 265

45. 7 × 4.25 = ?
(a) 29.75 (b) 34.5 (c) 28 (d) 27.95

46. 42 × 6.25 = ?
(a) 262.5 (b) 260.5 (c) 464 (d) 265

47. 14 × 2.25 = ?
(a) 34 (b) 32 (c) 31.5 (d) 33.5

48. 16 × 4.25 = ?
(a) 48 (b) 66 (c) 64 (d) 68

49. 88 × 8.25 = ?
(a) 726 (b) 762 (c) 267 (d) 672

50. 108 × 10.25 = ?
(a) 2017 (b) 1208 (c) 1107 (d) 1007

51. 200 × 10.25 = ?
(a) 2055 (b) 2050 (c) 2072 (d) 2075

52. 32 × 8.25 = ?
(a) 264 (b) 274 (c) 432 (d) 284

53. 44 × 15.25 = ?
(a) 666 (b) 761 (c) 672 (d) 671

54. 16 × 14.25 = ?
(a) 238 (b) 229 (c) 228 (d) 230

55. 4 × 8.125 = ?
(a) 33 (b) 32.5 (c) 33.5 (d) 35

56. 40 × 7.25 = ?
(a) 288 (b) 238 (c) 298 (d) 290

57. 100 × 9.125 = ?
(a) 912.5 (b) 980 (c) 643 (d) 256

58. 64 × 10.125 = ?
(a) 480 (b) 578 (c) 648 (d) 964

Type-6 Answer - Key

1.	(b)	13.	(d)	25.	(a)	37.	(b)	49.	(a)
2.	(d)	14.	(c)	26.	(c)	38.	(a)	50.	(c)
3.	(c)	15.	(a)	27.	(a)	39.	(c)	51.	(b)
4.	(a)	16.	(c)	28.	(d)	40.	(a)	52.	(a)
5.	(b)	17.	(a)	29.	(b)	41.	(c)	53.	(d)
6.	(d)	18.	(d)	30.	(a)	42.	(a)	54.	(c)
7.	(c)	19.	(c)	31.	(c)	43.	(d)	55.	(b)
8.	(b)	20.	(a)	32.	(d)	44.	(c)	56.	(d)
9.	(a)	21.	(c)	33.	(c)	45.	(a)	57.	(a)
10.	(d)	22.	(a)	34.	(b)	46.	(a)	58.	(c)
11.	(c)	23.	(b)	35.	(a)	47.	(c)		
12.	(b)	24.	(c)	36.	(d)	48.	(d)		

Type-7

☞ इस Type की सभी Equations Type 1 से Type 6 पर आधारित हैं Practice करने के लिए।

Exercise

1. 57.73647 to nearest hundredth
(a) 100 (b) 57 (c) 56.7 (d) 57.74

2. 78.09 + 19.367
(a) 58.723 (b) 87.357 (c) 97.457 (d) 87.457

3. 3.419 – 0.7
(a) 34.12 (b) 0.2719 (c) 2.719 (d) 0.3412

4. 3.491 – 0.7
(a) 2.791 (b) 2.301 (c) 2.331 (d) 2.412

5. 426 – 7.2
(a) 354 (b) 425.28 (c) 418.8 (d) 417.8

6. 6.35 × 5
(a) 31.75 (b) 30.75 (c) 3.175 (d) 317.5

7. 5.9 – 4.166
(a) 1.844 (b) 1.843 (c) 1.744 (d) 1.734

8. 172 × 0.56
(a) 9.632 (b) 96.32 (c) 963.2 (d) 0.9632

9. 0.63 × 0.42
(a) 26.46 (b) 2.646 (c) 0.2646 (d) 0.02646

10. 0.216 + 9.3 + 72
(a) 81.516 (b) 77.516 (c) 16.716 (d) 81.55

11. 0.49 × 0.07
(a) 34.3 (b) 0.0343 (c) 3.43 (d) 0.343

12. 9456 ÷ 24

(a) 3940 (b) 394 (c) 39.4 (d) 3.946

13. $(6.5 \times 10^{-6}) \div (3.25 \times 10^{-3})$

(a) 2×10^{-9} (b) 2×10^{-3} (c) 2×10^{2} (d) 2×10^{3}

14. 0.31 + 0.673

(a) 0.0983 (b) 0.983 (c) 0.967 (d) 9.83

15. 12.9991 + 78 + 0.9866

(a) 90.9857 (b) 90.0957 (c) 91.9857 (d) 91.9957

16. 2 – 0.42 – 0.1

(a) 14.8 (b) 1.48 (c) 1.048 (d) 1.0048

Type-7: Answer - Key

1.	(d)	4.	(a)	7.	(d)	10.	(a)	13.	(b)
2.	(c)	5.	(c)	8.	(b)	11.	(b)	14.	(b)
3.	(c)	6.	(a)	9.	(c)	12.	(b)	15.	(c)
								16.	(b)

SURDS (करणी)

Type-1

Concept:

☞ $\left(\sqrt{a}\right)^2 = a \rightarrow$ Root की power even (सम) है तो Root हट गया।

☞ $\left(\sqrt{a}\right)^3 = a\sqrt{a} \rightarrow$ Root की power odd (विषम) है तो Root नहीं हटेगा।

Example 1: $\left(\sqrt{13}\right)^4 = \boxed{169}$

Example 2: $\left(3\sqrt{3}\right)^2 = (3)^2 = (9)\times(3) = \boxed{27}$

Example 3: $\left(5\sqrt{2}\right)^3 \rightarrow$ Answer $\sqrt{2}$ में आएगा क्योंकि power odd है।

$(5)^3 = 125 \times 2\sqrt{2}$

$= 250\sqrt{2}$

Exercise

1. $\left(\sqrt{2}\right)^2$

(a) $\sqrt{2}$ (b) 4 (c) 2 (d) $2\sqrt{2}$

2. $\left(\sqrt{13}\right)^4$

(a) 26 (b) 13 (c) $13\sqrt{13}$ (d) 169

3. $\left(3\sqrt{3}\right)^2$

(a) $27\sqrt{3}$ (b) 27 (c) $9\sqrt{3}$ (d) 81

4. $\left(6\sqrt{6}\right)^2$

(a) $216\sqrt{6}$ (b) $36\sqrt{6}$ (c) 216 (d) 36

5. $\left(5\sqrt{2}\right)^3$

(a) 125 (b) $125\sqrt{2}$ (c) 250 (d) $250\sqrt{2}$

6. $\left(3\sqrt{2}\right)^2$

(a) 18 (b) 9 (c) $9\sqrt{2}$ (d) $18\sqrt{2}$

7. $\left(7\sqrt{7}\right)^2$

(a) 343 (b) 98 (c) 49 (d) $49\sqrt{7}$

8. $\left(3\sqrt{3}\right)^3$

(a) 27 (b) 81 (c) $81\sqrt{3}$ (d) $27\sqrt{3}$

9. $\left(\sqrt{5}\right)^4$

(a) 5 (b) 25 (c) 125 (d) 50

10. $\left(3\sqrt{7}\right)^2$

(a) $9\sqrt{7}$ (b) 21 (c) $63\sqrt{7}$ (d) 63

11. $\left(9\sqrt{10}\right)^2$

(a) 90 (b) 81 (c) $81\sqrt{10}$ (d) 810

12. $\left(11\sqrt{3}\right)^2$

(a) 363 (b) $121\sqrt{3}$ (c) $363\sqrt{3}$ (d) 121

13. $\left(12\sqrt{2}\right)^2$

(a) 144 (b) $144\sqrt{2}$ (c) 288 (d) 12

14. $\left(5\sqrt{5}\right)^2$

(a) 125 (b) 25 (c) 50 (d) 625

15. $\left(6\sqrt{6}\right)^2$

(a) $216\sqrt{6}$ (b) 216 (c) 36 (d) $36\sqrt{6}$

16. $\left(8\sqrt{2}\right)^2$

(a) $64\sqrt{2}$ (b) 64 (c) 128 (d) 32

17. $\left(7\sqrt{8}\right)^2$

(a) 56 (b) 392 (c) 98 (d) 176

18. $\left(8\sqrt{3}\right)^2$

(a) 96 (b) 72 (c) 192 (d) $64\sqrt{3}$

19. $\left(9\sqrt{9}\right)^2$

(a) 729 (b) $81\sqrt{3}$ (c) $72\sqrt{3}$ (d) 243

20. $\left(11\sqrt{11}\right)^2$

(a) $121\sqrt{11}$ (b) 121 (c) 1331 (d) 1089

21. $\left(10\sqrt{2}\right)^3$

(a) 1000 (b) $1000\sqrt{2}$ (c) $2000\sqrt{2}$ (d) 2000

22. $\left(\sqrt{3}\right)^4$

(a) $3\sqrt{3}$ (b) 6 (c) 3 (d) 9

23. $\left(\sqrt{14}\right)^2$

(a) 14 (b) 28 (c) $14\sqrt{14}$ (d) 7

24. $\left(\sqrt{5}\right)^4$

(a) 5 (b) 25 (c) $5\sqrt{5}$ (d) 50

25. $\left(3\sqrt{5}\right)^2$

(a) 45 (b) 15 (c) $9\sqrt{5}$ (d) 30

26. $\left(4\sqrt{5}\right)^2$

(a) $8\sqrt{5}$ (b) $16\sqrt{5}$ (c) 80 (d) 40

27. $\left(4\sqrt{2}\right)^2$

(a) 48 (b) 8 (c) 16 (d) 32

28. $\left(5\sqrt{6}\right)^2$

(a) 125 (b) 150 (c) 120 (d) 180

29. $\left(2\sqrt{2}\right)^3$

(a) $16\sqrt{2}$ (b) 8 (c) 16 (d) $8\sqrt{2}$

30. $\left(3\sqrt{2}\right)^3$

(a) 36 (b) $18\sqrt{2}$ (c) $54\sqrt{2}$ (d) 54

31. $\left(4\sqrt{2}\right)^3$

(a) 48 (b) 64 (c) $64\sqrt{2}$ (d) $128\sqrt{2}$

32. $\left(2\sqrt{3}\right)^3$

(a) $24\sqrt{3}$ (b) $12\sqrt{3}$ (c) 36 (d) 24

33. $\left(3\sqrt{3}\right)^3$

(a) 27 (b) 81 (c) $81\sqrt{3}$ (d) $27\sqrt{3}$

34. $\left(4\sqrt{3}\right)^2$

(a) $48\sqrt{3}$ (b) 48 (c) $16\sqrt{3}$ (d) 32

35. $\left(5\sqrt{3}\right)^2$

(a) 25 (b) 150 (c) 75 (d) $75\sqrt{3}$

36. $\left(8\sqrt{2}\right)^2$

(a) $128\sqrt{2}$ (b) $64\sqrt{2}$ (c) 128 (d) 64

37. $\left(6\sqrt{3}\right)^2$

(a) 108 (b) 36 (c) 72 (d) $108\sqrt{3}$

38. $\left(7\sqrt{6}\right)^2$

(a) 294 (b) $294\sqrt{6}$ (c) $49\sqrt{6}$ (d) $294\sqrt{3}$

39. $\left(9\sqrt{4}\right)^2$

(a) 324 (b) 162 (c) 36 (d) 108

40. $\left(10\sqrt{4}\right)^2$

(a) 1600 (b) 400 (c) 200 (d) 40

41. $\left(10\sqrt{5}\right)^2$

(a) 1250 (b) 500 (c) 250 (d) 100

42. $\left(11\sqrt{5}\right)^2$

(a) 506 (b) 555 (c) 550 (d) 605

43. $\left(\sqrt{4}\right)^2$

(a) 4 (b) 8 (c) 16 (d) 2

44. $\left(2\sqrt{2}\right)^2$

(a) 12 (b) 6 (c) 8 (d) 4

45. $\left(13\sqrt{5}\right)^2$

(a) 845 (b) 485 (c) 1690 (d) 1265

46. $\left(2\sqrt{7}\right)^2$

(a) 14 (b) $4\sqrt{7}$ (c) 28 (d) 56

47. $\left(2\sqrt{6}\right)^3$

(a) 144 (b) 12 (c) $12\sqrt{6}$ (d) $48\sqrt{6}$

48. $\left(5\sqrt{11}\right)^2$

(a) 55 (b) 275 (c) 121 (d) $55\sqrt{11}$

49. $\left(3\sqrt{11}\right)^2$

(a) 99 (b) 33 (c) $9\sqrt{11}$ (d) 66

50. $\left(5\sqrt{12}\right)^2$

(a) 60 (b) 120 (c) 720 (d) 300

51. $\left(3\sqrt{12}\right)^2$

(a) $27\sqrt{3}$ (b) $36\sqrt{3}$ (c) 108 (d) 36

52. $\left(2\sqrt{11}\right)^2$

(a) $4\sqrt{11}$ (b) 44 (c) 22 (d) $121\sqrt{2}$

53. $\left(11\sqrt{7}\right)^2$

(a) 154 (b) 77 (c) 539 (d) 847

54. $\left(10\sqrt{7}\right)^2$

(a) 350 (b) 700 (c) 1400 (d) 70

55. $\left(15\sqrt{3}\right)^2$

(a) 675 (b) 112 (c) 450 (d) $225\sqrt{3}$

56. $\left(\sqrt{7}\right)^3$

(a) $14\sqrt{7}$ (b) 49 (c) $7\sqrt{7}$ (d) 343

57. $\left(\sqrt{8}\right)^3$

(a) 8 (b) $8\sqrt{8}$ (c) 64 (d) $16\sqrt{2}$

58. $\left(\sqrt{9}\right)^3$

(a) 18 (b) 27 (c) 81 (d) $9\sqrt{3}$

59. $\left(2\sqrt{10}\right)^3$

(a) $80\sqrt{10}$ (b) 40 (c) 80 (d) $40\sqrt{5}$

60. $\left(3\sqrt{10}\right)^3$

(a) 90 (b) $270\sqrt{10}$ (c) 270 (d) $135\sqrt{3}$

61. $\left(4\sqrt{10}\right)^3$

(a) 320 (b) 640 (c) $640\sqrt{10}$ (d) 400

62. $\left(5\sqrt{10}\right)^3$

(a) $1250\sqrt{10}$ (b) 1250 (c) 625 (d) $1000\sqrt{10}$

63. $\left(6\sqrt{5}\right)^2$

(a) 108 (b) 90 (c) 120 (d) 180

64. $\left(\sqrt{5}\right)^3$

(a) $5\sqrt{5}$ (b) 5 (c) 25 (d) 125

65. $\left(4\sqrt{3}\right)^2$

(a) 24 (b) 48 (c) $16\sqrt{3}$ (d) 96

66. $\left(12\sqrt{5}\right)^2$

(a) 60 (b) 1440 (c) 720 (d) 360

67. $\left(4\sqrt{11}\right)^2$

(a) 176 (b) 88 (c) 44 (d) 484

68. $\left(7\sqrt{2}\right)^2$

(a) 49 (b) 196 (c) 98 (d) $98\sqrt{2}$

69. $\left(20\sqrt{5}\right)^2$

(a) 2000 (b) 1000 (c) 10000 (d) 4000

70. $\left(8\sqrt{2}\right)^3$

(a) 256 (b) 512 (c) 1024 (d) $1024\sqrt{2}$

71. $\left(4\sqrt{13}\right)^2$

(a) 104 (b) 208 (c) 52 (d) $52\sqrt{13}$

72. $\left(3\sqrt{7}\right)^2$

(a) 63 (b) 21 (c) 147 (d) 42

73. $\left(4\sqrt{7}\right)^2$

(a) 57 (b) 112 (c) 224 (d) 98

74. $\left(5\sqrt{7}\right)^2$

(a) 125 (b) 246 (c) 175 (d) 225

75. $\left(20\sqrt{3}\right)^2$

(a) 3600 (b) 60 (c) 1200 (d) 600

76. $\left(10\sqrt{3}\right)^2$

(a) $30\sqrt{3}$ (b) 150 (c) 30 (d) 300

77. $\left(7\sqrt{5}\right)^2$

(a) $49\sqrt{5}$ (b) 49 (c)75 (d) 245

78. $\left(2\sqrt{8}\right)^2$

(a) 32 (b) 16 (c) $32\sqrt{2}$ (d) $16\sqrt{2}$

79. $\left(3\sqrt{8}\right)^2$

(a) 108 (b) 72 (c) 36 (d) 24

80. $\left(5\sqrt{8}\right)^2$

(a) $40\sqrt{2}$ (b) 40 (c) 200 (d) 400

81. $\left(6\sqrt{8}\right)^2$

(a) 288 (b) 144 (c) 384 (d) $144\sqrt{2}$

82. $\left(2\sqrt{15}\right)^2$

(a) $30\sqrt{15}$ (b) 30 (c) 60 (d) 90

83. $\left(3\sqrt{15}\right)^2$

(a) 135 (b) 225 (c) 405 (d) 81

84. $\left(4\sqrt{15}\right)^2$

(a) $64\sqrt{5}$ (b) 60 (c) 120 (d) 240

85. $\left(\sqrt{7}\right)^3$

(a) $7\sqrt{7}$ (b) 49 (c) 98 (d) $14\sqrt{7}$

86. $\left(5\sqrt{2}\right)^2$

(a) 100 (b) 50 (c) 25 (d) $25\sqrt{2}$

87. $\left(6\sqrt{7}\right)^2$

(a) 42 (b) 147 (c) 252 (d) 294

88. $\left(15\sqrt{4}\right)^2$

(a) 800 (b) 180 (c) 300 (d) 900

89. $\left(3\sqrt{6}\right)^2$

(a) 54 (b) 27 (c) $18\sqrt{6}$ (d) $54\sqrt{3}$

90. $\left(25\sqrt{3}\right)^2$

(a) 225 (b) 1875 (c) 3750 (d) 1350

91. $\left(8\sqrt{5}\right)^2$

(a) $64\sqrt{5}$ (b) 160 (c) 320 (d) 200

92. $\left(11\sqrt{5}\right)^2$

(a) 605 (b) 360 (c) $144\sqrt{5}$ (d) 180

93. $\left(14\sqrt{5}\right)^2$

(a) 325 (b) 4225 (c) 980 (d) $169\sqrt{5}$

94. $\left(2\sqrt{25}\right)^2$

(a) 50 (b) 1000 (c) 75 (d) 100

95. $\left(3\sqrt{25}\right)^2$

(a) 250 (b) 225 (c) 500 (d) 450

96. $\left(2\sqrt{14}\right)^2$

(a) $28\sqrt{7}$ (b) 28 (c) 56 (d) $14\sqrt{2}$

97. $\left(2\sqrt{3}\right)^2$

(a) 12 (b) 6 (c) 18 (d) 24

98. $\left(4\sqrt{3}\right)^2$

(a) 48 (b) 24 (c) 12 (d) 96

99. $\left(5\sqrt{3}\right)^2$

(a) 50 (b) 75 (c) 150 (d) $75\sqrt{3}$

100. $\left(9\sqrt{2}\right)^2$

(a) 18 (b) 81 (c) 162 (d) $81\sqrt{2}$

101. $\left(11\sqrt{2}\right)^2$

(a) 484 (b) 22 (c) 242 (d) 220

102. $\left(15\sqrt{4}\right)^2$

(a) 300 (b) 120 (c) 800 (d) 900

103. $\left(20\sqrt{2}\right)^2$

(a) 800 (b) 1600 (c) 400 (d) 1200

104. $\left(30\sqrt{2}\right)^2$

(a) 1800 (b) 900 (c) 300 (d) 600

105. $\left(\sqrt{8}\right)^2$

(a) 8 (b) 16 (c) 64 (d) 512

106. $\left(\sqrt{18}\right)^3$

(a) 324 (b) $36\sqrt{3}$ (c) $54\sqrt{2}$ (d) 54

107. $\left(\sqrt{13}\right)^3$

(a) $26\sqrt{13}$ (b) $13\sqrt{13}$ (c) 169 (d) 13

108. $\left(6\sqrt{2}\right)^2$

(a) 72 (b) 36 (c) 24 (d) 12

109. $\left(\sqrt{14}\right)^3$

(a) 56 (b) 7 (c) $14\sqrt{14}$ (d) 14

110. $\left(4\sqrt{6}\right)^2$

(a) 96 (b) 49 (c) 48 (d) 24

111. $\left(9\sqrt{5}\right)^2$

(a) 2025 (b) $81\sqrt{5}$ (c) 81 (d) 405

112. $\left(3\sqrt{14}\right)^2$

(a) 126 (b) 53 (c) 63 (d) 42

113. $\left(\sqrt{17}\right)^3$

(a) 17 (b) 34 (c) $17\sqrt{17}$ (d) 289

114. $\left(\sqrt{29}\right)^2$

(a) 29 (b) 58 (c) $29\sqrt{2}$ (d) 9

115. $\left(\sqrt{30}\right)^3$

(a) 30 (b) 900 (c) $30\sqrt{30}$ (d) $90\sqrt{3}$

116. $\left(\sqrt{40}\right)^2$

(a) 20 (b) 40 (c) 60 (d) 80

117. $\left(\sqrt{50}\right)^3$

(a) 50 (b) $150\sqrt{3}$ (c) 150 (d) $250\sqrt{2}$

118. $\left(\sqrt{12}\right)^3$

(a) $24\sqrt{3}$ (b) 24 (c) 72 (d) 36

119. $\left(2\sqrt{2}\right)^3$

(a) $16\sqrt{2}$ (b) 512 (c) 64 (d) 16

120. $\left(3\sqrt{3}\right)^3$

(a) 27 (b) $81\sqrt{3}$ (c) 81 (d) 243

121. $\left(4\sqrt{2}\right)^3$

(a) 64 (b) 128 (c) $128\sqrt{2}$ (d) 48

122. $\left(5\sqrt{2}\right)^2$

(a) 50 (b) 25 (c) 100 (d) 75

123. $\left(6\sqrt{2}\right)^2$

(a) 36 (b) 48 (c) 72 (d) 120

124. $\left(\sqrt{11}\right)^3$

(a) $11\sqrt{11}$ (b) 11 (c) 121 (d) 111

125. $\left(9\sqrt{2}\right)^2$

(a) 81 (b) 36 (c) 162 (d) 343

Type-1: Answer - Key

1.	(c)	26.	(c)	51.	(c)	76.	(d)	101.	(c)
2.	(d)	27.	(d)	52.	(b)	77.	(d)	102.	(d)
3.	(b)	28.	(b)	53.	(d)	78.	(a)	103.	(a)
4.	(c)	29.	(a)	54.	(b)	79.	(b)	104.	(a)
5.	(d)	30.	(c)	55.	(a)	80.	(c)	105.	(a)
6.	(a)	31.	(d)	56.	(c)	81.	(a)	106.	(c)
7.	(a)	32.	(a)	57.	(b)	82.	(c)	107.	(b)
8.	(c)	33.	(c)	58.	(b)	83.	(a)	108.	(a)
9.	(b)	34.	(b)	59.	(a)	84.	(d)	109.	(c)
10.	(d)	35.	(c)	60.	(b)	85.	(a)	110.	(a)
11.	(d)	36.	(c)	61.	(c)	86.	(b)	111.	(d)
12.	(a)	37.	(a)	62.	(a)	87.	(c)	112.	(a)
13.	(c)	38.	(a)	63.	(d)	88.	(d)	113.	(c)
14.	(a)	39.	(a)	64.	(a)	89.	(a)	114.	(a)
15.	(b)	40.	(b)	65.	(b)	90.	(b)	115.	(c)
16.	(c)	41.	(b)	66.	(c)	91.	(c)	116.	(b)
17.	(b)	42.	(d)	67.	(a)	92.	(a)	117.	(d)
18.	(c)	43.	(a)	68.	(c)	93.	(c)	118.	(a)
19.	(a)	44.	(c)	69.	(a)	94.	(d)	119.	(a)
20.	(c)	45.	(a)	70.	(d)	95.	(b)	120.	(b)
21.	(c)	46.	(c)	71.	(b)	96.	(c)	121.	(c)
22.	(d)	47.	(d)	72.	(a)	97.	(a)	122.	(a)
23.	(a)	48.	(b)	73.	(b)	98.	(a)	123.	(c)
24.	(b)	49.	(a)	74.	(c)	99.	(b)	124.	(a)
25.	(a)	50.	(d)	75.	(c)	100.	(c)	125.	(c)

Type-2

☞ इस प्रकार के सवालों को हल करने के लिए हमें वर्ग (Square), वर्गमूल (Square Root), घन (Cube), घनमूल (Cube Root) आदि के बारे में पता होना चाहिए।

Hint:

$$\boxed{\left(\sqrt{7}\right)^2 + \left(\sqrt{4}\right)^2}$$

$7 + 4 = \boxed{11}$ Ans.

या

$$\left(\sqrt{7}\right)^2 + \left(\sqrt{4}\right)^2$$

☞ चूंकि Power (घात) 2 है और $\sqrt{}$ वर्गमूल (Square Root) है, इसलिए संख्या को वर्गमूल में 2 बार लिखेंगे और समान number का दो का जोड़ा (Pair) बनाएंगे और इस तरह ये number वर्गमूल (Square Root) से बाहर आ जाएगा और वर्गमूल (Square Root) हट जाएगा।

$$\sqrt{\underline{7 \times 7}} + \sqrt{\underline{4 \times 4}}$$

$7 + 4 = \boxed{11}$ Ans.

Hint:

$$\left(\sqrt{21}\right)^3 \times \frac{3}{7}$$

☞ चूंकि Power 3 है तो वर्गमूल (Square Root) वाले Number को 3 बार गुणा (Multiplication) करेंगे।

$$\sqrt{\underbrace{21 \times 21}\times 21} \times \frac{3}{7}$$

21 का जोड़ा (Pair) बन रहा है इसलिए जोड़े वाला 21 बाहर आ जाएगा और शेष 21 वर्गमूल में रहेगा क्योंकि इसका जोड़ा नहीं बना

$$\overset{3}{\cancel{21}} \times \sqrt{21} \times \frac{3}{\cancel{7}} = \boxed{9\sqrt{21}} \text{ Ans.}$$

Hint:

$$\left(\sqrt[3]{125}\right)^2 + \left(\sqrt[3]{343}\right)^2$$

☞ यहाँ $\sqrt[3]{\ }$ घनमूल (Cube Root) है इसलिए 3 का जोड़ा (Pair) बनाएंगे और जो जोड़ा (Pair) बन जाएगा वो $\sqrt[3]{\ }$ से बाहर आ जाएगा।

$$\left(\sqrt[3]{\underline{5 \times 5 \times 5}}\right)^2 + \left(\sqrt[3]{\underline{7 \times 7 \times 7}}\right)^2$$

$$\left(\sqrt[3]{5^3}\right)^2 + \left(\sqrt[3]{7^3}\right)^2$$

$= 25 + 49 = \boxed{74}$ Ans.

Exercise

- **FIND THE VALUE OF:-**

1. $\left(\sqrt{7}\right)^2 + \left(\sqrt{4}\right)^2$

(a) 57 (b) $\sqrt{11}$ (c) 10 (d) 11

2. $\left(\sqrt{3}\right)^2 + \left(\sqrt{5}\right)^2$

(a) 34 (b) $\sqrt{8}$ (c) 8 (d) $\sqrt{19}$

3. $\left(\sqrt{6}\right)^2 + \left(2\sqrt{2}\right)^2$

(a) 10 (b) $\sqrt{40}$ (c) 14 (d) 28

4. $5^2 + \left(\sqrt{3}\right)^2$

(a) 8 (b) 28 (c) 14 (d) 34

5. $2 \times \left(\sqrt{3}\right)^3$

(a) 54 (b) $9\sqrt{3}$ (c) $6\sqrt{3}$ (d) 18

6. $\left(\sqrt{21}\right)^3 \times \frac{3}{7}$

(a) $9\sqrt{21}$ (b) 9 (c) $3\sqrt{21}$ (d) 63

7. $2 \times \left(\sqrt{5}\right)^2$

(a) $4\sqrt{5}$ (b) 50 (c) 20 (d) 10

8. $6 \times \left(2\sqrt{2}\right)^2$

(a) 48 (b) 24 (c) 36 (d) 72

9. $\left(4\sqrt{2}\right)^2 + 9$

(a) 73 (b) 50 (c) 36 (d) 41

10. $\left(6\sqrt{3}\right)^2 - 4$

(a) 104 (b) 52 (c) 32 (d) 112

11. $9 \times \left(\sqrt{11}\right)^3$

(a) 99 (b) $33\sqrt{11}$ (c) $99\sqrt{11}$ (d) 99

12. $\left(\sqrt{17}\right)^2 + 13$

(a) 30 (b) 31 (c) 50 (d) 40

13. $\left(\sqrt{12}\right)^3 / 6$

(a) $6\sqrt{2}$ (b) $16\sqrt{3}$ (c) 24 (d) $4\sqrt{3}$

14. $\left(6\sqrt{2}\right)^2 + \left(3\sqrt{2}\right)^2$

(a) 60 (b) 70 (c) 80 (d) 90

15. $\left(9\sqrt{4}\right)^2 - 40$

(a) 364 (b) 324 (c) 284 (d) 244

16. $\left(\sqrt{21}\right)^3 \times \frac{2}{3}$

(a) $14\sqrt{21}$ (b) 42 (c) 98 (d) $28\sqrt{3}$

17. $5^2 + \left(\sqrt{7}\right)^2$

(a) 74 (b) 12 (c) 16 (d) 32

18. $9^2 - \left(\sqrt{5}\right)^2$

(a) 76 (b) 13 (c) 86 (d) 72

19. $8^2 - \left(2\sqrt{2}\right)^2$

(a) 58 (b) 48 (c) 28 (d) 56

20. $\left(6\sqrt{2}\right)^2 \times \frac{1}{4}$

(a) 9 (b) 12 (c) 18 (d) 24

21. $\left(7\sqrt{5}\right)^2 \times \frac{8}{5}$

(a) 392 (b) 350 (c) 400 (d) 560

22. $\left(5\sqrt{2}\right)^2 \times \frac{3}{5}$

(a) 30 (b) 60 (c) 90 (d) 45

23. $\left(9\sqrt{3}\right)^2 \times \frac{4}{81}$

(a) 162 (b) 6 (c) 12 (d) 18

24. $\left(2\sqrt{2}\right)^2 + 3$

(a) 11 (b) 19 (c) 7 (d) 15

25. $\left(5\sqrt{5}\right)^2 + 30$

(a) 120 (b) 150 (c) 155 (d) 175

26. $\left(\sqrt{17}\right)^3 \times 7$

(a) $119\sqrt{17}$ (b) 119 (c) 238 (d) $98\sqrt{17}$

27. $\left(\sqrt{20}\right)^3 \times \frac{5}{4}$

(a) 50 (b) $25\sqrt{5}$ (c) $50\sqrt{5}$ (d) 100

28. $\left(7\sqrt{5}\right)^2 + 25$

(a) 270 (b) 250 (c) 240 (d) 260

29. $\left(2\sqrt{7}\right)^2 + 16 \times 7$

(a) 150 (b) 140 (c) 120 (d) 130

30. $\left(9\sqrt{2}\right)^2 - \left(6\sqrt{2}\right)^2$

(a) 80 (b) 120 (c) 100 (d) 90

31. $\left(3\sqrt{3}\right)^2 + \left(2\sqrt{2}\right)^2$

(a) 35 (b) 30 (c) 70 (d) 40

32. $\left(2\sqrt{5}\right)^2 + \left(4\sqrt{2}\right)^2$

(a) 62 (b) 52 (c) 50 (d) 27

33. $\left(3\sqrt{6}\right)^2 + \left(6\sqrt{3}\right)^2$

(a) 172 (b) 168 (c) 162 (d) 160

34. $\left(2\sqrt{4}\right)^2 + \left(\sqrt[3]{15}\right)^3$

(a) 21 (b) 31 (c) 30 (d) 41

35. $\left(\sqrt[3]{17}\right)^3 - \left(\sqrt{8}\right)^2$

(a) 9 (b) 7 (c) 1 (d) 3

36. $\left(11\sqrt{2}\right)^2 - \left(3\sqrt{3}\right)^2$

(a) 220 (b) 215 (c) 210 (d) 225

37. $\left(\sqrt[3]{15}\right)^2$

(a) 30 (b) $15^{\frac{2}{3}}$ (c) $\sqrt[3]{30}$ (d) 60

38. $\left(\sqrt[3]{27}\right)^2 + \left(\sqrt[3]{64}\right)^2$

(a) 25 (b) 50 (c) 91 (d) 73

39. $\left(\sqrt[3]{125}\right)^2 + \left(\sqrt[3]{343}\right)^2$

(a) 72 (b) 73 (c) 74 (d) 75

40. $\left(\sqrt{625}\right)^2 - \left(\sqrt[3]{64}\right)^5$

(a) 100 (b) 399 (c) –400 (d) –399

41. $2\sqrt[3]{512} - 3\sqrt[3]{8}$

(a) 10 (b) 8 (c) 9 (d) 12

42. $\left(\sqrt[3]{729}\right)^2 - 3\sqrt[3]{8}$

(a) 75 (b) 15 (c) 16 (d) 14

43. $14 \times \sqrt[4]{16}$

(a) 112 (b) 28 (c) 14 (d) 32

44. $4 \times \sqrt[4]{81}$

(a) 54 (b) 24 (c) 12 (d) 18

45. $\left[\sqrt[5]{32}\right]^3 + \left[\sqrt[3]{125}\right]^2$

(a) 33 (b) 30 (c) 36 (d) 63

46. $\frac{\sqrt[4]{625}}{25} + 15$

(a) 15.20 (b) 25 (c) 16 (d) 15.25

47. $\left[\sqrt[3]{4}\right]^2 \div \sqrt[3]{2}$

(a) 2 (b) $4\sqrt[3]{2}$ (c) 4 (d) $2\sqrt[3]{2}$

48. $\left(\sqrt{32}\right)^2 - \left(\sqrt{15}\right)^2$

(a) 17 (b) 15 (c) 16 (d) $6\sqrt{3}$

49. $3\sqrt[3]{27} - 4\sqrt[4]{16}$

(a) 1 (b) 10 (c) 2 (d) 5

Type-2: Answer - Key

1.	(d)	**11.**	(c)	**21.**	(a)	**31.**	(a)	**41.**	(a)
2.	(c)	**12.**	(a)	**22.**	(a)	**32.**	(b)	**42.**	(a)
3.	(c)	**13.**	(d)	**23.**	(c)	**33.**	(c)	**43.**	(b)
4.	(b)	**14.**	(d)	**24.**	(a)	**34.**	(b)	**44.**	(c)
5.	(c)	**15.**	(c)	**25.**	(c)	**35.**	(a)	**45.**	(a)
6.	(a)	**16.**	(a)	**26.**	(a)	**36.**	(b)	**46.**	(a)
7.	(d)	**17.**	(d)	**27.**	(c)	**37.**	(b)	**47.**	(a)
8.	(a)	**18.**	(a)	**28.**	(a)	**38.**	(a)	**48.**	(a)
9.	(d)	**19.**	(d)	**29.**	(b)	**39.**	(c)	**49.**	(a)
10.	(a)	**20.**	(c)	**30.**	(d)	**40.**	(d)		

Type-3

Find the approximate value of:-

$\sqrt{5}$

☞ पहले 5 को 100 से गुणा करना (500) है अब देखना है कि किसके वर्ग (Square) के करीब है जो (22) के वर्ग (Square) करीब नजर आ रहा है तो उससे एक अंक (Digit) पहले Decimal लगा देना (2.2) या उससे थोड़ा ज्यादा तो (2.236) Answer होगा।

$\frac{1}{\sqrt{2}}$

☞ $\frac{1}{\sqrt{2}}$ का मतलब होता है $\frac{\sqrt{2}}{2}$ जिसे हम Rationalise कहते है।

$\frac{\sqrt{2}}{2} = \frac{1.414}{2} = 0.707$

$\sqrt{1.42}$

☞ $\sqrt{1.42} = \sqrt{144}$ जो 12 के बराबर है लेकिन उससे कम है तो 1.2 नहीं 1.19 Answer होगा।

$\sqrt{0.6}$

☞ $\sqrt{0.6} =$ को जब 100 से गुणा करेगे तो 60 बनेगा 6 के करीब 8 और 7 का वर्ग होता है तो 0.8 से 0.7 Answer जब No.

एक छोटा होता है तो

$$\begin{bmatrix} x<1 \ \sqrt{x}>x>x^2 \text{ जब ये pattern follow होता है} \\ x>1 \ \sqrt{x}<x<x^2 \end{bmatrix}$$

$0.5 \times \sqrt[3]{0.125}$

$= 0.5 \times 0.5 = 0.25$ Answer

$\sqrt[3]{0.008}$

☞ जब cube root निकालेंगे तब (1000) से गुणा करेगें और देखना है कि किसके cube के करीब है और एक अंक पहले Decimal लगा देगें।

☞ **Solution:** 0.008 को 1000 से गुणा करेगें तो (8) आ गया अब हमने देखा है कि (8) (2) का cube होता है तो एक अंक पहले Decimal लगा देंगे 0.2 जो हमारा Answer हो जाएगा।

Exercise

- **FIND APPROXIMATE VALUE:-**

1. $\sqrt{2}$

(a) 1.414 (b) 1.824 (c) 2.214 (d) 1.212

2. $\sqrt{3}$

(a) 1.236 (b) 1.732 (c) 2.244 (d) 1.984

3. $\sqrt{5}$

(a) 2.236 (b) 2.436 (c) 3.345 (d) 2.021

4. $\sqrt{6}$
(a) 2.654 (b) 2.449 (c) 3.345 (d) 3.432

5. $\sqrt{10}$
(a) 2.458 (b) 3.348 (c) 3.242 (d) 3.162

6. $1/\sqrt{2}$
(a) 0.707 (b) 0.52 (c) 0.12 (d) 1.2

7. $1/\sqrt{3}$
(a) 0.845 (b) 0.214 (c) 0.577 (d) 0.865

8. $\sqrt{2.25}$
(a) 1.5 (b) 0.15 (c) 15 (d) 0.25

9. $\sqrt{1.70}$
(a) 1.90 (b) 1.30 (c) 1.40 (d) 1.50

10. $\sqrt{1.42}$
(a) 1.20 (b) 1.19 (c) 1.60 (d) 1.45

11. $\sqrt{1.19}$
(a) 1.09 (b) 1.41 (c) 1.21 (d) 1.01

12. $\sqrt{3.2}$
(a) 1.92 (b) 1.45 (c) 2.24 (d) 1.78

13. $\sqrt{4.4}$
(a) 2.53 (b) 2.09 (c) 2.72 (d) 2.42

14. $\sqrt{7}$
(a) 2.235 (b) 2.123 (c) 2.645 (d) 2.245

15. $\sqrt{8}$

(a) 2.648 (b) 2.828 (c) 2.212 (d) 2.542

16. $\sqrt{9.6}$

(a) 3.09 (b) 3.52 (c) 3.4 (d) 4.1

17. $\sqrt{10.2}$

(a) 3.24 (b) 3.42 (c) 3.68 (d) 3.19

18. $\sqrt{6.8}$

(a) 2.90 (b) 2.80 (c) 2.60 (d) 3.12

19. $3\sqrt{2}$

(a) 4.243 (b) 4.424 (c) 6.424 (d) 4.836

20. $5\sqrt{2}$

(a) 7.824 (b) 10 (c) 7.071 (d) 9.06

21. $7\sqrt{2}$

(a) 9.89 (b) 9.43 (c) 10.9 (d) 6

22. $8\sqrt{2}$

(a) 10.48 (b) 11.31 (c) 12.42 (d) 11.96

23. $9\sqrt{3}$

(a) 24.42 (b) 11.48 (c) 12.42 (d) 15.58

24. $3\sqrt{3}$

(a) 5.196 (b) 5.987 (c) 4.642 (d) 4.562

25. $4\sqrt{3}$

(a) 6.2 (b) 7.42 (c) 6.928 (d) 8.928

26. $2\sqrt{5}$

(a) 6.42 (b) 4.47 (c) 8.96 (d) 5.67

27. $3\sqrt{5}$

(a) 7.68 (b) 8.428 (c) 6.242 (d) 6.708

28. $6\sqrt{5}$

(a) 13.38 (b) 12.43 (c) 15.98 (d) 11.67

29. $2\sqrt{6}$

(a) 12 (b) 8.2 (c) 4.8 (d) 6

30. $3\sqrt{6}$

(a) 8.3 (b) 7.34 (c) 9.34 (d) 4.34

31. $\frac{3}{\sqrt{2}}$

(a) 2.12 (b) 3.12 (c) 4.12 (d) 5.12

32. $\frac{5}{\sqrt{2}}$

(a) 1.54 (b) 3.54 (c) 2.54 (d) 4.54

33. $\frac{7}{\sqrt{2}}$

(a) 3.95 (b) 5.95 (c) 4.95 (d) 6.95

34. $\frac{2}{\sqrt{3}}$

(a) 2.864 (b) 1.154 (c) 2.234 (d) 3.765

35. $\frac{4}{\sqrt{3}}$

(a) 2.30 (b) 4.54 (c) 3.68 (d) 1.89

36. $\sqrt{2.89}$

(a) 0.17 (b) 3.4 (c) 1.7 (d) 0.017

37. $\sqrt{0.6}$

(a) 0.7 (b) 0.6 (c) 0.5 (d) 0.9

38. $\sqrt{0.5}$

(a) 0.4 (b) 0.7 (c) 0.5 (d) 0.2

39. $\sqrt{0.16}$

(a) 0.4 (b) 4 (c) 0.04 (d) 1.2

40. $\sqrt{0.26}$

(a) 0.81 (b) 0.41 (c) 0.51 (d) 0.24

41. $2\sqrt{10}$

(a) 6.32 (b) 5.65 (c) 8.48 (d) 4.42

42. $\sqrt[3]{0.008}$

(a) 0.5 (b) 0.2 (c) 2 (d) 0.02

43. $\sqrt[3]{0.001}$

(a) 0.01 (b) 1 (c) 0.1 (d) 0.001

44. $\sqrt[3]{0.125}$

(a) 0.25 (b) 0.05 (c) 0.5 (d) 5

45. $\sqrt[3]{0.064}$

(a) 0.4 (b) 0.04 (c) 0.8 (d) 0.004

46. $\sqrt[3]{0.216}$

(a) 0.6 (b) 6 (c) 0.3 (d) 0.06

47. $\sqrt[3]{0.350}$

(a) 0.63 (b) 0.704 (c) 0.8 (d) 0.9

48. $\sqrt[3]{0.520}$

(a) 0.5 (b) 0.65 (c) 0.408 (d) 0.804

49. $\sqrt[3]{0.729}$

(a) 0.3 (b) 0.9 (c) 1.1 (d) 1

50. $\sqrt[3]{1.330}$

(a) 1 (b) 11 (c) 0.11 (d) 1.1

51. $\sqrt[3]{1.729}$

(a) 12 (b) 1.2 (c) 0.12 (d) 1.12

52. $2\sqrt[3]{0.008}$

(a) 40 (b) 0.2 (c) 0.4 (d) 4

53. $3\sqrt[3]{0.008}$

(a) 0.006 (b) 0.6 (c) 6 (d) 0.06

54. $0.4\sqrt[3]{0.001}$

(a) 0.4 (b) 40 (c) 4 (d) 0.04

55. $0.5 \times \sqrt[3]{0.125}$

(a) 2.25 (b) 2.5 (c) 0.25 (d) 0.025

56. $\sqrt[3]{0.125} \times \sqrt{2.25}$

(a) 0.75 (b) 2.5 (c) 7.5 (d) 75

57. $\sqrt[3]{0.001} \times \sqrt{1.96}$

(a) 0.0014 (b) 1.4 (c) 0.14 (d) 0.014

58. $\sqrt[3]{1.331} \times \sqrt{0.25}$

(a) 0.55 (b) 5.5 (c) 10.2 (d) 1.5

59. $3 \times \sqrt[3]{1.728}$

(a) 7.2 (b) 1.8 (c) 3.6 (d) 1.2

60. $4 \times \sqrt[3]{0.064}$

(a) 1.6 (b) 0.32 (c) 0.16 (d) 3.2

61. $3 \times \sqrt[3]{0.125}$

(a) 0.15 (b) 1.8 (c) 1.5 (d) 1.2

62. $5 \times \sqrt[3]{0.216}$

(a) 3 (b) 6 (c) 0.3 (d) 0.6

63. $5 \times \sqrt{1.44}$

(a) 3 (b) 0.06 (c) 6 (d) 0.6

64. $6 \times \sqrt{6.25}$

(a) 15 (b) 1.5 (c) 30 (d) 3

65. $\sqrt[3]{0.216} \times \sqrt{0.25}$

(a) 0.003 (b) 0.03 (c) 0.3 (d) 3

66. $\sqrt[3]{0.729} \times \sqrt{0.81}$

(a) 0.81 (b) 1.6 (c) 0.36 (d) 8.1

67. $\sqrt[3]{0.026} \times \sqrt{2.89}$

(a) 1.7 (b) 0.89 (c) 0.51 (d) 3.4

68. $\sqrt{9.6} \times \sqrt[3]{0.008}$

(a) 4.2 (b) 0.24 (c) 0.62 (d) 1.02

69. $\sqrt{10.2} \times \sqrt[3]{1.330}$

(a) 5.36 (b) 3.51 (c) 4.25 (d) 3.81

70. $\sqrt{2} \times \sqrt[3]{0.216}$

(a) 0.36 (b) 1.2 (c) 0.72 (d) 0.84

71. $2\sqrt{2} \times \sqrt[3]{1.729}$

(a) 3.4 (b) 3.8 (c) 4.3 (d) 8.1

Type-3: Answer - Key

1.	(a)	**15.**	(b)	**29.**	(c)	**43.**	(c)	**57.**	(c)
2.	(b)	**16.**	(a)	**30.**	(b)	**44.**	(c)	**58.**	(a)
3.	(a)	**17.**	(d)	**31.**	(a)	**45.**	(a)	**59.**	(c)
4.	(b)	**18.**	(c)	**32.**	(b)	**46.**	(a)	**60.**	(a)
5.	(d)	**19.**	(a)	**33.**	(c)	**47.**	(b)	**61.**	(c)
6.	(a)	**20.**	(c)	**34.**	(b)	**48.**	(d)	**62.**	(a)
7.	(c)	**21.**	(a)	**35.**	(a)	**49.**	(b)	**63.**	(c)
8.	(a)	**22.**	(b)	**36.**	(c)	**50.**	(d)	**64.**	(a)
9.	(b)	**23.**	(d)	**37.**	(a)	**51.**	(b)	**65.**	(c)
10.	(b)	**24.**	(a)	**38.**	(b)	**52.**	(c)	**66.**	(a)
11.	(a)	**25.**	(c)	**39.**	(a)	**53.**	(b)	**67.**	(c)
12.	(d)	**26.**	(b)	**40.**	(c)	**54.**	(d)	**68.**	(c)
13.	(b)	**27.**	(d)	**41.**	(a)	**55.**	(c)	**69.**	(b)
14.	(c)	**28.**	(a)	**42.**	(b)	**56.**	(a)	**70.**	(d)
								71.	(a)

LCM

Hint :

10, 15

☞ LCM निकालने के लिए सबसे पहले बड़ी संख्या (15) को देखना है और देखकर पता करना है कि इसमें ऐसा कौन-सा Number नहीं है जो दूसरी संख्या (10) में है जो हमें (2) दिखाई दे रहा है तो इसलिए 15 को 2 से गुणा कर देगें तो Answer 30 आ जाएगा।

Example:

Non-common ↑ (2), Common ↷ (5)

$10 \Rightarrow \boxed{2} \times \boxed{5}$

$15 \Rightarrow \boxed{3} \times \boxed{5}$

बड़ी संख्या (15) को देखना है जो common नहीं है (10) में वो 2 है तो 15 × 2 = 30 Answer

Exercise

1. 10,15

(a) 50 (b) 30 (c) 15 (d) 20

2. 20, 30

(a) 120 (b) 40 (c) 60 (d) 100

3. 40, 70

(a) 420 (b) 240 (c) 280 (d) 210

4. 10,20,30
(a) 40 (b) 60 (c) 30 (d) 90

5. 60,15,30
(a) 120 (b) 180 (c) 90 (d) 60

6. 45,30,60
(a) 240 (b) 120 (c) 90 (d) 180

7. 90,120,80
(a) 120 (b) 720 (c) 360 (d) 240

8. 30,40,50
(a) 240 (b) 900 (c) 600 (d) 720

9. 18,30,60
(a) 90 (b) 120 (c) 60 (d) 180

10. 12,15,30
(a) 60 (b) 80 (c) 90 (d) 120

11. 40,80,120
(a) 250 (b) 120 (c) 240 (d) 360

12. 36,48,72
(a) 144 (b) 216 (c) 360 (d) 240

13. 30,45,90
(a) 180 (b) 120 (c) 160 (d) 90

14. 24,30,36
(a) 360 (b) 120 (c) 240 (d) 180

15. 12,9,15
(a) 120 (b) 180 (c) 60 (d) 150

16. 6,12,15
(a) 36 (b) 60 (c) 45 (d) 90

17. 8,12,15

(a) 120 (b) 100 (c) 60 (d) 80

18. 18,24,36

(a) 120 (b) 36 (c) 72 (d) 84

19. 20,25,30

(a) 150 (b) 360 (c) 180 (d) 300

20. 40,36,24

(a) 720 (b) 360 (c) 320 (d) 600

21. 16,24,48

(a) 36 (b) 48 (c) 72 (d) 120

22. 45,15,60

(a) 120 (b) 90 (c) 180 (d) 300

23. 12,18,36

(a) 36 (b) 18 (c) 72 (d) 180

24. 21,42,63

(a) 126 (b) 166 (c) 136 (d) 176

25. 55,66,50

(a) 1650 (b) 1100 (c) 1560 (d) 1210

26. 72,90,180

(a) 180 (b) 360 (c) 720 (d) 900

27. 24,6,16

(a) 48 (b) 36 (c) 60 (d) 72

28. $\frac{7}{2}, \frac{9}{4}, \frac{8}{3}$

(a) $\frac{72}{7}$ (b) 504 (c) $\frac{504}{12}$ (d) 252

29. $\frac{3}{4},\frac{4}{5},\frac{6}{7}$

(a) 12 (b) 16 (c) $\frac{12}{7}$ (d) $\frac{12}{35}$

30. $\frac{9}{2},\frac{9}{4},3$

(a) 3 (b) $\frac{9}{4}$ (c) 9 (d) $\frac{9}{2}$

31. **20,30,50**

(a) 300 (b) 240 (c) 250 (d) 150

32. **5,6,7**

(a) 240 (b) 84 (c) 70 (d) 210

33. **2,3,5**

(a) 15 (b) 30 (c) 7.5 (d) 12

34. **24,16**

(a) 72 (b) 32 (c) 48 (d) 60

35. $\frac{1}{2},\frac{3}{4},1$

(a) $\frac{3}{4}$ (b) 3 (c) $\frac{3}{2}$ (d) 9

36. **8,12,16**

(a) 60 (b) 24 (c) 48 (d) 64

37. 15,20,30

(a) 50 (b) 100 (c) 120 (d) 60

38. 8,9,10

(a) 240 (b) 720 (c) 72 (d) 360

39. 10,12,15

(a) 30 (b) 60 (c) 120 (d) 180

40. 24,72,36

(a) 72 (b) 144 (c) 360 (d) 180

41. 10,15,20,30

(a) 30 (b) 60 (c) 120 (d) 90

42. 6,5,7.5

(a) 60 (b) 12 (c) 30 (d) 15

43. 10,20,25

(a) 100 (b) 80 (c) 150 (d) 300

44. 20,30,15

(a) 90 (b) 120 (c) 30 (d) 60

45. 5,20,36

(a) 180 (b) 300 (c) 120 (d) 144

46. 14,16

(a) 64 (b) 112 (c) 42 (d) 84

47. 5,60,7.5

(a) 60 (b) 80 (c) 300 (d) 120

48. $24, \frac{120}{7}$

(a) 168 (b) 100 (c) 120 (d) 140

49. 0.3, 0.4, 0.6

(a) 1.2 (b) 0.12 (c) 12 (d) 1.02

50. $\sqrt{3}, 2\sqrt{3}, 4$

(a) $\sqrt{3}$ (b) $4\sqrt{3}$ (c) $2\sqrt{3}$ (d) 12

LCM : Answer - Key

1.	(b)	11.	(c)	21.	(b)	31.	(a)	41.	(b)
2.	(c)	12.	(a)	22.	(c)	32.	(d)	42.	(c)
3.	(c)	13.	(d)	23.	(a)	33.	(b)	43.	(a)
4.	(b)	14.	(a)	24.	(a)	34.	(c)	44.	(d)
5.	(d)	15.	(b)	25.	(a)	35.	(b)	45.	(a)
6.	(d)	16.	(b)	26.	(b)	36.	(c)	46.	(b)
7.	(b)	17.	(a)	27.	(a)	37.	(d)	47.	(a)
8.	(c)	18.	(c)	28.	(b)	38.	(d)	48.	(c)
9.	(d)	19.	(d)	29.	(a)	39.	(b)	49.	(a)
10.	(a)	20.	(b)	30.	(c)	40.	(a)	50.	(b)

HCF

☞ HCF के लिए option से ऐसा Number देखें जो बड़े से बड़ा हो और सभी दिए गए Number को भाग करें।

Hint :

29, 667

(a) 29 (b) 667 (c) 23 (d) 21

☞ Option से 667 लेने पर देखा कि दोनों number 667 से विभाजित (Divide) नहीं हो रहे हैं।

अब 29 से भाग किया तो दोनो number भाग (Divide) हो रहे हैं। इसलिए H.C.F.= 29 होगा।

Hint :

240, 480, 960

(a) 120 (b) 240 (c) 480 (d) 125

☞ Option में सबसे बड़ा number 480 है और इससे सभी number विभाजित (Divide) नहीं हो रहे हैं अब 240 से विभाजित किया तो सभी number 240 से विभाजित हो रहे हैं। इसलिए H.C.F. = 240 होगा।

☞ **जब संख्या दशमलव (Decimal) में हों**

जब संख्या (N) दशमलव (Decimal) में हों इस प्रकार के प्रश्नों को हल करने के लिए सबसे पहले हम दशमलव (Decimal) हटाएंगे।

☞ दशमलव (Decimal) हटाने के लिए हम संख्या (Number) में जितने दशमलव (Decimal) हैं संख्या (Number) के हर (Denominators) में 1 के बाद उतने ही zero लगा देते हैं।

यानि अगर दशमलव (Decimal) के बाद यदि एक अंक (Digit) है तो हर (Denominator) में 10 लिखेंगे।

यदि 2 अंक (Digit) है तो हर (Denominator) में 100 लिखेंगे।

और इसी तरह ....

Hint:

0.6, 9.6, 0.36

(a) 0.6 (b) 0.12 (c) 0.18 (d) 0.16

☞ सबसे पहले हम दशमलव (Decimal) हटाएंगे, दशमलव (Decimal) बाद जितने अंक (Digit) होंगे उतने ही हर (Denominator) में 1 के बाद zero लगा देंगे।

$\frac{60}{10}, \frac{96}{10}, \frac{36}{100}$

H.C.F. के लिए अब हम अंश (Numerator) का H.C.F. निकालेंगे और हर (Denominator) का L.C.M. निकालेंगे।

$\frac{60}{10}, \frac{96}{10}, \frac{36}{100}$

H.C.F. = 12 क्योंकि ये सभी को विभाजित (Divide) कर रहा है। इसलिए (B) 0.12 H.C.F. होगा।

☞ **जब भिन्न (Fraction) वाली संख्या हो**

जब कभी भिन्न (Fraction) वाली संख्याओं (numbers) का H.C.F. निकालना हो तो हम अंश (Numerator) का H.C.F. निकालेंगे (जिस तरह से H.C.F. निकालते हैं) और हर (Denominator) का L.C.M. निकालेंगे।

Hint:

Option पर नजर रखकर आसानी से हल होगा।

$\boxed{\frac{2}{3}, \frac{1}{2}, \frac{3}{5}}$

(a) $\frac{2}{5}$ (b) $\frac{1}{30}$ (c) $\frac{3}{10}$ (d) $\frac{7}{30}$

☞ अंश (Numerator) को देखने से पता चला कि 2, 1 और 3 को सिर्फ 1 ही विभाजित कर सकता है। इसलिए अंश (Numerator) में 1 आएगा।

☞ अब हम हर (Denominator) का L.C.M. निकालेंगे।

3, 2, 5 का L.C.M. = 30 है। इसलिए H.C.F. = (B) $\frac{1}{30}$ होगा।

Note: जब हमने Numerator का H.C.F = 1 निकाला और Option में सिर्फ (B) option में 1 था तो वहीं Answer हुआ।

☞ **मिश्रित भिन्न (Mix Fraction)**

इस तरह के सवालों में सबसे पहले मिश्रित भिन्न (Mix Fraction) को हल करेंगे, फिर उसी तरह से H.C.F. निकालेंगे जिस तरह भिन्न (Fraction) वाले Number का H.C.F. निकाला है।

Hint:

$$\mathbf{2\frac{1}{3}, 4\frac{2}{3}, 5\frac{1}{4}}$$

(a) $\frac{12}{7}$ (b) $\frac{7}{12}$ (c) $\frac{5}{3}$ (d) $\frac{5}{4}$

$\Rightarrow \frac{7}{3}, \frac{14}{3}, \frac{21}{4}$

अब उसी तरह हल करेंगे जिस तरह भिन्न (Fraction) वाले Number का H.C.F. निकाला है।

H.C.F. = $\frac{7}{12}$ Option (B) Ans.

Exercise

1. 5, 10

(a) 10 (b) 2.5 (c) 5 (d) 15

2. 7, 21

(a) 21 (b) 7 (c) 3.5 (d) 147

3. 29, 667

(a) 29 (b) 667 (c) 23 (d) 21

4. 852, 1491

(a) 852 (b) 1491 (c) 213 (d) 217

5. 153, 323

(a) 19 (b) 153 (c) 323 (d) 17

6. 875, 1225

(a) 35 (b) 245 (c) 875 (d) 1225

7. 128, 240

(a) 128 (b) 16 (c) 240 (d) 120

8. 117, 455

(a) 117 (b) 35 (c) 13 (d) 17

9. 945, 2475

(a) 45 (b) 105 (c) 99 (d) 75

10. 23, 667

(a) 29 (b) 23 (c) 27 (d) 667

11. 5, 10, 25

(a) 5 (b) 10 (c) 15 (d) 25

12. 3, 21, 63

(a) 7 (b) 3 (c) 21 (d) 63

13. 126, 144, 162

(a) 12 (b) 14 (c) 18 (d) 16

14. 121, 187, 286
(a) 121 (b) 11 (c) 22 (d) 13

15. 585, 945, 2475
(a) 55 (b) 45 (c) 35 (d) 75

16. 1397, 1651, 2032
(a) 127 (b) 123 (c) 137 (d) 129

17. 357, 833, 952
(a) 119 (b) 121 (c) 113 (d) 123

18. 240, 480, 960
(a) 120 (b) 240 (c) 480 (d) 125

19. 108, 288, 396
(a) 39 (b) 36 (c) 54 (d) 51

20. 192, 288, 336
(a) 48 (b) 47 (c) 49 (d) 192

21. 0.6, 9.6, 0.36
(a) 0.6 (b) 0.12 (c) 0.18 (d) 0.16

22. 1.75, 5.60, 7.00
(a) 0.35 (b) 0.25 (c) 7 (d) 5.6

23. 1.20, 22.5, 45
(a) 0.30 (b) 0.25 (c) 0.45 (d) 1.20

24. 0.48, 0.72, 0.108
(a) 0.12 (b) 0.012 (c) 1.2 (d) 0.48

25. 0.6, 1.5, 0.18
(a) 0.6 (b) 0.06 (c) 1.5 (d) 0.006

26. 1.5, 2.05, 3.5
(a) 1.5 (b) 0.5 (c) 0.005 (d) 0.05

27. 0.8, 0.125, 0.625, 0.5
(a) 0.25 (b) 0.0025 (c) 2.5 (d) 0.025

28. 0.216, 6, 2
(a) 2 (b) 0.8 (c) 0.008 (d) 0.08

29. **3, 2.7, 0.09**

(a) 3 (b) 0.3 (c) 0.003 (d) 0.03

30. **0.63, 0.84, 1.05**

(a) 0.21 (b) 2.1 (c) 0.021 (d) 0.63

31. $\frac{2}{3}, \frac{1}{2}, \frac{3}{5}$

(a) $\frac{2}{5}$ (b) $\frac{1}{30}$ (c) $\frac{3}{10}$ (d) $\frac{7}{30}$

32. $\frac{2}{3}, \frac{5}{8}, \frac{7}{9}, \frac{7}{12}$

(a) $\frac{5}{72}$ (b) $\frac{7}{72}$ (c) $\frac{1}{72}$ (d) $\frac{1}{12}$

33. $\frac{3}{8}, \frac{17}{19}, \frac{21}{23}$

(a) $\frac{3}{8}$ (b) $\frac{17}{3496}$ (c) $\frac{21}{3496}$ (d) $\frac{1}{3496}$

34. $\frac{2}{3}, \frac{8}{9}, \frac{16}{81}, \frac{10}{27}$

(a) $\frac{1}{81}$ (b) $\frac{16}{81}$ (c) $\frac{10}{81}$ (d) $\frac{2}{81}$

35. $\frac{16}{3}, \frac{48}{7}, \frac{96}{15}$

(a) $\frac{16}{7}$ (b) $\frac{16}{29}$ (c) $\frac{16}{105}$ (d) $\frac{19}{105}$

36. $\frac{21}{6}, \frac{98}{13}, \frac{154}{3}$

(a) $\frac{7}{78}$ (b) $\frac{154}{78}$ (c) $\frac{7}{13}$ (d) $\frac{21}{13}$

37. $\frac{15}{2}, \frac{30}{7}, \frac{105}{8}$

(a) $\frac{15}{8}$ (b) $\frac{15}{56}$ (c) $\frac{105}{56}$ (d) $\frac{56}{15}$

38. $\frac{852}{7}, \frac{1491}{14}, \frac{1065}{2}$

(a) $\frac{13}{14}$ (b) $\frac{27}{213}$ (c) $\frac{14}{213}$ (d) $\frac{213}{14}$

39. $\frac{8}{3}, \frac{12}{7}, \frac{64}{21}$

(a) $\frac{4}{21}$ (b) $\frac{8}{21}$ (c) $\frac{21}{4}$ (d) $\frac{21}{8}$

40. $\frac{2}{3}, \frac{6}{11}, \frac{10}{13}$

(a) $\frac{2}{429}$ (b) $\frac{429}{2}$ (c) $\frac{10}{429}$ (d) $\frac{429}{10}$

41. $4\frac{1}{2}, \frac{6}{5}, 10\frac{1}{2}$

(a) $\frac{3}{10}$ (b) $\frac{3}{2}$ (c) $\frac{10}{3}$ (d) $\frac{2}{3}$

42. $2\frac{1}{2}, 3\frac{1}{3}, 3\frac{3}{4}$

(a) $\frac{5}{12}$ (b) $\frac{12}{5}$ (c) $\frac{10}{3}$ (d) $\frac{5}{2}$

43. $9\frac{1}{11}, 19\frac{2}{22}$

(a) $\frac{11}{50}$ (b) $\frac{50}{11}$ (c) $\frac{10}{11}$ (d) $\frac{1}{11}$

44. $2\frac{1}{7}, 7\frac{1}{7}, 14\frac{2}{7}$

(a) $\frac{6}{7}$ (b) $\frac{7}{6}$ (c) $\frac{7}{5}$ (d) $\frac{5}{7}$

45. $12\frac{1}{2}, 8\frac{1}{3}, 16\frac{2}{3}$

(a) $\frac{25}{6}$ (b) $\frac{6}{25}$ (c) $\frac{3}{25}$ (d) $\frac{12}{25}$

46. $2\frac{1}{3}, 4\frac{2}{3}, 5\frac{1}{4}$

(a) $\frac{12}{7}$ (b) $\frac{7}{12}$ (c) $\frac{5}{3}$ (d) $\frac{5}{4}$

47. $5\frac{1}{5}, 7\frac{3}{7}, 3\frac{1}{4}$

(a) $\frac{140}{13}$ (b) $\frac{120}{7}$ (c) $\frac{7}{120}$ (d) $\frac{13}{140}$

48. $4\frac{1}{4}, 4\frac{6}{7}, 7\frac{5}{9}$

(a) $\frac{17}{9}$ (b) $\frac{17}{28}$ (c) $\frac{17}{252}$ (d) $\frac{252}{17}$

49. $14\frac{2}{7}, 16\frac{2}{3}, \frac{1}{4}$

(a) $\frac{100}{7}$ (b) $\frac{1}{84}$ (c) 84 (d) $\frac{9}{8.4}$

50. $33\frac{1}{3}, 66\frac{2}{3}, 6\frac{1}{4}$

(a) $\frac{12}{25}$ (b) $\frac{25}{12}$ (c) $\frac{33}{13}$ (d) $\frac{13}{33}$

HCF : Answer - Key

1.	(c)	**11.**	(a)	**21.**	(b)	**31.**	(b)	**41.**	(a)
2.	(b)	**12.**	(b)	**22.**	(a)	**32.**	(c)	**42.**	(a)
3.	(a)	**13.**	(c)	**23.**	(a)	**33.**	(d)	**43.**	(c)
4.	(c)	**14.**	(b)	**24.**	(b)	**34.**	(d)	**44.**	(d)
5.	(d)	**15.**	(b)	**25.**	(b)	**35.**	(c)	**45.**	(a)
6.	(a)	**16.**	(a)	**26.**	(d)	**36.**	(a)	**46.**	(b)
7.	(b)	**17.**	(a)	**27.**	(d)	**37.**	(b)	**47.**	(d)
8.	(c)	**18.**	(b)	**28.**	(c)	**38.**	(d)	**48.**	(c)
9.	(a)	**19.**	(b)	**29.**	(d)	**39.**	(a)	**49.**	(b)
10.	(b)	**20.**	(a)	**30.**	(a)	**40.**	(a)	**50.**	(b)

FRACTION (भिन्न)

Type-1

Hint :

$$1+\frac{2}{3}$$

☞ इस type में हर (Denominator) तो होगा ही mixed fraction में जो लिखा है उसे गुणा करना है और अंश (Numerator) में जोड़ देना है।

$$1+\frac{2}{3}=\frac{3\times1+2}{3}=\boxed{\frac{5}{3}}$$

Exercise

1. $1+\frac{2}{3}=?$

(a) 5/2 (b) 5/3 (c) 2/5 (d) 3/5

2. $3+\frac{1}{4}=?$

(a) 13/3 (b) 11/4 (c) 13/4 (d) 11/3

3. $\frac{7}{3}=1+?$

(a) 4/3 (b) 3/4 (c) 5/3 (d) 3/2

4. $\frac{9}{8} = 1 + ?$

(a) 8/9 (b) 1/9 (c) 7/8 (d) 1/8

5. $4 + \frac{1}{2} = ?$

(a) 9/4 (b) 7/2 (c) 9/2 (d) 5/2

6. $7 + \frac{1}{4} = ?$

(a) 29/4 (b) 29/2 (c) 27/4 (d) 27/2

7. $8 + \frac{1}{3} = ?$

(a) 8/3 (b) 25/3 (c) 3/8 (d) 23/3

8. $\frac{27}{33} = 1 - ?$

(a) 4/33 (b) 2/11 (c) 3/11 (d) 5/33

9. $\frac{13}{7} = 1 + ?$

(a) 8/7 (b) 5/7 (c) 4/7 (d) 6/7

10. $\frac{22}{5} =$ [illegible] + ?

(a) 2/5 (b) [illegible]5 (c) 5/2 (d) 4/5

11. $\frac{8}{11} = 1 - ?$

(a) 1/11 (b) 2/11 (c) 3/11 (d) 4/11

12. $\frac{19}{4} = 5 - ?$

(a) 1/4 (b) 1/5 (c) 5/4 (d) 4/5

13. $\frac{25}{8} = ? + \frac{1}{8}$

(a) 26/8 (b) 13/4 (c) 4 (d) 3

14. $7 + \frac{1}{7} = ?$

(a) 8/7 (b) 48/7 (c) 51/7 (d) 50/7

15. $9 + \frac{1}{9} = ?$

(a) 82/9 (b) 10/9 (c) 100/9 (d) 80/9

16. $8 + \frac{1}{4} = ?$

(a) 19/2 (b) 31/4 (c) 33/4 (d) 17/2

17. $5 + \frac{1}{3} = ?$

(a) 5/3 (b) 16/3 (c) 3/5 (d) 17/3

18. $6 + \frac{1}{4} = ?$

(a) 13/2 (b) 3/2 (c) 25/4 (d) 23/4

19. $8 + \frac{3}{7} = ?$

(a) 53/7 (b) 24/7 (c) 59/7 (d) 48/7

20. $9 + \frac{4}{5} = ?$

(a) 41/5 (b) 49/5 (c) 45/4 (d) 36/5

21. $2 + \frac{3}{5} = ?$

(a) 13/5 (b) 6/5 (c) 10/3 (d) 7/3

22. $4 + \frac{6}{11} = ?$

(a) 24/11 (b) 48/11 (c) 38/11 (d) 50/11

23. $9 + \frac{3}{7} = ?$

(a) 22/7 (b) 66/7 (c) 69/7 (d) 69/14

24. $10 + \frac{4}{13} = ?$

(a) 134/13 (b) 40/13 (c) 269/26 (d) 143/13

25. $15 + \frac{1}{2} = ?$

(a) 15/2 (b) 63/4 (c) 31/2 (d) 123/8

26. $\frac{18}{5} = 3 + ?$

(a) 8/15 (b) 3/5 (c) 4/4 (d) 5/3

27. $\frac{19}{7} = ? + \frac{5}{7}$

(a) 2 (b) 1 (c) 24/7 (d) 3

28. $\frac{28}{9} = 3 + ?$

(a) 1/3 (b) 2/9 (c) 2/3 (d) 1/9

29. $\frac{19}{16} = 1 + ?$

(a) 1/4 (b) 5/16 (c) 5/32 (d) 3/16

30. $\frac{58}{33} = 1 + ?$

(a) 26/33 (b) 23/33 (c) 25/33 (d) 29/33

31. $\frac{21}{43} = 1 - \frac{22}{?}$

(a) 21 (b) 43 (c) 86 (d) 34

32. $\frac{68}{3} = ? - \frac{1}{3}$

(a) 23 (b) 22 (c) 21 (d) 20

33. $\frac{46}{7} = 6 + ?$

(a) 4/7 (b) 7/4 (c) 5/7 (d) 7/5

34. $\frac{90}{7} = ? + \frac{6}{7}$

(a) 14 (b) 12 (c) 11 (d) 13

35. $\frac{25}{7} = 4 - ?$

(a) 2/7 (b) 4/7 (c) 5/14 (d) 3/7

36. $\frac{43}{9} = 4 + ?$

(a) 9/8 (b) 9/7 (c) 7/9 (d) 8/9

37. $\frac{96}{7} = ? + \frac{5}{7}$

(a) 12 (b) 14 (c) 13 (d) 15

38. $\frac{64}{3} = ? + \frac{1}{3}$

(a) 22 (b) 21 (c) 63 (d) 20

39. $\frac{28}{65} = 1 - ?$

(a) 37/65 (b) 27/65 (c) 73/130 (d) 67/130

40. $\frac{17}{36} = 1 - ?$

(a) 11/18 (b) 21/36 (c) 37/72 (d) 19/36

41. $\frac{19}{3} = 7 - ?$

(a) 7/6 (b) 4/3 (c) 2/3 (d) 1/3

Type-1: Answer - Key

1.	(b)	**10.**	(a)	**19.**	(c)	**28.**	(d)	**37.**	(c)
2.	(c)	**11.**	(c)	**20.**	(b)	**29.**	(d)	**38.**	(b)
3.	(a)	**12.**	(a)	**21.**	(a)	**30.**	(c)	**39.**	(a)
4.	(d)	**13.**	(d)	**22.**	(d)	**31.**	(b)	**40.**	(d)
5.	(c)	**14.**	(d)	**23.**	(b)	**32.**	(a)	**41.**	(c)
6.	(a)	**15.**	(a)	**24.**	(a)	**33.**	(a)		
7.	(b)	**16.**	(c)	**25.**	(c)	**34.**	(b)		
8.	(b)	**17.**	(b)	**26.**	(b)	**35.**	(d)		
9.	(d)	**18.**	(c)	**27.**	(a)	**36.**	(c)		

Type-2

Hint :

$\frac{2}{5} \times 3$

☞ 1 बारी में जाएगा एक शेषफल (Remainder) बचेगा 5 से भाग करने पर।

$\frac{2}{5} \times 3 = \frac{2 \times 3}{5} = \frac{6}{5} = 1\frac{1}{5}$

बिना लिखे Mind में Visualise करें

Exercise

1. $\frac{2}{5} \times 3 = ?$

(a) $1\frac{4}{5}$ (b) $1\frac{3}{5}$ (c) $1\frac{1}{5}$ (d) $1\frac{2}{5}$

2. $\frac{6 \times 7}{5} = ?$

(a) $7\frac{2}{5}$ (b) $8\frac{2}{5}$ (c) $9\frac{4}{5}$ (d) $10\frac{6}{5}$

3. $\frac{4 \times 8}{3} = ?$

(a) $10\frac{1}{3}$ (b) $9\frac{1}{3}$ (c) $9\frac{2}{3}$ (d) $10\frac{2}{3}$

4. $\dfrac{5 \times 7}{4} = ?$

(a) $9\frac{1}{2}$ (b) $9\frac{1}{4}$ (c) $7\frac{3}{4}$ (d) $8\frac{3}{4}$

5. $\dfrac{8 \times 4}{7} = ?$

(a) $4\frac{2}{7}$ (b) $3\frac{6}{7}$ (c) $4\frac{4}{7}$ (d) $3\frac{5}{7}$

6. $\dfrac{3 \times 7}{4} = ?$

(a) $5\frac{1}{4}$ (b) $5\frac{3}{4}$ (c) $4\frac{3}{4}$ (d) $5\frac{1}{2}$

7. $\dfrac{5}{8} \times 7 = ?$

(a) $4\frac{1}{4}$ (b) $4\frac{3}{8}$ (c) $4\frac{3}{4}$ (d) $4\frac{5}{8}$

8. $\dfrac{8}{6} \times 8 = ?$

(a) $10\frac{5}{6}$ (b) $11\frac{1}{6}$ (c) $10\frac{2}{3}$ (d) $15\frac{3}{4}$

9. $\frac{9}{7} \times 5 = ?$

(a) $9\frac{5}{7}$ (b) $6\frac{2}{7}$ (c) $7\frac{5}{7}$ (d) $6\frac{3}{7}$

10. $\frac{8}{11} \times 8 = ?$

(a) $5\frac{7}{11}$ (b) $5\frac{8}{11}$ (c) $5\frac{9}{11}$ (d) $6\frac{2}{11}$

11. $13 \times \frac{7}{5} = ?$

(a) $14\frac{2}{5}$ (b) $18\frac{1}{5}$ (c) $9\frac{1}{10}$ (d) $13\frac{5}{7}$

12. $11 \times \frac{7}{13} = ?$

(a) $5\frac{11}{13}$ (b) $11\frac{7}{13}$ (c) $5\frac{7}{13}$ (d) $5\frac{12}{13}$

13. $8 \times \frac{6}{11} = ?$

(a) $5\frac{3}{11}$ (b) $6\frac{8}{11}$ (c) $4\frac{4}{11}$ (d) $8\frac{6}{11}$

14. $\frac{6}{5} \times 8 = ?$

(a) $9\frac{3}{5}$ (b) $9\frac{1}{5}$ (c) $8\frac{2}{5}$ (d) $8\frac{5}{6}$

15. $\frac{9}{7} \times 11 = ?$

(a) $12\frac{2}{7}$ (b) $14\frac{2}{7}$ (c) $7\frac{1}{7}$ (d) $14\frac{1}{7}$

16. $\frac{9}{4} \times 13 = ?$

(a) $29\frac{1}{4}$ (b) $22\frac{3}{4}$ (c) $27\frac{3}{4}$ (d) $27\frac{1}{4}$

17. $13 \times \frac{4}{7} = ?$

(a) $7\frac{1}{7}$ (b) $7\frac{3}{7}$ (c) $13\frac{4}{7}$ (d) $7\frac{2}{7}$

18. $12 \times \frac{8}{5} = ?$

(a) $19\frac{1}{5}$ (b) $13\frac{3}{5}$ (c) $19\frac{3}{5}$ (d) $13\frac{1}{5}$

19. $7 \times \frac{6}{5} = ?$

(a) $8\frac{1}{5}$ (b) $8\frac{2}{5}$ (c) $9\frac{3}{5}$ (d) $9\frac{4}{5}$

20. $11 \times \frac{9}{13} = ?$

(a) $11\frac{6}{13}$ (b) $7\frac{5}{13}$ (c) $11\frac{9}{13}$ (d) $7\frac{8}{13}$

21. $12 \times \frac{7}{5} = ?$

(a) $12\frac{5}{7}$ (b) $13\frac{2}{5}$ (c) $16\frac{4}{5}$ (d) $17\frac{1}{5}$

22. $6 \times \frac{8}{13} = ?$

(a) $4\frac{4}{13}$ (b) $8\frac{6}{13}$ (c) $3\frac{9}{13}$ (d) $6\frac{8}{13}$

23. $4 \times \frac{16}{17} = ?$

(a) $4\frac{16}{17}$ (b) $3\frac{13}{17}$ (c) $16\frac{4}{17}$ (d) $5\frac{1}{17}$

24. $5 \times \frac{9}{17} = ?$

(a) $14\frac{2}{5}$ (b) $5\frac{9}{17}$ (c) $2\frac{11}{17}$ (d) $3\frac{1}{17}$

25. $6 \times \frac{13}{17} = ?$

(a) $6\frac{13}{17}$ (b) $10\frac{4}{17}$ (c) $5\frac{10}{17}$ (d) $4\frac{10}{17}$

26. $\frac{9}{17} \times 8 = ?$

(a) $4\frac{4}{17}$ (b) $4\frac{8}{17}$ (c) $8\frac{9}{17}$ (d) $9\frac{8}{17}$

27. $\frac{7}{20} \times 11 = ?$

(a) $3\frac{13}{20}$ (b) $3\frac{17}{20}$ (c) $11\frac{17}{20}$ (d) $7\frac{7}{10}$

28. $6 \times \frac{8}{25} = ?$

(a) $8\frac{6}{25}$ (b) $6\frac{8}{25}$ (c) $1\frac{23}{25}$ (d) $2\frac{4}{25}$

29. $5 \times \frac{9}{22} = ?$

(a) $4\frac{6}{11}$ (b) $4\frac{1}{11}$ (c) $5\frac{9}{22}$ (d) $2\frac{1}{22}$

30. $3 \times \frac{16}{17} = ?$

(a) $3\frac{16}{17}$ (b) $2\frac{14}{17}$ (c) $3\frac{1}{17}$ (d) $2\frac{11}{17}$

31. $19 \times \frac{5}{30} = ?$

(a) $3\frac{1}{6}$ (b) $21\frac{2}{6}$ (c) $19\frac{1}{6}$ (d) $2\frac{1}{6}$

32. $9 \times \frac{8}{13} = ?$

(a) $8\frac{9}{13}$ (b) $7\frac{5}{13}$ (c) $9\frac{8}{13}$ (d) $5\frac{7}{13}$

33. $12 \times \frac{6}{25} = ?$

(a) $3\frac{3}{25}$ (b) $12\frac{6}{25}$ (c) $2\frac{4}{5}$ (d) $2\frac{22}{25}$

34. $16 \times \frac{7}{25} = ?$

(a) $16\frac{7}{25}$ (b) $4\frac{2}{25}$ (c) $4\frac{12}{25}$ (d) $4\frac{22}{25}$

35. $\frac{9}{20} \times 7 = ?$

(a) $3\frac{3}{20}$ (b) $9\frac{7}{20}$ (c) $7\frac{3}{10}$ (d) $6\frac{3}{10}$

36. $18 \times \frac{5}{13} = ?$

(a) $5\frac{5}{13}$ (b) $19\frac{1}{13}$ (c) $6\frac{12}{13}$ (d) $18\frac{5}{13}$

37. $19 \times \frac{6}{5} = ?$

(a) $21\frac{3}{5}$ (b) $22\frac{4}{5}$ (c) $23\frac{1}{5}$ (d) $20\frac{1}{5}$

38. $24 \times \frac{7}{5} = ?$

(a) $25\frac{2}{5}$ (b) $33\frac{1}{5}$ (c) $33\frac{1}{3}$ (d) $33\frac{3}{5}$

39. $22 \times \frac{2}{5} = ?$

(a) $22\frac{2}{5}$ (b) $11\frac{1}{5}$ (c) $8\frac{4}{5}$ (d) $9\frac{1}{5}$

40. $28 \times \frac{5}{11} = ?$

(a) $12\frac{8}{11}$ (b) $28\frac{5}{11}$ (c) $13\frac{7}{11}$ (d) $19\frac{4}{11}$

41. $16 \times \frac{9}{7} = ?$

(a) $17\frac{1}{7}$ (b) $20\frac{4}{7}$ (c) $20\frac{2}{7}$ (d) $17\frac{2}{7}$

42. $15 \times \frac{7}{8} = ?$

(a) $16\frac{1}{4}$ (b) $15\frac{7}{8}$ (c) $13\frac{1}{8}$ (d) $12\frac{3}{4}$

43. $17 \times \frac{6}{5} = ?$

(a) $19\frac{1}{5}$ (b) $18\frac{1}{5}$ (c) $17\frac{2}{5}$ (d) $20\frac{2}{5}$

44. $22 \times \frac{4}{5} = ?$

(a) $22\frac{4}{5}$ (b) $17\frac{3}{5}$ (c) $15\frac{2}{5}$ (d) $16\frac{4}{5}$

45. $13 \times \frac{11}{4} = ?$

(a) $35\frac{3}{4}$ (b) $14\frac{3}{4}$ (c) $35\frac{1}{2}$ (d) $17\frac{3}{4}$

Type-2: Answer - Key

1.	(c)	**10.**	(c)	**19.**	(b)	**28.**	(c)	**37.**	(b)
2.	(b)	**11.**	(b)	**20.**	(d)	**29.**	(d)	**38.**	(d)
3.	(d)	**12.**	(d)	**21.**	(c)	**30.**	(b)	**39.**	(c)
4.	(d)	**13.**	(c)	**22.**	(c)	**31.**	(a)	**40.**	(a)
5.	(c)	**14.**	(a)	**23.**	(b)	**32.**	(d)	**41.**	(b)
6.	(a)	**15.**	(d)	**24.**	(c)	**33.**	(d)	**42.**	(c)
7.	(b)	**16.**	(a)	**25.**	(d)	**34.**	(c)	**43.**	(d)
8.	(c)	**17.**	(b)	**26.**	(a)	**35.**	(a)	**44.**	(b)
9.	(d)	**18.**	(a)	**27.**	(b)	**36.**	(c)	**45.**	(a)

Type-3

Hint :

$8\frac{1}{5}\times 7$

☞ इस प्रकार की calculation करने के लिए सबसे पहले (×) जिससे fraction वाले part को multiply करे $\left(\frac{1}{5}\times 7\right)$ आपको पता लगेगा कि शेषफल क्या होगा और पूर्णांक (Integer) कितनी बार जाएगा यदि हम $\frac{7}{5}$ करते हैं तो 1 बार में जाएगा और $\frac{2}{5}$ बच जाएगा जिसका मतलब है एक संख्या जुड़ेगी (8 × 7 = 56) में (56 + 1 = 57) तो Answer $57\frac{2}{5}$ निकल जाएगा बिना पेन पेपर के।

Exercise

- **Convert into integer or $a\frac{b}{c}$**

1. $8\frac{1}{5}\times 7 = ?$

(a) $57\frac{2}{5}$ (b) $56\frac{1}{5}$ (c) $42\frac{2}{5}$ (d) $48\frac{1}{5}$

2. $6\frac{1}{4} \times 8 = ?$

(a) 75 (b) 60 (c) 40 (d) 50

3. $7\frac{1}{6} \times 7 = ?$

(a) $48\frac{1}{6}$ (b) $49\frac{1}{6}$ (c) $50\frac{1}{6}$ (d) $51\frac{1}{6}$

4. $9\frac{1}{4} \times 12 = ?$

(a) 112 (b) 110 (c) 116 (d) 111

5. $8\frac{1}{7} \times 8 = ?$

(a) $65\frac{1}{7}$ (b) $64\frac{1}{7}$ (c) $64\frac{2}{7}$ (d) $65\frac{2}{7}$

6. $11\frac{1}{3} \times 5 = ?$

(a) $55\frac{1}{3}$ (b) $55\frac{2}{3}$ (c) $56\frac{2}{3}$ (d) $56\frac{1}{3}$

7. $3\frac{1}{11} \times 12 = ?$

(a) $38\frac{1}{11}$ (b) $37\frac{1}{11}$ (c) $36\frac{2}{11}$ (d) $36\frac{1}{11}$

8. $9\frac{1}{9} \times 13 = ?$

(a) $117\frac{4}{9}$ (b) $119\frac{1}{9}$ (c) $117\frac{5}{9}$ (d) $118\frac{4}{9}$

9. $8\frac{7}{8} \times 11 = ?$

(a) $88\frac{7}{8}$ (b) $97\frac{5}{8}$ (c) $98\frac{7}{8}$ (d) $89\frac{1}{8}$

10. $5\frac{1}{5} \times 20 = ?$

(a) 102 (b) 105 (c) 104 (d) 110

11. $6\frac{1}{11} \times 33 = ?$

(a) 201 (b) 189 (c) 203 (d) 198

12. $9\frac{1}{4} \times 40 = ?$

(a) 380 (b) 375 (c) 360 (d) 370

13. $8\frac{1}{2} \times 70 = ?$

(a) 596 (b) 592 (c) 595 (d) 590

14. $17\frac{3}{4} \times 5 = ?$

(a) $87\frac{3}{4}$ (b) $88\frac{3}{4}$ (c) $85\frac{3}{4}$ (d) $89\frac{1}{4}$

15. $9\frac{6}{7} \times 8 = ?$

(a) $76\frac{6}{7}$ (b) $72\frac{6}{7}$ (c) $77\frac{1}{7}$ (d) $78\frac{6}{7}$

16. $33\frac{1}{3} \times 2 = ?$

(a) $66\frac{2}{3}$ (b) $66\frac{1}{3}$ (c) $67\frac{1}{3}$ (d) $68\frac{1}{3}$

17. $6\frac{2}{3} \times 8 = ?$

(a) $48\frac{2}{3}$ (b) $50\frac{1}{3}$ (c) $53\frac{1}{3}$ (d) $52\frac{2}{3}$

18. $16\frac{2}{3} \times 4 = ?$

(a) $64\frac{2}{3}$ (b) $66\frac{2}{3}$ (c) $65\frac{2}{3}$ (d) $66\frac{1}{3}$

19. $16\frac{2}{3} \times 5 = ?$

(a) $80\frac{2}{3}$ (b) $83\frac{2}{3}$ (c) $82\frac{1}{3}$ (d) $83\frac{1}{3}$

20. $12\frac{1}{2} \times 7 = ?$

(a) $84\frac{1}{2}$ (b) $86\frac{1}{2}$ (c) $85\frac{1}{2}$ (d) $87\frac{1}{2}$

21. $11\frac{1}{9} \times 2 = ?$

(a) $22\frac{2}{9}$ (b) $22\frac{1}{9}$ (c) $23\frac{1}{9}$ (d) $22\frac{1}{3}$

22. $14\frac{2}{7} \times 3 = ?$

(a) $42\frac{2}{7}$ (b) $42\frac{6}{7}$ (c) $43\frac{1}{7}$ (d) $42\frac{1}{7}$

23. $14\frac{2}{7} \times 5 = ?$

(a) $71\frac{2}{7}$ (b) $70\frac{2}{7}$ (c) $71\frac{3}{7}$ (d) $70\frac{3}{7}$

24. $9\frac{1}{11} \times 3 = ?$

(a) $27\frac{2}{11}$ (b) $27\frac{1}{11}$ (c) $27\frac{6}{11}$ (d) $27\frac{3}{11}$

25. $8\frac{1}{3} \times 3 = ?$

(a) 26 (b) 27 (c) 25 (d) $24\frac{1}{3}$

26. $8\frac{1}{3} \times 9 = ?$

(a) 73 (b) 75 (c) 78 (d) 72

27. $6\frac{2}{3} \times 3 = ?$

(a) 20 (b) $18\frac{2}{3}$ (c) 21 (d) $19\frac{1}{3}$

28. $6\frac{2}{3} \times 4 = ?$

(a) $25\frac{1}{3}$ (b) $24\frac{2}{3}$ (c) $26\frac{2}{3}$ (d) $25\frac{2}{3}$

29. $9\frac{1}{11} \times 7 = ?$

(a) $64\frac{4}{11}$ (b) $63\frac{1}{11}$ (c) $64\frac{1}{11}$ (d) $63\frac{7}{11}$

30. $11\frac{1}{9} \times 10 = ?$

(a) $110\frac{1}{9}$ (b) $111\frac{1}{9}$ (c) $110\frac{2}{9}$ (d) $111\frac{2}{9}$

31. $26\frac{2}{3} \times 3 = ?$

(a) 72 (b) 90 (c) 52 (d) 80

32. $11\frac{1}{13} \times 13 = ?$

(a) 144 (b) 154 (c) 145 (d) $143\frac{1}{13}$

33. $22\frac{2}{9} \times 4 = ?$

(a) $89\frac{1}{9}$ (b) $88\frac{2}{9}$ (c) $88\frac{8}{9}$ (d) $88\frac{4}{9}$

34. $44\frac{4}{9} \times 5 = ?$

(a) $176\frac{5}{9}$ (b) $222\frac{2}{9}$ (c) $220\frac{4}{9}$ (d) $222\frac{5}{9}$

35. $66\frac{2}{3} \times 3 = ?$

(a) 180 (b) 132 (c) 200 (d) 270

36. $22\frac{3}{4} \times 8 = ?$

(a) 182 (b) 132 (c) 196 (d) 175

37. $91\frac{3}{4} \times 5 = ?$

(a) $455\frac{3}{4}$ (b) $457\frac{1}{4}$ (c) $460\frac{1}{4}$ (d) $458\frac{3}{4}$

38. $88\frac{3}{8} \times 8 = ?$

(a) 717 (b) 264 (c) 777 (d) 707

39. $102\frac{3}{7} \times 7 = ?$

(a) 306 (b) 707 (c) 717 (d) 777

40. $77\frac{7}{11} \times 22 = ?$

(a) 1078 (b) 1708 (c) 1087 (d) 1707

41. $214\frac{3}{8} \times 4 = ?$

(a) $857\frac{1}{2}$ (b) $860\frac{1}{2}$ (c) $856\frac{1}{2}$ (d) $642\frac{1}{2}$

42. $302\frac{4}{7} \times 5 = ?$

(a) $1510\frac{4}{7}$ (b) $1511\frac{3}{7}$ (c) $1512\frac{6}{7}$ (d) $1208\frac{5}{7}$

43. $16\frac{2}{3} \times 16 = ?$

(a) $264\frac{2}{3}$ (b) $256\frac{2}{3}$ (c) $265\frac{1}{3}$ (d) $266\frac{2}{3}$

44. $17\frac{1}{4} \times 8 = ?$

(a) 24 (b) 138 (c) 148 (d) 128

45. $14\frac{1}{7} \times 14 = ?$

(a) 28 (b) 198 (c) 140 (d) 180

46. $12\frac{2}{5} \times 8 = ?$

(a) $99\frac{1}{5}$ (b) $97\frac{3}{5}$ (c) $98\frac{4}{5}$ (d) $96\frac{2}{5}$

47. $16\frac{4}{5} \times 6 = ?$

(a) $96\frac{4}{5}$ (b) $97\frac{4}{5}$ (c) $102\frac{2}{5}$ (d) $100\frac{4}{5}$

48. $14\frac{2}{7} \times 2 = ?$

(a) $29\frac{2}{7}$ (b) $28\frac{2}{7}$ (c) $28\frac{4}{7}$ (d) $29\frac{4}{7}$

49. $9\frac{1}{11} \times 4 = ?$

(a) $37\frac{4}{11}$ (b) $36\frac{4}{11}$ (c) $37\frac{1}{11}$ (d) $36\frac{1}{11}$

50. $8\frac{1}{3} \times 5 = ?$

(a) $41\frac{2}{3}$ (b) $42\frac{1}{3}$ (c) $40\frac{1}{3}$ (d) $41\frac{1}{3}$

51. $12\frac{1}{2} \times 8 = ?$

(a) 100 (b) 48 (c) 104 (d) 98

52. $11\frac{1}{9} \times 3 = ?$

(a) $34\frac{1}{3}$ (b) $33\frac{2}{3}$ (c) $35\frac{1}{3}$ (d) $33\frac{1}{3}$

53. $14\frac{2}{7} \times 4 = ?$

(a) $56\frac{1}{7}$ (b) $57\frac{2}{7}$ (c) $57\frac{1}{7}$ (d) $56\frac{2}{7}$

54. $9\frac{1}{11} \times 5 = ?$

(a) $45\frac{1}{11}$ (b) $45\frac{5}{11}$ (c) $46\frac{1}{11}$ (d) $46\frac{5}{11}$

55. $11\frac{1}{9} \times 6 = ?$

(a) $66\frac{1}{9}$ (b) $66\frac{1}{3}$ (c) $66\frac{2}{3}$ (d) $66\frac{2}{9}$

56. $11\frac{1}{9} \times 7 = ?$

(a) $77\frac{1}{9}$ (b) $78\frac{1}{9}$ (c) $78\frac{7}{9}$ (d) $77\frac{7}{9}$

57. $8\frac{1}{3} \times 4 = ?$

(a) $33\frac{1}{3}$ (b) $32\frac{1}{3}$ (c) $33\frac{2}{3}$ (d) $32\frac{2}{3}$

58. $6\frac{2}{3} \times 6 = ?$

(a) 40 (b) 48 (c) 36 (d) 24

59. $14\frac{2}{7} \times 6 = ?$

(a) $85\frac{6}{7}$ (b) $84\frac{2}{7}$ (c) $85\frac{5}{7}$ (d) $85\frac{2}{7}$

60. $6\frac{2}{3} \times 5 = ?$

(a) $32\frac{2}{3}$ (b) $33\frac{1}{3}$ (c) $31\frac{1}{3}$ (d) $30\frac{2}{3}$

61. $12\frac{1}{2} \times 3 = ?$

(a) $36\frac{1}{2}$ (b) $38\frac{1}{2}$ (c) $35\frac{1}{2}$ (d) $37\frac{1}{2}$

62. $9\frac{1}{11} \times 8 = ?$

(a) $72\frac{2}{11}$ (b) $72\frac{1}{11}$ (c) $72\frac{8}{11}$ (d) $73\frac{8}{11}$

63. $12\frac{1}{2} \times 8 = ?$

(a) 108 (b) 100 (c) 98 (d) 48

64. $20\frac{1}{4} \times 8 = ?$

(a) 162 (b) 40 (c) 160 (d) 164

65. $21\frac{1}{2} \times 7 = ?$

(a) $147\frac{1}{2}$ (b) $148\frac{1}{2}$ (c) $151\frac{1}{2}$ (d) $150\frac{1}{2}$

66. $22\frac{4}{7} \times 5 = ?$

(a) $111\frac{6}{7}$ (b) $110\frac{4}{7}$ (c) $112\frac{6}{7}$ (d) $113\frac{4}{7}$

67. $44\frac{3}{4} \times 3 = ?$

(a) $132\frac{3}{4}$ (b) $134\frac{1}{4}$ (c) $133\frac{3}{4}$ (d) $135\frac{1}{4}$

68. $45\frac{1}{7} \times 4 = ?$

(a) $181\frac{1}{7}$ (b) $180\frac{2}{7}$ (c) $180\frac{4}{7}$ (d) $180\frac{1}{7}$

69. $10\frac{1}{4} \times 8 = ?$

(a) 85 (b) 84 (c) 20 (d) 82

70. $12\frac{1}{5} \times 11 = ?$

(a) $132\frac{1}{5}$ (b) $135\frac{1}{5}$ (c) $133\frac{1}{5}$ (d) $134\frac{1}{5}$

71. $13\frac{1}{4} \times 8 = ?$

(a) 106 (b) 104 (c) 52 (d) 26

72. $14\frac{7}{8} \times 7 = ?$

(a) $98\frac{7}{8}$ (b) $100\frac{7}{8}$ (c) $100\frac{1}{8}$ (d) $104\frac{1}{8}$

73. $24\frac{3}{5} \times 20 = ?$

(a) 492 (b) 288 (c) 496 (d) 490

74. $26\frac{2}{3} \times 6 = ?$

(a) 150 (b) 160 (c) 180 (d) 104

75. $28\frac{4}{5} \times 4 = ?$

(a) $113\frac{3}{5}$ (b) $112\frac{4}{5}$ (c) $115\frac{1}{5}$ (d) $114\frac{2}{5}$

76. $30\frac{4}{7} \times 7 = ?$

(a) 214 (b) 212 (c) 210 (d) 120

77. $14\frac{2}{7} \times 5 = ?$

(a) $72\frac{1}{7}$ (b) $70\frac{2}{7}$ (c) $70\frac{5}{7}$ (d) $71\frac{3}{7}$

78. $35\frac{1}{4} \times 20 = ?$

(a) 175 (b) 705 (c) 725 (d) 507

79. $25\frac{1}{8} \times 5 = ?$

(a) $126\frac{5}{8}$ (b) $126\frac{1}{8}$ (c) $125\frac{5}{8}$ (d) $125\frac{1}{8}$

80. $9\frac{1}{11} \times 2 = ?$

(a) $19\frac{2}{11}$ (b) $19\frac{1}{11}$ (c) $18\frac{2}{11}$ (d) $18\frac{1}{11}$

81. $8\frac{1}{3} \times 6 = ?$

(a) 60 (b) 16 (c) 32 (d) 50

82. $8\frac{1}{3} \times 7 = ?$

(a) $57\frac{1}{3}$ (b) $57\frac{2}{3}$ (c) $56\frac{1}{3}$ (d) $58\frac{1}{3}$

83. $8\frac{1}{3} \times 8 = ?$

(a) $64\frac{1}{3}$ (b) $66\frac{2}{3}$ (c) $66\frac{1}{3}$ (d) $64\frac{2}{3}$

84. $6\frac{2}{3} \times 10 = ?$

(a) $66\frac{2}{3}$ (b) $60\frac{2}{3}$ (c) $63\frac{1}{3}$ (d) $67\frac{1}{3}$

85. $11\frac{1}{9} \times 5 = ?$

(a) $55\frac{1}{9}$ (b) $56\frac{1}{9}$ (c) $55\frac{5}{9}$ (d) $56\frac{5}{9}$

86. $12\frac{1}{2} \times 6 = ?$

(a) 78 (b) 75 (c) 36 (d) 72

87. $6\frac{2}{3} \times 8 = ?$

(a) $50\frac{2}{3}$ (b) $51\frac{2}{3}$ (c) $53\frac{1}{3}$ (d) $48\frac{2}{3}$

88. $12\frac{1}{2} \times 5 = ?$

(a) $61\frac{1}{2}$ (b) $62\frac{1}{2}$ (c) $63\frac{1}{2}$ (d) $60\frac{1}{2}$

89. $9\frac{1}{11} \times 6 = ?$

(a) $54\frac{1}{11}$ (b) $54\frac{3}{11}$ (c) $54\frac{2}{11}$ (d) $54\frac{6}{11}$

90. $6\frac{2}{3} \times 12 = ?$

(a) 48 (b) 84 (c) 80 (d) 96

91. $6\frac{2}{3} \times 6 = ?$

(a) 54 (b) 48 (c) 40 (d) 24

92. $9\frac{1}{11} \times 9 = ?$

(a) $82\frac{1}{11}$ (b) $81\frac{9}{11}$ (c) $81\frac{2}{11}$ (d) $81\frac{1}{11}$

93. $29\frac{1}{3} \times 4 = ?$

(a) $117\frac{1}{3}$ (b) $116\frac{1}{3}$ (c) $118\frac{1}{3}$ (d) $116\frac{2}{3}$

94. $13\frac{7}{8} \times 8 = ?$

(a) 91 (b) 108 (c) 120 (d) 111

95. $18\frac{5}{11} \times 11 = ?$

(a) 203 (b) 90 (c) 220 (d) 180

96. $19\frac{6}{7} \times 4 = ?$

(a) $76\frac{6}{7}$ (b) $79\frac{3}{7}$ (c) $77\frac{1}{7}$ (d) $78\frac{4}{7}$

97. $102\frac{4}{5} \times 4 = ?$

(a) $410\frac{4}{5}$ (b) $412\frac{1}{5}$ (c) $411\frac{1}{5}$ (d) $408\frac{4}{5}$

98. $214\frac{4}{5} \times 5 = ?$

(a) 1070 (b) 1074 (c) 996 (d) 856

99. $1002\frac{2}{3} \times 6 = ?$

(a) 6016 (b) 4008 (c) 6064 (d) 5048

100. $2004\frac{1}{4} \times 3 = ?$

(a) $6024\frac{3}{4}$ (b) $6024\frac{1}{4}$ (c) $6012\frac{1}{4}$ (d) $6012\frac{3}{4}$

101. $121\frac{4}{7} \times 8 = ?$

(a) $984\frac{3}{7}$ (b) $972\frac{4}{7}$ (c) $978\frac{3}{7}$ (d) $968\frac{4}{7}$

102. $20\frac{1}{11} \times 22 = ?$

(a) 40 (b) 450 (c) 442 (d) 440

103. $30\frac{1}{13} \times 26 = ?$

(a) 782 (b) 786 (c) 750 (d) 60

104. $17\frac{1}{4} \times 8 = ?$

(a) 34 (b) 148 (c) 156 (d) 138

105. $100\frac{11}{12} \times 10 = ?$

(a) $1009\frac{1}{12}$ (b) $1000\frac{11}{12}$ (c) $1009\frac{1}{6}$ (d) $1009\frac{1}{3}$

106. $200\frac{20}{27} \times 27 = ?$

(a) 5400 (b) 4000 (c) 4400 (d) 5420

Type-3: Answer - Key

1.	(a)	**22.**	(b)	**43.**	(d)	**64.**	(a)	**85.**	(c)
2.	(d)	**23.**	(c)	**44.**	(b)	**65.**	(d)	**86.**	(b)
3.	(c)	**24.**	(d)	**45.**	(b)	**66.**	(c)	**87.**	(c)
4.	(d)	**25.**	(c)	**46.**	(a)	**67.**	(b)	**88.**	(b)
5.	(a)	**26.**	(b)	**47.**	(d)	**68.**	(c)	**89.**	(d)
6.	(c)	**27.**	(a)	**48.**	(c)	**69.**	(d)	**90.**	(c)
7.	(b)	**28.**	(c)	**49.**	(b)	**70.**	(d)	**91.**	(c)
8.	(d)	**29.**	(d)	**50.**	(a)	**71.**	(a)	**92.**	(b)
9.	(b)	**30.**	(b)	**51.**	(a)	**72.**	(d)	**93.**	(a)
10.	(c)	**31.**	(d)	**52.**	(d)	**73.**	(a)	**94.**	(d)
11.	(a)	**32.**	(a)	**53.**	(c)	**74.**	(b)	**95.**	(a)
12.	(d)	**33.**	(c)	**54.**	(b)	**75.**	(c)	**96.**	(b)
13.	(c)	**34.**	(b)	**55.**	(c)	**76.**	(a)	**97.**	(c)
14.	(b)	**35.**	(c)	**56.**	(d)	**77.**	(d)	**98.**	(b)
15.	(d)	**36.**	(a)	**57.**	(a)	**78.**	(b)	**99.**	(a)
16.	(a)	**37.**	(d)	**58.**	(a)	**79.**	(c)	**100.**	(d)
17.	(c)	**38.**	(d)	**59.**	(c)	**80.**	(c)	**101.**	(b)
18.	(b)	**39.**	(c)	**60.**	(b)	**81.**	(d)	**102.**	(c)
19.	(d)	**40.**	(b)	**61.**	(d)	**82.**	(d)	**103.**	(a)
20.	(d)	**41.**	(a)	**62.**	(c)	**83.**	(b)	**104.**	(d)
21.	(a)	**42.**	(c)	**63.**	(b)	**84.**	(a)	**105.**	(c)
								106.	(d)

Type-4

Hint :

$$44\frac{4}{9}\times\frac{7}{11}$$

☞ इस type की calculation करते समय सबसे पहले $\left(44\times\frac{7}{11}=28\right)$ हल करेंगे और दिमाग में रखना है उसके बाद $\left(\frac{4\times7}{9\times11}\right)=\frac{28}{99}$ आता है तो Answer $\left(28\frac{28}{99}\right)$ निकल जाता है।

दिमाग में Calculation करनी है।

Exercise

1. $\frac{1}{3}\times\frac{1}{4}=?$

(a) 1/12 (b) 1/6 (c) 1/24 (d) 3/4

2. $\frac{1}{7}\times\frac{3}{4}=?$

(a) 1/28 (b) 3/28 (c) 1/21 (d) 4/21

3. $\frac{1}{5}\times\frac{9}{7}=?$

(a) 7/45 (b) 3/54 (c) 9/35 (d) 5/63

4. $\frac{1}{3} \times \frac{14}{5} = ?$

(a) 7/30 (b) 7/15 (c) 7/20 (d) 14/15

5. $\frac{1}{5} \times \frac{27}{4} = ?$

(a) 27/40 (b) 9/10 (c) 9/20 (d) 27/20

6. $\frac{33}{7} \times \frac{1}{2} = ?$

(a) 7/11 (b) 11/7 (c) 33/14 (d) 11/14

7. $\frac{96}{13} \times \frac{1}{2} = ?$

(a) 96/13 (b) 48/13 (c) 43/13 (d) 13/48

8. $\frac{74}{5} \times \frac{1}{2} = ?$

(a) 37/5 (b) 37/10 (c) 5/37 (d) 10/37

9. $\frac{127}{14} \times \frac{1}{5} = ?$

(a) 70/127 (b) 127/70 (c) 140/127 (d) 127/140

10. $\frac{2}{3} \times \frac{7}{4} = ?$

(a) 3/14 (b) 6/7 (c) 7/6 (d) 14/3

11. $\frac{9}{4} \times \frac{8}{13} = ?$

(a) 9/26 (b) 13/18 (c) 16/13 (d) 18/13

12. $\frac{6}{7} \times \frac{14}{23} = ?$

(a) 12/23 (b) 6/23 (c) 21/46 (d) 2/7

13. $\frac{4}{5} \times \frac{13}{15} = ?$

(a) 26/65 (b) 13/12 (c) 52/75 (d) 26/75

14. $\frac{9}{8} \times \frac{7}{5} = ?$

(a) 35/72 (b) 63/40 (c) 42/35 (d) 40/63

15. $\frac{23}{4} \times \frac{7}{8} = ?$

(a) 14/23 (b) 161/32 (c) 32/161 (d) 23/14

16. $\frac{1}{6} \times \left(2\frac{1}{3}\right) = ?$

(a) 7/15 (b) 7/18 (c) 7/20 (d) 7/16

17. $\frac{1}{9} \times \left(4\frac{1}{4}\right) = ?$

(a) 17/36 (b) 36/17 (c) 15/32 (d) 13/36

18. $\frac{2}{3} \times \left(2\frac{2}{3}\right) = ?$

(a) $2\frac{4}{9}$ (b) $1\frac{8}{9}$ (c) $2\frac{1}{9}$ (d) $1\frac{7}{9}$

19. $\frac{5}{3} \times \left(66\frac{2}{3}\right) = ?$

(a) $67\frac{1}{9}$ (b) $121\frac{1}{9}$ (c) $111\frac{1}{9}$ (d) $67\frac{1}{3}$

20. $\left(44\frac{4}{9}\right) \times \frac{7}{11} = ?$

(a) $28\frac{28}{99}$ (b) $22\frac{28}{99}$ (c) $44\frac{28}{99}$ (d) $27\frac{28}{99}$

21. $\left(112\frac{5}{7}\right) \times \frac{5}{7} = ?$

(a) $112\frac{25}{49}$ (b) $80\frac{25}{49}$ (c) $56\frac{1}{7}$ (d) $57\frac{1}{7}$

22. $\left(264\frac{3}{4}\right) \times \frac{3}{11} = ?$

(a) $84\frac{9}{44}$ (b) $24\frac{9}{44}$ (c) $72\frac{9}{44}$ (d) $36\frac{9}{44}$

23. $\left(9\frac{1}{9}\right) \times \frac{2}{9} = ?$

(a) $2\frac{4}{81}$ (b) $9\frac{2}{81}$ (c) $4\frac{4}{81}$ (d) $2\frac{2}{81}$

24. $\left(14\frac{2}{7}\right) \times \frac{5}{14} = ?$

(a) $5\frac{5}{49}$ (b) $14\frac{5}{49}$ (c) $7\frac{5}{49}$ (d) $10\frac{5}{49}$

25. $\left(4\frac{4}{5}\right) \times \frac{3}{4} = ?$

(a) $4\frac{3}{5}$ (b) $3\frac{1}{5}$ (c) $3\frac{3}{5}$ (d) $4\frac{1}{5}$

26. $\left(8\frac{5}{8}\right) \times \frac{7}{2} = ?$

(a) $24\frac{3}{16}$ (b) $30\frac{3}{16}$ (c) $32\frac{3}{16}$ (d) $16\frac{3}{16}$

27. $\left(8\frac{7}{8}\right) \times \frac{11}{8} = ?$

(a) $11\frac{7}{8}$ (b) $12\frac{13}{64}$ (c) $8\frac{13}{64}$ (d) $10\frac{7}{8}$

28. $\left(14\frac{1}{4}\right) \times \frac{5}{7} = ?$

(a) $10\frac{5}{28}$ (b) $14\frac{5}{28}$ (c) $7\frac{5}{7}$ (d) $9\frac{5}{14}$

29. $\left(14\frac{1}{7}\right) \times \frac{15}{7} = ?$

(a) $15\frac{15}{49}$ (b) $14\frac{15}{49}$ (c) $28\frac{15}{49}$ (d) $30\frac{15}{49}$

30. $\left(22\frac{2}{9}\right) \times \frac{5}{11} = ?$

(a) $20\frac{10}{99}$ (b) $11\frac{10}{99}$ (c) $10\frac{10}{99}$ (d) $22\frac{10}{99}$

31. $\left(26\frac{2}{3}\right) \times \frac{7}{13} = ?$

(a) $26\frac{14}{39}$ (b) $14\frac{7}{13}$ (c) $14\frac{14}{39}$ (d) $13\frac{7}{39}$

32. $\left(33\frac{1}{3}\right) \times \frac{5}{11} = ?$

(a) $16\frac{5}{33}$ (b) $33\frac{5}{11}$ (c) $30\frac{5}{11}$ (d) $15\frac{5}{33}$

33. $\left(66\frac{2}{3}\right) \times \frac{5}{3} = ?$

(a) $111\frac{1}{9}$ (b) $166\frac{1}{9}$ (c) $111\frac{2}{9}$ (d) $166\frac{2}{3}$

34. $\left(11\frac{1}{9}\right) \times \frac{9}{11} = ?$

(a) $9\frac{1}{9}$ (b) $9\frac{1}{11}$ (c) $11\frac{1}{9}$ (d) $11\frac{1}{11}$

35. $\left(44\frac{4}{9}\right) \times \frac{5}{11} = ?$

(a) $25\frac{10}{99}$ (b) $22\frac{20}{99}$ (c) $16\frac{20}{99}$ (d) $20\frac{20}{99}$

36. $\left(16\frac{2}{3}\right) \times \frac{7}{8} = ?$

(a) $14\frac{7}{12}$ (b) $16\frac{7}{12}$ (c) $14\frac{2}{3}$ (d) $12\frac{7}{12}$

37. $\left(42\frac{3}{7}\right) \times \frac{5}{14} = ?$

(a) $30\frac{15}{98}$ (b) $21\frac{15}{98}$ (c) $15\frac{15}{98}$ (d) $42\frac{15}{98}$

38. $\left(56\frac{4}{7}\right)\times\frac{15}{14}=?$

(a) $64\frac{15}{49}$ (b) $90\frac{15}{49}$ (c) $60\frac{30}{49}$ (d) $66\frac{6}{49}$

39. $\left(83\frac{1}{3}\right)\times\frac{120}{83}=?$

(a) $144\frac{16}{83}$ (b) $120\frac{40}{83}$ (c) $132\frac{20}{83}$ (d) $83\frac{40}{83}$

40. $\left(102\frac{4}{7}\right)\times\frac{5}{17}=?$

(a) $30\frac{20}{119}$ (b) $102\frac{20}{119}$ (c) $51\frac{20}{119}$ (d) $60\frac{20}{119}$

41. $\left(150\frac{5}{8}\right)\times\frac{24}{17}=?$

(a) $212\frac{15}{17}$ (b) $150\frac{15}{17}$ (c) $450\frac{15}{17}$ (d) $212\frac{11}{17}$

42. $\left(112\frac{5}{8}\right)\times\frac{5}{7}=?$

(a) $80\frac{25}{56}$ (b) $16\frac{25}{56}$ (c) $32\frac{25}{56}$ (d) $40\frac{25}{56}$

43. $\left(12\frac{3}{7}\right) \times \frac{5}{4} = ?$

(a) $9\frac{5}{7}$ (b) $12\frac{15}{28}$ (c) $15\frac{15}{28}$ (d) $27\frac{3}{7}$

44. $\left(28\frac{11}{15}\right) \times \frac{5}{14} = ?$

(a) $14\frac{11}{42}$ (b) $28\frac{11}{42}$ (c) $7\frac{11}{42}$ (d) $10\frac{11}{42}$

45. $\left(42\frac{2}{7}\right) \times \frac{7}{14} = ?$

(a) $21\frac{2}{7}$ (b) $21\frac{1}{7}$ (c) $42\frac{1}{14}$ (d) $42\frac{1}{7}$

46. $\left(93\frac{11}{12}\right) \times \frac{3}{31} = ?$

(a) $9\frac{11}{31}$ (b) $9\frac{11}{124}$ (c) $93\frac{11}{31}$ (d) $93\frac{11}{124}$

47. $\left(14\frac{3}{5}\right) \times \frac{5}{7} = ?$

(a) $10\frac{3}{7}$ (b) $14\frac{3}{7}$ (c) $15\frac{5}{7}$ (d) $12\frac{2}{7}$

48. $\left(19\frac{4}{5}\right)\times\frac{5}{7}=?$

(a) $19\frac{4}{7}$ (b) $14\frac{2}{7}$ (c) $15\frac{2}{7}$ (d) $14\frac{1}{7}$

49. $\left(23\frac{3}{7}\right)\times\frac{11}{23}=?$

(a) $11\frac{22}{161}$ (b) $11\frac{23}{161}$ (c) $11\frac{33}{161}$ (d) $23\frac{11}{161}$

50. $\left(50\frac{5}{11}\right)\times\frac{23}{10}=?$

(a) $116\frac{5}{110}$ (b) $116\frac{1}{110}$ (c) $110\frac{1}{110}$ (d) $115\frac{5}{110}$

Type-4: Answer - Key

1.	(a)	11.	(d)	21.	(b)	31.	(c)	41.	(d)
2.	(b)	12.	(a)	22.	(c)	32.	(d)	42.	(a)
3.	(c)	13.	(c)	23.	(d)	33.	(a)	43.	(c)
4.	(d)	14.	(b)	24.	(a)	34.	(b)	44.	(d)
5.	(d)	15.	(b)	25.	(c)	35.	(d)	45.	(b)
6.	(c)	16.	(b)	26.	(b)	36.	(a)	46.	(b)
7.	(b)	17.	(a)	27.	(b)	37.	(c)	47.	(a)
8.	(a)	18.	(d)	28.	(a)	38.	(c)	48.	(d)
9.	(b)	19.	(c)	29.	(d)	39.	(b)	49.	(c)
10.	(c)	20.	(a)	30.	(c)	40.	(a)	50.	(a)

Type-5

Example 1:

$$\frac{72}{96}$$

☞ जब भी हमें $\frac{N}{D}$ अंश/हर को काटना हो तो हम दोनो संख्याओं का HCF निकालते है और देखते हैं कितने गुना संख्याएँ है। सब कुछ दिमाग में करना है।

$$\left.\frac{72}{96}\right) \text{HCF} \Rightarrow 24$$

$$\Rightarrow \frac{\cancel{72}}{\cancel{96}} \quad \boxed{\frac{3}{4}}$$

Example 2:

$$\frac{7}{8} - \frac{3}{8}$$

☞ अगर fraction का denominator same है तो numerator में से घटा देते है।

$$\frac{7}{8} - \frac{3}{8} = \frac{4}{8} = \boxed{\frac{1}{2}}$$

Example 3:

$$\frac{1}{6}+\frac{7}{12}+\frac{2}{3}$$

☞ दी गई fraction का denominator (हर) different है तो पहले denominator को same करने वाले multiplier से numerator (अंश) में multiply करके add करेंगे फिर दिमाग में Answer निकाल लेंगे।

$\frac{1}{6}+\frac{7}{12}+\frac{2}{3}=\boxed{\frac{17}{12}}$ (लिखना नहीं है सब दिमाग में करना है)

Example 4:

$$2\frac{1}{4}+3+1\frac{1}{4}$$

☞ Mixed fraction में number वाला भाग अलग लेना है (2 + 3 + 1 = 6) जोड़ देना है फिर Denominator देखना है same है $\frac{\text{Numerator}}{\text{Denominator}}$ को जोड़ देना है $\left(\frac{1}{4}+\frac{1}{4}\right)$ जो $\left(\frac{1}{2}\right)$ के बराबर है तो Answer $\left(6\frac{1}{2}\right)$ निकल जाएगा।

Exercise

1. $\frac{72}{96}=?$

(a) 2/3 (b) 3/4 (c) 7/8 (d) 7/9

2. $\frac{7}{8}-\frac{3}{8}=?$

(a) 1/4 (b) 1/2 (c) 5/8 (d) 11/4

3. $\frac{1}{6}+\frac{7}{12}+\frac{2}{3}=?$

(a) $1\frac{5}{12}$ (b) $2\frac{1}{6}$ (c) $1\frac{3}{5}$ (d) $1\frac{3}{10}$

4. $2\frac{1}{4}+3+1\frac{1}{4}=?$

(a) $5\frac{1}{4}$ (b) $6\frac{1}{8}$ (c) $6\frac{1}{4}$ (d) $6\frac{1}{2}$

5. $4\frac{7}{10}-3\frac{1}{10}=?$

(a) $\frac{3}{5}$ (b) $1\frac{1}{2}$ (c) $1\frac{3}{5}$ (d) $1\frac{3}{10}$

6. $\frac{5}{12}-\frac{3}{8}=?$

(a) 1/10 (b) 1/24 (c) 5/48 (d) 19/24

7. $56\frac{3}{8}-10\frac{5}{6}=?$

(a) $46\frac{1}{7}$ (b) $46\frac{13}{14}$ (c) $45\frac{1}{3}$ (d) $45\frac{13}{24}$

8. $-\frac{3}{10}-\frac{1}{5}=?$

(a) $-\frac{1}{2}$ (b) $\frac{2}{3}$ (c) $-\frac{3}{50}$ (d) $\frac{3}{50}$

9. $\frac{1}{3}-\frac{2}{7}=?$

(a) $2\frac{4}{5}$ (b) $\frac{1}{21}$ (c) $2\frac{1}{7}$ (d) $1\frac{1}{5}$

10. $\frac{7}{8}-\frac{3}{5}=?$

(a) $\frac{11}{40}$ (b) $1\frac{1}{3}$ (c) $\frac{1}{10}$ (d) $1\frac{19}{40}$

11. $4\frac{3}{5}+\left(-1\frac{2}{5}\right)=?$

(a) $3\frac{1}{5}$ (b) 4 (c) $3\frac{1}{2}$ (d) $5\frac{1}{5}$

12. $76\frac{1}{2}+11\frac{5}{6}=?$

(a) $87\frac{1}{2}$ (b) $88\frac{1}{3}$ (c) $88\frac{5}{6}$ (d) $89\frac{1}{6}$

13. $20\frac{5}{7} - 15\frac{1}{7} = ?$

(a) $5\frac{2}{7}$ (b) $5\frac{3}{7}$ (c) $5\frac{4}{7}$ (d) $5\frac{6}{7}$

14. $43\frac{2}{3} + 36\frac{3}{9} = ?$

(a) 100 (b) 90 (c) 80 (d) 70

15. $\frac{6}{7} + \frac{4}{5} = ?$

(a) $\frac{25}{44}$ (b) $\frac{35}{49}$ (c) $\frac{58}{35}$ (d) $\frac{14}{33}$

16. $3\frac{3}{4} \times \frac{4}{5} = ?$

(a) $\frac{3}{4}$ (b) 3 (c) $3\frac{3}{4}$ (d) $4\frac{11}{16}$

17. $2\frac{1}{4} \div 2\frac{4}{7} = ?$

(a) $\frac{9}{14}$ (b) $\frac{7}{8}$ (c) $1\frac{2}{7}$ (d) $5\frac{11}{14}$

18. $1\frac{1}{2} \div 1\frac{5}{13} = ?$

(a) $1\frac{3}{10}$ (b) $1\frac{1}{12}$ (c) $2\frac{1}{13}$ (d) $3\frac{9}{10}$

19. $2\frac{1}{3} \times 1\frac{1}{14} \times 1\frac{4}{5} = ?$

(a) $1\frac{7}{18}$ (b) $2\frac{1}{2}$ (c) $3\frac{6}{7}$ (d) $4\frac{1}{2}$

20. $\frac{2}{3} \div \frac{5}{12} = ?$

(a) $1\frac{3}{5}$ (b) $1\frac{5}{18}$ (c) $1\frac{7}{36}$ (d) $1\frac{5}{6}$

21. $6\frac{2}{9} - \frac{1}{6} = ?$

(a) $6\frac{1}{18}$ (b) $6\frac{5}{27}$ (c) $6\frac{5}{28}$ (d) $5\frac{8}{9}$

22. $9\frac{3}{7} + 4\frac{2}{5} = ?$

(a) $13\frac{5}{12}$ (b) $13\frac{3}{4}$ (c) $13\frac{29}{35}$ (d) $13\frac{37}{52}$

23. $3\frac{5}{6} \times 4\frac{2}{3} = ?$

(a) $17\frac{8}{9}$ (b) $12\frac{7}{18}$ (c) $16\frac{2}{3}$ (d) $13\frac{3}{5}$

24. $1\frac{1}{2} \div 2\frac{1}{4} = ?$

(a) $\frac{2}{3}$ (b) $1\frac{1}{2}$ (c) $2\frac{3}{8}$ (d) $33\frac{1}{2}$

25. $7\frac{3}{5} \div \frac{1}{4} = ?$

(a) $24\frac{2}{7}$ (b) $27\frac{3}{8}$ (c) $30\frac{2}{5}$ (d) $33\frac{1}{2}$

Type-5: Answer - Key

1.	(b)	**6.**	(b)	**11.**	(b)	**16.**	(b)	**21.**	(a)
2.	(b)	**7.**	(d)	**12.**	(b)	**17.**	(b)	**22.**	(c)
3.	(a)	**8.**	(a)	**13.**	(c)	**18.**	(b)	**23.**	(a)
4.	(d)	**9.**	(b)	**14.**	(c)	**19.**	(d)	**24.**	(a)
5.	(c)	**10.**	(a)	**15.**	(c)	**20.**	(a)	**25.**	(c)

FRACTION (भिन्न)

Fraction Division

Type-1

Hint :

$\frac{1}{4} \div 3$

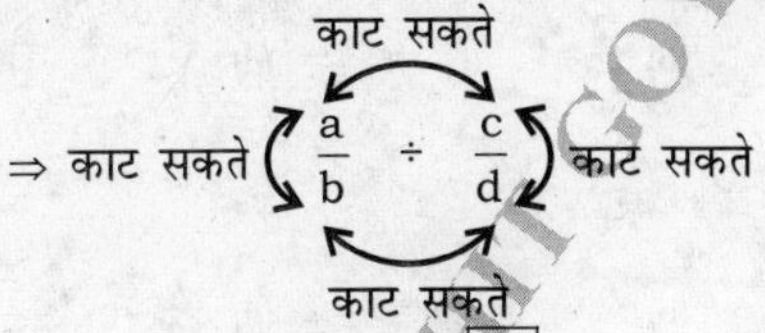

Result ⇒ $\frac{a}{b} \div \frac{c}{d} = \boxed{\frac{ad}{bc}}$

Example:

☞ $\left(\frac{1}{4} \div 3\right)$ है तो (3) Denominator से Multiply और $\left(\frac{1}{12}\right)$ Answer निकल जाएगा।

Exercise

1. $\frac{1}{4} \div 3$

(a) $\frac{1}{12}$ (b) $\frac{3}{4}$ (c) $\frac{4}{3}$ (d) 12

2. $\frac{1}{7} \div 5$

(a) $\frac{5}{7}$ (b) $\frac{7}{5}$ (c) $\frac{1}{35}$ (d) 35

3. $\frac{2}{5} \div 3$

(a) $\frac{6}{5}$ (b) $\frac{2}{15}$ (c) 7.5 (d) $\frac{2}{15}$

4. $\frac{3}{7} \div 4$

(a) $\frac{12}{7}$ (b) $\frac{28}{3}$ (c) $\frac{12}{5}$ (d) $\frac{3}{28}$

5. $\frac{8}{9} \div 12$

(a) $\frac{4}{27}$ (b) $\frac{2}{27}$ (c) $\frac{32}{3}$ (d) 6

6. $\frac{14}{5} \div 3$

(a) $\frac{42}{5}$ (b) $\frac{2}{3}$ (c) $\frac{15}{14}$ (d) $\frac{14}{15}$

7. $\frac{9}{7} \div 5$

(a) $\frac{9}{35}$ (b) $\frac{5}{63}$ (c) $\frac{35}{9}$ (d) $\frac{9}{7}$

8. $\frac{24}{7} \div 2$

(a) $\frac{7}{12}$ (b) $1\frac{5}{7}$ (c) $1\frac{3}{7}$ (d) $6\frac{6}{7}$

9. $\frac{22}{4} \div 5$

(a) $\frac{20}{27}$ (b) $1\frac{1}{10}$ (c) $1\frac{7}{20}$ (d) $\frac{4}{20}$

10. $\frac{33}{7} \div 2$

(a) $\frac{3}{14}$ (b) $2\frac{5}{14}$ (c) $\frac{14}{33}$ (d) 42

11. $\frac{96}{13} \div 2$

(a) $\frac{21}{26}$ (b) $2\frac{4}{13}$ (c) $3\frac{9}{13}$ (d) $5\frac{5}{13}$

12. $\frac{74}{5} \div 3$

(a) $\frac{15}{74}$ (b) $4\frac{14}{15}$ (c) 110 (d) $5\frac{4}{15}$

13. $\frac{127}{14} \div 5$

(a) $2\frac{57}{70}$ (b) $\frac{7}{15}$ (c) 2.4 (d) $1\frac{57}{70}$

14. $\frac{25}{8} \div 4$

(a) $\frac{25}{32}$ (b) $\frac{7}{25}$ (c) $1\frac{25}{32}$ (d) $1\frac{7}{25}$

15. $\frac{16}{17} \div 4$

(a) $3\frac{13}{17}$ (b) $\frac{5}{17}$ (c) $\frac{4}{17}$ (d) $2\frac{4}{17}$

16. $\frac{6}{5} \div 7$

(a) $8\frac{2}{5}$ (b) $\frac{6}{7}$ (c) $\frac{4}{5}$ (d) $\frac{6}{35}$

17. $\frac{8}{25} \div 6$

(a) $18\frac{3}{4}$ (b) $\frac{4}{75}$ (c) $1\frac{23}{25}$ (d) 21

18. $\frac{9}{22} \div 5$

(a) $2\frac{1}{22}$ (b) $\frac{9}{110}$ (c) $\frac{3}{22}$ (d) $\frac{9}{22}$

19. $\frac{17}{16} \div 3$

(a) $\frac{17}{48}$ (b) $2\frac{14}{17}$ (c) $\frac{14}{17}$ (d) $\frac{17}{42}$

20. $\frac{28}{5} \div 2$

(a) $\frac{5}{4}$ (b) $2\frac{4}{5}$ (c) $2\frac{5}{8}$ (d) $5\frac{3}{5}$

21. $\frac{114}{5} \div 10$

(a) $2\frac{4}{15}$ (b) $5\frac{4}{20}$ (c) $2\frac{7}{25}$ (d) $2\frac{6}{25}$

22. $\frac{74}{5} \div 3$

(a) $\frac{15}{74}$ (b) $\frac{13}{74}$ (c) $\frac{14}{15}$ (d) $4\frac{14}{15}$

23. $\frac{26}{5} \div 3$

(a) $1\frac{11}{15}$ (b) $1\frac{3}{5}$ (c) $\frac{9}{15}$ (d) $\frac{15}{26}$

24. $\frac{13}{4} \div 7$

(a) $\frac{13}{64}$ (b) $5\frac{3}{13}$ (c) $\frac{13}{28}$ (d) $\frac{17}{52}$

25. $\frac{19}{5} \div 16$

(a) $\frac{16}{95}$ (b) $\frac{19}{80}$ (c) $4\frac{4}{19}$ (d) $4\frac{3}{4}$

26. $\frac{16}{3} \div 4$

(a) $\frac{12}{17}$ (b) $\frac{3}{4}$ (c) 1 (d) $1\frac{1}{3}$

27. $\frac{17}{18} \div 3$

(a) $\frac{17}{54}$ (b) $4\frac{16}{17}$ (c) $\frac{7}{17}$ (d) $\frac{12}{17}$

28. $\frac{100}{11} \div 7$

(a) $\frac{33}{7}$ (b) $1\frac{23}{77}$ (c) $1\frac{3}{8}$ (d) $\frac{4}{11}$

29. $\frac{200}{9} \div 4$

(a) $\frac{800}{9}$ (b) $9\frac{5}{90}$ (c) $5\frac{5}{9}$ (d) 200

30. $\frac{120}{7} \div 15$

(a) $\frac{7}{8}$ (b) $1\frac{5}{7}$ (c) $1\frac{3}{35}$ (d) $1\frac{1}{7}$

31. $\frac{300}{13} \div 20$

(a) $1\frac{2}{13}$ (b) $\frac{13}{15}$ (c) 130 (d) $\frac{13}{30}$

32. $\frac{150}{19} \div 10$

(a) $\frac{15}{21}$ (b) $\frac{7}{19}$ (c) $\frac{15}{19}$ (d) $\frac{19}{15}$

Type-1: Answer - Key

1.	(a)	8.	(b)	15.	(c)	22.	(d)	29.	(c)
2.	(c)	9.	(b)	16.	(d)	23.	(a)	30.	(d)
3.	(b)	10.	(b)	17.	(b)	24.	(c)	31.	(a)
4.	(d)	11.	(c)	18.	(b)	25.	(b)	32.	(c)
5.	(b)	12.	(b)	19.	(a)	26.	(d)		
6.	(d)	13.	(d)	20.	(b)	27.	(a)		
7.	(a)	14.	(a)	21.	(c)	28.	(b)		

Type-2

Hint :

$$\frac{2}{3} \div \frac{7}{4}$$

☞ Cross multiply करके दिमाग में solve करना है और जो संख्या आपस मे कट जाती है उसे काट देना है जैसा Type 1 में बताया है।

$$\frac{2}{3} \times \frac{7}{4} = \frac{8}{21}$$

Exercise

1. $\frac{2}{3} \div \frac{7}{4}$

(a) $\frac{21}{8}$ (b) $\frac{8}{21}$ (c) $\frac{6}{7}$ (d) $1\frac{1}{6}$

2. $\frac{9}{4} \div \frac{8}{13}$

(a) $4\frac{21}{32}$ (b) $\frac{18}{13}$ (c) $3\frac{21}{32}$ (d) 2

3. $\frac{6}{7} \div \frac{14}{23}$

(a) $1\frac{20}{49}$ (b) $\frac{23}{12}$ (c) 46 (d) $\frac{84}{161}$

4. $\frac{4}{5} \div \frac{13}{15}$

(a) $\frac{13}{12}$ (b) $\frac{12}{13}$ (c) 4.5 (d) $\frac{15}{13}$

5. $\frac{9}{8} \div \frac{17}{5}$

(a) 1.6 (b) $3\frac{1}{45}$ (c) $\frac{45}{136}$ (d) $\frac{3}{17}$

6. $\frac{23}{4} \div \frac{7}{8}$

(a) $1\frac{2}{7}$ (b) $6\frac{4}{7}$ (c) $\frac{7}{23}$ (d) $2\frac{1}{7}$

7. $\frac{1}{3} \div \frac{1}{4}$

(a) $\frac{3}{4}$ (b) 12 (c) $\frac{1}{12}$ (d) $1\frac{1}{3}$

8. $\frac{1}{7} \div \frac{4}{3}$

(a) $\frac{3}{28}$ (b) $9\frac{1}{3}$ (c) 84 (d) $\frac{4}{21}$

9. $\frac{1}{5} \div \frac{7}{9}$

(a) $6\frac{3}{7}$ (b) $3\frac{8}{9}$ (c) $\frac{9}{35}$ (d) $\frac{7}{45}$

10. $\frac{1}{3} \div \frac{5}{14}$

(a) $\frac{14}{15}$ (b) $1\frac{1}{14}$ (c) $\frac{7}{9}$ (d) $\frac{4}{5}$

11. $\frac{33}{7} \div \frac{2}{5}$

(a) $\frac{66}{35}$ (b) $11\frac{3}{7}$ (c) $11\frac{11}{14}$ (d) $11\frac{1}{14}$

12. $\frac{2}{3} \div \frac{4}{7}$

(a) $\frac{8}{21}$ (b) $1\frac{1}{6}$ (c) $\frac{6}{7}$ (d) $2\frac{5}{8}$

13. $\frac{9}{4} \div \frac{13}{8}$

(a) $\frac{5}{13}$ (b) $\frac{13}{18}$ (c) $1\frac{5}{13}$ (d) $\frac{7}{8}$

14. $\frac{17}{4} \div \frac{2}{9}$

(a) $5\frac{2}{17}$ (b) $19\frac{1}{8}$ (c) 306 (d) $42\frac{1}{2}$

15. $\frac{8}{3} \div \frac{3}{2}$

(a) $\frac{3}{4}$ (b) $\frac{7}{9}$ (c) $1\frac{7}{9}$ (d) $\frac{9}{16}$

16. $\frac{200}{3} \div \frac{3}{5}$

(a) 360 (b) $111\frac{1}{9}$ (c) $33\frac{4}{5}$ (d) $\frac{1}{30}$

17. $\frac{15}{7} \div \frac{8}{14}$

(a) $\frac{7}{30}$ (b) $\frac{4}{15}$ (c) 60 (d) $3\frac{3}{4}$

18. $\frac{16}{13} \div \frac{5}{7}$

(a) 2 (b) $1\frac{47}{65}$ (c) $\frac{47}{65}$ (d) $\frac{65}{112}$

19. $\frac{19}{7} \div \frac{4}{3}$

(a) $\frac{21}{76}$ (b) $\frac{4}{19}$ (c) $2\frac{1}{28}$ (d) 2

20. $\frac{18}{7} \div \frac{9}{5}$

(a) $1\frac{3}{7}$ (b) $\frac{4}{7}$ (c) $3\frac{1}{3}$ (d) $\frac{80}{65}$

21. $\frac{26}{5} \div \frac{1}{20}$

(a) $3\frac{1}{4}$ (b) 26 (c) $\frac{4}{13}$ (d) 104

22. $\frac{71}{8} \div \frac{1}{11}$

(a) $\frac{71}{88}$ (b) $\frac{11}{568}$ (c) $97\frac{5}{8}$ (d) $\frac{8}{781}$

23. $\frac{6}{13} \div \frac{4}{7}$

(a) $\frac{21}{26}$ (b) $\frac{13}{21}$ (c) 52 (d) $1\frac{5}{21}$

24. $\frac{5}{12} \div \frac{13}{14}$

(a) 210 (b) $\frac{35}{78}$ (c) $2\frac{8}{35}$ (d) $\frac{7}{6}$

25. $\frac{8}{23} \div \frac{3}{7}$

(a) $1\frac{2}{69}$ (b) $\frac{14}{23}$ (c) $\frac{7}{23}$ (d) $\frac{56}{69}$

26. $\frac{25}{8} \div \frac{4}{3}$

(a) $2\frac{11}{32}$ (b) $\frac{25}{32}$ (c) $6\frac{9}{11}$ (d) 37.5

27. $\frac{16}{17} \div \frac{4}{5}$

(a) $\frac{17}{20}$ (b) $2\frac{6}{17}$ (c) $1\frac{3}{17}$ (d) $\frac{17}{40}$

28. $\frac{6}{5} \div \frac{7}{6}$

(a) $1\frac{1}{35}$ (b) $7\frac{2}{6}$ (c) 35 (d) $\frac{35}{36}$

29. $\frac{3}{7} \div \frac{4}{13}$

(a) 56 (b) $1\frac{11}{28}$ (c) $3\frac{6}{11}$ (d) $1\frac{1}{14}$

30. $\frac{8}{9} \div \frac{12}{5}$

(a) $\frac{20}{27}$ (b) $2\frac{7}{10}$ (c) $5\frac{2}{5}$ (d) $\frac{10}{27}$

31. $\frac{14}{5} \div \frac{3}{4}$

(a) $3\frac{9}{15}$ (b) $3\frac{11}{15}$ (c) $\frac{15}{56}$ (d) $\frac{11}{14}$

32. $\frac{108}{5} \div \frac{36}{4}$

(a) 2.5 (b) 60 (c) $1\frac{1}{4}$ (d) $2\frac{2}{5}$

33. $\frac{114}{7} \div \frac{3}{2}$

(a) $10\frac{5}{7}$ (b) $10\frac{6}{7}$ (c) $11\frac{6}{7}$ (d) $\frac{7}{8}$

Type-2: Answer - Key

1.	(b)	8.	(a)	15.	(c)	22.	(c)	29.	(b)
2.	(c)	9.	(c)	16.	(b)	23.	(a)	30.	(d)
3.	(a)	10.	(a)	17.	(d)	24.	(b)	31.	(b)
4.	(b)	11.	(c)	18.	(b)	25.	(d)	32.	(d)
5.	(c)	12.	(b)	19.	(c)	26.	(a)	33.	(b)
6.	(b)	13.	(c)	20.	(a)	27.	(c)		
7.	(d)	14.	(b)	21.	(d)	28.	(a)		

Type-3

Hint :

$9\frac{1}{4} \div 20$

Step-1 = Solve mixed fraction $\frac{37}{4}$

Step-2 = $\frac{37}{4} \div 20$

Step-3 = $\frac{37}{80}$ Ans.

$14\frac{2}{7} \div 5$

☞ इस type में $\left(14\frac{2}{7}\right)$ को $\left(\frac{100}{7}\right)$ भी लिख सकते है percentage में पढ़ा था। 100 कटेगा 5 से तो $\frac{20}{7}$ Answer निकल जाएगा।

ये thought process भी रखनी है दिमाग में।

Exercise

1. $9\frac{1}{4} \div 5$

(a) $2\frac{9}{20}$ (b) $1\frac{1}{4}$ (c) $1\frac{17}{20}$ (d) 1.2

2. $8\frac{7}{10} \div 3$

(a) $2\frac{9}{10}$ (b) 2.8 (c) $2\frac{2}{15}$ (d) $2\frac{1}{3}$

3. $14\frac{2}{7} \div 5$

(a) $2\frac{6}{7}$ (b) $2\frac{1}{35}$ (c) $2\frac{3}{14}$ (d) $2\frac{1}{3}$

4. $16\frac{2}{3} \div 7$

(a) 2.8 (b) $2\frac{3}{21}$ (c) $2\frac{8}{21}$ (d) $2\frac{1}{7}$

5. $33\frac{1}{3} \div 4$

(a) $8\frac{1}{4}$ (b) $8\frac{1}{3}$ (c) $8\frac{1}{12}$ (d) 8.66

6. $42\frac{3}{5} \div 20$

(a) 2.26 (b) $2\frac{3}{50}$ (c) $2\frac{13}{100}$ (d) $2\frac{13}{25}$

7. $8\frac{3}{4} \div 7$

(a) 1.13 (b) $1\frac{1}{4}$ (c) 1.50 (d) $1\frac{3}{4}$

8. $9\frac{1}{12} \div 8$

(a) 1.187 (b) $1\frac{5}{96}$ (c) $1\frac{13}{96}$ (d) $1\frac{3}{24}$

9. $11\frac{2}{3} \div 9$

(a) $1\frac{3}{27}$ (b) $1\frac{8}{27}$ (c) $1\frac{5}{27}$ (d) 1.2

10. $22\frac{2}{5} \div 10$

(a) 2.5 (b) $2\frac{7}{25}$ (c) $2\frac{6}{25}$ (d) $2\frac{8}{25}$

11. $2\frac{2}{3} \div 3$

(a) $\frac{8}{9}$ (b) $\frac{9}{10}$ (c) 0.72 (d) $1\frac{1}{9}$

12. $2\frac{1}{3} \div 6$

(a) .5 (b) $\frac{1}{3}$ (c) $\frac{1}{18}$ (d) $\frac{7}{18}$

13. $44\frac{4}{9} \div 3$

(a) $14\frac{22}{27}$ (b) 14.02 (c) $14\frac{4}{9}$ (d) $14\frac{2}{27}$

14. $11\frac{1}{9} \div 2$

(a) 5.45 (b) $5\frac{1}{9}$ (c) $5\frac{5}{9}$ (d) $5\frac{5}{18}$

15. $33\frac{1}{3} \div 5$

(a) 6.33 (b) $6\frac{2}{3}$ (c) $6\frac{1}{15}$ (d) $6\frac{3}{5}$

16. $16\frac{2}{3} \div 4$

(a) $4\frac{1}{3}$ (b) $4\frac{1}{6}$ (c) $4\frac{2}{3}$ (d) $4\frac{1}{12}$

17. $66\frac{2}{3} \div 3$

(a) $22\frac{1}{3}$ (b) $22\frac{2}{3}$ (c) $22\frac{2}{9}$ (d) 22.18

18. $14\frac{2}{7} \div 4$

(a) $3\frac{4}{7}$ (b) 3.33 (c) $3\frac{5}{7}$ (d) $3\frac{6}{7}$

19. $83\frac{1}{3} \div 50$

(a) 1.33 (b) $1\frac{3}{4}$ (c) $1\frac{2}{3}$ (d) $1\frac{3}{5}$

20. $28\frac{4}{7} \div 25$

(a) $1\frac{2}{7}$ (b) $1\frac{1}{7}$ (c) $1\frac{1}{35}$ (d) 1.3

21. $42\frac{6}{7} \div 15$

(a) 2.4 (b) $2\frac{6}{7}$ (c) $2\frac{1}{35}$ (d) $2\frac{5}{7}$

22. $57\frac{1}{7} \div 8$

(a) $7\frac{7}{8}$ (b) 7.07 (c) $7\frac{1}{56}$ (d) $7\frac{1}{7}$

23. $71\frac{3}{7} \div 20$

(a) $3\frac{4}{7}$ (b) 3.2 (c) $3\frac{3}{7}$ (d) $3\frac{3}{14}$

24. $85\frac{5}{7} \div 15$

(a) 5.45 (b) $5\frac{3}{5}$ (c) $5\frac{5}{7}$ (d) $5\frac{4}{7}$

25. $37\frac{1}{2} \div 13$

(a) $2\frac{23}{26}$ (b) $2\frac{5}{13}$ (c) 2.5 (d) $2\frac{12}{13}$

26. $37\frac{1}{2} \div 15$

(a) 2.33 (b) $2\frac{2}{3}$ (c) $2\frac{1}{15}$ (d) $2\frac{1}{2}$

27. $62\frac{1}{2} \div 3$

(a) $20\frac{2}{3}$ (b) $20\frac{5}{6}$ (c) $21\frac{5}{6}$ (d) 20.33

28. $87\frac{1}{2} \div 4$

(a) 21 (b) $20\frac{1}{4}$ (c) $21\frac{1}{8}$ (d) $21\frac{7}{8}$

29. $11\frac{1}{9} \div 4$

(a) $2\frac{7}{9}$ (b) $2\frac{1}{4}$ (c) $2\frac{2}{7}$ (d) 2.63

30. $22\frac{2}{9} \div 8$

(a) 2.63 (b) $2\frac{5}{9}$ (c) $2\frac{7}{9}$ (d) $\frac{7}{9}$

31. $44\frac{4}{9} \div 15$

(a) 2.1 (b) $2\frac{5}{27}$ (c) $2\frac{5}{15}$ (d) $2\frac{26}{27}$

32. $55\frac{5}{9} \div 25$

(a) $2\frac{2}{9}$ (b) $2\frac{1}{3}$ (c) $\frac{6}{5}$ (d) 2.18

33. $77\frac{7}{9} \div 14$

(a) 5.45 (b) $4\frac{4}{9}$ (c) $5\frac{5}{9}$ (d) $5\frac{2}{3}$

34. $88\frac{8}{9} \div 16$

(a) 5.45 (b) $5\frac{4}{9}$ (c) $5\frac{8}{9}$ (d) $5\frac{5}{9}$

35. $9\frac{1}{11} \div 4$

(a) 2.4 (b) $2\frac{3}{11}$ (c) $2\frac{5}{11}$ (d) $\frac{9}{44}$

36. $18\frac{2}{11} \div 25$

(a) $\frac{9}{11}$ (b) $\frac{7}{11}$ (c) $\frac{8}{11}$ (d) 0.9

37. $27\frac{3}{11} \div 15$

(a) $1\frac{10}{11}$ (b) $1\frac{9}{11}$ (c) $1\frac{7}{11}$ (d) 1.02

38. $36\frac{4}{11} \div 16$

(a) 2.8 (b) $8\frac{1}{3}$ (c) $2\frac{5}{11}$ (d) $2\frac{3}{11}$

39. $45\frac{5}{11} \div 25$

(a) $1\frac{9}{11}$ (b) 2.4 (c) $11\frac{1}{9}$ (d) $\frac{100}{99}$

40. $54\frac{6}{11} \div 15$

(a) $\frac{5}{77}$ (b) $3\frac{2}{11}$ (c) $2\frac{3}{11}$ (d) $3\frac{7}{11}$

41. $63\frac{7}{11} \div 7$

(a) $9\frac{1}{11}$ (b) $\frac{11}{9}$ (c) $\frac{9}{11}$ (d) 99

42. $72\frac{8}{11} \div 16$

(a) 15 (b) $8\frac{2}{3}$ (c) $4\frac{6}{11}$ (d) $5\frac{5}{11}$

43. $81\frac{9}{11} \div 18$

(a) 4 (b) $4\frac{6}{11}$ (c) $8\frac{2}{3}$ (d) $3\frac{5}{11}$

44. $90\frac{10}{11} \div 500$

(a) 22 (b) $5\frac{1}{2}$ (c) $\frac{2}{11}$ (d) $\frac{1}{11}$

Type-3: Answer - Key

1.	(c)	**10.**	(c)	**19.**	(c)	**28.**	(d)	**37.**	(b)
2.	(a)	**11.**	(a)	**20.**	(b)	**29.**	(a)	**38.**	(d)
3.	(a)	**12.**	(d)	**21.**	(b)	**30.**	(c)	**39.**	(a)
4.	(c)	**13.**	(a)	**22.**	(d)	**31.**	(d)	**40.**	(d)
5.	(b)	**14.**	(c)	**23.**	(a)	**32.**	(a)	**41.**	(a)
6.	(c)	**15.**	(b)	**24.**	(c)	**33.**	(c)	**42.**	(c)
7.	(b)	**16.**	(b)	**25.**	(a)	**34.**	(d)	**43.**	(b)
8.	(c)	**17.**	(c)	**26.**	(d)	**35.**	(b)	**44.**	(c)
9.	(b)	**18.**	(a)	**27.**	(b)	**36.**	(c)		

Type-4

Hint :

$1\frac{1}{4} \div \frac{3}{7}$

Step-1 $\Rightarrow \frac{5}{4}$

Step-2 $\Rightarrow \frac{5}{4} \times \frac{3}{7} = \boxed{\frac{35}{12}}$

लिखना नहीं है दिमाग में रोक कर करो

Exercise

1. $1\frac{1}{4} \div \frac{3}{7}$

(a) $\frac{5}{7}$ (b) $2\frac{11}{12}$ (c) $\frac{12}{35}$ (d) $2\frac{1}{7}$

2. $3\frac{1}{7} \div \frac{2}{3}$

(a) $4\frac{2}{7}$ (b) $\frac{7}{33}$ (c) $\frac{21}{44}$ (d) $4\frac{5}{7}$

3. $9\frac{1}{2} \div \frac{4}{7}$

(a) $15\frac{5}{8}$ (b) $16\frac{5}{8}$ (c) $17\frac{3}{8}$ (d) $\frac{5}{14}$

4. $4\frac{1}{5} \div \frac{8}{3}$

(a) $1\frac{3}{40}$ (b) $\frac{23}{40}$ (c) $\frac{40}{63}$ (d) $1\frac{23}{40}$

5. $9\frac{7}{4} \div \frac{11}{4}$

(a) $4\frac{3}{10}$ (b) $3\frac{10}{11}$ (c) $\frac{11}{16}$ (d) $3\frac{5}{11}$

6. $8\frac{4}{3} \div \frac{7}{5}$

(a) $4\frac{18}{4}$ (b) $4\frac{2}{3}$ (c) $6\frac{1}{3}$ (d) $6\frac{2}{3}$

7. $\frac{9}{5} \div 12\frac{1}{4}$

(a) $\frac{36}{245}$ (b) $\frac{2}{49}$ (c) $\frac{3}{7}$ (d) $\frac{5}{49}$

8. $\frac{8}{3} \div 13\frac{1}{4}$

(a) $\frac{24}{159}$ (b) $1\frac{1}{53}$ (c) $\frac{32}{159}$ (d) $\frac{11}{53}$

9. $\frac{2}{7} \div 4\frac{1}{8}$

(a) $\frac{4}{77}$ (b) $\frac{16}{231}$ (c) $\frac{2}{11}$ (d) $\frac{1}{7}$

10. $\frac{11}{7} \div 6\frac{1}{5}$

(a) $\frac{11}{217}$ (b) $\frac{7}{31}$ (c) $\frac{5}{31}$ (d) $\frac{55}{217}$

11. $\frac{21}{5} \div 3\frac{1}{2}$

(a) $\frac{6}{5}$ (b) $\frac{7}{6}$ (c) $\frac{5}{6}$ (d) $\frac{6}{7}$

12. $\frac{48}{7} \div 2\frac{1}{5}$

(a) $3\frac{9}{11}$ (b) $3\frac{4}{77}$ (c) $3\frac{4}{7}$ (d) $3\frac{9}{77}$

13. $66\frac{2}{3} \div \frac{3}{5}$

(a) $110\frac{1}{9}$ (b) $111\frac{1}{9}$ (c) $111\frac{1}{11}$ (d) $112\frac{8}{11}$

14. $9\frac{1}{9} \div \frac{9}{2}$

(a) $9\frac{1}{2}$ (b) $2\frac{2}{9}$ (c) $2\frac{2}{81}$ (d) $2\frac{1}{27}$

15. $14\frac{2}{7} \div \frac{14}{5}$

(a) $5\frac{1}{35}$ (b) $5\frac{5}{49}$ (c) $5\frac{5}{7}$ (d) $5\frac{15}{49}$

16. $8\frac{5}{8} \div \frac{2}{7}$

(a) $30\frac{3}{16}$ (b) $30\frac{1}{4}$ (c) $30\frac{1}{16}$ (d) $30\frac{3}{4}$

17. $8\frac{7}{8} \div \frac{8}{11}$

(a) $12\frac{21}{64}$ (b) $12\frac{7}{16}$ (c) $12\frac{3}{4}$ (d) $12\frac{13}{64}$

18. $11\frac{1}{9} \div \frac{11}{9}$

(a) $9\frac{2}{11}$ (b) $9\frac{1}{11}$ (c) $11\frac{1}{9}$ (d) $11\frac{2}{9}$

Type-4: Answer - Key

1. (b)	5. (b)	9. (b)	13. (b)	17. (d)
2. (d)	6. (d)	10. (d)	14. (c)	18. (b)
3. (b)	7. (a)	11. (a)	15. (b)	
4. (d)	8. (c)	12. (d)	16. (a)	

Type-5

Example-1:

$$1\frac{1}{4} \div 2\frac{1}{7}$$

Step-1 $\Rightarrow$ Solved mixed fraction $\frac{5}{4} \div \frac{15}{7}$

Step-2 $\Rightarrow$ Cancel out if possible $\frac{\cancel{5}}{4} \div \frac{\cancel{15}^{3}}{7}$

Step-3 $\Rightarrow$ $\frac{7}{12}$ Answer by above explanation

Example-2:

$$33\frac{1}{3} \div 7\frac{1}{7}$$

☞ इस Type के लिए $\left(33\frac{1}{3}\right)$ को $\left(\frac{100}{3}\right)$ बोलते है और $\left(7\frac{1}{7}\right)$ को $\left(\frac{50}{7}\right)$ बोलते है

Step-1 $\Rightarrow$ $\frac{\overset{2}{\cancel{100}}}{3} \times \frac{\cancel{50}}{7}$

Step-2 $\Rightarrow$ $\boxed{\frac{14}{3}}$ Answer

Percentage का application दिमाग में करके।

FRACTION (भिन्न)

Exercise

1. $1\frac{1}{4} \div 2\frac{1}{7}$

(a) $\frac{7}{12}$ (b) $\frac{7}{60}$ (c) $\frac{14}{12}$ (d) $\frac{14}{12}$

2. $2\frac{1}{3} \div 3\frac{1}{4}$

(a) $\frac{39}{28}$ (b) $\frac{14}{13}$ (c) $\frac{28}{39}$ (d) $\frac{7}{13}$

3. $9\frac{1}{7} \div 7\frac{1}{9}$

(a) $\frac{8}{7}$ (b) $1\frac{2}{7}$ (c) $1\frac{3}{7}$ (d) $\frac{63}{81}$

4. $4\frac{1}{16} \div 5\frac{1}{2}$

(a) $\frac{5}{11}$ (b) $\frac{52}{88}$ (c) $\frac{65}{88}$ (d) $\frac{5}{8}$

5. $9\frac{1}{2} \div 7\frac{1}{8}$

(a) $1\frac{1}{3}$ (b) $1\frac{2}{3}$ (c) $\frac{2}{3}$ (d) $1\frac{1}{4}$

6. $8\frac{4}{3} \div 3\frac{5}{8}$

(a) $2\frac{2}{29}$ (b) $2\frac{3}{29}$ (c) $2\frac{50}{87}$ (d) $2\frac{25}{87}$

7. $11\frac{1}{5} \div 7\frac{1}{4}$

(a) $1\frac{79}{145}$ (b) $\frac{3}{20}$ (c) $1\frac{3}{29}$ (d) $1\frac{89}{145}$

8. $10\frac{1}{4} \div 3\frac{1}{2}$

(a) $2\frac{2}{7}$ (b) $2\frac{13}{14}$ (c) $1\frac{2}{7}$ (d) $2\frac{8}{14}$

9. $9\frac{1}{11} \div 7\frac{4}{13}$

(a) $1\frac{19}{31}$ (b) $1\frac{18}{31}$ (c) $1\frac{41}{209}$ (d) $1\frac{51}{209}$

10. $22\frac{1}{4} \div 4\frac{1}{3}$

(a) $\frac{8}{13}$ (b) $5\frac{5}{52}$ (c) $5\frac{7}{52}$ (d) $5\frac{1}{13}$

11. $33\frac{1}{4} \div 5\frac{1}{5}$

(a) $6\frac{41}{104}$ (b) $6\frac{59}{104}$ (c) $6\frac{51}{104}$ (d) $6\frac{1}{3}$

12. $33\frac{1}{3} \div 7\frac{1}{7}$

(a) $4\frac{1}{6}$ (b) $3\frac{1}{3}$ (c) $4\frac{1}{3}$ (d) $4\frac{2}{3}$

13. $66\frac{2}{3} \div 7\frac{1}{7}$

(a) $9\frac{1}{7}$ (b) $9\frac{1}{3}$ (c) $9\frac{11}{21}$ (d) $9\frac{1}{21}$

14. $33\frac{1}{3} \div 11\frac{1}{9}$

(a) 6 (b) $\frac{1}{3}$ (c) 3 (d) $\frac{1}{9}$

15. $11\frac{1}{9} \div 7\frac{1}{7}$

(a) $1\frac{2}{9}$ (b) $1\frac{5}{9}$ (c) $1\frac{1}{9}$ (d) $1\frac{7}{9}$

16. $66\frac{2}{3} \div 11\frac{1}{9}$

(a) 6 (b) $\frac{5}{9}$ (c) $\frac{1}{9}$ (d) $6\frac{1}{9}$

17. $22\frac{2}{9} \div 66\frac{2}{3}$

(a) $\frac{1}{6}$ (b) $\frac{1}{9}$ (c) $\frac{1}{3}$ (d) $\frac{2}{3}$

18. $44\frac{4}{9} \div 36\frac{4}{11}$

(a) $1\frac{8}{11}$ (b) $1\frac{2}{9}$ (c) $1\frac{1}{9}$ (d) $\frac{9}{11}$

19. $62\frac{1}{2} \div 37\frac{1}{2}$

(a) $1\frac{1}{3}$ (b) $\frac{1}{3}$ (c) $1\frac{2}{3}$ (d) $\frac{2}{3}$

20. $90\frac{10}{11} \div 62\frac{1}{2}$

(a) $1\frac{5}{11}$ (b) $1\frac{6}{11}$ (c) $1\frac{5}{22}$ (d) $\frac{9}{11}$

21. $14\frac{2}{7} \div 54\frac{6}{11}$

(a) $\frac{18}{42}$ (b) $\frac{5}{21}$ (c) $\frac{11}{42}$ (d) $\frac{1}{14}$

22. $16\frac{2}{3} \div 7\frac{1}{7}$

(a) $2\frac{1}{7}$ (b) $2\frac{1}{3}$ (c) $2\frac{2}{3}$ (d) $3\frac{2}{3}$

23. $8\frac{1}{3} \div 27\frac{3}{11}$

(a) $\frac{13}{36}$ (b) $\frac{5}{36}$ (c) $\frac{7}{36}$ (d) $\frac{11}{36}$

24. $57\frac{1}{7} \div 83\frac{1}{3}$

(a) $\frac{24}{35}$ (b) $\frac{4}{5}$ (c) $\frac{4}{7}$ (d) $\frac{3}{5}$

25. $87\frac{1}{2} \div 18\frac{2}{11}$

(a) $4\frac{1}{22}$ (b) $4\frac{13}{16}$ (c) $4\frac{11}{16}$ (d) $4\frac{6}{11}$

Type-5: Answer - Key

1.	(a)	6.	(c)	11.	(a)	16.	(a)	21.	(c)
2.	(c)	7.	(a)	12.	(d)	17.	(c)	22.	(b)
3.	(b)	8.	(b)	13.	(b)	18.	(b)	23.	(d)
4.	(c)	9.	(d)	14.	(c)	19.	(c)	24.	(a)
5.	(a)	10.	(c)	15.	(b)	20.	(a)	25.	(b)

PERCENTAGE (प्रतिशत)

Type-1

Hint :

1% of 19 =

⇒ 1%, 10%, 100%, 150%, 200%

Concept used:

☞ एक (1%) का मतलब 2 place पहले Decimal लगा देना (10%) का मतलब 1 place पहले Decimal लगा देना (100%) का मतलब (1 गुना) (150%) का मतलब (1.5) गुना और (200%) का मतलब 2 गुना

Ex: 1% of 19

☞ 1% का मतलब दो place पहले Decimal लगा देना। जो 0.19 हो जाएगा।

Exercise

1. 1% of 19 =

(a) 0.19 (b) 1.9 (c) 0.019 (d) 19

2. 50% of 19 =

(a) 19 (b) 9.5 (c) 38 (d) 95

3. 150% of 19 =

(a) 19 (b) 38 (c) 28.5 (d) 22.5

4. 10% of 118 =

(a) 1.18 (b) 11.8 (c) 18.1 (d) 8.11

5. 150 % of 118 =
(a) 236 (b) 118 (c) 59 (d) 177

6. 200% of 118 =
(a) 236 (b) 354 (c) 177 (d) 218

7. 10% of 206 =
(a) 2.06 (b) 20.6 (c) 206 (d) 2.60

8. 200% of 206 =
(a) 206 (b) 20.6 (c) 406 (d) 412

9. 1% of 143 =
(a) 1.43 (b) 14.3 (c) 143 (d) 13.4

10. 50% of 143 =
(a) 73.55 (b) 71.5 (c) 214.5 (d) 72.5

11. 150% of 143 =
(a) 143 (b) 286 (c) 214.5 (d) 71.5

12. 1% of 27.5 =
(a) 0.275 (b) 27.5 (c) 25.7 (d) 275

13. 200% of 27.5 =
(a) 55 (b) 27.5 (c) 41.25 (d) 82.5

14. 150% of 27.5 =
(a) 27.5 (b) 55 (c) 41.25 (d) 82.5

15. 1% of 298 =
(a) 2.98 (b) 29.8 (c) 28.9 (d) 298

16. 50% of 298 =
(a) 223.5 (b) 298 (c) 447 (d) 149

17. 150% of 298 =
(a) 149 (b) 223.5 (c) 298 (d) 447

18. 1% of 6.04 =
(a) 0.0604 (b) 0.604 (c) 6.04 (d) 60.4

19. 10% of 6.04 =
(a) 0.0604 (b) 0.604 (c) 6.04 (d) 60.4

20. 50% of 6.04 =
(a) 60.4 (b) 0.302 (c) 3.02 (d) 30.2

21. 150% of 6.04 =
(a) 90.6 (b) 9.06 (c) 12.08 (d) 60.4

22. 200% of 6.04 =
(a) 18.12 (b) 9.06 (c) 12.08 (d) 24.16

23. 1% of 529 =
(a) 0.529 (b) 5.29 (c) 52.9 (d) 529

24. 50% of 529 =
(a) 26.45 (b) 211.6 (c) 260.45 (d) 264.5

25. 150% of 529 =
(a) 634.8 (b) 793.5 (c) 740.6 (d) 1322.5

26. 1% of 0.04 =
(a) 0.04 (b) 0.004 (c) 0.0004 (d) 0.4

27. 10% of 0.04 =
(a) 0.04 (b) 0.004 (c) 0.0004 (d) 0.4

28. 50% of 0.04 =
(a) 0.0002 (b) 0.002 (c) 0.08 (d) 0.02

29. 150% of 0.04 =
(a) 0.0006 (b) 0.06 (c) 0.08 (d) 0.006

30. 1% of 0.78 =
(a) 0.0078 (b) 0.078 (c) 0.00078 (d) 0.78

31. 10% of 0.78 =
(a) 0.0078 (b) 0.078 (c) 7.8 (d) 0.78

32. 50% of 0.78 =
(a) 0.117 (b) 0.039 (c) 3.9 (d) 0.39

33. 150% of 0.78 =
(a) 0.117 (b) 1.17 (c) 11.7 (d) 1.56

34. 50% of 27.54 =
(a) 13.77 (b) 11.016 (c) 2.754 (d) 1.377

35. 150% of 27.54 =
(a) 43.33 (b) 40.3 (c) 42.32 (d) 41.31

36. 50% of 89.6 =
(a) 44.8 (b) 43.3 (c) 40.32 (d) 134.4

37. 200% of 89.6 =
(a) 143.36 (b) 161.28 (c) 179.2 (d) 134.4

38. 1% of 512 =
(a) 0.512 (b) 51.2 (c) 5.12 (d) 0.0512

39. 50% of 512 =
(a) 256 (b) 51.2 (c) 768 (d) 1024

40. 1% of 2032 =
(a) 203.2 (b) 20.32 (c) 2.032 (d) 0.2032

41. 10% of 2032 =
(a) 203.2 (b) 20.32 (c) 2.032 (d) 0.2032

42. 50% of 2032 =
(a) 4064 (b) 2032 (c) 3048 (d) 1016

43. 150% of 830 =
(a) 1328 (b) 1245 (c) 1162 (d) 996

44. 200% of 625 =
(a) 625 (b) 1250 (c) 1875 (d) 750

45. 1% of 350 =
(a) 3.5 (b) 0.035 (c) 35 (d) 0.35

46. 10% of 350 =
(a) 3.5 (b) 70 (c) 35 (d) 0.35

47. 50% of 960 =

(a) 480 (b) 96 (c) 48 (d) 720

48. 150% of 960 =

(a) 2400 (b) 1152 (c) 1536 (d) 1440

Type-1: Answer - Key

1.	(a)	**11.**	(c)	**21.**	(b)	**31.**	(b)	**41.**	(a)
2.	(b)	**12.**	(a)	**22.**	(c)	**32.**	(d)	**42.**	(d)
3.	(c)	**13.**	(a)	**23.**	(b)	**33.**	(b)	**43.**	(b)
4.	(b)	**14.**	(c)	**24.**	(d)	**34.**	(a)	**44.**	(b)
5.	(d)	**15.**	(a)	**25.**	(b)	**35.**	(d)	**45.**	(a)
6.	(a)	**16.**	(d)	**26.**	(c)	**36.**	(a)	**46.**	(c)
7.	(b)	**17.**	(d)	**27.**	(b)	**37.**	(c)	**47.**	(a)
8.	(d)	**18.**	(a)	**28.**	(d)	**38.**	(c)	**48.**	(d)
9.	(a)	**19.**	(b)	**29.**	(b)	**39.**	(a)		
10.	(b)	**20.**	(c)	**30.**	(a)	**40.**	(b)		

Type-2

Hint :

$\frac{1}{3}$

☞ $\frac{1}{3}$ को हम percentage में 33.33% लिखते हैं, जब बोला जाए $\left(\frac{2}{3}\right)$ तो $\left(\frac{1}{3}\right)$ का दोगुना नजर आ रहा है तो उत्तर 33.33 का दोगुना 66.66% आएगा।

Conclusion:

☞ Percentage के multiple देखकर Answer calculate करना है।

Example = $\frac{1}{3} = 33.33$ है ऐसे ही $\frac{2}{3} = 66.66$ है- दोगुना कर दिया है।

Exercise

- **Convert the following fractions into percentage:**

1. 1 / 3 =

(a) 66.66 (b) 33.33 (c) 63.33 (d) 36.66

2. 2 / 3 =

(a) 66.66 (b) 33.33 (c) 63.33 (d) 36.66

3. 1 / 4 =

(a) 20 (b) 25 (c) 27.5 (d) 50

4. 3 / 4 =

(a) 25 (b) 50 (c) 65 (d) 75

5. 1 / 5 =

(a) 15 (b) 25 (c) 20 (d) 50

6. 2 / 5 =

(a) 40 (b) 50 (c) 20 (d) 60

7. 3 / 5 =

(a) 40 (b) 60 (c) 75 (d) 80

8. 4 / 5 =

(a) 60 (b) 40 (c) 75 (d) 80

9. 7 / 5 =

(a) 115 (b) 140 (c) 120 (d) 160

10. 9 / 5 =

(a) 90 (b) 190 (c) 180 (d) 145

11. 1 / 6 =

(a) 13.33 (b) 16.66 (c) 15.75 (d) 33.33

12. 5 / 6 =

(a) 78.33 (b) 120 (c) 63.33 (d) 83.33

13. 7 / 6 =

(a) 116.66 (b) 166.66 (c) 136.66 (d) 126.66

14. 11 / 6 =

(a) 185 (b) 163.33 (c) 183.33 (d) 166.66

15. 1 / 7 =

(a) 7.28 (b) 14.28 (c) 28.56 (d) 16.56

16. 2 / 7 =

(a) 35.71 (b) 28.57 (c) 14.28 (d) 42.84

17. 3 / 7 =
(a) 42.85 (b) 35.71 (c) 28.56 (d) 21.42

18. 4 / 7 =
(a) 57.14 (b) 71.42 (c) 64.28 (d) 42.85

19. 5 / 7 =
(a) 64.28 (b) 85.68 (c) 57.12 (d) 71.42

20. 6 / 7 =
(a) 85.71 (b) 71.82 (c) 64.28 (d) 92.82

21. 8 / 7 =
(a) 121.42 (b) 107.14 (c) 112.24 (d) 114.28

22. 9 / 7 =
(a) 128.57 (b) 142.85 (c) 157.14 (d) 135.72

23. 12 / 7 =
(a) 157.14 (b) 171.42 (c) 128.57 (d) 142.85

24. 1 / 8 =
(a) 13.5 (b) 16.5 (c) 12.5 (d) 18.5

25. 3 / 8 =
(a) 35.7 (b) 37.5 (c) 38.5 (d) 36.5

26. 5 / 8 =
(a) 62.5 (b) 60 (c) 67.5 (d) 72

27. 7 / 8 =
(a) 82.5 (b) 85 (c) 92 (d) 87.5

28. 9 / 8 =
(a) 102.5 (b) 108 (c) 117 (d) 112.5

29. 11 / 8 =
(a) 137.5 (b) 132.5 (c) 142 (d) 136

30. 1 / 9 =
(a) 22.22 (b) 11.11 (c) 11.22 (d) 18.18

31. 2 / 9 =

(a) 18.18 (b) 22.22 (c) 36.36 (d) 33.33

32. 4 / 9 =

(a) 33.33 (b) 22.22 (c) 44.44 (d) 36.36

33. 5 / 9 =

(a) 55.55 (b) 44.44 (c) 54.54 (d) 45.45

34. 7 / 9 =

(a) 88.88 (b) 66.66 (c) 63.63 (d) 77.77

35. 8 / 9 =

(a) 77.77 (b) 88.88 (c) 84.84 (d) 72.72

36. 11 / 9 =

(a) 122.22 (b) 111.11 (c) 133.33 (d) 101.01

37. 13 / 9 =

(a) 136.36 (b) 144.44 (c) 133.33 (d) 145.45

38. 1 / 10 =

(a) 10 (b) 20 (c) 5 (d) 25

39. 3 / 10 =

(a) 35 (b) 33.33 (c) 3 (d) 30

40. 7 / 10 =

(a) 50 (b) 35 (c) 7 (d) 70

41. 11 / 10 =

(a) 111 (b) 11 (c) 110 (d) 55

42. 13 / 10 =

(a) 133 (b) 130 (c) 13 (d) 133.33

43. 17 / 10 =

(a) 170 (b) 17 (c) 185 (d) 175

44. 23 / 10 =

(a) 23 (b) 250 (c) 230 (d) 233.33

45. 1 / 11 =

(a) 18.18 (b) 9.09 (c) 10.10 (d) 11.11

46. 2 / 11 =
(a) 36.36 (b) 22.22 (c) 18.36 (d) 18.18

47. 3 / 11 =
(a) 27.27 (b) 36.36 (c) 18.36 (d) 18.18

48. 4 / 11 =
(a) 36.36 (b) 44.44 (c) 36 (d) 33.33

49. 5 / 11 =
(a) 55.55 (b) 54.54 (c) 45 (d) 45.45

50. 6 / 11 =
(a) 63.63 (b) 54.54 (c) 55.55 (d) 66.66

51. 7 / 11 =
(a) 63.63 (b) 77.77 (c) 72.72 (d) 66.66

52. 8 / 11 =
(a) 88.88 (b) 81.81 (c) 72.72 (d) 72

53. 9 / 11 =
(a) 90.90 (b) 99.99 (c) 81.81 (d) 88.88

54. 10 / 11 =
(a) 99.99 (b) 90.90 (c) 89.89 (d) 110.10

55. 12 / 11 =
(a) 112.12 (b) 110.10 (c) 108.08 (d) 109.09

56. 13 / 11 =
(a) 136.36 (b) 118.18 (c) 124.24 (d) 127.27

57. 14 / 11 =
(a) 127.27 (b) 136.36 (c) 145.45 (d) 144.44

58. 15 / 11 =
(a) 155.55 (b) 145.45 (c) 144.44 (d) 136.36

59. 16 / 11 =
(a) 154.54 (b) 163.63 (c) 145.45 (d) 166.66

60. 1 / 12 =

(a) 7.5 (b) 8.25 (c) 8.33 (d) 8.5

61. 5 / 12 =

(a) 42.5 (b) 45 (c) 41.66 (d) 46.66

62. 7 / 12 =

(a) 56.5 (b) 58.33 (c) 62.5 (d) 56.66

63. 11 / 12 =

(a) 88.75 (b) 92.5 (c) 87.5 (d) 91.66

64. 1 / 13 =

(a) 7.69 (b) 7.91 (c) 6.79 (d) 8.33

65. 1 / 14 =

(a) 7.14 (b) 7.07 (c) 14.28 (d) 7.28

66. 3 / 14 =

(a) 24.48 (b) 28.56 (c) 27.54 (d) 21.42

67. 5 / 14 =

(a) 42.85 (b) 57.12 (c) 35.71 (d) 71.42

68. 1 / 15 =

(a) 6.33 (b) 7.5 (c) 6.66 (d) 6.5

69. 2 / 15 =

(a) 13.33 (b) 16.66 (c) 12.5 (d) 15.7

70. 4 / 15 =

(a) 26.66 (b) 26.5 (c) 23.33 (d) 27.5

71. 7 / 15 =

(a) 43.44 (b) 46.66 (c) 47.5 (d) 37.5

72. 8 / 15 =

(a) 52 (b) 56.66 (c) 57.5 (d) 53.33

73. 11 / 15 =

(a) 72.5 (b) 76.66 (c) 73.33 (d) 67.5

74. 1 / 16 =

(a) 6.33 (b) 6.75 (c) 6.25 (d) 7.25

75. 3 / 16 =

(a) 18.75 (b) 18.25 (c) 27.5 (d) 24

76. 5 / 16 =

(a) 32 (b) 31.25 (c) 36 (d) 37.5

77. 7 / 16 =

(a) 42.5 (b) 45 (c) 40 (d) 43.75

78. 9 / 16 =

(a) 56.25 (b) 57.5 (c) 56 (d) 54.75

79. 11 / 16 =

(a) 68.75 (b) 67.5 (c) 65.75 (d) 64

80. 1 / 20 =

(a) 4 (b) 5 (c) 15 (d) 6

81. 7 / 20 =

(a) 42 (b) 35 (c) 28 (d) 40

82. 11 / 20 =

(a) 66 (b) 44 (c) 55 (d) 33

83. 13 / 20 =

(a) 78 (b) 52 (c) 65 (d) 39

84. 16 / 15 =

(a) 103.33 (b) 106.66 (c) 110.5 (d) 107.25

85. 16 / 7 =

(a) 214.28 (b) 228.57 (c) 207.14 (d) 225.28

86. 45 / 8 =

(a) 562.5 (b) 550 (c) 542.5 (d) 560

87. 1 / 24 =

(a) 4.133 (b) 4.33 (c) 4.166 (d) 4.66

88. 23 / 12 =

(a) 191.66 (b) 191.76 (c) 192.68 (d) 192.76

89. 1 / 25 =

(a) 4 (b) 5 (c) 6 (d) 2.5

90. 1 / 30 =

(a) 3.33 (b) 33.33 (c) 3 (d) 3.5

91. 1 / 40 =

(a) 3.75 (b) 2.5 (c) 4 (d) 7.5

92. 1 / 50 =

(a) 3 (b) 5 (c) 2.5 (d) 2

93. 38 / 13 =

(a) 293.3 (b) 295 (c) 292.3 (d) 285

94. 1 / 17 =

(a) 6.33 (b) 5.75 (c) 6.25 (d) 5.88

95. 1 /18 =

(a) 4.44 (b) 6.66 (c) 5.66 (d) 5.55

96. 1 / 19 =

(a) 5.25 (b) 5.75 (c) 5.26 (d) 5.5

97. 1 / 21 =

(a) 4.76 (b) 4.25 (c) 4.75 (d) 4.5

98. 1 / 12 =

(a) 8.25 (b) 8.5 (c) 8.33 (d) 8.75

99. 1 / 23 =

(a) 4.43 (b) 4.34 (c) 3.34 (d) 3.43

100. 35 / 6 =

(a) 583.33 (b) 586.66 (c) 583 (d) 586

101. 29 / 3 =

(a) 950 (b) 933.33 (c) 975 (d) 966.66

102. 41 / 8 =

(a) 537.5 (b) 525 (c) 512.5 (d) 527.5

103. 37 / 15 =
(a) 241.66 (b) 243.33 (c) 246.66 (d) 241.33

104. 71 / 12 =
(a) 593.33 (b) 591.66 (c) 591.33 (d) 593.66

105. 13 / 12 =
(a) 112.33 (b) 108.66 (c) 112.66 (d) 108.33

106. 59 / 15 =
(a) 393.66 (b) 396.66 (c) 393.33 (d) 396.33

107. 17 / 6 =
(a) 283.33 (b) 286.33 (c) 283.66 (d) 286.66

108. 1 / 70 =
(a) 1.49 (b) 1.42 (c) 1.35 (d) 1.24

109. 1 / 60 =
(a) 1.36 (b) 1.66 (c) 1.63 (d) 1.33

110. 1 / 90 =
(a) 1.81 (b) 1.90 (c) 1.18 (d) 1.11

111. 1 / 110 =
(a) 0.85 (b) 0.818 (c) 0.909 (d) 0.99

112. 1 / 120 =
(a) 0.833 (b) 0.866 (c) 0.875 (d) 0.825

113. 1 / 140 =
(a) 0.714 (b) 0.75 (c) 0.728 (d) 0.76

114. 1 / 150 =
(a) 0.36 (b) 0.63 (c) 0.75 (d) 0.66

115. 1 / 22 =
(a) 5.45 (b) 4.54 (c) 4.63 (d) 5.54

116. 1/18 =
(a) 4.44 (b) 6.66 (c) 9.99 (d) 5.55

Type-2: Answer - Key

1.	(b)	24.	(c)	47.	(a)	70.	(a)	93.	(c)
2.	(a)	25.	(b)	48.	(a)	71.	(b)	94.	(d)
3.	(b)	26.	(a)	49.	(d)	72.	(d)	95.	(d)
4.	(d)	27.	(d)	50.	(b)	73.	(c)	96.	(c)
5.	(c)	28.	(d)	51.	(a)	74.	(c)	97.	(a)
6.	(a)	29.	(a)	52.	(c)	75.	(a)	98.	(c)
7.	(b)	30.	(b)	53.	(c)	76.	(b)	99.	(b)
8.	(d)	31.	(b)	54.	(b)	77.	(d)	100.	(a)
9.	(b)	32.	(c)	55.	(d)	78.	(a)	101.	(d)
10.	(c)	33.	(a)	56.	(b)	79.	(a)	102.	(c)
11.	(b)	34.	(d)	57.	(a)	80.	(b)	103.	(c)
12.	(d)	35.	(b)	58.	(d)	81.	(b)	104.	(b)
13.	(a)	36.	(a)	59.	(c)	82.	(c)	105.	(d)
14.	(c)	37.	(b)	60.	(c)	83.	(c)	106.	(c)
15.	(b)	38.	(a)	61.	(c)	84.	(b)	107.	(a)
16.	(b)	39.	(d)	62.	(b)	85.	(b)	108.	(b)
17.	(a)	40.	(d)	63.	(d)	86.	(a)	109.	(b)
18.	(a)	41.	(c)	64.	(a)	87.	(c)	110.	(d)
19.	(d)	42.	(b)	65.	(a)	88.	(a)	111.	(c)
20.	(a)	43.	(a)	66.	(d)	89.	(a)	112.	(a)
21.	(d)	44.	(c)	67.	(c)	90.	(a)	113.	(a)
22.	(a)	45.	(b)	68.	(c)	91.	(b)	114.	(d)
23.	(b)	46.	(d)	69.	(a)	92.	(d)	115.	(b)
								116.	(d)

Type-3

Hint :

4%

☞ इसमें देखना है की किस संख्या से गुणा किया जाए जिससे दी गई संख्या (100) हो जाए।

Ex. 1: 4% को किससे गुणा करें कि 100 बन जाए यानि 25 से गुणा करने से 1/25 Ans. हो जाएगा।

Ex. 2: $30\% = \left(\frac{3}{10}\right)$ यदि $\left(\frac{1}{10}\right)$ 10% के बराबर है तो 30% हमे उसका $\left(\frac{3}{10}\right)$ प्राप्त हो जाएगा। कहने का मतलब है प्रतिशत देखकर उसका multiplier से भी Answer आ जाएगा।

Exercise

- **Convert the following percentage into fractions:**

1. 4% =

(a) 1/20 (b) 1/25 (c) 1/16 (d) 1/30

2. 5% =

(a) 1/20 (b) 1/25 (c) 1/50 (d) 1/10

3. 10% =

(a) 1/5 (b) 1/10 (c) 1/20 (d) 1/25

4. 15% =

(a) 3/20 (b) 4/25 (c) 7/40 (d) 3/10

5. **20% =**
(a) 1/4 (b) 1/10 (c) 1/5 (d) 1/20

6. **25% =**
(a) 1/4 (b) 1/10 (c) 1/5 (d) 1/20

7. **30% =**
(a) 6/10 (b) 3/10 (c) 2/5 (d) 1/3

8. **35% =**
(a) 5/7 (b) 7/25 (c) 2/7 (d) 7/20

9. **40% =**
(a) 1/5 (b) 4/5 (c) 1/2 (d) 2/5

10. **60% =**
(a) 3/5 (b) 3/10 (c) 3/2 (d) 2/3

11. **70% =**
(a) 2/5 (b) 7/10 (c) 3/5 (d) 7/5

12. **80% =**
(a) 2/5 (b) 8/15 (c) 4/5 (d) 9/10

13. **90% =**
(a) 3/5 (b) 9/10 (c) 7/10 (d) 4/5

14. **45% =**
(a) 7/15 (b) 9/16 (c) 9/20 (d) 9/25

15. **55% =**
(a) 11/20 (b) 5/11 (c) 11/25 (d) 5/9

16. **65% =**
(a) 13/10 (b) 13/25 (c) 26/35 (d) 13/20

17. **75% =**
(a) 3/5 (b) 3/4 (c) 4/5 (d) 4/3

18. **85% =**
(a) 17/10 (b) 17/25 (c) 17/20 (d) 10/17

19. 95% =

(a) 19/20 (b) 9/10 (c) 17/18 (d) 19/25

20. 105% =

(a) 15/14 (b) 20/21 (c) 8/7 (d) 21/20

21. 12% =

(a) 1/8 (b) 3/25 (c) 4/25 (d) 3/20

22. 14% =

(a) 7/25 (b) 14/25 (c) 7/50 (d) 14/75

23. 18% =

(a) 9/20 (b) 9/50 (c) 18/25 (d) 9/25

24. 34% =

(a) 17/50 (b) 17/25 (c) 17/75 (d) 25/17

25. 42% =

(a) 25/42 (b) 14/25 (c) 7/20 (d) 21/50

26. 56% =

(a) 7/10 (b) 14/20 (c) 14/25 (d) 5/7

27. 84% =

(a) 25/42 (b) 21/25 (c) 17/20 (d) 17/25

28. 28% =

(a) 17/50 (b) 14/25 (c) 5/14 (d) 7/25

29. 68% =

(a) 17/20 (b) 19/25 (c) 17/25 (d) 20/27

30. 72% =

(a) 18/25 (b) 8/9 (c) 9/10 (d) 3/5

31. $33\frac{1}{3}\% =$

(a) 1/3 (b) 2/3 (c) 3/10 (d) 1/6

32. $66\frac{2}{3}\% =$

(a) 3/5 (b) 2/3 (c) 5/6 (d) 3/2

33. **120% =**

(a) 4/3 (b) 5/6 (c) 6/5 (d) 17/15

34. **140% =**

(a) 5/4 (b) 8/5 (c) 4/3 (d) 7/5

35. $133\frac{1}{3}\% =$

(a) 7/6 (b) 5/3 (c) 3/2 (d) 4/3

36. $266\frac{2}{3}\% =$

(a) 25/9 (b) 7/3 (c) 8/3 (d) 26/9

37. $16\frac{2}{3}\% =$

(a) 1/3 (b) 1/6 (c) 1/9 (d) 1/7

38. $83\frac{1}{3}\% =$

(a) 5/6 (b) 6/7 (c) 8/9 (d) 7/8

39. $116\frac{2}{3}\% =$

(a) 8/7 (b) 10/9 (c) 7/6 (d) 4/3

40. $114\frac{2}{7}\% =$

(a) 8/7 (b) 10/9 (c) 7/6 (d) 4/3

41. $28\frac{4}{7}\% =$

(a) 1/7 (b) 2/7 (c) 3/7 (d) 3/14

42. $37\frac{1}{2}\% =$

(a) 2/5 (b) 3/8 (c) 8/15 (d) 5/12

43. $162\frac{1}{2}\% =$

(a) 13/8 (b) 11/8 (c) 5/4 (d) 7/4

44. $9\frac{1}{11}\% =$

(a) 1/9 (b) 2/9 (c) 1/11 (d) 2/11

45. $163\frac{7}{11}\% =$

(a) 15/7 (b) 14/11 (c) 18/11 (d) 17/11

46. $281\frac{9}{11}\% =$

(a) 31/11 (b) 32/11 (c) 25/9 (d) 29/11

47. $42\frac{6}{7}\% =$

(a) 5/8 (b) 3/7 (c) 5/7 (d) 4/7

48. $87\frac{1}{2}\% =$

(a) 3/4 (b) 8/7 (c) 4/3 (d) 7/8

49. $157\frac{1}{7}\% =$

(a) 12/7 (b) 10/7 (c) 13/7 (d) 11/7

50. $444\frac{4}{9}\% =$

(a) 40/11 (b) 40/9 (c) 50/11 (d) 44/9

51. $142\frac{6}{7}\% =$

(a) 10/7 (b) 11/7 (c) 9/7 (d) 12/7

52. $77\frac{7}{9}\% =$

(a) 2/3 (b) 8/9 (c) 7/9 (d) 11/18

53. $55\frac{5}{9}\% =$

(a) 5/9 (b) 4/9 (c) 5/12 (d) 11/18

54. $27\frac{3}{11}\% =$

(a) 4/11 (b) 3/11 (c) 2/9 (d) 2/11

55. $108\frac{1}{3}\% =$

(a) 10/9 (b) 14/13 (c) 16/15 (d) 13/12

56. $58\frac{1}{3}\% =$

(a) 4/9 (b) 5/12 (c) 5/9 (d) 7/12

57. $107\frac{1}{7}\% =$

(a) 17/16 (b) 16/15 (c) 8/7 (d) 15/14

58. $21\frac{3}{7}\% =$

(a) 3/14 (b) 2/15 (c) 3/7 (d) 2/7

59. $35\frac{5}{7}\% =$

(a) 5/7 (b) 4/7 (c) 5/14 (d) 3/7

60. $42\frac{6}{7}\% =$

(a) 5/14 (b) 4/7 (c) 3/7 (d) 3/14

61. $64\frac{2}{7}\% =$

(a) 4/7 (b) 5/7 (c) 9/14 (d) 11/14

62. $6\frac{2}{3}\% =$

(a) 2/15 (b) 1/16 (c) 1/6 (d) 1/15

63. $13\frac{1}{3}\% =$

(a) 1/16 (b) 2/15 (c) 2/13 (d) 1/13

64. $126\frac{2}{3}\% =$

(a) 19/15 (b) 11/6 (c) 7/5 (d) 4/3

65. $46\frac{2}{3}\% =$

(a) 8/15 (b) 5/9 (c) 7/15 (d) 4/9

66. $106\frac{1}{4}\% =$

(a) 9/8 (b) 17/16 (c) 35/32 (d) 5/4

67. $23\frac{1}{3}\% =$

(a) 5/18 (b) 13/60 (c) 7/20 (d) 7/30

68. $57\frac{1}{7}\% =$

(a) 4/7 (b) 5/7 (c) 11/14 (d) 9/14

69. $137\frac{1}{2}\% =$

(a) 5/4 (b) 13/8 (c) 7/4 (d) 11/8

70. $62\frac{1}{2}\% =$

(a) 11/16 (b) 7/8 (c) 5/8 (d) 9/16

71. $377\frac{7}{9}\% =$

(a) 37/9 (b) 34/9 (c) 37/11 (d) 35/9

72. $18\frac{2}{11}\% =$

(a) 2/11 (b) 3/11 (c) 4/11 (d) 5/11

73. $290\frac{10}{11}\% =$

(a) 26/9 (b) 125/44 (c) 32/11 (d) 31/11

74. $41\frac{2}{3}\% =$

(a) 5/12 (b) 5/13 (c) 7/12 (d) 7/13

75. $158\frac{1}{3}\% =$

(a) 11/6 (b) 17/12 (c) 13/6 (d) 19/12

76. $191\frac{2}{3}\% =$

(a) 13/6 (b) 11/6 (c) 5/3 (d) 23/12

77. $106\frac{2}{3}\% =$

(a) 17/16 (b) 16/15 (c) 10/9 (d) 13/12

78. $113\frac{1}{3}\% =$

(a) 15/13 (b) 15/14 (c) 17/15 (d) 16/15

79. $6\frac{1}{4}\% =$

(a) 1/15 (b) 1/12 (c) 1/16 (d) 1/18

80. $36\frac{2}{3}\% =$

(a) 1/3 (b) 10/33 (c) 11/30 (d) 4/9

81. $71\frac{3}{7}\% =$

(a) 5/7 (b) 6/7 (c) 4/7 (d) 3/7

82. $237\frac{1}{2}\% =$

(a) 9/4 (b) 11/4 (c) 21/8 (d) 19/8

83. $255\frac{5}{9}\% =$

(a) 20/9 (b) 22/9 (c) 25/9 (d) 23/9

84. $36\frac{4}{11}\% =$

(a) 5/11 (b) 3/11 (c) 6/11 (d) 4/11

85. $172\frac{8}{11}\% =$

(a) 20/11 (b) 18/11 (c) 19/11 (d) 17/11

86. $81\frac{9}{11}\% =$

(a) 9/11 (b) 10/11 (c) 7/11 (d) 8/11

87. $91\frac{2}{3}\% =$

(a) 11/12 (b) 13/15 (c) 9/10 (d) 8/9

88. $213\frac{1}{3}\% =$

(a) 30/13 (b) 32/15 (c) 20/9 (d) 12/5

89. $26\frac{2}{3}\% =$

(a) 2/7 (b) 2/9 (c) 4/15 (d) 5/16

90. $18\frac{3}{4}\% =$

(a) 2/9 (b) 5/21 (c) 3/20 (d) 3/16

91. $77\frac{7}{9}\% =$

(a) 7/9 (b) 12/11 (c) 8/9 (d) 11/12

92. $85\frac{5}{7}\% =$

(a) 24/25 (b) 6/7 (c) 27/25 (d) 8/7

93. $22\frac{2}{9}\% =$

(a) 5/11 (b) 4/9 (c) 2/9 (d) 5/9

94. $188\frac{8}{9}\% =$

(a) 16/9 (b) 68/35 (c) 5/3 (d) 17/9

95. $45\frac{5}{11}\% =$

(a) 7/11 (b) 6/11 (c) 4/11 (d) 5/11

96. $141\frac{2}{3}\% =$

(a) 15/13 (b) 17/12 (c) 13/9 (d) 19/17

97. $118\frac{3}{4}\% =$

(a) 19/16 (b) 13/12 (c) 16/19 (d) 25/24

Type-3: Answer - Key

1.	(b)	21.	(b)	41.	(b)	61.	(c)	81.	(a)
2.	(a)	22.	(c)	42.	(b)	62.	(d)	82.	(d)
3.	(b)	23.	(b)	43.	(a)	63.	(b)	83.	(d)
4.	(a)	24.	(a)	44.	(c)	64.	(a)	84.	(d)
5.	(c)	25.	(d)	45.	(c)	65.	(c)	85.	(c)
6.	(a)	26.	(c)	46.	(a)	66.	(b)	86.	(a)
7.	(b)	27.	(b)	47.	(b)	67.	(d)	87.	(a)
8.	(d)	28.	(d)	48.	(d)	68.	(a)	88.	(b)
9.	(d)	29.	(c)	49.	(d)	69.	(d)	89.	(c)
10.	(a)	30.	(a)	50.	(b)	70.	(c)	90.	(d)
11.	(b)	31.	(a)	51.	(a)	71.	(b)	91.	(a)
12.	(c)	32.	(b)	52.	(c)	72.	(a)	92.	(b)
13.	(b)	33.	(c)	53.	(a)	73.	(c)	93.	(c)
14.	(c)	34.	(d)	54.	(b)	74.	(a)	94.	(d)
15.	(a)	35.	(d)	55.	(d)	75.	(d)	95.	(d)
16.	(d)	36.	(c)	56.	(d)	76.	(d)	96.	(b)
17.	(b)	37.	(b)	57.	(d)	77.	(b)	97.	(a)
18.	(c)	38.	(a)	58.	(a)	78.	(c)		
19.	(a)	39.	(c)	59.	(c)	79.	(c)		
20.	(d)	40.	(a)	60.	(c)	80.	(c)		

Type-4

Hint :

43.33%

☞ इस प्रकार के प्रश्न के प्रतिशत मान को हम अपने अनुसार याद वाले प्रतिशत मानों को मान लेना जैसे 43.33 (40% + 3.33%) या (50 – 6.66%) और दोनों को दिमाग में रखना है $\left(\frac{2}{5}+\frac{1}{30}\right)$ इस Type की fraction को बताया है Denominator को same करके add करना है जिससे $\left(\frac{13}{30}\right)$ Answer निकल जाएगा।

Exercise

- **Convert percentage into fraction :**

1. 43.33% =

(a) 11/30 (b) 13/30 (c) 7/15 (d) 17/30

2. 53.33% =

(a) 8/15 (b) 7/15 (c) 19/30 (d) 17/30

3. 63.33% =

(a) 11/15 (b) 17/30 (c) 2/3 (d) 19/30

4. 73.33% =

(a) 11/15 (b) 17/30 (c) 13/15 (d) 19/30

5. 22.5% =

(a) 11/40 (b) 9/40 (c) 7/40 (d) 7/20

6. 42.5% =

(a) 13/40 (b) 17/40 (c) 3/8 (d) 19/40

7. 46.66% =

(a) 11/30 (b) 13/30 (c) 4/15 (d) 7/15

8. 24.28% =

(a) 2/7 (b) 8/35 (c) 17/70 (d) 3/14

9. 34.28% =

(a) 11/35 (b) 13/35 (c) 31/70 (d) 12/35

10. 38.56% =

(a) 27/70 (b) 29/70 (c) 31/70 (d) 33/70

11. 52.84% =

(a) 18/35 (b) 37/70 (c) 33/70 (d) 39/70

12. 67.14% =

(a) 27/70 (b) 37/70 (c) 47/70 (d) 57/70

13. 81.4% =

(a) 57/70 (b) 47/70 (c) 55/70 (d) 59/70

14. 47.5% =

(a) 19/40 (b) 17/40 (c) 12/25 (d) 21/40

15. 72.5% =

(a) 3/4 (b) 31/40 (c) 11/15 (d) 29/40

16. 97.5% =

(a) 29/30 (b) 39/40 (c) 19/20 (d) 49/50

17. 21.11% =

(a) 29/90 (b) 19/99 (c) 19/90 (d) 29/99

18. 32.22% =

(a) 29/99 (b) 39/90 (c) 39/99 (d) 29/90

19. 54.44% =

(a) 59/99 (b) 59/90 (c) 49/90 (d) 49/99

20. 65.55% =

(a) 59/99 (b) 59/90 (c) 69/90 (d) 69/99

21. 87.77% =

(a) 79/99 (b) 79/90 (c) 69/90 (d) 69/99

22. 98.88% =

(a) 89/90 (b) 88/90 (c) 88/99 (d) 89/99

23. 19.09% =

(a) 17/90 (b) 2/11 (c) 21/110 (d) 19/110

24. 28.18% =

(a) 2/11 (b) 29/110 (c) 3/11 (d) 31/110

25. 37.27% =

(a) 21/55 (b) 41/110 (c) 19/55 (d) 37/110

26. 47.27% =

(a) 26/55 (b) 51/110 (c) 47/110 (d) 27/55

27. 46.36% =

(a) 51/110 (b) 53/110 (c) 26/55 (d) 27/55

28. 55.45% =

(a) 31/55 (b) 51/110 (c) 29/55 (d) 61/110

29. 64.54% =

(a) 61/110 (b) 31/55 (c) 71/110 (d) 34/55

30. 73.63% =

(a) 81/110 (b) 71/110 (c) 41/55 (d) 61/90

31. 82.72% =

(a) 81/110 (b) 91/110 (c) 71/110 (d) 71/90

32. 100.90% =

(a) 100/99 (b) 110/111 (c) 51/50 (d) 111/110

33. 18.33% =

(a) 13/60 (b) 2/13 (c) 11/60 (d) 3/16

34. 28.33% =

(a) 11/30 (b) 7/30 (c) 17/60 (d) 19/60

35. 36.66% =

(a) 13/30 (b) 11/30 (c) 13/33 (d) 4/15

36. 16.25% =

(a) 7/40 (b) 17/80 (c) 27/160 (d) 13/80

37. 26.25% =

(a) 7/20 (b) 21/80 (c) 41/160 (d) 11/40

38. 36.25% =

(a) 17/40 (b) 13/40 (c) 29/80 (d) 31/80

39. 56.25% =

(a) 17/32 (b) 7/16 (c) 19/35 (d) 9/16

40. 83.33% =

(a) 5/6 (b) 23/30 (c) 11/15 (d) 6/7

Type-4: Answer - Key

1.	(b)	**9.**	(d)	**17.**	(c)	**25.**	(b)	**33.**	(c)
2.	(a)	**10.**	(a)	**18.**	(d)	**26.**	(a)	**34.**	(c)
3.	(d)	**11.**	(b)	**19.**	(c)	**27.**	(a)	**35.**	(b)
4.	(a)	**12.**	(c)	**20.**	(b)	**28.**	(d)	**36.**	(d)
5.	(b)	**13.**	(a)	**21.**	(b)	**29.**	(c)	**37.**	(b)
6.	(b)	**14.**	(a)	**22.**	(a)	**30.**	(a)	**38.**	(c)
7.	(d)	**15.**	(d)	**23.**	(c)	**31.**	(b)	**39.**	(d)
8.	(c)	**16.**	(b)	**24.**	(d)	**32.**	(d)	**40.**	(a)

Type-5

Hint :

10% ↑

☞ 10% को fraction में $\left(\frac{1}{10}\right)$ लिखते है और numerator को देखना है कि कितना बढ़ रहा है तो Denominator में जोड़कर ऊपर Numerator में लिख देंगे $\left(\frac{1}{10}\right)\uparrow = \left(\frac{11}{10}\right)$ Answer आ जाएगा।

10% ↓

☞ 10% कम का मतलब Denominator में जो Numerator है उसे घटा देंगे $\left(\frac{1}{10}\right)\downarrow = \left(\frac{9}{10}\right)$ Answer आ जाएगा

Exercise

- **Convert these percentage to smallest fraction form:**

1. 10%↑

(a) $\frac{9}{10}$ (b) $\frac{11}{10}$ (c) $\frac{99}{100}$ (d) $\frac{1}{10}$

2. 10%↓

(a) $\frac{9}{10}$ (b) $\frac{3}{10}$ (c) $\frac{1}{10}$ (d) $\frac{11}{10}$

3. 20%↑

(a) $\frac{2}{5}$ (b) $\frac{6}{5}$ (c) $\frac{3}{5}$ (d) $\frac{4}{5}$

4. **20%↓**

(a) $\frac{3}{5}$ (b) $\frac{5}{6}$ (c) $\frac{4}{5}$ (d) $\frac{4}{10}$

5. **30%↑**

(a) $\frac{7}{10}$ (b) $\frac{13}{10}$ (c) $\frac{3}{5}$ (d) $\frac{7}{5}$

6. **40%↓**

(a) $\frac{2}{5}$ (b) $\frac{3}{5}$ (c) $\frac{7}{5}$ (d) $\frac{9}{10}$

7. **50%↑**

(a) $\frac{3}{5}$ (b) $\frac{1}{5}$ (c) $\frac{3}{2}$ (d) $\frac{1}{2}$

8. **30%↓**

(a) $\frac{7}{10}$ (b) $\frac{5}{8}$ (c) $\frac{3}{5}$ (d) $\frac{3}{10}$

9. **70%↑**

(a) $\frac{7}{10}$ (b) $\frac{3}{10}$ (c) $\frac{17}{10}$ (d) $\frac{1}{7}$

10. **80%↓**

(a) $\frac{2}{5}$ (b) $\frac{4}{5}$ (c) $\frac{1}{10}$ (d) $\frac{1}{5}$

11. **40%↑**

(a) $\frac{7}{10}$ (b) $\frac{7}{5}$ (c) $\frac{2}{5}$ (d) $\frac{3}{5}$

12. **60%↑**

(a) $\frac{2}{5}$ (b) $\frac{8}{5}$ (c) $\frac{4}{5}$ (d) $\frac{5}{4}$

13. 70%↓

(a) $\frac{3}{10}$ (b) $\frac{7}{10}$ (c) $\frac{17}{10}$ (d) $\frac{5}{6}$

14. 25%↑

(a) $\frac{1}{5}$ (b) $\frac{6}{5}$ (c) $\frac{1}{4}$ (d) $\frac{5}{4}$

15. 60%↓

(a) $\frac{3}{5}$ (b) $\frac{2}{5}$ (c) $\frac{3}{10}$ (d) $\frac{5}{4}$

16. 15%↑

(a) $\frac{17}{10}$ (b) $\frac{23}{20}$ (c) $\frac{17}{20}$ (d) $\frac{13}{10}$

17. 35%↑

(a) $\frac{7}{10}$ (b) $\frac{27}{50}$ (c) $\frac{27}{20}$ (d) $\frac{7}{20}$

18. 25%↓

(a) $\frac{3}{5}$ (b) $\frac{3}{4}$ (c) $\frac{4}{5}$ (d) $\frac{1}{5}$

19. 15%↓

(a) $\frac{17}{10}$ (b) $\frac{3}{20}$ (c) $\frac{23}{10}$ (d) $\frac{17}{20}$

20. 35%↓

(a) $\frac{7}{10}$ (b) $\frac{3}{10}$ (c) $\frac{13}{20}$ (d) $\frac{5}{17}$

21. 45%↑

(a) $\frac{9}{10}$ (b) $\frac{19}{10}$ (c) $\frac{29}{20}$ (d) $\frac{11}{20}$

22. 55%↑

(a) $\frac{31}{20}$ (b) $\frac{9}{20}$ (c) $\frac{11}{20}$ (d) $\frac{22}{30}$

23. 55%↓

(a) $\frac{19}{20}$ (b) $\frac{9}{20}$ (c) $\frac{31}{20}$ (d) $\frac{11}{20}$

24. 75%↑

(a) $\frac{8}{5}$ (b) $\frac{3}{4}$ (c) $\frac{7}{4}$ (d) $\frac{7}{8}$

25. 85%↓

(a) $\frac{17}{10}$ (b) $\frac{3}{20}$ (c) $\frac{7}{20}$ (d) $\frac{13}{20}$

26. 75%↓

(a) $\frac{1}{4}$ (b) $\frac{1}{5}$ (c) $\frac{3}{4}$ (d) $\frac{4}{5}$

27. 2%↑

(a) $\frac{49}{50}$ (b) $\frac{22}{25}$ (c) $\frac{24}{25}$ (d) $\frac{51}{50}$

28. 4%↑

(a) $\frac{24}{25}$ (b) $\frac{49}{25}$ (c) $\frac{26}{25}$ (d) $\frac{6}{5}$

29. $3\frac{1}{3}$%↑

(a) $\frac{1}{30}$ (b) $\frac{31}{30}$ (c) $\frac{29}{30}$ (d) $\frac{19}{20}$

30. 2%↓

(a) $\frac{49}{50}$ (b) $\frac{51}{50}$ (c) $\frac{24}{25}$ (d) $\frac{7}{15}$

31. 5%↑

(a) $\frac{11}{10}$ (b) $\frac{55}{29}$ (c) $\frac{21}{20}$ (d) $\frac{19}{20}$

32. 5%↓

(a) $\frac{9}{10}$ (b) $\frac{1}{20}$ (c) $\frac{22}{25}$ (d) $\frac{19}{20}$

33. $3\frac{1}{3}$%↓

(a) $\frac{29}{30}$ (b) $\frac{2}{3}$ (c) $\frac{1}{9}$ (d) $\frac{8}{9}$

34. 4%↓

(a) $\frac{2}{5}$ (b) $\frac{24}{25}$ (c) $\frac{26}{25}$ (d) $\frac{1}{16}$

35. $4\frac{1}{6}$%↑

(a) $\frac{3}{8}$ (b) $\frac{25}{24}$ (c) $\frac{3}{4}$ (d) $\frac{13}{12}$

36. $6\frac{2}{3}$%↓

(a) $\frac{9}{20}$ (b) $\frac{22}{15}$ (c) $\frac{5}{9}$ (d) $\frac{14}{15}$

37. $6\frac{1}{4}$%↑

(a) $\frac{1}{15}$ (b) $\frac{14}{15}$ (c) $\frac{17}{16}$ (d) $\frac{15}{16}$

38. $7\frac{1}{7}$%↑

(a) $\frac{15}{14}$ (b) $\frac{49}{50}$ (c) $\frac{21}{20}$ (d) $\frac{8}{7}$

39. $4\frac{1}{6}$%↓

(a) $\frac{25}{24}$ (b) $\frac{23}{25}$ (c) $\frac{24}{23}$ (d) $\frac{23}{24}$

40. $6\frac{1}{4}$%↓

(a) $\frac{14}{15}$ (b) $\frac{16}{15}$ (c) $\frac{15}{16}$ (d) $\frac{9}{16}$

41. $6\frac{2}{3}\%\uparrow$

(a) $\frac{14}{15}$ (b) $\frac{16}{15}$ (c) $\frac{17}{16}$ (d) $\frac{14}{16}$

42. $7\frac{1}{7}\%\downarrow$

(a) $\frac{14}{15}$ (b) $\frac{49}{50}$ (c) $\frac{6}{7}$ (d) $\frac{13}{14}$

43. $8\frac{1}{3}\%\uparrow$

(a) $\frac{13}{12}$ (b) $\frac{11}{15}$ (c) $\frac{13}{15}$ (d) $\frac{1}{6}$

44. $9\frac{1}{11}\%\downarrow$

(a) $\frac{9}{11}$ (b) $\frac{10}{11}$ (c) $\frac{8}{9}$ (d) $\frac{9}{10}$

45. $11\frac{1}{9}\%\uparrow$

(a) $\frac{9}{10}$ (b) $\frac{11}{10}$ (c) $\frac{10}{9}$ (d) $\frac{12}{11}$

46. $12\frac{1}{2}\%\uparrow$

(a) $\frac{9}{8}$ (b) $\frac{9}{10}$ (c) $\frac{13}{12}$ (d) $\frac{1}{12}$

47. $9\frac{1}{11}\%\uparrow$

(a) $\frac{11}{10}$ (b) $\frac{9}{11}$ (c) $\frac{12}{11}$ (d) $\frac{11}{12}$

48. $8\frac{1}{3}\%\downarrow$

(a) $\frac{10}{11}$ (b) $\frac{5}{6}$ (c) $\frac{11}{12}$ (d) $\frac{7}{8}$

49. $12\frac{1}{2}\%\downarrow$

(a) $\frac{9}{8}$ (b) $\frac{1}{8}$ (c) $\frac{7}{8}$ (d) $\frac{11}{12}$

50. $14\frac{2}{7}\%\uparrow$

(a) $\frac{8}{7}$ (b) $\frac{15}{14}$ (c) $\frac{7}{8}$ (d) $\frac{11}{12}$

51. $16\frac{2}{3}\%\downarrow$

(a) $\frac{2}{3}$ (b) $\frac{15}{16}$ (c) $\frac{7}{8}$ (d) $\frac{5}{6}$

52. $18\frac{3}{4}\%\downarrow$

(a) $\frac{11}{12}$ (b) $\frac{11}{8}$ (c) $\frac{19}{16}$ (d) $\frac{13}{16}$

53. $33\frac{1}{3}\%\downarrow$

(a) $\frac{3}{4}$ (b) $\frac{1}{9}$ (c) $\frac{2}{3}$ (d) $\frac{1}{3}$

54. $14\frac{2}{7}\%\downarrow$

(a) $\frac{13}{14}$ (b) $\frac{1}{14}$ (c) $\frac{7}{8}$ (d) $\frac{6}{7}$

55. $16\frac{2}{3}\%\uparrow$

(a) $\frac{7}{8}$ (b) $\frac{7}{6}$ (c) $\frac{4}{3}$ (d) $\frac{16}{15}$

56. $87\frac{1}{2}\%\downarrow$

(a) $\frac{5}{6}$ (b) $\frac{19}{16}$ (c) $\frac{1}{8}$ (d) $\frac{15}{8}$

57. $33\frac{1}{3}\%\uparrow$

(a) $\frac{2}{3}$ (b) $\frac{10}{9}$ (c) $\frac{13}{12}$ (d) $\frac{4}{3}$

58. $66\frac{2}{3}\%\uparrow$

(a) $\frac{5}{3}$ (b) $\frac{4}{3}$ (c) $\frac{11}{9}$ (d) $\frac{15}{12}$

59. $66\frac{2}{3}\%\downarrow$

(a) $\frac{1}{3}$ (b) $\frac{5}{6}$ (c) $\frac{2}{3}$ (d) $\frac{1}{6}$

60. $125\%\uparrow$

(a) $\frac{5}{4}$ (b) $\frac{9}{4}$ (c) $\frac{6}{5}$ (d) $\frac{4}{3}$

61. $120\%\uparrow$

(a) $\frac{6}{5}$ (b) $\frac{11}{5}$ (c) $\frac{5}{4}$ (d) $\frac{4}{3}$

62. $28\frac{4}{7}\%\downarrow$

(a) $\frac{2}{7}$ (b) $\frac{9}{7}$ (c) $\frac{3}{8}$ (d) $\frac{5}{7}$

63. $44\frac{4}{9}\%\uparrow$

(a) $\frac{13}{9}$ (b) $\frac{4}{7}$ (c) $\frac{11}{7}$ (d) $\frac{5}{9}$

64. $55\frac{5}{9}\%\downarrow$

(a) $\frac{4}{9}$ (b) $\frac{14}{9}$ (c) $\frac{4}{11}$ (d) $\frac{5}{11}$

65. $37\frac{1}{2}\%\uparrow$

(a) $\frac{3}{8}$ (b) $\frac{11}{8}$ (c) $\frac{5}{8}$ (d) $\frac{4}{5}$

66. $62\frac{1}{2}\%\uparrow$

(a) $\frac{5}{8}$ (b) $\frac{13}{8}$ (c) $\frac{5}{12}$ (d) $\frac{7}{12}$

67. $28\frac{4}{7}\%\downarrow$

(a) $\frac{5}{7}$ (b) $\frac{2}{7}$ (c) $\frac{3}{8}$ (d) $\frac{9}{7}$

68. $44\frac{4}{9}\%\downarrow$

(a) $\frac{5}{9}$ (b) $\frac{4}{9}$ (c) $\frac{2}{9}$ (d) $\frac{13}{9}$

69. $55\frac{5}{9}\%\uparrow$

(a) $\frac{14}{9}$ (b) $\frac{14}{11}$ (c) $\frac{5}{11}$ (d) $\frac{16}{11}$

70. $37\frac{1}{2}\%\downarrow$

(a) $\frac{5}{12}$ (b) $\frac{5}{8}$ (c) $\frac{5}{16}$ (d) $\frac{3}{16}$

71. $62\frac{1}{2}\%\downarrow$

(a) $\frac{2}{3}$ (b) $\frac{5}{12}$ (c) $\frac{7}{8}$ (d) $\frac{3}{8}$

72. $9\frac{1}{11}\%\uparrow$

(a) $\frac{9}{10}$ (b) $\frac{11}{10}$ (c) $\frac{12}{11}$ (d) $\frac{10}{9}$

73. $11\frac{1}{9}\%\downarrow$

(a) $\frac{9}{10}$ (b) $\frac{8}{9}$ (c) $\frac{10}{11}$ (d) $\frac{12}{11}$

74. $42\frac{6}{7}\%\uparrow$

(a) $\frac{10}{7}$ (b) $\frac{6}{7}$ (c) $\frac{15}{14}$ (d) $\frac{9}{10}$

75. $87\frac{1}{2}\%\uparrow$

(a) $\frac{3}{8}$ (b) $\frac{23}{16}$ (c) $\frac{1}{8}$ (d) $\frac{15}{8}$

76. $57\frac{1}{7}\%\downarrow$

(a) $\frac{1}{7}$ (b) $\frac{3}{7}$ (c) $\frac{6}{7}$ (d) $\frac{13}{14}$

77. $77\frac{7}{9}\%\uparrow$

(a) $\frac{16}{9}$ (b) $\frac{2}{9}$ (c) $\frac{7}{18}$ (d) $\frac{5}{3}$

78. $33\frac{6}{18}\%\uparrow$

(a) $\frac{5}{4}$ (b) $\frac{4}{3}$ (c) $\frac{11}{9}$ (d) $\frac{23}{18}$

79. $12\frac{7}{14}\%\downarrow$

(a) $\frac{1}{12}$ (b) $\frac{13}{14}$ (c) $\frac{6}{7}$ (d) $\frac{7}{8}$

Type-5: Answer - Key

1.	(b)	17.	(c)	33.	(a)	49.	(c)	65.	(b)
2.	(a)	18.	(b)	34.	(b)	50.	(a)	66.	(b)
3.	(b)	19.	(d)	35.	(b)	51.	(d)	67.	(a)
4.	(c)	20.	(c)	36.	(d)	52.	(d)	68.	(a)
5.	(b)	21.	(c)	37.	(c)	53.	(c)	69.	(a)
6.	(b)	22.	(a)	38.	(a)	54.	(d)	70.	(b)
7.	(c)	23.	(b)	39.	(d)	55.	(b)	71.	(d)
8.	(a)	24.	(c)	40.	(c)	56.	(c)	72.	(c)
9.	(c)	25.	(b)	41.	(b)	57.	(d)	73.	(b)
10.	(d)	26.	(a)	42.	(d)	58.	(a)	74.	(a)
11.	(b)	27.	(d)	43.	(a)	59.	(a)	75.	(d)
12.	(b)	28.	(c)	44.	(b)	60.	(b)	76.	(b)
13.	(a)	29.	(b)	45.	(c)	61.	(b)	77.	(a)
14.	(d)	30.	(a)	46.	(a)	62.	(d)	78.	(b)
15.	(b)	31.	(c)	47.	(c)	63.	(a)	79.	(d)
16.	(b)	32.	(d)	48.	(c)	64.	(a)		

Type-6

Hint :

2% ↑ & 3% ↑

☞ Net increase करते वक्त सबसे पहले हमे दोनों संख्याओं को जोड़कर दिमाग में रखना है
(2 + 3 = 5) फिर दोनों संख्याओं का गुणा (2 × 3 = 6) दो अंक (digit) पहले Decimal लगाकर दिमाग में रखी संख्या जोड़कर Ans. निकालना है।

$$5 + 0.06 = 5.06$$

$$x + y + \frac{xy}{100}$$

[Focus $\frac{xy}{100}$ पर रखकर दिमाग में Calculate करें]

Exercise

- **FIND NET INCREASE%:-**

1. **2%↑ & 3%↑=**
(a) 5.50% (b) 5.05% (c) 6.06% (d) 5.06%

2. **4%↑ & 5%↑=**
(a) 20.09% (b) 9.20% (c) 9.02% (d) 9.09%

3. **6%↑ & 7%↑=**
(a) 13.13% (b) 12.87% (c) 13.42% (d) 12.15%

4. **8%↑ & 5%↑=**
(a) 13.40% (b) 13.60% (c) 12.45% (d) 13.04%

5. 10%↑ & 5%↑=

(a) 15.06% (b) 15.20% (c) 15.50% (d) 16.06%

6. 10%↑ & 15%↑=

(a) 27.50% (b) 25.15% (c) 26.50% (d) 25.50%

7. 5%↑ & 5%↑=

(a) 25.25% (b) 10.75% (c) 13.25% (d) 10.25%

8. 10%↑ & 20%↑=

(a) 32.2% (b) 32% (c) 31.20% (d) 30.2%

9. 20%↑ & 30%↑=

(a) 54% (b) 50% (c) 56% (d) 66%

10. 30%↑ & 40%↑=

(a) 82% (b) 72% (c) 80.12% (d) 81.12%

11. 20%↑ & 15%↑=

(a) 33% (b) 38% (c) 35.30% (d) 36%

12. 20%↑ & 25%↑=

(a) 45% (b) 55% (c) 50% (d) 48%

13. 50%↑ & 20%↑=

(a) 70% (b) 80% (c) 71% (d) 81.81%

14. 35%↑ & 20%↑ =

(a) 72% (b) 55% (c) 62% (d) 68%

15. 12%↑ & 10%↑ =

(a) 23.20% (b) 22.20% (c) 20.20% (d) 24.40%

16. 14%↑ & 12%↑=

(a) 30.32% (b) 27.68% (c) 28.24% (d) 27.16%

17. 13%↑ & 12%↑=

(a) 25.25% (b) 24.44% (c) 27.56% (d) 26.56%

18. 15%↑ & 12%↑=

(a) 27.28% (b) 27.80% (c) 28.80% (d) 30.60%

19. 9%↑ & 20%↑=

(a) 30.80% (b) 29.08% (c) 30.06% (d) 28.80%

20. 24%↑ & 10%↑=

(a) 35.40% (b) 36.40% (c) 36.60% (d) 37.40%

21. 15%↑ & 8%↑=

(a) 25.6% (b) 24.16% (c) 24.20% (d) 23.8%

22. 24%↑ & 7%↑=

(a) 31.28% (b) 30.68% (c) 32.48% (d) 32.68%

23. 16%↑ & 13%↑ =

(a) 29.08% (b) 31.08% (c) 32.18% (d) 30.06%

24. 30%↑ & 12%↑=

(a) 45.6% (b) 41.06% (c) 43.6% (d) 44.6%

25. 25%↑ & 4%↑=

(a) 29% (b) 31.58% (c) 30% (d) 28.10%

26. 28%↑ & 3%↑=

(a) 31.84% (b) 32.16% (c) 30.84% (d) 32.63%

- **FIND NET DECREASE%:-**

27. 8%↓ & 5%↓=

(a) 12% (b) 13.40% (c) 12.6% (d) 11.6%

28. 4%↓ & 5%↓=

(a) 9.09% (b) 9.8% (c) 8.8% (d) 8.2%

29. 2%↓ & 3%↓=

(a) 5.05% (b) 4.94% (c) 4.6% (d) 3.96%

30. 7%↓ & 6%↓=

(a) 12.16% (b) 12.58% (c) 13.42% (d) 12.42%

31. 10%↓ & 5%↓=

(a) 15.55% (b) 12.5% (c) 14.50% (d) 15%

32. 5%↓ & 5%↓=

(a) 2.25% (b) 9.75% (c) 6.25% (d) 10.25%

33. 10%↓ & 20%↓=

(a) 25% (b) 27% (c) 28% (d) 29%

34. 20%↓ & 30%↓=
(a) 16% (b) 56% (c) 46% (d) 44%

35. 30%↓ & 40%↓=
(a) 72% (b) 58% (c) 48% (d) 68%

36. 20%↓ & 15%↓=
(a) 32% (b) 35% (c) 33% (d) 30%

37. 50%↓ & 20%↓=
(a) 50% (b) 60% (c) 65% (d) 70%

38. 35%↓ & 20%↓=
(a) 55% (b) 45% (c) 48% (d) 50%

39. 25%↓ & 25%↓=
(a) 55.75% (b) 43.75% (c) 45.75% (d) 42.25%

40. 12%↓ & 10%↓=
(a) 20.8% (b) 22% (c) 21.6% (d) 20.2%

41. 14%↓ & 12%↓=
(a) 26.68% (b) 24.32% (c) 24.68% (d) 25.32%

42. 13%↓ & 12%↓=
(a) 22.66% (b) 25.66% (c) 23.44% (d) 22.44%

43. 15%↓ & 12%↓=
(a) 27.2% (b) 25.2% (c) 28.2% (d) 26.2%

44. 9%↓ & 20%↓=
(a) 28.2% (b) 29.2% (c) 26.2% (d) 27.2%

45. 24%↓ & 30%↓=
(a) 46.8% (b) 50.8% (c) 45.2% (d) 48.5%

46. 15%↓ & 8%↓=
(a) 20.8% (b) 22.8% (c) 21.8% (d) 23.2%

47. 24%↓ & 10%↓=
(a) 34.16% (b) 31.6% (c) 30.16% (d) 30.60%

48. 16%↓ & 13%↓=
(a) 26.92% (b) 29.08% (c) 28.92% (d) 30.16%

49. 30%↓ & 12%↓=

(a) 38.60% (b) 38.40% (c) 40.40% (d) 36.50%

50. 28%↓ & 3%↓=

(a) 30.16% (b) 42.16% (c) 18.16% (d) 28.16%

51. 25%↓ & 4%↓=

(a) 28% (b) 26% (c) 27% (d) 25%

- **FIND INCREASE OR DECREASE % :-**

52. 2%↑ & 3%↓=

(a) -1.06% (b) +1.06% (c) -1.20% (d) -2.06%

53. 4%↑ & 5%↓=

(a) -0.2% (b) +1.2% (c) - 1.2% (d) +0.8%

54. 7%↑ & 6%↓=

(a) +0.58% (b) +0.42% (c) +1.42% (d) -0.42%

55. 25%↑ & 20%↓=

(a) +5% (b) -5% (c) +4.5% (d) No change

56. 15%↓ & 10%↑=

(a) -6.5% (b) -4.5% (c) -5.5% (d) -5%

57. 8%↑ & 5%↓=

(a) -2% (b) +3% (c) +2.6% (d) -0.6%

58. 10%↑ & 5%↓=

(a) +4% (b) +6% (c) +5% (d) +4.5%

59. 15%↑ & 10%↓=

(a) +3.5% (b) +2.6% (c) +4.5% (d) +5%

60. 35%↑ & 20%↓=

(a) +6% (b) +10% (c) +8% (d) +15%

61. 20%↑ & 10%↓=

(a) +2% (b) +8% (c) +10% (d) 5%

62. 30%↑ & 20%↓=
(a) +4% (b) +6% (c) +8% (d) +5%

63. 40%↓ & 30%↑=
(a) -10% (b) -22% (c) -12% (d) -24%

64. 20%↑ & 15%↓=
(a) -1.2% (b) +3% (c) +2% (d) +4%

65. 50%↑ & 20%↓=
(a) +20% (b) +26% (c) +30% (d) +16%

66. 35%↑ & 20%↓=
(a) +6% (b) +10% (c) +12.5% (d) +8%

67. 12%↑ & 10%↓=
(a) -0.2% (b) +0.6% (c) +2% (d) +0.8%

68. 14%↑ & 12%↓=
(a) -0.32% (b) +0.32% (c) +0.68% (d) +1.6%

69. 13%↑ & 12%↓=
(a) -1.44% (b) -0.56% (c) -0.44% (d) +1.56%

70. 15%↑ & 12%↓=
(a) -1.2% (b) +2.2% (c) +1.2% (d) -2.2%

71. 20%↑ & 11%↓=
(a) +6.6% (b) +6.8% (c) +8.6% (d) +9.6%

72. 30%↑ & 22%↓=
(a) +8.33% (b) +7.66% (c) +0.6% (d) +1.4%

73. 15%↑ & 8%↓=
(a) +5.6% (b) +5.8% (c) +6.8% (d) +7.6%

74. 24%↓ & 7%↑=
(a) -18.68% (b) -13.32% (c) -14.68% (d) -16.64%

75. 16%↓ & 13%↑=
(a) -5.08% (b) -3.08% (c) -4.02% (d) -6.02%

76. 30%↓ & 12%↑=
(a) -21.36% (b) -21.6% (c) -18.6% (d) -22.6%

77. 25%↑ & 4%↓=
(a) +20.6% (b) +21% (c) +20% (d) +22%

78. 28%↓ & 3%↑=
(a) -25.16% (b) -26.16% (c) -25.84% (d) -25.16%

79. 22%↑ & 21%↓=
(a) +1.62% (b) +.06% (c) -1.60% (d) -3.62%

80. 14%↑ & 7%↓=
(a) +6.02% (b) +7.06% (c) +6.06% (d) +7.02%

81. 32%↑ & 5%↓=
(a) +27.4% (b) +25.4% (c) -27% (d) +26.6%

Type-6: Answer - Key

1.	(d)	17.	(d)	33.	(c)	49.	(b)	65.	(a)
2.	(b)	18.	(c)	34.	(d)	50.	(a)	66.	(d)
3.	(c)	19.	(a)	35.	(b)	51.	(a)	67.	(d)
4.	(a)	20.	(b)	36.	(a)	52.	(a)	68.	(b)
5.	(c)	21.	(c)	37.	(b)	53.	(c)	69.	(b)
6.	(c)	22.	(d)	38.	(c)	54.	(a)	70.	(c)
7.	(d)	23.	(b)	39.	(b)	55.	(d)	71.	(b)
8.	(b)	24.	(a)	40.	(a)	56.	(a)	72.	(d)
9.	(c)	25.	(c)	41.	(b)	57.	(c)	73.	(b)
10.	(a)	26.	(a)	42.	(c)	58.	(d)	74.	(a)
11.	(b)	27.	(c)	43.	(b)	59.	(a)	75.	(a)
12.	(c)	28.	(c)	44.	(d)	60.	(c)	76.	(b)
13.	(b)	29.	(b)	45.	(a)	61.	(b)	77.	(c)
14.	(c)	30.	(b)	46.	(c)	62.	(a)	78.	(c)
15.	(a)	31.	(c)	47.	(b)	63.	(b)	79.	(d)
16.	(b)	32.	(b)	48.	(a)	64.	(c)	80.	(a)
								81.	(b)

Type-7

Hint :

Find Net increase or decrease (% or fraction)

$33\frac{1}{3}\% \uparrow$ & $10\% \uparrow$

☞ Net fraction की percentage को solve करते वक्त सबसे पहले fraction के form में $\left(\frac{1}{3}\uparrow \text{ and } \frac{1}{10}\uparrow\right)$ दिमाग में रखें। हर (Denominator) से बराबर करना है मतलब (LCM 30) दिमाग में रखना है अंश (Numerator) (4, 11) मतलब 44 हो जाएगा यानि कोई भी वस्तु 30 से 44 हो रही है मतलब 14 बढ़ गई 30 पर तो Answer $\frac{14}{30}$ आ जाएगा। सारी calculation दिमाग में करनी है।

$$\frac{4}{3}\times\frac{11}{10}=\frac{44}{30} \rightarrow \frac{14}{30} = \frac{7}{15}$$

Exercise

- **FIND NET INCREASE OR DECREASE (% OR FRACTION):-**

1. $33\frac{1}{3}\%\uparrow$ & $10\%\uparrow$ =

(a) $\frac{11}{30}$ (b) $\frac{14}{30}$ (c) $\frac{11}{25}$ (d) $\frac{1}{2}$

2. $14\frac{2}{7}\%\uparrow$ & $20\%\uparrow$ =

(a) $\frac{13}{35}$ (b) $\frac{2}{5}$ (c) $\frac{12}{39}$ (d) $\frac{21}{25}$

3. $6\frac{1}{4}\%\uparrow$ & $10\%\uparrow$ =

(a) 15.75% (b) 16.875% (c) 16.625% (d) 18.33%

4. $6\frac{2}{3}\%\uparrow$ & $25\%\uparrow$ =

(a) 33% (b) 32.5% (c) 30% (d) 33.33%

5. $6\frac{2}{3}\%\downarrow$ & $15\%\uparrow$ =

(a) 7.33% (b) 9.09% (c) $\frac{1}{13}$ (d) 8.33%

6. $33\frac{1}{3}\%\uparrow$ & $20\%\uparrow$ =

(a) 55.55% (b) $\frac{3}{5}$ (c) 66.66% (d) 62.5%

7. $16\frac{2}{3}\%\uparrow$ & $20\%\uparrow$ =

(a) 38% (b) 44.44% (c) $\frac{1}{5}$ (d) $\frac{2}{5}$

8. $16\frac{2}{3}\%\downarrow$ & $10\%\uparrow$ =

(a) $\frac{1}{12}$ (b) 7.5% (c) $\frac{1}{5}$ (d) 9.09%

9. $14\frac{2}{7}\%\uparrow$ & $25\%\uparrow$ =

(a) $\frac{7}{13}$ (b) $\frac{1}{2}$ (c) 40% (d) $\frac{3}{7}$

10. $30\%\uparrow$ & $14\frac{2}{7}\%\downarrow$

(a) 11.42% (b) 10% (c) 11.11% (d) 12.5%

11. $25\%\uparrow$ & $14\frac{2}{7}\%\downarrow$ =

(a) $\frac{3}{14}$ (b) $\frac{1}{14}$ (c) $\frac{1}{7}$ (d) $\frac{2}{7}$

12. $12.5\%\uparrow$ & $6\frac{1}{4}\%\downarrow$ =

(a) 5% (b) 5.46% (c) $\frac{1}{21}$ (d) 4.84%

13. $12.5\%\uparrow$ & $10\%\uparrow$

(a) $\frac{29}{60}$ (b) 23.75% (c) $\frac{19}{80}$ (d) 22.22%

14. $11\frac{1}{9}\%\uparrow$ & $20\%\uparrow$ =

(a) $\frac{1}{4}$ (b) 33.33% (c) 30% (d) 35%

15. $11\frac{1}{9}\%\uparrow$ & $10\%\downarrow$ =

(a) $\frac{1}{100}$ (b) 0% (c) $\frac{1}{20}$ (d) $\frac{1}{80}$

16. $11\frac{1}{9}\%\downarrow$ & $25\%\uparrow$ =

(a) 10% (b) 11.11% (c) $\frac{1}{11}$ (d) 11%

17. $22\frac{2}{9}\%\uparrow$ & $20\%\downarrow$ =

(a) $\frac{44}{45}$ (b) $\frac{1}{40}$ (c) $\frac{1}{50}$ (d) $\frac{1}{45}$

18. $44\frac{4}{9}\%\uparrow$ $15\%\downarrow$ =

(a) 24% (b) 20% (c) $\frac{1}{4}$ (d) 22.77%

19. $9\frac{1}{11}\%\uparrow$ & $12\frac{1}{2}\%\downarrow$ =

(a) $\frac{1}{21}$ (b) 5% (c) 4.2% (d) $\frac{1}{22}$

20. $9\frac{1}{11}\%\uparrow$ & $20\%\uparrow$ =

(a) $\frac{1}{25}$ (b) $\frac{1}{24}$ (c) $\frac{17}{55}$ (d) 5%

21. $7\frac{1}{7}\%\uparrow$ & $25\%\uparrow$ =

(a) 33% (b) 33.92% (c) $\frac{11}{25}$ (d) 35.92%

22. $6\frac{1}{4}\%\uparrow$ & $20\%\uparrow$ =

(a) $\frac{3}{8}$ (b) 27.5% (c) 28.56% (d) 30%

23. $3\frac{1}{3}\%\uparrow$ & $10\%\uparrow$ =

(a) $\frac{13}{80}$ (b) $\frac{1}{7}$ (c) $\frac{41}{300}$ (d) $\frac{51}{300}$

24. $2\frac{1}{2}\%\uparrow$ & $10\%\downarrow$ =

(a) 6.25% (b) 7.75% (c) $\frac{3}{16}$ (d) $\frac{1}{14}$

25. $62\frac{1}{2}\%\uparrow$ & $12.5\%\downarrow$ =

(a) $\frac{25}{64}$ (b) $\frac{27}{64}$ (c) $\frac{3}{7}$ (d) $\frac{1}{3}$

26. $37\frac{1}{2}\%\uparrow$ & $30\%\uparrow$ =

(a) $\frac{7}{8}$ (b) 78.75% (c) 75% (d) 77.77%

27. $87\frac{1}{2}\%\uparrow$ & $20\%\uparrow$ =

(a) 150% (b) $\frac{6}{5}$ (c) $\frac{5}{4}$ (d) $\frac{3}{4}$

28. $42\frac{6}{7}\%\uparrow$ & $30\%\uparrow$ =

(a) 81.42% (b) $\frac{6}{7}$ (c) $\frac{5}{7}$ (d) 82.5%

29. $57\frac{1}{7}\%\uparrow$ & $40\%\uparrow$ =

(a) $\frac{3}{2}$ (b) $\frac{6}{5}$ (c) $\frac{3}{4}$ (d) $\frac{5}{4}$

30. $16\frac{2}{3}\%\uparrow$ & $22\frac{2}{9}\%\uparrow$ =

(a) $\frac{4}{7}$ (b) 42.6% (c) 44.44% (d) 52%

31. $14\frac{2}{7}\%\uparrow$ & $33\frac{1}{3}\%\uparrow$ =

(a) 50% (b) $\frac{11}{21}$ (c) $\frac{13}{21}$ (d) 55.55%

32. $66\frac{2}{3}\%\uparrow$ & $33\frac{1}{3}\%\uparrow$ =

(a) 122.22% (b) $\frac{11}{8}$ (c) $\frac{9}{11}$ (d) $\frac{10}{9}$

33. $33\frac{1}{3}\%\uparrow$ & $14\frac{2}{7}\%\downarrow$ =

(a) $\frac{8}{21}$ (b) $\frac{1}{14}$ (c) $\frac{1}{7}$ (d) 15%

34. $22\frac{2}{9}\%\uparrow$ & $12\frac{1}{2}\%\uparrow$ =

(a) $\frac{3}{8}$ (b) $\frac{7}{20}$ (c) 36.36% (d) 36%

35. $9\frac{1}{11}\%\uparrow$ & $22\frac{2}{9}\%\uparrow$ =

(a) $\frac{1}{3}$ (b) $\frac{3}{8}$ (c) 30% (d) 33%

36. $11\frac{1}{9}\%\uparrow$ & $16\frac{2}{3}\%\downarrow$ =

(a) $\frac{1}{9}$ (b) 6.06% (c) 7.40% (d) $\frac{1}{27}$

37. $16\frac{2}{3}\%\uparrow$ & $6\frac{2}{3}\%\downarrow$ =

(a) $\frac{1}{12}$ (b) 9.09% (c) 8.8% (d) $\frac{1}{9}$

38. $62\frac{1}{2}\%\uparrow$ & $33\frac{1}{3}\%\downarrow$ =

(a) 8.8% (b) $\frac{1}{6}$ (c) $\frac{1}{12}$ (d) $\frac{1}{4}$

39. $12\frac{1}{2}\%\uparrow$ & $37\frac{1}{2}\%\uparrow$ =

(a) 54.54% (b) $\frac{35}{64}$ (c) $\frac{7}{16}$ (d) 52.5%

40. $87\frac{1}{2}\%\uparrow$ & $33\frac{1}{3}\%\uparrow$ =

(a) $\frac{5}{4}$ (b) $\frac{2}{1}$ (c) $\frac{1}{6}$ (d) $\frac{3}{2}$

41. $57\frac{1}{7}\%\uparrow$ & $16\frac{2}{3}\%\uparrow$ =

(a) 81.81% (b) $\frac{16}{21}$ (c) $\frac{5}{6}$ (d) $\frac{6}{7}$

42. $22\frac{2}{9}\%\uparrow$ & $44\frac{4}{9}\%\uparrow$ =

(a) $\frac{8}{9}$ (b) $\frac{7}{9}$ (c) 76.54% (d) 75%

43. $55\frac{5}{9}\%\uparrow$ & $28\frac{4}{7}\%\uparrow$ =

(a) $\frac{3}{2}$ (b) 100% (c) $\frac{60}{63}$ (d) 111.11%

44. $42\frac{6}{7}\%\uparrow$ & $55\frac{5}{9}\%\downarrow$ =

(a) 35.5% (b) $\frac{16}{21}$ (c) 36.50% (d) $\frac{3}{8}$

45. $22\frac{2}{9}\%\uparrow$ & $18\frac{2}{11}\%\uparrow$ =

(a) 45% (b) $\frac{4}{11}$ (c) 44% (d) $\frac{4}{9}$

46. $6\frac{1}{4}\%\uparrow$ & $45\frac{5}{11}\%\uparrow$ =

(a) 54.54% (b) $\frac{7}{11}$ (c) 50% (d) $\frac{7}{9}$

Type-7: Answer - Key

1.	(b)	11.	(b)	21.	(b)	31.	(b)	41.	(c)
2.	(a)	12.	(b)	22.	(b)	32.	(a)	42.	(c)
3.	(b)	13.	(c)	23.	(c)	33.	(c)	43.	(b)
4.	(d)	14.	(b)	24.	(b)	34.	(a)	44.	(c)
5.	(a)	15.	(b)	25.	(b)	35.	(a)	45.	(d)
6.	(b)	16.	(b)	26.	(b)	36.	(c)	46.	(a)
7.	(d)	17.	(d)	27.	(c)	37.	(c)		
8.	(a)	18.	(d)	28.	(b)	38.	(c)		
9.	(d)	19.	(d)	29.	(b)	39.	(b)		
10.	(a)	20.	(c)	30.	(b)	40.	(d)		

Type-1

Note: Discount हमेशा अंकित मूल्य पर दिया जाता है।

MP	D	P

Question बनता है इन तीन चीज़ें में से किन्हीं दो का मान दे दिया जाता है और तीसरे का पूछ लिया जाता है।

$$\frac{MP}{CP} = \frac{(100+P)}{(100-D)} = \frac{(1+P)}{(1-D)}$$ → जब P और D भिन्न (Fraction) में हो

Hint:

$28\frac{4}{7}$ markup and discount $11\frac{1}{9}$% profit or loss = ?

☞ Percentage में हमने देखा था कोई वस्तु $\left(28\frac{4}{7}\right)$ यानि $\left(\frac{2}{7}\right)$ मतलब 7 की वस्तु 2 unit ऊपर अंकित किया तो $\left[\frac{9}{7}\right]$, इसके बाद अंकित मूल्य (Marked Price) पर छूट दी जाती $\left(11\frac{1}{9}\right) = \left(\frac{1}{9}\right)$, 9 की वस्तु पर 1 की छूट हो तो 8 हो जाती है।

पहले CP, 7 था और SP 8 है तो 1 का फायदा हुआ 7 पर $\left(\frac{1}{7}\right)$ का मतलब 14.28%।

सारी calculation दिमाग में करनी है।

Exercise

Markup/MP ☞ अंकित मूल्य

Discount ☞ छूट

1. **Markup = $28\frac{4}{7}$% and discount = $11\frac{1}{9}$%.**

   Profit or Loss%=?

   (a) 42.85 (b) 14.28 (c) 16.66 (d) 12.5

2. **Markup = $16\frac{2}{3}$% and discount = $28\frac{4}{7}$%.**

   Profit or Loss% = ?

   (a) 12.5 (b) 14.28 (c) 20 (d) 16.66

3. **Markup = $37\frac{1}{2}$% and discount = $18\frac{2}{11}$%.**

   Profit or Loss% = ?

   (a) 12.5 (b) 14.28 (c) 20 (d) 16.66

4. **Markup = 45.45% and discount = 6.25%.**

   Profit or Loss % = ?

   (a) 33.33 (b) 36.36 (c) 44.44 (d) 45.45

5. **Markup = 20% and profit = 8%. Discount% = ?**
(a) 12 (b) 12.5 (c) 8.5 (d) 10

6. **Markup = 30% and Profit = 4%, Discount% = ?**
(a) 25 (b) 10 (c) 20 (d) 16.66

7. **Markup = 40% and Loss = 2%. Discount% =?**
(a) 50 (b) 30 (c) 40 (d) 33.33

8. **Markup = 50% and Loss = 25%. Discount% = ?**
(a) 50 (b) 16.66 (c) 40 (d) 33.33

9. **Markup = $33\frac{1}{3}\%$ and Profit = $16\frac{2}{3}\%$. Discount% = ?**
(a) 10 (b) 12.5 (c) 20 (d) 16.66

10. **Markup = $16\frac{2}{3}\%$ and Loss = $16\frac{2}{3}\%$. Discount% = ?**
(a) 0 (b) 14.28 (c) 20 (d) 28.57

11. **Markup = $37\frac{1}{2}\%$ and Profit = $12\frac{1}{2}\%$. Discount% = ?**
(a) 18.18 (b) 28.57 (c) 27.27 (d) 12.5

12. **After allowing a discount of $11\frac{1}{9}\%$, profit is $14\frac{2}{7}\%$. Markup% = ?**
(a) 37.5 (b) 28.57 (c) 25 (d) 22.22

13. After allowing a discount of $28\frac{4}{7}\%$, loss is $16\frac{2}{3}\%$. Markup% = ?

(a) 10 (b) 20 (c) 16.66 (d) 14.28

14. After allowing a discount of $22\frac{2}{9}\%$, loss is $12\frac{1}{2}\%$. Markup% = ?

(a) 10 (b) 11.11 (c) 12.5 (d) 20

15. After allowing a discount of $6\frac{1}{4}\%$, profit is 36.36%. Markup% = ?

(a) 9.09 (b) 45.45 (c) 12.5 (d) 10

Type-1: Answer - Key

1.	(b)	4.	(b)	7.	(b)	10.	(d)	13.	(c)
2.	(d)	5.	(d)	8.	(a)	11.	(a)	14.	(c)
3.	(a)	6.	(c)	9.	(b)	12.	(b)	15.	(b)

Type-2

Hint:

Markup = 20% and discount = 10% है

Profit or Loss % is?

☞ 100 रु. की एक वस्तु थी (20%) से अंकित किया मतलब (120) हो गई और अंकित मूल्य पर 10% की छूट (108) को हो गई तो (100) रु. की वस्तु (108) रु. मे बेची गई तो 8% का लाभ हुआ सारी calculation दिमाग में रखकर करनी है।

आप इसमें $x - y - \frac{xy}{100}$ भी लगा सकते हैं

$$\left[20 - 10 - \frac{20 \times 10}{100} = 8\right]$$

Exercise

1. **Markup = 20% and discount = 10%. Profit or Loss % = ?**
   (a) 5 (b) 4 (c) 8 (d) 6

2. **Markup = 30% and discount = 5%. Profit or Loss% = ?**
   (a) 23.5 (b) 24.5 (c) 25 (d) 20

3. Markup = 36% and discount = 40%. Profit or Loss % = ?

(a) 15.6 (b) 18.4 (c) 14.8 (d) 16.5

4. Markup = 20% and discount = 5%. Profit or Loss % = ?

(a) 15 (b) 14 (c) 12 (d) 16

5. Markup = 30% and discount = 20%. Profit or Loss% = ?

(a) 5 (b) 10 (c) 4 (d) 6

6. Markup = 20% with no discount. Profit or Loss% = ?

(a) 25 (b) 16.66 (c) 50 (d) 20

7. Markup = 30% with no discount. Profit or Loss % = ?

(a) 42.85 (b) 33.33 (c) 45 (d) 30

8. Markup = 35% and discount = 22.22%. Profit or Loss% = ?

(a) 5 (b) 11.11 (c) 10 (d) 33.33

9. Markup = x%, discount = 30% and Profit = 5%. x = ?

(a) 5 (b) 25 (c) 50 (d) 150

10. Markup = y%, discount = 13% and Profit = 45%. y = ?

(a) 26 (b) 33.33 (c) 30 (d) 66.66

11. Markup = z%, discount = 19% and Profit 8%. z = ?

(a) 29 (b) 33.33 (c) 30 (d) 66.66

12. MP increased by 45.45% and sold at CP. Discount% = ?

(a) 33.33 (b) 31.25 (c) 32.50 (d) 45.45

13. MP increased by 10% and sold at original MP. Discount% = ?

(a) 12.5 (b) 10 (c) 11.11 (d) 9.09

14. Discount of 45% on MP and sold at CP. Markup% = ?

(a) 55 (b) 22.22 (c) 81.81 (d) 72.72

15. After allowing a discount of 12.5%, profit is 12% markup% = ?

(a) 37.5 (b) 32.84 (c) 28 (d) 33.33

16. After allowing a discount of 8%, profit is $22\frac{2}{3}\%$. Markup% = ?

(a) 37.5 (b) 32.84 (c) 32.5 (d) 33.33

17. After allowing a discount of 11%, profit is $22\frac{3}{8}\%$. Markup% = ?

(a) 37.5 (b) 27.5 (c) 36 (d) 42

18. Profit is 32% and discount 12%. Markup% = ?

(a) 5/4 (b) 1/2 (c) 4/5 (d) 2/3

19. Profit is $16\frac{2}{3}\%$ and discount $7\frac{1}{7}\%$. Markup% = ?

(a) $36\frac{1}{9}$ (b) $24\frac{1}{3}$ (c) 25.6 (d) 26.5

Type-2: Answer - Key

1.	(c)	5.	(c)	9.	(c)	13.	(d)	17.	(a)
2.	(a)	6.	(d)	10.	(d)	14.	(c)	18.	(b)
3.	(b)	7.	(d)	11.	(b)	15.	(c)	19.	(c)
4.	(b)	8.	(a)	12.	(b)	16.	(d)		

Type-1

☞ Find Net Rate/Fraction

(1) 2% @ CI for 2 years

$\boxed{2a.\dfrac{a^2}{100}} \Rightarrow$ C.I. for 2 years

$\boxed{3a\ .\ 3a^2a^3} \Rightarrow$ C.I. for 3 years

$\Rightarrow 2 \times 2 + 0.4 = 4.04\%$ Ans.

दिमाग में सीधा click होना चाहिए।

$\Rightarrow 14\frac{2}{7}\%$ @ C.I. for 2 years

☞ इस Type में जब Rate fraction दी हुई हो तो $\left(14\frac{2}{7}\right) = \left(\frac{1}{7}\right)$ यानि $\left(\frac{8}{7}\right)$ दो वर्ष के लिए है $\left(\frac{8}{7}\right)^2 = \left(\frac{64}{49}\right)$ यानि 15 C.I. है और मूलधन 49 है तो $\left(\frac{15}{49}\right)$ का जो percentage होगा वो ही Net rate कहलाएगा जो Answer होगा, दिमाग में करना है।

(2) 10% @ CI for 2.5 years

☞ हम जानते है दो वर्ष के लिए 10% की दर से Net Rate 21% होता है। अब आधा साल यानि 5% लगाना है तो $\left(21+5+\frac{21\times5}{100}\right)=27.05$ Answer निकल जाएगा।

(3) 20% @ CI for 2.5 years

☞ 20% के हिसाब से 2 वर्ष के लिए Net rate 44% होती है और इसे हमने दिमाग में रोक लिया अब 44 और 10 में Net rate निकालना है, तो $\left(44+10+\frac{44\times10}{100}\right)=$ तो 58.4 Answer निकल जाएगा।

लिखना नहीं है ये ही दिमाग के लिए Challenge है

(4) 20% @ CI for $2\frac{2}{5}$ years

☞ 20% के हिसाब से 2 वर्ष का Net (44%) होता है $\left(20 \text{ का } \frac{2}{5}\right)$ निकालते है तो (8%) अब (44) और (8%) का नेट निकालेगे।

52 + 3.52 = 55.52 Answer निकल जाएगा।

दिमाग में बिना लिखे अभ्यास करें।

(5) 15% @ CI for $2\frac{2}{5}$ years

☞ (15%) की दर से 2 वर्ष के नेट (32.25) होता है $\frac{2}{5}$ वर्ष के लिए 6% तो नेट 38.25 + $\frac{3825 \times 6}{100}$ = 41.28 Answer इसमें काम करना पड़ेगा।

(6) 2% CI for 3 years :

☞ $3a.3a^2a^3$ = 6.1208 ⇒ दिमाग में पूरा solve करना है। यहाँ दो अंक (Digit) आएंगे इसलिए zero लगानी हैं अगर दो अंक (Digit) नहीं बन पाएँ।

(7) $16\frac{2}{3}$ % @ CI for 3 years

☞ $\left(16\frac{2}{3}\right)$ का मतलब $\left(\frac{1}{6}\right)$ है जो $\left(\frac{7}{6}\right)$ हो जाएगा तीन वर्ष दिया है तो (cube) कर देंगे $\left(\frac{7}{6}\right)^3 = \left(\frac{343}{216}\right)$ 127 ब्याज मिल रहा 216 पर तो $\frac{127}{216}$ Answer हो जाएगा।

Exercise

- **FIND NET RATE/FRACTION:-**

1. 2% @ CI for 2 years.

(a) 4% (b) 4.04% (c) 4.16% (d) 4.4%

2. 3% @ CI for 2 years.

(a) 6% (b) 6.06% (c) 6.09% (d) 6.12%

3. 4% @ CI for 2 years.

(a) 8% (b) 8.08% (c) 8.16% (d) 8.64%

4. 5% @ CI for 2 years.

(a) 10% (b) 10.10% (c) 10.50% (d) 10.25%

5. 6% @ CI for 2 years.

(a) 12.64% (b) 12.36% (c) 12.12% (d) 12%

6. 7% @ CI for 2 years.

(a) 14.49% (b) 14.14% (c) 14.07% (d) 14%

7. 9% @ CI for 2 years.

(a) 18% (b) 18.18% (c) 18.81% (d) 18.09%

8. 10% @ CI for 2 years.

(a) 20% (b) 20.20% (c) 21% (d) 20.40%

9. 12% @ CI for 2 years.

(a) 24% (b) 24.44% (c) 24.48% (d) 25.44%

10. 13% @ CI for 2 years.

(a) 27.69% (b) 27.96% (c) 26.69% (d) 26.96%

11. 15% @ CI for 2 years.

(a) 32.75% (b) 32.25% (c) 31.75% (d) 31.25%

12. $14\frac{2}{7}$ % @ CI for 2 years.

(a) 8/49 (b) 15/49 (c) 2/7 (d) 17/49

13. $16\frac{2}{3}$ % @ CI for 2 years.

(a) 1/3 (b) 11/36 (c) 13/36 (d) 7/36

14. $11\frac{1}{9}$ % @ CI for 2 years.

(a) 2/9 (b) 7/27 (c) 17/81 (d) 19/81

15. $9\frac{1}{11}$ % @ CI for 2 years.

(a) 2/11 (b) 21/121 (c) 23/121 (d) 19/121

16. 10% @ CI for $2\frac{1}{3}$ years.

(a) 25.03% (b) 27.05% (c) 28.25% (d) 29.15%

17. 10% @ CI for 2.5 years.

(a) 20% (b) 27.05% (c) 21% (d) 20.40%

18. 20% @ CI for 2.5 years.

(a) 56.2% (b) 58.4% (c) 60% (d) 54.8%

19. 20% @ SI for $2\frac{2}{5}$ years.

(a) 45% (b) 46% (c) 48% (d) 47.5%

20. 20% @ CI for $2\frac{2}{5}$ years.

(a) 55.52% (b) 57.5% (c) 55% (d) 57%

21. 10% @ CI for $2\frac{2}{5}$ years.

(a) 25% (b) 24% (c) 24.84% (d) 25.84%

22. 15% @ CI for $2\frac{2}{5}$ years.

(a) 38.75% (b) 42.25% (c) 40.18% (d) 41.28%

23. 14% @ SI for $2\frac{5}{7}$ years.

(a) 32% (b) 35% (c) 36% (d) 38%

24. 8% @ CI for $2\frac{5}{8}$ years.

(a) 21.76% (b) 18.72% (c) 21% (d) 22.47%

25. 2% @ CI for 3 years.

(a) 6.27% (b) 6.3% (c) 6.12% (d) 6.21%

26. 3% @ CI for 3 years.

(a) 9.18% (b) 9.27% (c) 9.36% (d) 9.54%

27. 4% @ CI for 3 years.

(a) 12.48% (b) 12.84% (c) 12.6% (d) 12.96%

28. 5% @ CI for 3 years.

(a) 15.25% (b) 15.5% (c) 15.76% (d) 15.8%

29. 6% @ CI for 3 years.

(a) 18% (b) 19.3% (c) 20% (d) 19.1%

30. 10% @ CI for 3 years.

(a) 30% (b) 33% (c) 33.1% (d) 33.33%

31. $16\frac{2}{3}$% @ CI for 3 years.

(a) 7/12 (b) 19/36 (c) 127/216 (d) 127/256

32. 5% @ SI for 3.5 years.

(a) 16.5% (b) 17.5% (c) 18% (d) 18.5%

33. 15% @ SI for $3\frac{4}{5}$ years.

(a) 57% (b) 49% (c) 58% (d) 53%

34. 3.7% @ SI for 4 years.

(a) 13.8% (b) 14.4% (c) 14.6% (d) 14.8%

35. 6.5% @ SI for 4 years.

(a) 24% (b) 25% (c) 26% (d) 27%

36. 8.75% @ SI for 4 years.

(a) 30% (b) 35% (c) 36% (d) 33%

37. $2\frac{3}{4}$% @ SI for 4 years.

(a) 9% (b) 9.8% (c) 11% (d) 10.4%

38. 9.8% @ SI for 6 years.

(a) 58.8% (b) 54.72% (c) 54.48% (d) 56.4%

39. $6\frac{2}{3}$% @ SI for $4\frac{1}{5}$ years.

(a) 30% (b) 25% (c) $33\frac{1}{3}$% (d) 28%

40. 9.7% @ SI for 6 years.

(a) 56% (b) 58.2% (c) 56.4% (d) 59.4%

41. 12% @ SI for $6\frac{2}{3}$ years.

(a) 60% (b) 64% (c) 80% (d) 90%

42. 4% @ SI for 8.5 years.

(a) 35% (b) 32% (c) 34% (d) 36%

Type-1 : Answer - Key

1.	(b)	10.	(a)	19.	(c)	28.	(c)	37.	(c)
2.	(c)	11.	(b)	20.	(a)	29.	(d)	38.	(a)
3.	(c)	12.	(b)	21.	(d)	30.	(c)	39.	(d)
4.	(d)	13.	(c)	22.	(c)	31.	(c)	40.	(b)
5.	(b)	14.	(d)	23.	(d)	32.	(b)	41.	(c)
6.	(a)	15.	(c)	24.	(d)	33.	(a)	42.	(c)
7.	(c)	16.	(a)	25.	(c)	34.	(d)		
8.	(c)	17.	(b)	26.	(b)	35.	(c)		
9.	(d)	18.	(b)	27.	(a)	36.	(b)		

Type-2

☞ **Difference CI – SI:-**

(1) 2% for 2 years

दो साल का Difference $\left(\frac{R^2}{100}\right)$ होता है $\frac{4}{100} = 0.04$ Answer आ जाएगा।

(2) 2% CI for 3 years

तीन साल का अंतर $3a^2a^3$ होता है $(2)^3 = (08)$

$(3a^2) = 0.1208$ Answer निकल जाएगा।

(3) $14\frac{2}{7}$ % for 2 years

$= \left(\frac{1}{7}\right) = \left(\frac{8}{7}\right)$ दो साल का करेगें तो $\left(\frac{64}{49}\right)$ हो जाएगा यानि 15 जो हो गया वो CI होगा

7

7 1 Difference

हो गया तो $\frac{1}{49}$ Answer आ जाएगा दिमाग में होने वाली चीज है।

(4) $26\frac{2}{3}$% for 2 years

$\left(26\frac{2}{3}\right)$ का मतलब होता है $\left(6\frac{2}{3}\right)$ का 4 गुना यानि $\left(\frac{4}{15}\right)$

$= (15)^2 = 225$

225
→ 60
60 [16] → अंतर

$\boxed{\frac{16}{225}}$ Answer ऐसे करके Answer दिमाग में आना चाहिए।

(5) 10% for 4 years

I	II	III	IV
10%	21%	33.1	46.41%

+10 +10 +10

⇒ याद रखना

Answer 6.41% निकल जाएगा।

(6) $11\frac{1}{9}\%$ for 3 years

$$11\frac{1}{9} = \frac{1}{9} = \left(\frac{10}{9}\right)^3 = \frac{1000}{729}$$

↳ 729

↳ 81

$\boxed{\frac{28}{729}}$

81

81

9	
18	1

Difference

Exercise

- **Find difference between SI and CI (% or fraction):-**

1. 2% for 2 years.

(a) 0.2% (b) 0.04% (c) 0.02% (d) 0.4%

2. 3% for 2 years.

(a) 0.6% (b) 0.09% (c) 0.06% (d) 0.9%

3. 4% for 2 years.

(a) 0.4% (b) 0.08% (c) 0.16% (d) 0.8%

4. 8% for 2 years.

(a) 0.8% (b) 0.46% (c) 0.16% (d) 0.64%

5. 10% for 2 years.

(a) 1% (b) 2% (c) 1.5% (d) 2.5%

6. 11% for 2 years.

(a) 1.2% (b) 1.21% (c) 2.2% (d) 1.22%

7. 12% for 2 years.

(a) 1.44% (b) 1.12% (c) 1.24% (d) 1.4%

8. 2% for 3 years.

(a) 0.1406% (b) 0.1802%
(c) 0.1208% (d) 0.1008%

9. 3% for 3 years.

(a) 0.2121% (b) 0.2727%
(c) 0.2424% (d) 0.1818%

10. 4% for 3 years.

(a) 0.6464% (b) 0.6484%
(c) 0.4648% (d) 0.4864%

11. 5% for 3 years.

(a) 0.7625% (b) 0.6725%
(c) 0.567% (d) 0.625%

12. 10% for 3 years.

(a) 3% (b) 3.31% (c) 3.1% (d) 3.6%

13. $14\frac{2}{7}$**% for 2 years.**

(a) 1/14 (b) 1/49 (c) 2/49 (d) 3/49

14. $11\frac{1}{9}$**% for 2 years.**

(a) 1/18 (b) 1/27 (c) 1/81 (d) 2/81

15. $26\frac{2}{3}$ **% for 2 years.**

(a) 1/45 (b) 2/45 (c) 4/125 (d) 16/225

16. $33\frac{1}{3}$ **% for 2 years.**

(a) $11\frac{1}{9}\%$ (b) $9\frac{1}{11}\%$ (c) $16\frac{2}{3}\%$ (d) $8\frac{1}{3}\%$

17. $66\frac{2}{3}$ **% for 2 years.**

(a) $40\frac{4}{9}\%$ (b) $44\frac{4}{9}\%$ (c) $30\frac{1}{3}\%$ (d) $33\frac{1}{3}\%$

18. $16\frac{2}{3}$ **% for 2 years.**

(a) 1/36 (b) 1/9 (c) 1/64 (d) 1/30

19. 10% for 4 years.

(a) 6.41% (b) 2.41% (c) 4.61% (d) 4.41%

20. $9\frac{1}{11}$ **% for 2 years.**

(a) 1/90 (b) 1/121 (c) 1/99 (d) 1/110

21. $8\frac{1}{3}$ **% for 2 years.**

(a) 1/96 (b) 1/60 (c) 1/156 (d) 1/144

22. $57\frac{1}{7}$**% for 2 years.**

(a) 4/49 (b) 8/49 (c) 16/49 (d) 12/49

23. $14\frac{2}{7}$**% for 3 years.**

(a) 1/343 (b) 1/49 (c) 22/343 (d) 11/343

24. $11\frac{1}{9}$**% for 3 years.**

(a) 28/729 (b) 1/81 (c) 11/729 (d) 19/729

25. $16\frac{2}{3}$**% for 3 years.**

(a) 1/216 (b) 19/216 (c) 1/36 (d) 13/216

26. $12\frac{1}{2}$**% for 3 years.**

(a) 3/64 (b) 1/512 (c) 25/512 (d) 17/512

27. $9\frac{1}{11}$**% for 3 years.**

(a) 1/121 (b) 23/1331 (c) 1/1331 (d) 34/1331

28. 20% for 3 years.

(a) 15.68% (b) 1.56% (c) 12.8% (d) 1.28%

29. 25% for 3 years.

(a) 13.3% (b) 20.3% (c) 17.5% (d) 23%

30. 10% for 1st year and 20% for 2nd year.

(a) 2% (b) 4% (c) 1% (d) 5%

31. 15% for 1st year and 5% for 2nd year.

(a) 0.45% (b) 1.75% (c) 0.75% (d) 1.5%

32. 5% for 1st year and 10% for 2nd year.

(a) 0.25% (b) 0.75% (c) 0.5% (d) 1.5%

33. 25% for 1st year and 20% for 2nd year.

(a) 4% (b) 5% (c) 10% (d) 2.5%

34. $33\frac{1}{3}$% for 1st year and $14\frac{2}{7}$% for 2nd year.

(a) 1/14 (b) 1/42 (c) 1/21 (d) 1/35

35. $16\frac{2}{3}$% for 1st year and $33\frac{1}{3}$% for 2nd year.

(a) 1/9 (b) 1/18 (c) 1/27 (d) 1/24

36. 20% for 1st year and $33\frac{1}{3}$% for 2nd year.

(a) 1/12 (b) 1/15 (c) 1/18 (d) 1/20

37. 10% for 1st year and $11\frac{1}{9}$% for 2nd year.

(a) 1/45 (b) 2/45 (c) 1/90 (d) 1/81

38. $14\frac{2}{7}\%$ for 1st year and $16\frac{2}{3}\%$ for 2nd year.

(a) 1/49 (b) 1/56 (c) 1/48 (d) 1/42

39. $12\frac{1}{2}\%$ for 1st year and $9\frac{1}{11}\%$ for 2nd year.

(a) 1/72 (b) 1/88 (c) 1/84 (d) 1/108

40. 25% for 1st year and $12\frac{1}{2}\%$ for 2nd year.

(a) 1/16 (b) 1/24 (c) 1/32 (d) 1/48

Type-2: Answer - Key

1.	(b)	9.	(b)	17.	(b)	25.	(b)	33.	(b)
2.	(b)	10.	(d)	18.	(a)	26.	(c)	34.	(c)
3.	(c)	11.	(a)	19.	(a)	27.	(d)	35.	(b)
4.	(d)	12.	(c)	20.	(b)	28.	(c)	36.	(b)
5.	(a)	13.	(b)	21.	(d)	29.	(b)	37.	(c)
6.	(b)	14.	(c)	22.	(c)	30.	(a)	38.	(d)
7.	(a)	15.	(d)	23.	(c)	31.	(c)	39.	(b)
8.	(c)	16.	(a)	24.	(a)	32.	(c)	40.	(c)

Type-3

(1) 12% p.a. @ CI compounded 5 monthly in 10 months

यहाँ (12) महीने की Rate (12%) है (5) महीने की (5%) हो जाएगी (5%) के हिसाब से 2 बार cycle चलेगी जो 10.25 Answer आ जाएगा।

(2) $33\frac{1}{3}$ p.a. @ C.I. half yearly in 1 year

$\left(33\frac{1}{3}\right)$ का मतलब होता है $\left(\frac{1}{3}\right)$ Half yearly के हिसाब से $\left(\frac{1}{6}\right)$ हो जाएगा तो $\left(\frac{7}{6}\right)^2 = \left(\frac{49}{36}\right)$ हो जाएगा तो 13 ब्याज मिलेगा 36 मूलधन होगा $\left(\frac{13}{36}\right)$ Answer हो जाएगा।

(3) 12% p.a. @ CI compounded 8 monthly in 2 years

Rate 12% है p.a. लागू है CI पर 8 monthly 2 साल मतलब 24 महीने यानि cycle तीन बार चलेगी 12 महीने Rate 12% है तो 8 महीने का Rate 8% तो 3a . $3a^2a^3$ पर 81 का मान डालेगे तो 25.9712 Answer निकल जाएगा। दिमाग का प्रयोग करना है समझने के लिए और दिमाग में Answer निकालना है।

(4) 12%p.a. CI compounded 5 montly in 10 months

यहाँ cycle दो बार की है 12 महीने का 12% 5 महीने का 5% के हिसाब से दो बार का 10.25 होता है।

(5) 10% p.a, @ CI compounded half yearly for 15 months

10% के हिसाब से half yearly है तो 5% होगी 15 महीने की बात है तो 3 बार cycle चलेगी 15.7625 Answer निकल जाएगा।

(6) 12% p.a. @ CI compounded 7 monthly in $1\frac{3}{4}$ years

12% Rate है CI पर 7 monthly $\frac{7}{\cancel{4}} \times \cancel{12}^{3} = 21$ months मतलब तीन बार cycle चलेगी 12 month की 12% 7 months की 7% तो 7% वाली 3 बार लगती है तो 22.5043% Answer निकल जाएगा।

(7) $13\frac{1}{3}$% p.a. @ CI compounded 9 monthly for $2\frac{1}{4}$ years

$13\frac{1}{3}$% p.a. के हिसाब से 9 महीने के लिए

$\left(\frac{9}{\not{4}} \times \not{12}^{3} = 27\right)$ का समय हो गया और 3 बार लगेगा यदि 12 की value $\left(13\frac{1}{3} = \frac{2}{15}\right)$ तो 1 की value $\left(\frac{1}{90}\right)$ तो 9 महीने का $\frac{1}{10}$ आ गया अब 10% 3 बार लगाते है तो 33.1 हो गया।

Exercise

- **FIND THE COMPOUND INTEREST (in %) IN EACH CASE:-**

1. 10% p.a. @ CI half yearly in 1 year?

(a) 5.25% (b) 6.25%

(c) 11.25% (d) 10.25%

2. 20% p.a. @ CI half yearly in 1 year?

(a) 22% (b) 21%

(c)22.5% (d) 21.50%

3. 8% p.a. @ CI half yearly in 1 year?

(a) 9.16% (b) 8.25%

(c) 8.16% (d) 8.64%

4. 14% p.a. @ CI half yearly in 1 year?

(a) 14.49% (b)15.28%

(c) 14.28% (d)14.14%

5. 10% p.a. @ CI half yearly in $1\frac{1}{2}$ year?

(a) 16.6725%
(b) 15.225%
(c) 15.6250%
(d) 15.7625%

6. 20% p.a. @ CI half yearly in $1\frac{1}{2}$ year?

(a) 33.01%
(b) 33.5%
(c) 33.3%
(d) 33.1%

7. 4% p.a. @ CI half yearly in $1\frac{1}{2}$ year?

(a) 6.1208%
(b) 6.2108%
(c) 6.1728%
(d) 6.512%

8. 8% p.a. @ CI half yearly in $1\frac{1}{2}$ year?

(a) 12.6464%
(b) 12.5124%
(c) 12.4864%
(d) 12.4684%

9. $33\frac{1}{3}$% p.a. @ CI half yearly in 1 year?

(a) 35.21%
(b) 36.11%
(c) 36.36%
(d) 36.89%

10. $28\frac{4}{7}$% p.a. @ CI half yearly in 1 year?

(a) 30.512% (b) 32.312%

(c) 30.612% (d) 31.662%

11. $22\frac{2}{9}$% p.a. @ CI half yearly in 1 year?

(a) 25.25% (b) 36.36%

(c) 24.50% (d) 23.45%

12. $18\frac{2}{11}$% p.a. @ CI half yearly in 1 year?

(a) 20.5% (b) 21%

(c) 20% (d)19%

13. $12\frac{1}{2}$% p.a. @ CI half yearly in 1 year?

(a) 14.9% (b) 15%

(c) 12.9% (d) 13.5%

14. $14\frac{2}{7}$% p.a. @ CI half yearly in 1 year?

(a) 14.8% (b)15%

(c) 15.8% (d) 14.6%

15. $6\frac{2}{3}$% p.a. @ CI half yearly in 1 year?

(a) 7.70% (b) 6.77%

(c) 6.96% (d) 7.07%

16. $9\frac{1}{11}$% p.a. @ CI half yearly in 1 year?

(a) 9.29% (b) 11.11%

(c) 10.09% (d) 9.90%

17. 12% p.a. @ CI compounded 8 monthly in 2 year?

(a) 24.96% (b) 25.97%

(c) 28.84% (d) 26.96%

18. 12% p.a. @ CI compounded 5 monthly in 10 months?

(a) 11% (b) 11.25%

(c) 12.25% (d) 10.25%

19. 40% p.a. @ CI compounded quarterly in 1 year?

(a) 42.12% (b) 45.42%

(c) 46.41% (d) 48.41%

20. 15% p.a. @ CI compounded 8 monthly in 2 year?

(a) 33.1% (b) 30.1%

(c) 45.3% (d) 32.5%

21. 12% p.a. @ CI compounded 8 monthly in $1\frac{1}{3}$ years?

(a) 24.46% (b) 12.45%

(c) 18.64% (d) 16.64%

22. 12% p.a. @ CI compounded 5 monthly in $1\frac{1}{4}$ years?

(a) 15.7625% (b) 16.6725%

(c) 24.7526% (d) 18.7525%

23. 15% p.a. @ CI compounded 10 monthly in $2\frac{1}{2}$ years?

(a) 37.50% (b) 45.30%

(c) 42.38% (d) 40.50%

24. 15% p.a. @ SI compounded annually for $4\frac{4}{5}$ years?

(a) 72% (b) 72.2%

(c) 72.5% (d) 70.6%

25. 16% p.a. @ SI compounded annually for $4\frac{3}{5}$ years?

(a) 71.7% (b) 73.6%

(c) 74.5% (d) 75.2%

26. 10% p.a. @ CI compounded half yearly for 18 months?

(a) 15.73% (b) 15.76%

(c) 15.79% (d) 15.81%

27. 12% p.a. @ CI compounded 7 monthly in $1\frac{3}{4}$ year?

(a) 21.50% (b) 20.50%

(c) 22.50% (d) 23.50%

28. 20% p.a. @ CI compounded 3 monthly in $\frac{3}{4}$ year?

(a) 25.7625% (b) 16.6250%

(c) 15.7625% (d) 20.5672%

29. 18% p.a. @ CI compounded 4 monthly for $\frac{2}{3}$ year?

(a) 13.30% (b) 12.36%

(c) 19.36% (d) 15.30%

30. 12% p.a. @ CI compounded 14 monthly in $2\frac{1}{3}$ year?

(a) 28.36% (b) 30.96% (c) 24.96% (d) 29.96%

31. $13\frac{1}{3}$% p.a. @ CI compounded 9 monthly for $2\frac{1}{4}$ year?

(a) 35.3% (b) 30.1% (c) 32.3% (d) 33.1%

32. $14\frac{2}{7}$ % p.a. @ CI compounded 4 monthly in $\frac{2}{3}$ year?

(a) 10.25% (b) 9.75% (c) 15.25% (d) 11.75%

33. $11\frac{1}{9}$% p.a. @ CI compounded 6 monthly for 1 year?

(a) 12.21% (b) 13.84% (c) 11.42% (d) 12.42%

34. $16\frac{2}{3}$ % p.a. @ CI compounded 6 monthly for 1 year?

(a) 17.36% (b)18.66% (c) 32.45% (d) 20.26%

35. $44\frac{4}{9}$% p.a. @ CI compounded quarterly for 9 month?

(a) 36.1% (b) 35.1% (c) 33.1% (d) 37.1%

36. 10% p.a. @ CI for 2nd year?

(a) 12% (b) 13.31% (c) 11% (d) 10.5%

37. 20% p.a. @ CI for 2nd year?

(a) 22% (b) 24% (c) 25% (d) 23%

38. 10% p.a. @ CI for 3rd year?

(a) 13.1% (b) 11.1% (c) 12.1% (d) 11.9%

39. 5% p.a. @ CI for 2nd year?

(a) 7.25% (b) 5.25% (c) 6.25% (d) 6%

40. 2% p.a. @ CI for 2nd year?

(a) 3.02% (b) 2.5% (c) 2.08% (d) 2.04%

41. 10% p.a. @ CI for 4th year?

(a) 13.31% (b) 15.21% (c) 11.11% (d) 14.6%

42. 6% p.a. @ CI for 2nd year?

(a) 6.76% (b) 7.36% (c) 6.36% (d) 6.66%

43. 14% p.a. @ CI for 3rd year?

(a) 16.66% (b) 18.19% (c) 17.49% (d) 18.69%

44. 8% p.a. @ CI for 2nd year?

(a) 8.96% (b) 9.32% (c) 8.64% (d) 8.04%

45. 15% p.a. @ CI for 2nd year?

(a) 16.50% (b) 17.25% (c) 18.25% (d) 30.25%

46. 25% p.a. @ CI for 2nd year?

(a) 31.25% (b) 30.25% (c) 32.75% (d) 28.25%

47. $14\frac{2}{7}$% p.a. @ CI for 2nd year?

(a) 15.64% (b) 16.32% (c) 16.08% (d) 18.36%

48. 20% p.a. @ CI for 3rd year?

(a) 25.6% (b) 30.8% (c) 29.6% (d) 28.8%

49. $9\frac{1}{11}$% p.a. @ CI for 2nd year?

(a) 9.92% (b) 11.29% (c) 10.18% (d) 8.12%

50. $16\frac{2}{3}$% p.a. @ CI for 2nd year?

(a) 18.24% (b) 20.64% (c) 19.44% (d) 18.33%

51. 5% p.a. @ CI for 3rd year?

(a) 6.3515% (b) 5.5125% (c) 5.0562% (d) 6.2515%

52. 9% p.a. @ CI for 2nd year?

(a) 10.21% (b) 11.11% (c) 9.11% (d)9.81%

53. $6\frac{1}{4}$% p.a. @ CI for 2nd year?

(a) 7.24% (b) 6.64% (c) 6.28% (d) 8.32%

54. $6\frac{2}{3}$% p.a. @ CI for 2nd year?

(a) 6.96% (b) 8.21% (c) 7.11% (d) 7.90%

55. $16\frac{2}{3}$% p.a. @ CI for 3rd year?

(a) 20.58% (b) 24.48% (c) 22.68% (d) 18.28%

56. $14\frac{2}{7}$% p.a. @ CI for 1st year and $16\frac{2}{3}$% for 2nd year then compound interest for 2nd year?

(a) 19.04% (b) 18.64% (c) 20.24% (d) 16.08%

57. 10% p.a. @ CI for 1st year and 20% for 2nd year then compound interest for 2nd year?

(a) 21% (b) 24% (c) 22% (d) 23%

58. 10% p.a. @ CI for 1st year and 40% for 2nd year then compound interest for 2nd year?

(a) 42% (b) 44% (c) 45% (d) 43%

59. 40% p.a. @ CI for 1st year and 10% for 2nd year then compound interest for 2nd year?

(a) 12% (b) 13% (c) 16% (d) 14%

60. 20% p.a. @ CI for 1st year and 25% for 2nd year then compound interest for 2nd year?

(a) 28% (b) 32% (c) 30% (d) 29%

Type-3 : Answer - Key

1.	(d)	13.	(c)	25.	(b)	37.	(b)	49.	(a)
2.	(b)	14.	(a)	26.	(b)	38.	(c)	50.	(c)
3.	(c)	15.	(b)	27.	(c)	39.	(b)	51.	(b)
4.	(a)	16.	(a)	28.	(c)	40.	(d)	52.	(d)
5.	(d)	17.	(b)	29.	(b)	41.	(a)	53.	(b)
6.	(d)	18.	(d)	30.	(d)	42.	(c)	54.	(c)
7.	(a)	19.	(c)	31.	(d)	43.	(b)	55.	(c)
8.	(c)	20.	(a)	32.	(b)	44.	(c)	56.	(a)
9.	(b)	21.	(d)	33.	(c)	45.	(b)	57.	(c)
10.	(c)	22.	(a)	34.	(a)	46.	(a)	58.	(b)
11.	(d)	23.	(c)	35.	(d)	47.	(b)	59.	(d)
12.	(d)	24.	(a)	36.	(c)	48.	(d)	60.	(c)

TIME AND WORK (समय एवं कार्य)

Type-1

☞ If A does $\frac{2}{5}$ part of the work in 10 days, then in how many days whole work will be compeleted?

यदि A किसी कार्य का $\frac{2}{5}$ भाग 10 दिनों में करता है, तो कार्य कितने दिनों में पूरा हो जाएगा?

Options

20	25
30	40

Ans.

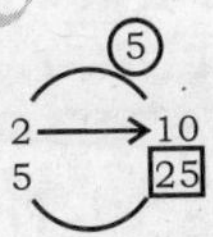

सीधा देखना है 2 की value 10 है मतलब 5 गुना, इसलिए 5 की value 5 गुना 25 होगी।

Exercise

1. If A does 2/5 part of the work in 10 days, then in how many days whole work will be completed?

यदि A कार्य का 2/5 भाग 10 दिनों में करता है, तो पूरा कार्य कितने दिनों में पूरा होगा?

(a) 20
(b) 25
(c) 30
(d) 40

2. **If A does 3/4 part of the work in 27 days, then in how many days whole work will be completed?**

यदि A कार्य का 3/4 भाग 27 दिनों में करता है, तो पूरा कार्य कितने दिनों में पूरा होगा?

(a) 20 (b) 24
(c) 36 (d) 30

3. **If A does 5/17 part of the work in 25 days, then in how many days whole work will be completed?**

यदि A कार्य का 5/17 भाग 25 दिनों में करता है, तो पूरा कार्य कितने दिनों में पूरा होगा?

(a) 68 (b) 85
(c) 102 (d) 91

4. **If A does 7/13 part of the work in 21 days, then in how many days whole work will be completed?**

यदि A कार्य का 7/13 भाग 21 दिनों में करता है, तो पूरा कार्य कितने दिनों में पूरा होगा?

(a) 91 (b) 36
(c) 26 (d) 39

5. **If A does 13/20 part of the work in 39 days, then in how many days whole work will be completed?**

यदि A कार्य का 13/20 भाग 39 दिनों में करता है, तो पूरा कार्य कितने दिनों में पूरा होगा?

(a) 60 (b) 26
(c) 57 (d) 65

6. **If A does $33\frac{1}{3}$% of the work in 17 days, then in how many days whole work will be completed?**

यदि A $33\frac{1}{3}$% कार्य 17 दिनों में करता है, तो पूरा कार्य कितने दिनों में पूरा होगा?

(a) 50 (b) 51
(c) 68 (d) 34

7. **If A does $14\frac{2}{7}$% of the work in $7\frac{1}{7}$ days, then in how many days whole work will be completed?**

यदि A $14\frac{2}{7}$% कार्य $7\frac{1}{7}$ दिनों में करता है, तो पूरा कार्य कितने दिनों में पूरा होगा?

(a) 100 (b) 40
(c) 50 (d) 60

8. If A does $28\frac{4}{7}\%$ of the work in 7 days, then in how many days whole work will be complted?

यदि A $28\frac{4}{7}\%$ कार्य 7 दिनों में करता है, तो पूरा कार्य कितने दिनों में पूरा होगा?

(a) 20
(b) 25
(c) $20\frac{1}{2}$
(d) $24\frac{1}{2}$

9. If A does $11\frac{1}{9}\%$ of the work in $6\frac{1}{3}$ days, then in how many days whole work will be completed?

यदि A $11\frac{1}{9}\%$ कार्य को $6\frac{1}{3}$ दिनों में करता है, तो पूरा कार्य कितने दिनों में पूरा होगा?

(a) 57
(b) 39
(c) 38
(d) $5\frac{7}{10}$

10. If A does $9\frac{1}{11}$ % of the work in $2\frac{1}{11}$ days, then in how many days whole work will be completed?

यदि A $9\frac{1}{11}$ % कार्य को $2\frac{1}{11}$ दिनों में करता है, तो पूरा कार्य कितने दिनों में पूरा होगा?

(a) 22 (b) 20
(c) 23 (d) 21

11. If A does $66\frac{2}{3}$ % of the work in 5 days, then in how many days whole work will be completed?

यदि A $66\frac{2}{3}$ % कार्य 5 दिनों में करता है, तो पूरा कार्य कितने दिनों में पूरा होगा?

(a) 5 (b) $7\frac{1}{2}$

(c) $6\frac{1}{2}$ (d) $8\frac{1}{2}$

12. **If A does $22\frac{2}{9}$% of the work in 18 days, then in how many days whole work will be completed?**

यदि A $22\frac{2}{9}$% कार्य 18 दिनों में करता है, तो पूरा कार्य कितने दिनों में पूरा होगा?

(a) 36 (b) 72
(c) 81 (d) 54

13. **If A does $36\frac{4}{11}$% of the work in $4\frac{4}{11}$ days, then in how many days whole work will be completed?**

यदि A $36\frac{4}{11}$% कार्य $4\frac{4}{11}$ दिनों में करता है, तो पूरा कार्य कितने दिनों में पूरा होगा?

(a) 16 (b) 12
(c) 20 (d) 22

14. **If A does 17/25 part of the work in 68 days, then in how may days whole work will be**

यदि A कार्य का 17/25 भाग 68 दिनों में करता है, तो पूरा कार्य कितने दिनों में पूरा होगा?

(a) 80 (b) 75
(c) 100 (d) 120

15. **If A does 20% of the work in 30 days, then in how many days whole work will be completed?**

यदि A 20% कार्य को 30 दिनों में करता है, तो पूरा कार्य कितने दिनों में पूरा होगा?

(a) 120
(b) 100
(c) 150
(d) 250

16. **If A does 30% of the work in 20 days, then in how many days whole work will be completed?**

यदि A कार्य का 30%, 20 दिनों में करता है, तो पूरा कार्य कितने दिनों में पूरा होगा?

(a) $66\frac{2}{3}$
(b) 75
(c) 60
(d) $62\frac{1}{2}$

17. **If A does $37\frac{1}{2}\%$ of the work in 21 days, then in how many days whole work will be completed?**

यदि A कार्य का $37\frac{1}{2}\%$, 21 दिनों में करता है, तो पूरा कार्य कितने दिनों में पूरा होगा?

(a) 21
(b) 56
(c) 14
(d) 28

18. If A does $58\frac{1}{3}\%$ of the work in 10.5 days, then in how many days whole work will be completed?

यदि A $58\frac{1}{3}\%$ कार्य 10.5 दिनों में करता है, तो पूरा कार्य कितने दिनों में पूरा होगा?

(a) 36
(b) 21
(c) 20
(d) 18

19. If A does 4/5 of the work in 10 days, then in how many days 2/3 of work will be completed?

यदि A किसी कार्य का 4/5 भाग 10 दिनों में करता है, तो 2/3 कार्य कितने दिनों में पूरा होगा?

(a) $6\frac{1}{3}$
(b) $8\frac{1}{3}$
(c) $6\frac{2}{3}$
(d) $9\frac{1}{3}$

20. **If A does 3/5 of the work in 10 days, then in how many days 2/5 of work will be completed?**

यदि A किसी कार्य का 3/5 भाग 10 दिनों में करता है, तो 2/5 कार्य कितने दिनों में पूरा होगा?

(a) $6\frac{1}{3}$ (b) $9\frac{1}{3}$ (c) 8 (d) $6\frac{2}{3}$

21. **If A does 4/7 of the work in 20 days, then in how many days 3/7 of work will be completed?**

यदि A कार्य का 4/7 भाग 20 दिनों में करता है, तो 3/7 कार्य कितने दिनों में पूरा होगा?

(a) 15 (b) 10
(c) 21 (d) 12

22. **If A does 20% of the work in 24 days, then in how many days 15% of work will be completed?**

यदि A 20% कार्य 24 दिनों में करता है, तो 15% कार्य कितने दिनों में पूरा होगा?

(a) 15 (b) 16
(c) 18 (d) 20

23. If A does 30% of the work in 18 days, then in how many days $33\frac{1}{3}$% of work will be completed?

यदि A 30% कार्य 18 दिनों में पूरा करता है, तो $33\frac{1}{3}$% कार्य कितने दिनों में पूरा होगा?

(a) 25 (b) 20

(c) 30 (d) 40

24. If A does 5/11 of the work in $16\frac{2}{3}$ days, then in how many days 15/22 of work will be completed?

यदि A कार्य का 5/11 भाग $16\frac{2}{3}$ दिनों में करता है, तो कार्य का 15/22 भाग कितने दिनों में पूरा होगा?

(a) 22 (b) 20

(c) 30 (d) 25

25. If A does $14\frac{2}{7}\%$ of the work in 22 days, then in how many days $9\frac{1}{11}\%$ of work will be completed?

यदि A कार्य का $14\frac{2}{7}\%$ 22 दिनों में करता है, तो $9\frac{1}{11}\%$ कार्य कितने दिनों में पूरा होगा?

(a) 21
(b) 14
(c) 22
(d) 18

26. If A does 6/11 of the work in 21 days, then in how many days 14/11 of work will be completed?

यदि A उस कार्य 6/11 भाग 21 दिनों में करता है, तो 14/11 का काम कितने दिनों में पूरा होगा?

(a) 98
(b) 49
(c) 42
(d) 50

27. If A does $16\frac{2}{3}\%$ of the work in $37\frac{1}{2}$ days, then in how many days $44\frac{4}{9}\%$ of work will be completed?

यदि A $16\frac{2}{3}\%$ कार्य $37\frac{1}{2}$ दिनों में करता है, तो $44\frac{4}{9}\%$ कार्य कितने दिनों में पूरा होगा?

(a) 100 (b) 50

(c) 90 (d) 80

28. If A does $66\frac{2}{3}\%$ of the work in 48 days, then in how many days 50% of 3/4 work will be completed?

यदि A $66\frac{2}{3}\%$ कार्य 48 दिनों में करता है, तो पूरे कार्य का 50% का 3/4 भाग कार्य कितने दिनों में पूरा होगा?

(a) 36 (b) 24

(c) 27 (d) 32

29. **If A does 35% of the work in 140 days, then in how many days $33\frac{1}{3}\%$ of $\frac{3}{4}$ work will be completed?**

यदि A 35% कार्य 140 दिनों में करता है, तो कार्य का $33\frac{1}{3}\%$ का $\frac{3}{4}$ भाग कितने दिनों में पूरा होगा?

(a) 60
(b) 100
(c) 80
(d) 120

30. **If A does 62.5% of the work in 25 days, then in how many days $14\frac{2}{7}\%$ of 7/9 work will be completed?**

यदि A 62.5% कार्य 25 दिनों में करता है, तो $14\frac{2}{7}\%$ का 7/9 कार्य कितने दिनों में पूरा होगा?

(a) $11\frac{1}{3}$
(b) $5\frac{2}{11}$
(c) $5\frac{2}{7}$
(d) $4\frac{4}{9}$

31. **If A does 5/12 of the work in 12.5 days, the in how many days 2/3 of work will be completed?**

यदि A 5/12 कार्य 12.5 दिनों में करता है, तो 2/3 कार्य कितने दिनों में पूरा होगा?

(a) 20 (b) 60 (c) 40 (d) 15

32. **If A does 1/4 of the work in 24 days, then in how many days $66\frac{2}{3}\%$ of work will be completed?**

यदि A 1/4 कार्य को 24 दिनों में करता है, तो $66\frac{2}{3}\%$ कार्य कितने दिन में पूरा होगा?

(a) 32 (b) 60 (c) 64 (d) 80

33. **If A does 3/4 of the work in $42\frac{6}{7}$ days, then in how many days 5/8 of work will be completed?**

यदि A 3/4 कार्य $42\frac{6}{7}$ दिनों करता है, तो 5/8 कार्य कितने दिनों में पूरा होगा?

(a) $30\frac{2}{3}$ (b) $42\frac{6}{7}$ (c) 35 (d) $35\frac{5}{7}$

34. If A does 50% of 2/3 work in $33\frac{1}{3}$ days, then in how many days $14\frac{2}{7}$% of 7/11 of 11/4 work will be completed?

यदि A 50% का 2/3 कार्य $33\frac{1}{3}$ दिनों में करता है, तो $14\frac{2}{7}$% का 7/11 का 11/4 कार्य कितने दिनों में पूरा होगा?

(a) 25 (b) 20 (c) 15 (d) 45

35. If A does $44\frac{4}{9}$% of 18/25 work in 32 days, then in how many days $18\frac{2}{11}$% of 22/25 work will be completed?

यदि A $44\frac{4}{9}$% का 18/25 कार्य 32 दिनों में करता है, तो $18\frac{2}{11}$% का 22/25 कार्य कितने दिनों में पूरा होगा?

(a) 11 (b) 16 (c) 10 (d) $12\frac{3}{4}$

36. If A does $57\frac{1}{7}\%$ of 7/36 work in $6\frac{1}{3}$ days, then in how many days $83\frac{1}{3}\%$ of 6/5 work will be completed?

यदि A $57\frac{1}{7}\%$ का 7/36 कार्य $6\frac{1}{3}$ दिनों में करता है, तो $83\frac{1}{3}\%$ का 6/5 कार्य कितने दिनों में पूरा होगा?

(a) $52\frac{1}{2}$ (b) 76 (c) 57 (d) $57\frac{1}{7}$

37. If A does $28\frac{4}{7}\%$ of $16\frac{2}{3}\%$ of a work in 4 days, then in how many days 100% work will be completed?

यदि A $28\frac{4}{7}\%$ का $16\frac{2}{3}\%$ कार्य 4 दिन में करता है, तो 100% कार्य कितने दिनों में पूरा होगा?

(a) 42 (b) 21 (c) 72 (d) 84

38. **If A does a work in 10 days, then in how many days $6\frac{1}{4}\%$ of 16/25 work will be completed?**

यदि A एक कार्य 10 दिनों में करता है, तो $6\frac{1}{4}\%$ का 16/25 कार्य कितने दिनों में पूरा होगा?

(a) 8/15 (b) 10/25 (c) 1/25 (d) 4

39. **If A does 3/10 of 5/11 of the work in 30 days, then in how many days 4/3 of 6/22 work will be completed?**

यदि A 3/10 का 5/11 कार्य 30 दिन में करता है, तो 4/3 का 6/22 कार्य कितने दिनों में पूरा होगा?

(a) 80 (b) 100 (c) 72 (d) 88

40. **If A does 75% of the work in 60 days, then in how many days 3 times of 20% work will be completed?**

यदि A 75% कार्य 60 दिनों में करता तो 20% कार्य का 3 गुना कितने दिनों में पूरा होगा?

(a) 24 (b) 72 (c) 48 (d) 36

41. **If A does 60% of 3/2 the work in 180 days, then in how many days $1\frac{1}{2}$ times of 3/10 work will be completed?**

यदि A 60% का 3/2 कार्य 180 दिन में करता है, तो 3/10 का $1\frac{1}{2}$ गुना कितने दिनों में पूरा होगा?

(a) 45
(b) 60
(c) 180
(d) 90

42. **If A does 4 times the 20% of the 3/5 work in 96 days, then in how many days 1.25 times of 40% work will be completed?**

यदि A 3/5 का 20% का 4 गुना कार्य 96 दिनों में करता है, तो 40% कार्य का 1.25 गुना कितने दिनों में पूरा होगा?

(a) 120
(b) 60
(c) 100
(d) 150

43. If A does 11.11% of the work in 20 days, then in how many days 9.09% work will be completed?

यदि A 11.11% कार्य 20 दिनों में करता है, तो 9.09% कार्य कितने दिनों में पूरा होगा?

(a) $16\frac{4}{11}$
(b) $16\frac{2}{3}$
(c) $15\frac{5}{9}$
(d) 20

44. If A does 20% of 30% work in 20% of 60 days, then in how many days work will be completed?

यदि A 30% का 20% कार्य 60 दिनों के 20% में करता है, तो कितने दिनों में कार्य पूरा होगा?

(a) 180
(b) 200
(c) 100
(d) 120

Time and Work : Answer - Key

1.	(b)	10.	(c)	19.	(b)	28.	(c)	37.	(d)
2.	(c)	11.	(b)	20.	(d)	29.	(b)	38.	(b)
3.	(b)	12.	(c)	21.	(a)	30.	(d)	39.	(a)
4.	(d)	13.	(b)	22.	(c)	31.	(a)	40.	(c)
5.	(a)	14.	(c)	23.	(b)	32.	(c)	41.	(d)
6.	(b)	15.	(c)	24.	(d)	33.	(d)	42.	(c)
7.	(c)	16.	(a)	25.	(b)	34.	(a)	43.	(a)
8.	(d)	17.	(b)	26.	(b)	35.	(b)	44.	(b)
9.	(a)	18.	(d)	27.	(a)	36.	(c)		

मेरे प्रिय दोस्तों,

उम्मीद है यह मेरा पत्र और यह पुस्तक आपको मिल गई होगी। मेरा मकसद हमेशा से आपके लिए निरंतर कुछ नया और सबसे अलग प्रयास करने का हैं और आगे भी अपने बच्चों के लिए करता रहूंगा। यह पुस्तक को मै काफी समय से बना रहा था और देख रहा था बच्चों को कहाँ–कहाँ Calculation से जुड़ी कठिनाइयों का सामना करना पड़ता है। आगे भी मेरा हमेशा एक सपना रहेगा कि आपके लिए जल्द से जल्द Math से जुड़ी सभी समस्याओं का समाधान निकाल सकूं।

जल्दी आप लोग Inspector बने दिल से दुआ है ❤

आपका अपना

मोहित गोयल

amazon Flipkart पर★★★★★ 5 Star Rating देकर अपना प्यार और सहयोग जरूर करें दोस्तों। आपका प्यार ही हमारा सब कुछ है।

Thank You for your love and support. Please give 5 Stars and Review for us. Please share your feedback on Whatsapp – 9711113573

Calculation
Rough Worksheet

Calculation
Rough Worksheet

Calculation

Rough Worksheet

Calculation

Rough Worksheet

Calculation

Rough Worksheet

Calculation
Rough Worksheet